THE
FIGHT
OF HIS
LIFE

THE FIGHT OF HIS LIFE

JOE LOUIS'S BATTLE FOR FREEDOM DURING WORLD WAR II

JOHNNY SMITH and **RANDY ROBERTS**

BASIC BOOKS

New York

Copyright © 2025 by John Matthew Smith and Randy Roberts
Cover design by Chin-Yee Lai
Cover images © Bettmann via Getty Images
Cover copyright © 2025 by Hachette Book Group, Inc.

Hachette Book Group supports the right to free expression and the value of copyright. The purpose of copyright is to encourage writers and artists to produce the creative works that enrich our culture.

The scanning, uploading, and distribution of this book without permission is a theft of the author's intellectual property. If you would like permission to use material from the book (other than for review purposes), please contact permissions@hbgusa.com. Thank you for your support of the author's rights.

Basic Books
Hachette Book Group
1290 Avenue of the Americas, New York, NY 10104
www.basicbooks.com

Printed in the United States of America

First Edition: November 2025

Published by Basic Books, an imprint of Hachette Book Group, Inc. The Basic Books name and logo is a registered trademark of the Hachette Book Group.

The Hachette Speakers Bureau provides a wide range of authors for speaking events. To find out more, go to hachettespeakersbureau.com or email HachetteSpeakers@hbgusa.com.

Basic books may be purchased in bulk for business, educational, or promotional use. For more information, please contact your local bookseller or the Hachette Book Group Special Markets Department at special.markets@hbgusa.com.

The publisher is not responsible for websites (or their content) that are not owned by the publisher.

Print book interior design by Amy Quinn.

Library of Congress Cataloging-in-Publication Data
Names: Smith, Johnny (John Matthew) author | Roberts, Randy, 1951– author
Title: The fight of his life : Joe Louis's battle for freedom during World War II / Johnny Smith and Randy Roberts.
Other titles: Joe Louis's battle for democracy during World War II
Description: First edition. | New York : Basic Books, 2025. | Includes bibliographical references and index.
Identifiers: LCCN 2025004814 | ISBN 9781541605060 hardcover | ISBN 9781541605077 ebook
Subjects: LCSH: Louis, Joe, 1914–1981 | African American boxers—Biography | Boxers (Sports)—United States—Biography | World War, 1939–1945—African Americans—Biography | African American soldiers—Biography | United States—Race relations—History—20th century | LCGFT: Biographies
Classification: LCC GV1132.L6 S65 2025 | DDC 796.83092—dc23/eng/20250818
LC record available at https://lccn.loc.gov/2025004814

ISBNs: 9781541605060 (hardcover), 9781541605077 (ebook)

LSC-C

Printing 1, 2025

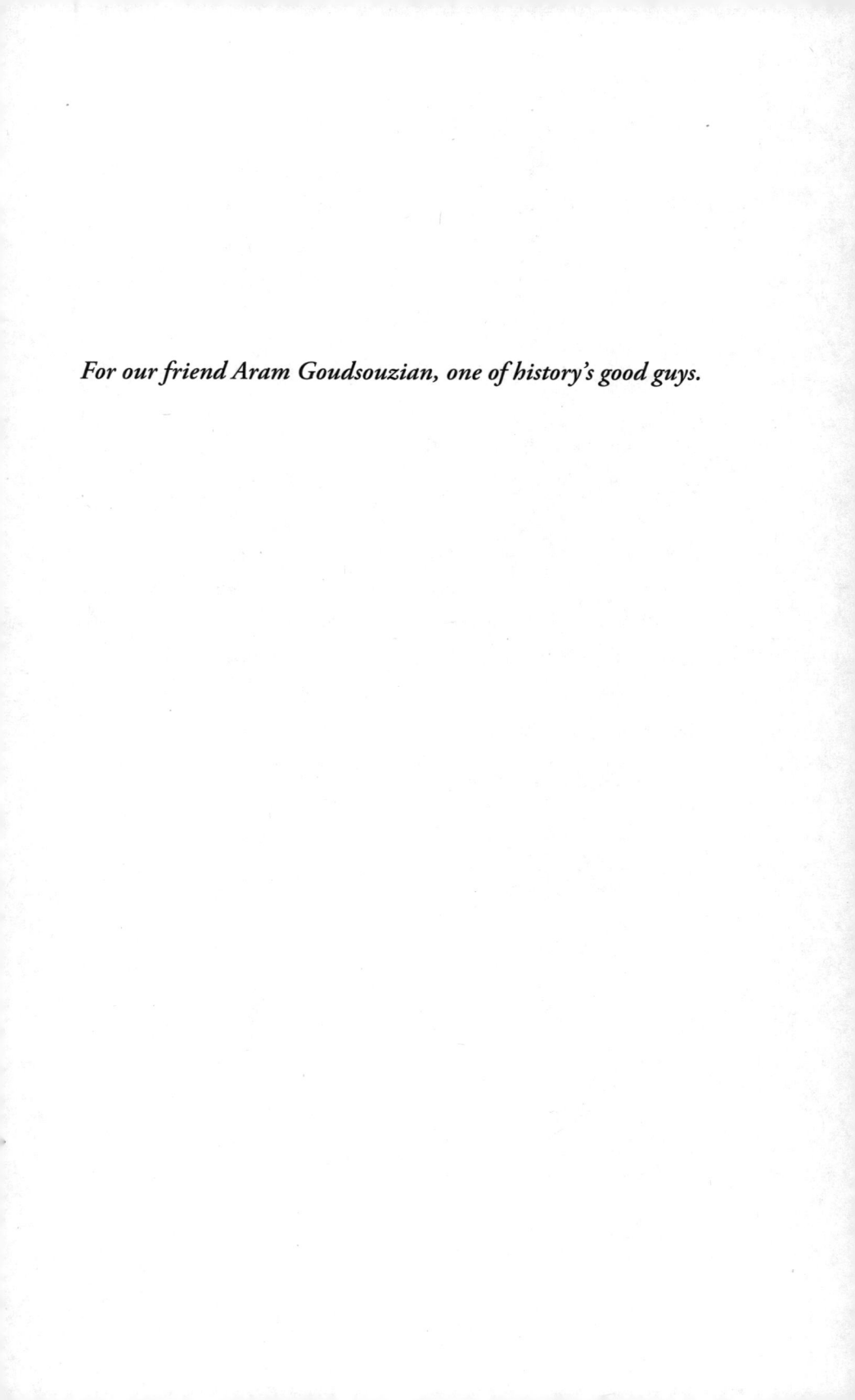

For our friend Aram Goudsouzian, one of history's good guys.

A book could be written of the thoughts behind Louis' inscrutable countenance as he saw his people pushed aside, treated like cattle on public conveyances such as trains, and trolley cars decorated with war slogans about saving the world for democracy; spreading the Four Freedoms, down with Fascism, and so on. Yes, a volume could be written about what Louis thought when he saw his own people unable to spend their money where they wanted to, insulted almost daily by newspaper "darky" stories; having to read about Congressmen and Senators publicly condemning those in uniform, those in war plants to an inferior status below that of the Japs or the Germans, our official enemies; saw them beaten, trampled upon.

—Columnist Dan Burley, *New York Amsterdam News*, April 15, 1944

CONTENTS

PREFACE:	A Silent Revolutionary	1
PROLOGUE:	He Belongs to Us	9
ONE:	Black Moses	21
TWO:	The Campaign	47
THREE:	Against the Ropes	69
FOUR:	King Joe	93
FIVE:	Anchors Aweigh	107
SIX:	God's War	127
SEVEN:	War Boxing, Inc.	149
EIGHT:	Stormy Weather	169
NINE:	The American Gestapo	191
TEN:	Over There	217
ELEVEN:	Homecoming	243
EPILOGUE:	The Final Round	265
	Acknowledgments	*283*
	Notes	*287*
	Index	*327*

Preface

A SILENT REVOLUTIONARY

I have fought the good fight, I have finished the race, I have kept the faith.

—2 Timothy 4:7 (New International Version)

IT WAS NOT A BOXER'S FUNERAL. JOE LOUIS WAS A HEAVYWEIGHT champion, arguably the greatest in the history of the sport. But his life as a fighter took him well beyond the confines of the boxing ring. In death, he was honored with a soldier's burial.

On April 21, 1981, six pallbearers in full military dress, wearing dark blue trimmed with gold—the colors of the Union Army—carried Joe's flag-covered casket to section 7A of Arlington National Cemetery. Situated on a gentle green slope near the Tomb of the Unknown Soldier, the gravesite was shaded by majestic trees with colorful patches of dogwood, magnolia, and cherry blossoms. On that glorious sunny day, seven riflemen from the Third US Infantry Regiment—The Old Guard—fired three volley shots into the cool spring air. Then Sergeant Washington James, an army bugler, played "Taps," a somber signal that the light would soon fade from sight.[1]

Nine days after Louis suffered a heart attack and died in Las Vegas at age sixty-six, hundreds of people gathered around his grave. The diverse congregation included people from different races and religions, politicians, civil rights activists, military officials, and athletes. A legion of famous fighters honored America's champion. Muhammad Ali, Joe Frazier, Larry Holmes, Floyd Patterson, Billy Conn, and Joe Walcott all paid their respects, but none of them had been as close to him as Sugar Ray Robinson, the middleweight sensation who had served with Louis during World War II.

President Ronald Reagan could not attend the funeral. Though he was still recovering from an assassin's bullet that had punctured one of his lungs, Reagan had waived the eligibility restrictions that would have prevented Louis's interment at the military cemetery. A longtime admirer of the former champion, Reagan had cheered for Louis during his fighting days and became his friend when they filmed *This Is the Army* together in 1943. Bound to a wheelchair, Louis had spent his final years in retreat from public view, but Reagan issued a public statement reminding the country of his importance: "His career was an indictment of racial bigotry and a source of pride and inspiration to millions of white and black people around the world."[2]

As heavyweight champion and the most admired Black American of his time, Joe Louis's career was virtually nonpareil. Between the late 1930s and the mid-1940s, no single athlete captured the nation's attention more than Louis. Recalling his reign as champion, a writer from the *Detroit Free Press* reminisced, "It is not likely that we will ever again know the magic of those yesterdays when the streets emptied, and commerce stopped and America huddled by its radios to listen to the exploits of the man with the jackhammer fists." For "a nation battered by the uncertainties of the Great Depression and World War II, there was comfort in the ring announcer's reassuring affirmation: 'The winner and still heavyweight champion of the world . . . Joe Louis!'"[3]

Yet he did not provide temporary relief from those global crises as much as he embodied resistance against racial oppression. During a crucial period between 1938, when Nazi Germany annexed Austria, and 1945, when Adolf Hitler died, the heavyweight champion defined Black Americans' fight for freedom on two fronts: against fascism abroad and white supremacy at home. His career as a boxer and as a soldier was framed by the rise of the Nazis and America's response. It all began in June 1938, when Louis knocked out German heavyweight Max Schmeling at Yankee Stadium in a fight that came to be seen as a prelude to war between the United States and Nazi Germany. That fight carried great significance for people all around the world, especially Black Americans and Jews.

Three and a half years later, after Louis joined the army in 1942, military officers introduced him to crowds of soldiers as the first American to knock out a Nazi. Although he never saw combat, Louis served in the army's Morale Branch as a goodwill ambassador, promoting patriotism and unity across American military bases crackling with racial tension. Performing boxing exhibitions and delivering short speeches, he entertained soldiers and urged them to fight for democracy. In his public appearances, he reassured the government—and white America—that Black folks would fight for the United States and remain completely committed to the mission. In private conversations, he reminded Black servicemen that despite the segregated conditions in the armed forces, they too had a stake in the war. Defending America, a land that they had helped build with their sweat and blood, signaled that the country belonged to them as much as anyone else. Like many Black politicians, activists, soldiers, and civilians, Louis thought that service in the military would earn them the respect of white Americans and ultimately advance their cause for full citizenship. At least, that's what he thought when the United States entered the international conflict.

Civil rights leaders and Black officials in the War Department believed Joe's role in the army could generate greater enthusiasm among Black men who were reluctant to serve in a segregated military. They also thought publicizing his interactions with admiring white servicemen could improve race relations. Walter White, the head of the National Association for the Advancement of Colored People (NAACP), recognized the cultural importance of the heavyweight champion. He believed that popular culture—sports, songs, and movies—could shape the struggle for civil rights during the war. And Louis, more than any other Black soldier, could undermine stereotypically negative perceptions of Black GIs as weak, unmotivated cowards. In the fight for freedom at home and abroad, producing positive images of Joe Louis, White thought, was as important as manufacturing rifles and planes.[4]

For the War Department, Louis seemed an ideal figure for dealing with the army's "Negro problem." No other Black celebrity or athlete personified American strength, courage, and achievement like Louis. His exhibitions in the ring, cheered on by Black and white American GIs, were celebrated in the press as powerful examples of democracy in action. For the first time in history, the US government built a propaganda campaign around the heroism of a Black soldier, featuring Louis in newspapers, magazines, movies, newsreels, posters, and pamphlets. Remarkably, while many white Americans questioned the fortitude and fighting ability of Black soldiers, the War Department made Louis, not a white man, *the symbol* of American manpower.[5]

The War Department also chose Louis because military officials did not expect that he would question the hypocrisy of America battling totalitarianism with a Jim Crow Army. While the United States conducted a war—in part—to end the reign of Nazi racism, the War Department maintained segregated armed forces, which included separating blood banks into "white" and "colored." And yet during Joe's tour, government officials pressed him to advance the idea that there should be no racial divisions in the military. However, as Louis became more aware of the cruel realities of a segregated army, he began to bristle about his assignment as a goodwill ambassador, promoting racial unity where it did not exist.

Throughout the war Louis wrestled with the challenge of being Black *and* being an American. It was a paradox known to all Black people navigating the color line, striving to advance in a country that denied their humanity and home. Black scholar W. E. B. Du Bois described that "peculiar sensation" of "double consciousness" as a "two-ness" that Louis undoubtedly felt, "an American, a Negro; two souls, two thoughts, two unreconciled strivings; two warring ideals in one dark body, whose dogged strength alone keeps it from being torn asunder."[6] Yet Louis came to believe that the war presented Black people an opportunity to integrate these dueling and warring selves. When he joined the army, he expressed a deep love for a country that had not always loved him. His public displays of patriotism served as a powerful reminder to anyone who questioned the loyalty of Black people that they, too, were Americans.

Decades later, his only son, Joe Louis Barrow Jr., came to appreciate his father's perspective. During the funeral service, Barrow praised his dad as a great American and a genuine folk hero—a man of the people who had always been accessible and generous. Speaking in a thoughtful, quiet manner, Barrow recalled a conversation he had with his dad during the Vietnam War, a time when political divisions fractured the country. Barrow expressed his own frustrations and doubts about the war and America. Louis looked him in the eye and said, "This is a beautiful country, son, and it's most important we stand by it. It may make its mistakes. It may not be exactly right, but you have to stand by it." Glancing at his father's flag-draped casket, Barrow concluded in a whisper, "We are going to miss you an awful lot, because you were the greatest, truly the greatest."⁷

JOE LOUIS NEVER BOASTED THAT HE WAS THE GREATEST. NOR WAS he known for speaking openly about racial justice. Before the Second World War, Louis rarely uttered a word, at least not publicly, about the American Dilemma—what Swedish author Gunnar Myrdal described as the gulf between the country's democratic ideals and the persistent denial of Black citizens' civil rights. During the second half of the 1930s, in the throes of the Great Depression, Louis was known for being a modest, soft-spoken champion whose victories over white opponents made him into a righteous symbol uplifting his people. When he died, journalists wrote obituaries memorializing him more as a cultural phenomenon than as a political force. A columnist at *The New York Times* quoted Louis's longtime friend Billy Rowe, a veteran reporter, who said, "Joe did everything quietly. In a way, Joe was a silent revolutionary."⁸

But that was only partially true. There's a certain myth that Louis never spoke out against racism and that he did not think it was appropriate for him to be anything more than a boxer. However, his experience in a segregated army sparked his political awakening. That awakening—a growing determination to fight for freedom and full citizenship—swept across Black America in large cities and small towns, in defense plants and diners, on army posts and naval bases. During the war Louis advocated for Black soldiers facing discrimination in the United States Army. And when he returned home from the service, while Black veterans were being attacked by lynch mobs, he spoke out against racial violence and white supremacy. Joining veterans and civil rights activists, he urged Black citizens to fight for voting rights

A Silent Revolutionary

and demand racial equality. In short, the Second World War transformed Louis into the first prominent Black athlete turned activist, a crucial role that has been overlooked.[9]

That story unfolds in *The Fight of His Life*. Our book demonstrates that Louis was not an incidental or invisible actor in the long struggle for civil rights. Rather, his actions during and after the war made Black Americans see him as more than a symbol; they saw him as a leader. Tracing his ascendance in American culture, we follow him from his training camp in Pompton Lakes to his fights at the Polo Grounds and Madison Square Garden, from New York nightclubs to Hollywood studios, from America's stateside military posts to army bases in Europe and North Africa. Investigating his forty-six months in the army, we explore how the federal government exploited his fame for propaganda purposes and how Louis emerged from the war as a voice of an oppressed people, a freedom fighter.

Telling that Joe Louis story entailed reconstructing his daily life inside and outside the ring using a treasure trove of archival sources: War Department records, official military personnel files, and Federal Bureau of Investigation (FBI) files; the papers of President Franklin Roosevelt; the records of the NAACP; hundreds of newspapers, especially accounts from Black journalists who knew Louis well; newsreels, movies, magazines, and photographs; speeches and songs; memoirs and oral histories; and a variety of other published and unpublished materials.

Those sources allowed us to separate the man from the legend and uncover how much more there was to Joe Louis than the stoic mask he wore in the ring. He was born in rural Alabama, but he was really a product of the Great Migration, having moved to Detroit during his childhood. He grew up hardly knowing his father, but he found paternal influences in the gym. Boxing gave him purpose, but golf brought him joy. Although he lacked a formal education, Louis had a remarkable memory for names, faces, and phone numbers, especially if they belonged to attractive women. He loved his first wife, Marva, but he romanced countless other women too. It seemed that he spent more nights sleeping in hotels than at home. He attracted large crowds at nightclubs, where he gladly picked up the tab even though during his fighting days, he didn't imbibe anything stronger than a Coca-Cola. Joe could be reticent with reporters but completely comfortable with strangers he met on the street. He indulged in the trappings of fame. Nearly every morning, he had his valet draw a bath and lay out his fine clothes. He made far more money than any other athlete of his generation, but he finished his career completely broke.

Joe Louis had no regrets. "The thing you have to understand about Joe," said his longtime friend Truman Gibson, "is that he lived every day." A Black lawyer from Chicago, Gibson understood Louis better than most. "I went to school, planned for the future," he said. But "Joe Louis *lived* every day."[10]

Prologue

HE BELONGS TO US

One hundred years from now, some historian may theorize, in a footnote at least, that the decline of Nazi prestige began with a left hook delivered by a former unskilled automobile worker who had never studied the politics of Neville Chamberlain and had no opinion whatsoever in regard to the situation in Czechoslovakia.

—Heywood Broun, *New York World-Telegram*, June 24, 1938

Reporters told Joe that Max was dead.

Once the darling of Nazi sports and Joe's greatest boxing rival, Max Schmeling had taken part in the 1941 German invasion of Crete. Though poorly trained for his mission, the German boxer was part of the first wave of paratroopers dropped just south of Chania. It was a night jump from a low altitude into enemy fire, and Schmeling's unit suffered high casualties. Schmeling landed awkwardly in a vineyard, aggravating an injury from his second fight against Louis: a meniscus tear and crushed vertebrae.[1]

According to a British report out of Alexandria, Egypt, on May 28, English soldiers captured the "wounded" boxer before the "truculent" Schmeling could make a daring escape. The United Press recounted that he snatched an injured man's rifle during his transfer to a prison camp, but before he could fire, a contingent of New Zealanders cut him down.[2]

The story spread to every corner of the world. Radio reports in Berlin lamented the former champion's passing, and the Italian *Corriere Della Sera* praised his choice to serve the Axis "in the most dangerous corps." The *Times of India* and the *South China Morning Post* also noted his death. In the United States, and especially in New York City, where Max had fought his most famous matches, journalists parsed his life and career, his upset victories and dramatic defeats. Former heavyweight champion Max Baer, who had knocked out Schmeling in 1933, exploded when he heard the news: "I hate war and fighting—I mean fighting to kill. And I think Schmeling did too. He probably didn't want to fight, but Hitler made him do it."[3]

Louis heard about Schmeling's death as he walked through the grand lobby of the Hotel Theresa in Harlem. "That's bad," he said. Then, as the news sank in, he added, "I'm sorry to hear that. This war is a terrible thing." From the lobby he went to the bar and ordered a glass of lemonade.[4]

At that moment the quiet, handsome champion stood incontrovertibly as the most famous athlete in the world. No one else was even remotely close. He had won the heavyweight title in 1937 and defended his crown an unprecedented twenty-one times. Lyricists composed songs about him, poets penned odes to him, sportswriters earned their wages reporting on his daily activities, and fans stood slack-jawed when they saw him on the streets. By the end of the war, Margery Miller, a young white woman who was perhaps the only female boxing writer in America, would publish a biography simply titled *Joe Louis: American*, identifying him as the best his nation had to offer.[5]

When Miller was just fifteen years old, she attended her first prizefight at Yankee Stadium with her father—the 1938 title rematch between Joe Louis and Max Schmeling. No sports rivalry quite matched that of Louis and Schmeling—not for drama, intensity, or political importance.

But as monumental as the 1938 Louis–Schmeling rematch was, their first meeting had none of the lavish prefight hullabaloo or international political significance. At Yankee Stadium on June 19, 1936, Louis entered the ring with an undefeated record and ten-to-one betting odds that he would win. It appeared that his likely victory would be little more than a cherry on top of a Juneteenth sundae.

By then, Louis was universally acclaimed as the biggest attraction in boxing. Rising through the heavyweight division, he seemed destined to become the next world champion. And virtually every Black person in America felt their fate was tied to his ascendance. A year earlier, Black novelist Richard Wright recognized the radical meaning of Louis as an inarticulate prophet unleashing violent upheaval. "Four centuries of repression," Wright observed, "of frustrated hope, of black bitterness, felt even in the bones of the bewildered young, were rising to the surface. Yes, unconsciously they had imputed to the brawny image of Joe Louis all the balked dreams of revenge, all the secretly visualized moments of retaliation." Without uttering a word, Louis had become a revolutionary force. Every time he knocked out a white man, Louis struck a mighty blow against the fallacy of white supremacy. "You see, Joe was the consciously-felt symbol," Wright wrote. "Joe was the concentrated essence of black triumph over white."[6]

If Louis had become an avenger for his race, Max Schmeling, Hitler's favorite boxer, was cast in Nazi Germany as a national hero. But American boxing insiders considered Schmeling another sacrificial lamb to be butchered for the sake of nourishing Louis's record. In 1930 Schmeling had won the title (while clutching his groin after a low blow delivered by Jack Sharkey), defended it once, then promptly lost it to Sharkey in 1932. After that he suffered a knockout in one fight, a loss and a draw in two others, and a downward plunge in his ranking and reputation. Although in 1934 he scored two victories in his native Germany against European boxers, when he sailed to the United States in the spring of 1936 to battle Joe Louis, few American sportswriters—or German ones, for that matter—gave him much of a chance.

Although Nazi leaders privately wished him luck against Louis, they were too coldly realistic to make much of a public fuss about the stakes of his fight. Syndicated columnist Westbrook Pegler wrote, "At no time during the months when Schmeling was preparing to fight Louis did the Nazi government accept any responsibility in the matter. Schmeling did not then enjoy the status of official patriot and representative of Nazi manhood. He was absolutely on his own, because there seemed an excellent chance that having already been knocked out by a Jew [Max Baer] he would now be stretched in the resin at the feet of a cotton-field Negro." In the end, Schmeling departed his fatherland without fanfare in the middle of the night.[7]

Yet the sacrificial lamb had the teeth of a wolf. Max clubbed Joe to the canvas with a perfectly delivered right in the fourth and continued to land the same punch for most of the next eight rounds. By the time Schmeling knocked out Louis in the twelfth round, the Brown Bomber's face looked like a ghoulish Halloween mask. The left side, which had absorbed all of Schmeling's right punches, had an unnatural quality, as if it had been stuffed with unshelled walnuts. Sitting in the fifth row, close enough to see Schmeling disfigure Louis's face, Joe's wife, Marva, gasped with every punch. "He's hurt. He's hurt bad," she cried. His mother, Lillie, dropped to her knees and prayed for her son's survival.[8]

Black America wept. Stunned, *Pittsburgh Courier* sportswriter Wendell Smith couldn't shake the sight of Louis being peeled off the canvas and carried back to his corner by the very German who had knocked him off his feet. Nearly twenty years later, poet and playwright Langston Hughes could still feel the trembling silence and sadness that reverberated throughout Harlem that night. After Schmeling punished Louis, Hughes walked down Seventh Avenue in Harlem, where he witnessed "grown men weeping like children, and women sitting on the curbs with their heads in their hands." No other Black figure, Hughes wrote, had "ever had such an effect on Negro emotions—or mine."[9]

Lena Horne would never forget how she felt when Louis collapsed. The singer was in Cincinnati that evening, entertaining an all-white audience with Noble Sissle's orchestra at the Moonlight Gardens. Band members had a radio backstage, and during breaks they listened to the broadcast, their fears growing as the fight moved toward a seemingly inevitable conclusion. Louis, "the one invincible Negro, the one who stood up to the white man," was so badly beaten that some of the musicians openly wept. Lena recalled that she was "near hysteria." He "carried so many of our hopes, maybe even our dreams of vengeance," she wrote. "But this night he became just another Negro getting beaten by a white man."[10]

Tears stained her face and emotions marred her performance. Her mother, Edna, was appalled and urged Lena to keep singing. "Why, you don't even know the man," she scolded her daughter.

"I don't care, I don't care," Lena yelled. "He belongs to us."

Two years later, Louis's rematch against Schmeling captured the tense anticipation of a world on the brink. Civil war raged in Spain, Japanese forces marauded the coast of China, and the Sudetenland crisis threatened to embroil Europe in another world war. Jews in Germany were being stripped of their civil, political, and even human rights by the Nuremberg laws and other draconian dictates, and were subject to harassment and physical assaults and shuffled into concentration camps for any arbitrary infraction. When Schmeling first fought Louis in 1936, Adolf Hitler had yet to begin his campaign of conquest. But by 1938, after his absorption of Austria and aggressive designs on Czechoslovakia, the scale of his ambition was undeniable.

In this heated atmosphere, the rematch between Louis and Schmeling on June 22, 1938, was transformed into something far greater than an athletic contest. American journalists turned the German boxer into a Nazi proxy—detailing his meetings with Hitler and his friendship with Joseph Goebbels, the Reich's minister of propaganda. Reporters noted that on Hitler's forty-ninth birthday Schmeling honored the Führer with a personal narration of his most recent fight. Throughout Germany, Max became the living embodiment of the Volk's lightning reflexes, decisive actions, and indomitable will, the very characteristics that Hitler praised in *Mein Kampf*.

That night Yankee Stadium oozed political theater. An enormous cartoon drawn by Burris Jenkins Jr., published in the *New York Journal-American* that day, embodied the worldwide fascination with the event. As two tiny boxers, one Black, one white, advance toward each other inside the ring, an anthropomorphic globe sits outside the ropes, bug-eyed. The globe holds a small sign that reads: MAIN BOUT, JOE LOUIS, U.S. VS. MAX SCHMELING, GERMANY. "Wars, involving the fate of nations, rage elsewhere on this globe," noted the *New York Mirror* earlier that day, "but the eyes of the world will be focused on a two-man battle in a ribbon of light stabbing the darkness of the Yankee Stadium."[11]

The match itself proved a short, sweet affirmation of what many Americans desperately wanted to think about themselves and their country. Joe Louis dispatched the idol of the German

Volk in less than a round as ringside fight fans shouted, "Kill that Nazi, Joe! Kill him!" In two minutes and four seconds, Louis nearly destroyed Schmeling. He knocked Max senseless and left him lying on the canvas, bleeding from his mouth, with several ribs shattered. Joe's triumph took place two generations after his grandparents' enslavement and less than one generation since the first Black heavyweight champion, Jack Johnson, whipped a "great white hope" named Jim Jeffries in a fight that sparked race riots across the nation. Now, though, there were no riots. Instead, Black and white Americans celebrated together, and even embraced one another as if "another World War had just ended."[12]

While many white reporters and columnists adopted the Black boxer as a representative of America's democratic values—freedom, equality, and fair play—battling against the racist ideology of Nazi Germany, Richard Wright wanted none of it. "The drama of the event," he wrote in 1938, "manipulated the common symbols and impulses in the minds and bodies of millions of people so effectively as to put to shame our professional playwrights." In a segregated country, where skin color all but determined his civil rights, Joe Louis wasn't fighting for some mythical racial unity. No, he was fighting to preserve the racial pride and dignity of twelve million Black Americans. For them, Louis "symbolized the living refutation of the hatred spewed forth daily over radios, in newspapers, in movies, and in books about their lives. Day by day, since their alleged emancipation, they have watched a picture of themselves being painted as lazy, stupid, and diseased. In hapless horror they have suffered the attacks and exploitation which followed in the wake of their being branded as 'inferiors.'" The heavyweight champion battled for a people who had been "Jim Crowed in the army and navy, barred from many trades and professions, excluded from commerce and finance, relegated to menial positions in government, segregated residentially, denied the right of franchise for the most part; in short, forced to live a separate and impoverished life."[13]

Wright reminded readers that only among Black Americans did Louis enjoy universal support. There were still reactionaries in the United States who preached the same racist creed as the fascists in Nazi Germany. And those forces had gloated when Schmeling had knocked out "the Negro" two years earlier, citing the match as proof of white supremacy. But Louis had promised to settle that old score. Vengeance for Louis would mean vengeance for his race.

When it was over, the champ found himself surrounded by dozens of scribes in his dressing room, the glow of victory illuminated by flashbulbs. Sitting on a dressing table, covered in sweat-soaked towels, he answered reporters' questions. Louis said he had never felt stronger in the ring than he did that night in Yankee Stadium. "I got what folks call revenge—and how," he said.[14]

JOE LOUIS MAY HAVE BURIED MAX SCHMELING BENEATH THE Yankee Stadium ring in 1938, but the reports of the German's death three years later in Crete proved premature. "MAX SCHMELING IS ALIVE," announced *The Star* from Nazi-occupied Guernsey in the English Channel Islands. *The New York Times* retracted its original reporting from a week earlier, informing readers that the former champion was, in effect, still punching, though he was laid up, suffering from some tropical disease in an undisclosed air force hospital. Contacted by a *Times* reporter, Schmeling summarized the Crete operation as one of German valor overcoming desperate odds. "We fought under tough and difficult conditions, as the enemy had the advantage of superior positions and heavy weapons," he explained. But in the end, superior German soldiers proved victorious.[15]

A day before the false report that Schmeling had died in battle, President Franklin D. Roosevelt had declared a national state of emergency. During a fireside chat, he explained that Nazi Germany had overrun Czechoslovakia, Poland, Denmark, Norway, Belgium, Luxembourg, and France. Britain was teetering and might fall any day. German forces were on the move in the Mediterranean and their subs were prowling the North Atlantic, threatening the "freedom of the seas." "The first and fundamental fact is that what started as a European war has developed into a world war for domination," intoned Roosevelt.[16]

The president needed to convince Americans that they had a stake in the war. Neutrality was no longer an option. He understood that when—not if—the United States entered the war, the nation had to be unified. Democrats and Republicans, men and women, young and old, Blacks and whites—Americans of all ethnic groups, religions, races, and income levels had to support the fight against fascism. But how could FDR build consensus in a nation bitterly divided over the prospect of fighting a world war? How could his administration forge racial unity in a segregated country with a Jim Crow military?

George B. Murphy Jr., the administrative secretary for the National Negro Congress, a civil rights organization founded during the New Deal, believed that Joe Louis, the preeminent symbol of democracy, could coalesce the nation in support of Roosevelt's defense program. On October 6, 1941, about a week before Louis reported for his preliminary army physical, Murphy, a former writer for the *Baltimore Afro-American*, urged Secretary of War Henry L. Stimson to let Louis fight in Uncle Sam's Army. Murphy believed that Louis, more than anyone, could unify Black troops and white soldiers. The champion, he wrote, "has won . . . the love and respect of the entire American people. More than any other single individual in the history of American sports,

Joe Louis represents the highest expression of our country's democratic tradition."[17]

Murphy noted that Louis had recently said, "Maybe my next fight will be against Max Schmeling somewhere in no-man's-land, and I won't be pulling punches." Take him at his word, Murphy implored. At a time when many Black Americans questioned the idea of fighting "a white man's war," Murphy believed that Louis's desire to suit up against the Nazis could mobilize Black men in the fight against "the menace of Hitler slavery which faces our country today." Louis could become "a key factor in building national unity, in giving America the strength to administer a knockout blow to the forces of Hitlerism."

Yet Stimson believed that Black men were unfit for military service. He considered them inferior to white soldiers, lacking the character, courage, and intellect required for combat, stereotypes that pervaded the military. Drawing on Army War College evaluations that assessed the performance of Black troops during World War I, Stimson confided to his diary, "Leadership is not embedded in the Negro race yet and to try to make commissioned officers to lead them into battle—colored men—is to work disaster for both." Furthermore, he maintained that segregation in the military must not be overturned. The army could not function as "a sociological laboratory" as it prepared for war.[18]

In the cramped offices of the War Department, the question was not how to integrate the armed forces or how to improve the conditions for Black soldiers, but how to *manage* "the Negro problem." After conducting extensive research and holding endless debates, the War Department maintained its separate but equal policy of "segregation without discrimination" as a necessity for avoiding a race war inside America's military camps, most of them located in the South. Rejecting Black Americans' cry for "the right to fight" for democracy at home and abroad, the Roosevelt administration needed a silent symbol, someone who inspired hope among millions of Black Americans without agitating for civil rights or racial equality. For that mission, Uncle Sam called on Joe Louis.[19]

But the federal government misjudged his plasticity. When he was inducted into the US Army, officers handed Louis a uniform, separated him from white soldiers, and directed him to the "colored" quarters. After his induction, Louis told *Pittsburgh Courier* columnist Billy Rowe that the segregated barracks were "the real battlefield" for Black troops. Talking with his fellow Black soldiers, Louis learned that he had to do more than entertain them with boxing exhibitions and short speeches about fighting Nazis. Encountering racism in military camps, Louis realized that his popularity as a famous athlete had done little to expand democracy. Being the heavyweight champion didn't insulate him from racism either. In the US Army, Joe Louis would discover that the fight against Hitler was important, but his greatest fight would be a battle against enemies on the home front.[20]

Chapter One

BLACK MOSES

You will hear the Louis saga in detail—how he was born in Alabama, the grandson of slaves belonging to the Barrows . . . a quiet unassuming colored boy of correct habits; a boy who has never smoked, used alcoholic drinks or chewed tobacco; whose early environment held the bravest of the brave . . . He has fought fair and square in his record in every instance, without ballahoo or bluster. Early in his career, his shrewd managers reminded him of his handicap of race and color, and impressed on him the value of modesty. Not to be ashamed of his race, but to help build it up in the eyes of the world, was, they urged, the best policy. The lesson stuck.

—Harry Stillwell Edwards, *Atlanta Journal*, June 19, 1936

"AT THE AGE OF 26, JOE LOUIS, HEAVYWEIGHT BOXING CHAMPION of the world, is the most famous and successful Negro on earth," began Earl Brown's *Life* magazine profile of the boxer. Published in June 1940, the seven-page article featured fifteen photographs, taking readers inside the champ's private world. Henry Luce's middlebrow publication seldom addressed issues of race, but Louis's popularity, particularly his fanatical hold on Black America, made him unique. In a 1941 cover story, *Time*, another Luce publication, would characterize him as a "Black Moses"—a leader, only two generations removed from slavery, who lifted "the children of Ham out of bondage" and delivered them to the promised land. Fittingly, Brown commented, "a picture of [Louis] hangs in the living room of almost every Negro home in the U.S." Across the country, Black women "named their cats, dogs and children after him" and, according to legend, the night Joe met his only defeat nine Black men died of heart attacks listening to the bout on the radio.[1]

Louis had reigned supreme in the American press from the time of his arrival in New York City in 1935 for a match against former heavyweight champion Primo Carnera, a six-foot-seven-inch, 260-pound Italian giant who had been plucked out of the circus and turned into a prizefighter by the mob. Joe's rags-to-riches biography, though sketchy, was widely known, especially to readers of the nation's Black newspapers, whose reporters had endowed the boxer with near superhuman qualities. From the onset of Joe's career, his manager, John Roxborough, cultivated mutually beneficial relationships with Black writers who, in exchange for access, wrote favorable columns presenting Louis as humble and dignified, a righteous force and the answer to Black America's prayers. In 1936, the *Pittsburgh Courier*'s Chester Washington, a writer who would serve as Joe's Boswell in the coming years, wrote, "He's quiet and reserved. He doesn't say much, but he's got an infectious, friendly grin that endears him to people. He's cocksure without being cocky; confident without being condescending. He's the type which everyone likes. Nothing Uncle-Tom about him."[2]

By 1940, Roxborough had come to expect that if a Black reporter was writing about Louis, not a disparaging word would be published about the champion. The unwritten rule for Black writers covering Louis was that they were expected to write fluff pieces—not hatchet jobs. Roxborough assumed, therefore, that a *Life* profile would further enhance his fighter's legend. *Life*'s editors selected Earl Brown to write the story. The Harvard-educated

Brown, a former Negro League ballplayer turned reporter and managing editor of the *New York Amsterdam News*, had covered the rise of Louis since at least the Carnera match. Ebeneezer Ray, a columnist for *The New York Age* who knew Brown, wrote that his counterpart "effects a quiet, unassuming manner—a dopey sort of 'unassuming.'" But, as another editorialist of the *Age* commented, Brown had a reputation for "coloring stories of those he liked and blasting away at those he disliked; it meant personal journalism; it meant inaccurate journalism."[3]

Roxborough welcomed the publicity. He carefully managed Louis's career and, even more importantly, his image. From the moment Joe turned professional, Roxborough and his business partner, Julian Black, set down several unbreakable rules that governed the fighter's conduct inside and outside the ring, knowing that white boxing fans preferred "Negro fighters virtuous, and remembering the stigma that still clung to colored fighters as a result of Jack Johnson's flamboyant wenching when he was the world's heavyweight champion" between 1908 and 1915. In short, noted a writer for *Time*, Roxborough and Black "decided that their boy was going to be pure." Inside the ropes, Joe became a gentleman killer—pummeling opponents into pugilistic graves, but never verbally humiliating them or suggesting in any way that they were anything less than worthy fighters. His deadpan expression before, during, and after matches and his brief, generous praise for his opponent—no matter how quickly dispatched—distanced him from the looming, gloating image of "Papa Jack" Johnson. Avoiding fixed fights and crooked entanglements with white mobsters, Louis said, "I want to fight honest so that the next colored boy can get the same kinda break I got. If I 'cut the fool,' I'll let my people down."[4]

Outside the ring, Louis traveled in a Black and brown world. His managers, trainers, friends, and wife were all Black. When he visited New York, he stayed uptown in Harlem at the Hotel Theresa between 124th and 125th Streets. When he landed in Chicago, he settled down on the South Side. And in Detroit, he mixed in his old Black Bottom neighborhood with longtime friends. No matter what city or town, Louis, unlike Johnson, treated any public social interaction with white women like handling vipers.

To protect his fighter, Roxborough established some ground rules for Earl Brown and John Fields, the *Life* editor. They assured him that they only had a human-interest piece in mind, a "complimentary and uplifting" story. Further, they promised the suspicious manager that he could read, and presumably suggest changes to, the final draft before publication. On this basis, Roxborough ushered Brown into Louis's inner circle. Brown received "every courtesy and consideration," Roxborough claimed. The quiet, "unassuming" reporter interviewed Roxborough, Joe's family, and several of his friends, and even the champion himself, always a difficult assignment. To make the assignment easier for Brown, the manager hosted the reporter at his home for several nights. Yet when the final draft was completed, Roxborough never saw it, though he requested to read it several times. Whether or not Brown planned from the first to ridicule and belittle Louis, to expose a member of his own race to public humiliation, is uncertain. But that's the way it turned out.[5]

On the surface, Brown's product touched all the bases. By 1940 the Joe Louis story had been told and retold in countless newspaper and magazine articles, blues recordings and calypso songs, and even one movie, *The Spirit of Youth*, with the prizefighter playing the lead. Somehow the standard narrative of his life never revealed the man in full, but his rise spoke to the important role he played as *the hero* in Black America. In 1936, Edward Van Every, a white reporter for *The Sun* and Joe's first biographer, believed, remarkably, that a young Black boxer with little formal education was meant to fulfill some divine mission for brokering peace between the races. "It is, and not extravagant to set down, as though the finger of God had singled this youth out for purposes of His own," Van Every wrote. "That the Negro race should find a Black Moses who was to prove of incalculable assistance to the great leaders of his people in lighting the way to a broader tolerance on the part of his white brother, and that this ambassador to the finer brotherhood should come up from the mayhap brutalizing paths and byways of pugilism, is as irreconcilable with plausibility as that a Negro could be acceptable in the role of heavyweight champion of the prize ring."[6]

The Joe Louis Barrow legend began in red-clay LaFayette, Alabama, in a dilapidated sharecropper's shack nestled close to the Georgia line. Born on May 13, 1914, the seventh of eight children, young Joe endured a hardscrabble existence with his family in the Chambers County countryside, laboring long hours in the sun-soaked cotton fields and often going to bed hungry at night. Virtually uneducated, burdened by a speech impediment, he faced daunting odds, which did not improve much when his overworked and often withdrawn father was committed to the Searcy Hospital for the Colored Criminally Insane in Mount Vernon, when Joe was about two years old. If chroniclers favored rags-to-riches stories, Louis's rags phase was as bad as they come.

His life took a slight turn upward when his mother and her second husband moved the family from Alabama to Detroit, Michigan, joining the Great Migration of Southern Black people to the urban Midwest and Northeast. If his educational opportunities didn't improve much, he did find regular work delivering ice and hauling truck bodies on a conveyor belt at a Ford auto plant. But the arrival of the Great Depression in 1929 made finding any paying work more difficult, particularly for Black Detroiters. In the spring of 1932 at the age of seventeen, shortly before the Hoover

Depression became the Roosevelt Depression, Louis found his gold mine—boxing, first as an amateur and then as a professional. He rose through the ranks with astonishing speed. Dropping Barrow from his name and fighting as Joe Louis, in 1933 and 1934 he won the Golden Gloves and several other national championships before turning professional under the management of Roxborough and Julian Black, who were often referred to as civic leaders in the Black enclaves of Detroit and Chicago.

The last piece in Louis's Horatio Alger tale was the promotional deal he signed with Mike Jacobs, who was on the cusp of becoming the most powerful operator in the sport. Jacobs could guarantee Louis important matches on the best dates in the largest venues. Summer bouts in New York at Yankee Stadium or the Polo Grounds, Chicago's Comiskey Park, and Philadelphia's Municipal Stadium—outdoor facilities that could seat tens of thousands of paying customers and generate million-dollar gates—were now open to the Brown Bomber. Jacobs would make Louis wealthy, and Joe would make the promoter a country squire on an estate in Rumson, New Jersey.

This was the well-worn Joe Louis saga—from Alabama to Detroit to New York, aided by several benevolent race men and a promoter who convinced Louis and his Black managers that as a proud Jew he knew something about discrimination in America. Roxborough, Black, and Jacobs promised to guide the fighter's career, watch over him, and make sure that he did not end up punch-drunk and broke. It was a comforting tale of decent men and a great athlete, of the meritocracy in sports and the democratic nature of America.

But that comforting tale was not fully accurate. Not by a long shot. By mid-1940, the successful triumvirate of Louis, Roxborough, and Jacobs confronted joint and individual problems. Money welded the three men together. Between 1935 and 1939, spurred by Jacobs's shrewd matchmaking and promotional genius, Louis became a veritable cash machine, giving life to the song "We're in the Money." His matches against former champions Primo Carnera, Max Baer, Max Schmeling, Jack Sharkey, and reigning title holder Jimmy Braddock saw the largest gates of the decade, and his contests against such contenders as "Two Ton" Tony Galento and King Levinsky were blockbusters. But in 1940 the gates began to shrink in proportion to the popularity of Louis's opponents. Added to this problem, the three men came under a level of scrutiny that was less than flattering.

Earl Brown's widely read profile, for instance, veered dramatically from the standard treatment of Joe's life story. In his article, Louis emerges as the most unlikely athlete to receive an invitation to a cotillion. Brown treats Louis as an illiterate, voiceless fighter, interested only in eating, sleeping, and watching movies. "Serious thoughts about his position in the world do not bother the champion." Instead, he spends his days chomping on apples, downing ice cream by the quart, and lounging on a sofa. With a sniff of superiority, Brown noted, "Louis's deportment, though better than it used to be, is not yet Chesterfieldian. At [the] table he sprawls like a huge puppy dog, with feet and elbows drifting in all directions. He snores like a Mack truck when asleep and wallows like a walrus when washing." Brown reported that the champion owned twenty-five pairs of shoes, though he frequently complained that they hurt his feet and enjoyed walking barefoot indoors and out. Adding anecdotes that would make Louis look most ridiculous, *Life*'s reporter observed, "One of [Joe's] small luxuries is having his corns trimmed by his wife, Marva, with whom his relations are otherwise not altogether flawless."[7]

Brown's frontal assault on the marriage between Joe and Marva incensed millions of Black readers. At the time, the two were the unofficial first family of Black America. Out for a stroll along an avenue in Harlem, dressed flawlessly and stunningly good-looking, they could draw a crowd any day of the week. Children and adults scrambled for the best view and trailed behind the couple for blocks. In the Black press, there was no saturation point for news stories about them. Joe training for an upcoming fight, Marva preparing at their Spring Hill estate in Michigan for a horse show, Joe blistering another white challenger, Marva attending Vogue Designing School, or both opening their fabulous closets to delighted reporters—every story seemed as if it had been filed from the land of Oz. Rich, famous, beautiful—there was not another success story for Black Americans like it.

Yet Brown suggested, sometimes with just a wisp of a detail, that there was trouble in paradise. Joe and Marva came from different worlds. Marva grew up in a religious upwardly mobile middle-class family that valued education and refinement. She enjoyed social gatherings but disliked her husband's childhood friends. Joe believed Marva's Sugar Hill soirees were pretentious and, even worse, boring. Marva thought that her husband's friends were parasites, estimating that he had spent about $200,000—an outrageous sum in 1940—entertaining them. Added to all this was the widely recognized, if seldom mentioned, fact that "Louis likes to make friends in democratic fashion with the entertainers in Harlem cafes." Translated from the magazine's circumspect editorial policy—Joe had dozens of meaningless affairs. Perhaps as a result, Brown included the couple's sleeping arrangements—twin beds. Nonetheless, he reported, "Joe and Marva have never had a rift serious enough to endanger Louis' position as an example of his race."[8]

Virtually everyone close to Louis was cut by Brown's axe. Roxborough and Black, generally characterized by Black writers as successful businessmen and benevolent guardians of Joe, emerged as criminals. "Roxborough is currently trying to establish his innocence in a Detroit policy-racket case," the journalist noted. "Black has a rather impressive police record. Fortunately, the fact that both Louis managers are undoubtedly well acquainted with the shadier side of Detroit's sporting and commercial life has operated for the good of all concerned," he added. Brown even made Joe's mother, Lillie Barrow Brooks, look foolish when he quoted her in Uncle Remus dialogue. "Dat boy was born in 1914. . . . He's always been healthy and strong 'cause I fed him plenty of collard greens, fat back, and corn pone."[9]

If Earl Brown's profile revealed uncomfortable truths about the champion—his flaws and shortcomings, and the seedy side of his career—it also provoked great anger from Black readers who believed the *Life* writer was determined to correct the "fictionized accounts of Joe Louis" spun by the Black press on a near daily basis. In order to understand the fierce defense of Joe Louis and his universal admiration among Black Americans, "we must try to grasp the meaning of the immense prestige that the Negro community attaches to those who are successful," Roi Ottley explained in his 1943 book *'New World A-Coming': Inside Black America*. Ottley argued that for Black Americans the success of one individual translated into a success for the entire race. "Close track is kept of Negroes who have been successful in all fields, but especially in those fields in which Negroes excel in competition with white men." That's what made Louis, a boxer, so important. Every Black kid who looked like him lived vicariously through the champ's triumphs. He gave Black folks reason to "shout and yell—and indeed to brag and boast." The Joe Louis story had "encouraged and inspired, moved and stirred, and set . . . examples of exemplary conduct." The power of the Louis tale was that it made Black people "unafraid of tomorrow." But if it turned out that the Louis story wasn't true—or that it was built on lies—that would shatter the hopes and dreams of millions of Black people.[10]

One unshakable rule that followed from Ottley's view was that Black folks should not attack a hero of the race, especially in front of white Americans. And there were not many publications whiter than Henry Luce's *Life* magazine. That made the backlash immediate—and damning. In his *New York Age* column, Ebeneezer Ray accused Earl Brown of stripping "the champion of everything complimentary but his ability to defeat his opponents. Any illusions that Louis admirers may have of him being the gentleman he appears to be on the surface is effectively dispelled. . . . Even Joe's conjugal life is mentioned." Going even further, another columnist for *The New York Age* labeled Brown a "pet" of the editors of *Time* and *Life*, essentially calling him the white publisher's "boy." The columnist predicted that Brown was through as a Black press man.[11]

The importance of the *Life* profile extended beyond Brown's questionable journalistic practices. Because Louis belonged to all of Black America, an assault on his character, even if true, became a highly politicized event. Walter White expressed outrage when he read the magazine article. A longtime admirer of Louis, the head of the NAACP kept a picture of the champ in his office, and he often uttered gratitude for Joe's generous donations to the civil rights organization. Lashing out at Brown, White wrote, "You and I know that there are any number of white people who don't want to see <u>any</u> Negro earn as much money or stay on top." The inclusion of a picture of Brown at the beginning of the article would make it easier for white critics to attack Louis. Why, White wondered, had Brown not focused on all the "commendable things" Louis had done?[12]

White was more direct in his correspondence with the editor of *Life*. Had White not known the fighter and his managers, not known the good they had done for their communities and their race, after reading the article he would have been misled to believe that Joe was "exceedingly stupid and Messrs. Roxborough and Black [were] cold-blooded Svengalis." But he knew better, and in a two-page letter elucidated the record. Inside the ropes, the boxer and his managers had never engaged in a fixed fight or been involved in any "shady business of that sort." Joe "refused to endorse products simply to get money." In fact, on one occasion the NAACP leader witnessed Louis turn down a "huge cheque" to endorse a brand of whiskey. He recalled Joe saying, "a lot of kids think they should do what the Champion does and I am not going to cause any of them to think drinking whiskey is right." Altogether, White lamented the decision of the magazine to print such a one-sided, inaccurate article of a vital Black idol.[13]

No one was more incensed by Earl Brown's article than John Roxborough. Infuriated and embarrassed that he had failed to protect Joe from "a sinister campaign" launched by a "white magazine," he took his complaints to the press. Not only was it "probably the worst story ever written about Joe," he told a *Detroit Tribune* reporter, but the humiliation was compounded by the fact that "it was written by a member of his own race." In Roxy's eyes, Brown "proved himself just another 'Uncle Tom,' who if he had his own way, would sell the Negroes of America down the river and back into slavery." Worse, Brown was a Judas, betraying a good and decent man for personal gain. But instead of thirty pieces of silver, the reporter "sold his racial pride for a mess of pottage."[14]

Joe Louis never uttered a word about Earl Brown, at least not publicly. He often said that he let his fighting do his talking. Roxborough had urged him to avoid arguments with reporters even if they spread bitter lies. For a boxer, even bad publicity was good publicity, his manager once said. "You just got to keep clean so they can't write you into scandal," Roxborough advised. It was a hard lesson his manager had learned from experience.[15]

THE FIGHT OF HIS LIFE

THERE WERE FEW STRAIGHT LINES IN JOE LOUIS'S LIFE. People drifted in and out, like they were passing through a revolving hotel door. Some he came to know well, others barely, and many not at all. Janet MacDonald, a thirty-four-year-old divorced émigré from England, fell into the last category. Joe Louis had no role in her sensational story, but the fallout of MacDonald's drama would have a profound impact on his life.

In 1937, MacDonald lived with her nine-year-old daughter Pearl in a boardinghouse on the east side of Detroit, working as a cashier in a small market. Then her life changed dramatically. She met William McBride, a mid-level hood who managed Detroit's Great Lakes Mutual Numbers House, an illegal gambling organization. They fell in love. Or at least she did. He arranged for her to work in his organization. McBride spent freely, tipped grandly, and enjoyed influential "friends" in Detroit's criminal, political, and law enforcement circles. He was, it turned out, especially close to Richard Reading Jr., son and right-hand man of Mayor Richard "Little Dick" Reading Sr. himself.[16]

But after a few good years, McBride sank into something that resembled a crisis of conscience. In July 1939 he ended his affair with MacDonald. It was for her "own good," he said. He generously counseled her to find "some nice fellow," a man such as he wasn't. MacDonald took the brush-off badly, vowing that only over her dead body would McBride take up with another woman.

Several anguished weeks later, Janet MacDonald made good on her words. On August 5th she retrieved her daughter from her sister's house, saying that they were going horseback riding, though the pink taffeta dress Pearl wore seemed more appropriate for an afternoon tea. Instead of galloping on horses, she prowled through the streets of Detroit until her daughter had fallen asleep. Only then did she pull into a tiny rented garage and attach a hose from the car's exhaust to its rear window. The carbon monoxide killed them both.

Before Janet MacDonald died, in a fine, steady hand she wrote a series of letters addressed to the Detroit police commissioner, several newspapers, Michigan's governor, and Detroit's FBI head outlining McBride's operation. The epistles precisely detailed the leading numbers organization's police bribes and political payoffs. Naming names and detailing the inner workings of the operation and the police protection arrangements, her remarkable j'accuse letters and dramatic death outraged city residents.

Mayor "Little Dick" Reading and his superintendent of police quickly formed racket squads to investigate and absolve themselves of the charges. "It's a lot of nonsense," claimed Reading. "I don't know what it is all about." But the evidence said otherwise. On April 24, 1940, a Detroit judge indicted Reading and 134 others of giving and accepting graft payments that allowed the city's $10 million a year numbers racket to thrive. Of the 135 indicted, 28 were Black. And one of them was a prominent businessman and committed "race man" in the Motor City: Joe Louis's manager, John Roxborough. Asked for a comment, Roxborough brushed the reporter aside. Smiling as he puffed a cigar, he explained, "I've been out of town and do not know what it is all about, but maybe I ought to check up and see if I stubbed my toe."[17]

The truth was that Roxborough knew the indictment was coming. *New York Daily News* columnist Jimmy Powers suggested that Roxborough had exploited public appearances by Louis to gain political favors in Michigan. And if investigators conducted an audit of Roxy's accounting, Powers wrote, they would find several sportswriters on the take. Outraged by Powers's column, Roy Wilkins, the NAACP's assistant secretary, rushed to defend Roxborough. Wilkins believed that countless white writers resented the fact that the champion's Black managers—"the Louis mob,"

Powers called them—were financially independent and not beholden to the white sports establishment. And now those same columnists, "tired of a Negro being heavyweight champion of the world," read Roxborough's indictment and planned to use it to destroy Joe's reputation since no white man could beat him in the ring.[18]

Pittsburgh Courier columnist Wendell Smith could not believe a grand jury would "railroad" "Genial John," a man who had "conducted himself above reproach in so many other lines of endeavor." Most Black reporters who knew Roxborough described him as a gentleman, "a credit to the Negro race," and the pride of Detroit. He had been born into a socially and politically influential biracial family and was well educated and business wise. His father had been a successful lawyer, a pillar of Detroit's Paradise Valley. His brother Charles was also a lawyer and politico, becoming the first Black person elected to the Michigan Senate. But John Roxborough was more interested in business than the law. He ran a real estate company, had banking and other commercial interests, and contributed generously to various charities supporting Black Detroit. Always interested in sports, he funded several local baseball teams. Soft-spoken and impeccably dressed, the bespectacled, moon-faced benefactor attended track meets and baseball games, boxing matches and football contests, eager to help a talented athlete reach for his dreams.[19]

Roxborough had spotted Joe Louis early in the boxer's amateur career. Recognizing Joe's talent, the businessman facilitated his development. He gave the fighter training money, but beyond that, he educated Joe, providing instruction on how to dress, speak, and behave socially. He even boarded the fighter in his own home. Was Roxborough's generosity a savvy investment? Perhaps. When Louis turned pro in 1934, Roxborough was his comanager, claiming 25 percent of every one of the boxer's purses, an amount that eventually rose above a million dollars. Yet in several crucial ways, Roxborough became a surrogate father to Louis. In a sport where exploitation was routine, where managers regularly gobbled, used up, and spit out their fighters, Roxborough looked out for Louis, trying as much as he could to save him from the sad fate of so many other boxers. At least that was the popular belief in the 1930s, and it was at least partially true.[20]

Gentleman, business tycoon, philanthropist, race man, and benevolent manager—Roxborough laid claim to all these titles. And one more—numbers operator. Out of a building on St. Antoine Street, he ran the Big Four Policy and Numbers House, generating an estimated $800,000 annually. He took chances and made a small fortune. When the police arrested Roxborough, he didn't try to make deals or implicate others to save himself—especially Louis, whom he insisted knew nothing about his businesses. "I liked the way he stood up to that Detroit indictment," wrote a Black columnist for the *Norfolk Journal and Guide*. "No whimpering. No mealy-mouthed hypocritical statements. Only the savage insistence that Joe Louis is not implicated. . . . He has his own code of right and wrong and has practiced it in its broadest sense always with the good name of his race in view."[21]

Even so, Roxborough's trouble soon became Joe Louis's problem. With his numbers business shut down and his legal expenses soaring, he desperately needed cash. In the past he had occasionally lent money to Louis when the improvident champion needed five or ten thousand dollars. Now the manager began to call in the loans, which Joe could only repay with his ring earnings. Roxborough and Louis required another major fight, another million-dollar gate. But Joe had already beaten all the big draws. It was a problem of supply and demand. In any era, quality heavyweights are a rare commodity. They require talent and dedication, as well as years of seasoning and promotional buildup. But

Louis had already rampaged through *The Ring*'s top ten list. The more he fought, the more he reduced the limited supply of capable and compelling opponents. By the end of 1940, with Roxborough more focused on staying out of prison than on Louis's career, Joe's schedule had been effectively turned over to promoter Mike Jacobs. Roxborough had often promised that he would take care of Joe. He insisted it was a question of race as well as decency. Jacobs, however, had made other promises, including arranging a shot at the title. Beyond that, he offered no commitments.

Mike Jacobs knew something about robbery. On April 7, 1940, a half dozen armed thieves invaded Jacobs's Rumson, New Jersey, home. At the time, the promoter, his wife, and some friends were watching television, which had begun regular broadcasts a year earlier. Jacobs described the gunmen as "nice and friendly," as gunmen went. "There were no arguments. I asked for a cigarette, and they gave me one." Then he did what he did best—negotiate. In the end, the robbers left the home with $700 and a cheap watch, and the women got to keep their diamonds. Though the victims reported the heist, Jacobs was vague about the entire affair, refusing at first to disclose the names of his friends and dollar amounts. Even so, the county prosecutor let it be known that he would "solve the horrid crime." But the investigation, if there was one, completely disappeared from newspapers.[22]

The entire story displayed the nature of Jacobs's career. There was something strange about it. A gang of "friendly" gunmen robbing a mansion and walking away with a few hundred dollars and an inexpensive lady's watch? No diamonds, no search of the house, no attempt to extort even more money from the wealthy group? But then, that was the story of Jacobs's improbable life, a tale where the lines between fact and fiction blurred, where accounting numbers were apt to suddenly change, and where exact details were hard to find. Of only two things could an observer be certain: No deal was exactly what it seemed, and at the end of the day Mike Jacobs worked out a favorable deal.

Everyone in the boxing game called the promoter "Uncle Mike." He encouraged that informality. It endowed him with a charming, familiar, harmless air, one that was accentuated by the cut of his cheap suits and the rattle of his store-bought false teeth. But the sobriquet Uncle Mike fit him about as well as "Uncle Joe" suited Stalin. Peering through his glasses with the small birdlike eyes of a predator, dark and intense, he unnerved anyone negotiating a deal with him. "When you heard his teeth clack and looked into those dark eyes," recalled boxing writer Dan Daniel, "you instinctively felt for your wallet."[23]

A son of Jewish immigrants born in a filthy, rough-edged Irish neighborhood close to the New York City Battery, Jacobs hustled nickels and dimes as soon as he was old enough to hustle. And he kept on hustling for the remainder of his life. With an uncanny sense of what New Yorkers and out-of-towners wanted to see, he accumulated a fortune speculating on tickets to Broadway plays, sporting events, and the Metropolitan Opera House. From hawking ducats to backing productions and assorted ventures was a small but lucrative step. Trafficking in everything from plays and six-day bicycle races to the Buffalo Bill Wild West Show and the Fifth Avenue fashion show, Uncle Mike took his cut. And in the 1920s, when New York legalized boxing and the sport entered its golden age, Jacobs bankrolled promoter George "Tex" Rickard, raking in enormous profits.[24]

Uncle Mike's finest day came in 1935 when he convinced Joe Louis's management team to sign an exclusive promotional contract with him. The deal eventually paved the way for Jacobs to take over promotions at Madison Square Garden and the prime summer dates for major fights at Yankee Stadium. Beginning in June 1935 with Primo Carnera, the House that Ruth Built and where the Bronx Bombers played became the Home of the Brown Bomber. By the end of 1941 Jacobs had featured Louis in eight Yankee Stadium bouts, including both contests with Max Schmeling.

Uncle Mike's plans for Louis were not made with Joe's health in mind. He believed that he had made Louis champion, and that meant Joe owed him. Jacobs played a critical role in arranging a title shot for Louis. By all rights—a slippery concept in the boxing racket—champion James J. Braddock should have defended his title in 1937 against Max Schmeling. The logic of a Braddock–Schmeling championship fight was irrefutable, the fairness unassailable. The German had won his last four fights, three by knockout and all against quality opponents. His signature victory in the streak was a decisive twelve-round knockout of Joe Louis. The win jumped Schmeling above Louis as number one contender, convincing the New York boxing commission to order Braddock to defend his title against Max.

Jacobs had other ideas. Control of the heavyweight champion was essential to his plans to dominate the entire sport. Virtually every authority predicted that a Louis–Braddock fight would be a mismatch. The Brown Bomber, they said, would dispatch the Cinderella Man in short order. The same boxing scribes expressed confidence that Schmeling would also defeat Braddock. Undoubtedly, the next champion would be the first of the two leading challengers to fight Braddock. Given the march toward war in Europe, coupled with Adolf Hitler's racist ideology, Jacobs suspected that if Schmeling won the heavyweight crown, it would come under the Führer's control, and Louis would never get a chance to fight for it. Somehow the crafty promoter had to convince Braddock and his manager Joe Gould to ignore the New York boxing commission and sidestep Schmeling.

His first strategy centered on anti-fascism. By the summer of 1937, Hitler had made his political and social designs abundantly evident. He had re-established mandatory military service in the Reich, remilitarized the Rhineland, renounced the Versailles Peace Treaty, signed defense treaties with fascist Italy and Imperial Japan, and fought alongside other fascists in Spain. Inside Germany, he had all but eliminated Jews from every corner of the fatherland's political, social, and cultural life. The fate of Jews in boxing, in fact, had been settled in the first months of his regime. On March 30, 1933, two months after Hitler became chancellor, the head of amateur boxing announced that Jews could no longer belong to his organization. Professional boxing soon eliminated Jewish participants altogether. According to the antisemitic newspaper *Der Angriff*, there was simply no place in German boxing for Jews—not as pugilists, trainers, doctors, lawyers, promotors, managers, or "whatever else those bloodsuckers call themselves."[25]

At that time Schmeling had not officially joined the Nazi party. He still enjoyed outstanding relations with the American press, and employed a Jewish manager—the flamboyant, cigar-chomping Joe Jacobs, a character who seemed to have emerged from the typewriter of Damon Runyon. But the fact that the boxer was German quickly tarnished everything else. In this frigid US–German political climate, anything that Hitler supported instantly became a commodity for opposition among "patriotic Americans." Some of the opposition groups that arose in this political climate were the Non-Sectarian Anti-Nazi League, the Jewish War Veterans, the American League Against War and Fascism, and like-minded groups and individuals. Although Mike Jacobs (no relation to Joe Jacobs) rarely ventured into deep and swirling political waters, he did develop some strong anti-fascist opinions about the scheduled Braddock–Schmeling fight. Expressing his newly discovered political conscience, he echoed the various anti-Nazi groups, suggesting that a Braddock–Schmeling fight would, in effect, be a stain on the American Declaration of Independence and the US Constitution. And even worse, with so many groups calling for a boycott, the fight wouldn't draw flies.[26]

On the other hand, a Braddock–Louis title match proved a quick fix to some prickly ethical, political, and financial problems. Ethically it removed the promoter from doing anything that resembled accommodating the Nazis; politically it supported a wide band of constituencies, Jewish organizations, and Black groups, in fact most interested American groups except for the German–American Bund; and financially the entire kerfuffle had generated so much soap-opera publicity that the fight was sure to kill at the box office. Neither Uncle Mike nor Joe Gould cared an iota about fairness for Schmeling or demands made by the New York boxing commission. They focused on the dollars—but on that subject the promoter and the manager disagreed.

Gould, representing Braddock, wanted the best deal possible, not only because the Cinderella Man was champion but because when he entered the ring against Louis, in all likelihood, the clock would strike midnight and he would end up flat on his back. A mediocre heavyweight with a long and undistinguished record, his fight against Louis would probably be his last, or close to it. That being the case, Gould felt that his man's end of the purse should be extra generous. Not only did he insist on 50 percent of the gate, he demanded an unprecedented bonus—20 percent of the net profits from every Joe Louis heavyweight championship bout that Jacobs promoted over the next decade. The deal would have staggered the imagination of P. T. Barnum or John D. Rockefeller. If Mike Jacobs had been able to evaluate the proposal in the abstract, he might even have envied it. But he took a more practical view. His ultimate plans, which included near-monopolistic control of professional boxing, depended on Louis winning the title. Therefore, he took the deal, undoubtedly plotting to maneuver out of it somewhere down the road.[27]

Louis won the title in Chicago's Comiskey Park on June 22, 1937, brutally knocking out Braddock in the eighth round after pummeling him for most of the fight. The former champion earned his share of the gate—and the extra unpublicized bonus. Jacobs's Twentieth Century Sporting Club captured the one prize it needed to dominate the sport. Of course, the promoter attempted to worm out of the deal, generating suits and countersuits, and in the process exposing the financial relationship between Louis and Jacobs. By March 1940, Gould and Braddock claimed that Jacobs owed them just over $104,000 for their cut from nine Louis title defenses. For some reporters the financial breakdown involved in the suit was just numbers in a ledger book, but several Black columnists noticed that the Brown Bomber's share from his fights was considerably less than what was generally reported. Joe received only 50 percent of his share of the gate. Roxborough and Black each received 25 percent. When all the divisions and subtractions were made, Uncle Mike made significantly more from each Louis defense than the Brown Bomber.[28]

However, by 1940, three years after Louis won the championship, Jacobs struggled to find fighters who could legitimately challenge him for the heavyweight title. In February, when Jacobs arranged for Louis to defend his crown against Chilean Arturo Godoy, an unranked ring veteran, virtually no sportswriter gave the contender a chance of winning. They undoubtedly agreed with the *Daily Worker*'s Lester Rodney that the challenger "will be a hero if he lasts more than five rounds." A few days before the contest Rodney reflected on the Louis phenomenon. Perhaps it was because there appeared to be no serious contenders remaining in the heavyweight ranks; maybe it was because a few blocks away from the Garden a large electric sign advertised *Gone with the Wind*, a nostalgic film that romanticized the antebellum South and presented Black people as servants and field hands. The communist sportswriter knew it had something to do with the explosion of humanity in Harlem after each victory of the Brown Bomber. The people "pour down the rickety steps into the street as soon as the radio tells them that he's won again—and somebody always digs up an old Ethiopian flag for a parade down 7th Avenue." The scribe thought that Joe was the greatest fighter who had ever lived—and something else, he was "much more significant than just a sports figure."[29]

Surprisingly, Godoy lasted past the fifth round. The rugged Chilean scrapper went the distance in an odd, unorthodox contest. His style defied description, confounding Louis. Like Tony Galento, another contender who frustrated the champion, Godoy fought from a deep crouch, bending at the knees and the waist. At times he dipped so low that his chest and chin almost scraped the canvas. Then, when it seemed he could not contort his body any lower, he would suddenly pogo-stick upward, launching left and right hooks at Louis's head. If he missed with the hooks—which he usually did—he closed tight to the champion—smothering Joe's punches, using his head and shoulders and elbows to hurt Louis, and then holding on until the referee split the two men. "Joe was slapped, laughed at, wrestled from corner to corner, taunted and provoked into probably the worst exhibition he has ever given in a prize ring since he was knocked out by Max Schmeling," judged Jimmy Powers.[30]

Louis's problem was that his jabs and hooks went over Godoy's head whenever the South American fighter stooped into his ludicrous crouch. But Louis landed enough punches to slice open Godoy's face in a dozen or more spots. And certainly, he scored enough to eke out a split decision. Although some writers believed the verdict was fair, several more cynical reporters thought that

Louis carried Godoy, allowing him to last the full fifteen rounds and keeping the fight close. Why? With so few viable contenders, a close decision would allow Jacobs and the reporters in his pocket to beat the drum for a summer stadium rematch. A photograph in *The Ring* showing Godoy locked onto Uncle Mike in a two-fisted hug while he planted a kiss on the promoter's cheek did nothing to dispel the rematch hypothesis. Nor did Godoy's startling jump from an unranked heavyweight to number one contender.[31]

Everything in the match seemed backward. Celebrated columnist Richards Vidmer touched the heart of the matter: "Louis won, but was not pleased. Godoy lost, but was jumping with joy an hour afterward, for the champion in victory had fought a bad fight and the challenger in defeat had accomplished the seemingly impossible by staying on his feet through fifteen rounds. Joe Louis was depressed, Godoy delighted."[32]

Joe took his Pyrrhic loss in stride. How could he fight an opponent who spent so much of the match looking like he was preparing to lower himself onto a mattress? "If a guy wants to stay and crawls on the ground you can't do much about it," commented the champion. "Maybe that's the way they fight south of the border." Even worse, it was his lowest-grossing Madison Square Garden fight. All he could do was shake his head and apologize for his performance.[33]

The bad match provided kindling for reporters critical of the champion. Since his 1936 loss to Max Schmeling, white boxing writers had filed hundreds of stories focused on Louis's flaws. He carried his right too low, he lacked the intelligence to adjust in the heat of battle, the good life had made him soft. Their conclusion: The champion's days were numbered. Better he leave the fight game on top than suffer another humiliating victory.[34]

Robert Considine advanced another reason Louis should exit. Like Alexander the Great, the champion had no more worlds to conquer. "I know it will be tough to quit," Considine wrote. "You want to; you've wanted to for some time. But there are complications. You are the central meal ticket of the 20th Century Sport Club." But Joe deserved retirement. He had been the "fairest, cleanest and most honest fighter any of us ever saw . . . You never had an alibi or unkind word about an opponent." Gracious in victory, honest in his one defeat, he had been that rarest of title holders—"a fighting champion" who never handpicked opponents. Considine ended by imploring, "Quit it, Joe. You've been an inspiration to your race and you've given boxing more than it probably deserves."[35]

Considine may have overestimated Louis's wealth, but his evaluation of the champion's importance to Jacobs's Twentieth Century Sporting Club was accurate. The main drawing card, the most dependable source of money, he had made Jacobs a very wealthy man. The promoter had no plans for Louis's retirement; just the opposite, his strategy called for an increase in the Bomber's title defenses. After the match, Jacobs began to think that Louis was vulnerable and that a stable of challengers could test him in matches that would generate packed arenas. "We're loaded to the barrel, now," he said. "The day before yesterday it looked as if we'd never find anybody to stand up against Louis, and now, because of what Godoy did, I can put the champion in against any one of nine contenders."[36]

Appropriately, nearly six weeks after facing Godoy, Louis returned to the Garden for a Finnish Relief Fund fight against Johnny Paychek, an unimpressive though ranked contender. Less than twelve thousand people paid to watch the contest, and judging from the boos most thought they did not get their money's worth. Paychek climbed into the ring visibly shaken. Nat Fleischer wrote that he appeared "more scared than any pugilist I have ever seen in my long association with the sport." Another ringside reporter quipped, "Did you ever see a ghost walking? I did." Once the bell rang, Paychek's fears materialized. From start to finish, Louis dominated the fight, knocking Paychek out cold in the second round. It took a bucket of ice water poured over his head to return him to consciousness.[37]

After demolishing Johnny Paychek, Louis's June rematch against Arturo Godoy erased all doubts about his fitness as champion. For seven rounds at Yankee Stadium, working with the methodical precision of a "butcher," he sliced and carved Godoy's face in one of the goriest bouts of his career. Streams of blood leaked from Arturo's flattened nose. His bloodstained chin looked as if a barber had shaved him with a rusty razor. "I took my time because I knew he would open up sooner or later," Louis said. In the eighth round, Joe thrashed him repeatedly and "almost tore Godoy's nose off." After the champ leveled Godoy twice, the referee stopped the mismatch on a technical knockout. When he rose to his feet, Godoy tried chasing Louis, but his handlers intercepted him. When it was all over, Louis declared it was the worst beating he had ever inflicted on another man.[38]

Only about twenty-seven thousand spectators witnessed the dramatic display of Louis's redemption. Always concerned about the bottom line, Mike Jacobs grumbled that he had lost money at the gate. For an outdoor title match at Yankee Stadium, it was a pathetic turnout. Was it the news from Europe that France was collapsing under the German blitzkrieg? Or was Joe so dominant that white fans had become tired of watching him knock out one white contender after another? Either way, Jacobs needed a new strategy to capitalize on Louis before the war reached America.

Chapter Two

THE CAMPAIGN

We're conducting a colored blitzkrieg. We're crusaders for Negroes. Joe is a fine politician.

—John Roxborough, on the eve of the 1940 presidential election

ON JUNE 10, 1940, THE SAME DAY JOE LOUIS SIGNED A CONTRACT for his rematch against Arturo Godoy, Franklin Roosevelt boarded US Train Car No. 1 at Union Station. A journalist observed the president looking "grave and pale" as he contemplated the dire news from Europe. While FDR prepared to deliver a commencement speech at the University of Virginia, German armies were cutting across the Marne southeast of Paris. In the previous two months, the Germans had vanquished much of northwestern Europe with lightning speed, conquering Denmark, Norway, Belgium, the Netherlands, and Luxembourg. It seemed only a matter of time before the Nazis would seize the French capital. Although most Americans wanted to believe that the war in Europe would not disrupt their lives, that the United States could and should remain neutral, the sheer speed of the Nazi blitzkrieg disabused the most clear-eyed citizens of that isolationist fantasy.[1]

About an hour before departing Washington, DC, Roosevelt seethed when he learned that Italian dictator Benito Mussolini had declared war on France and Great Britain. Incensed, he considered Mussolini's expansion of the war into the Mediterranean Sea an opportunistic and treacherous act. As the presidential train rolled beneath a somber sky through the green foothills of Virginia, Roosevelt pored over the typed draft of his speech, scribbling entirely new lines in the margins with a pencil. The president knew that he would have to use his pulpit to convince Americans of the escalating danger creeping at their doorstep. "On this tenth day of June, 1940," he wrote, "the hand that held the dagger has struck it into the back of its neighbor."[2]

As his train pulled into Charlottesville, a relentless rain soaked the campus. Faculty, students, parents, photographers, and reporters moved from the Lawn into Memorial Gymnasium. There, FDR ascended the stage in a cap and gown with his Harvard crimson hood to the strains of "Hail to the Chief." Standing before a crowd of eight thousand people, including his son Franklin Jr., a freshly minted UVA Law School grad, Roosevelt gave what *Time* magazine called "a fighting speech, more powerful and more determined than any he had delivered since the war began." Broadcasted on radio across the country and translated into seven languages for shortwave transmission around the globe, Roosevelt spoke forcefully against isolationists who insisted that the United States could remain an island of democracy in a world of totalitarianism. "Such an island," he said, represented "a helpless nightmare of a people without freedom, a people lodged in prison, handcuffed, hungry, and fed through the bars from day to day by the contemptuous, unpitying masters of other continents."[3]

At a moment when most Americans opposed entering the war against Germany, Roosevelt's message signaled an end to any pretense of American neutrality. He declared the United States would extend material supplies to the Allies and accelerate war production so that America would have the necessary manpower and munitions for defending democracy at home and abroad. Fearing an imminent German invasion of Britain as France teetered on the brink of collapse, Roosevelt called for unity and urgency in wartime mobilization. The American people would not hesitate, he said. "We will not slow down or detour. Signs and signals call for speed—full speed ahead."[4]

Roosevelt's speech aroused boisterous applause, but after he returned to the White House his most vocal critics denounced him as a belligerent warmonger plunging the country into an unnecessary conflict. Charles Lindbergh, the famous aviator whose solo flight across the Atlantic in 1927 had turned him into a national hero, emerged as the unofficial spokesman for the isolationists, condemning the president. An admirer of Hitler and German aviation, Lindbergh argued that Roosevelt was fueling "defense hysteria" and threatening peace with the Nazis. Perpetuating old antisemitic myths, Lindbergh suggested that a Jewish conspiracy was responsible for undermining America's racial solidarity with white Europeans and provoking war with Germany. Furthermore, he thought it was unlikely that the United States could defeat the German army—the strongest military in the world. In a national radio address delivered on June 15, the day after Paris fell to the Nazis, Lindbergh insisted that Hitler's domination of Europe would be preferable to America embarking on a suicidal military mission intended to stop it.[5]

With a presidential election fast approaching, the great debate between Roosevelt and Lindbergh, interventionists and isolationists, raged over the summer of 1940. After considering the possibilities of an unprecedented third term, Roosevelt decided he would run again, "determined to stay in the White House until the Nazis were defeated." During an early July press conference from his study at Hyde Park, he outlined what would become the central message of his wartime presidency. The United States must fight to preserve "certain freedoms," what he later called the Four Freedoms: freedom of speech, freedom of religion, freedom from want, and freedom from fear. Hitler's version of freedom, he said, would allow the Nazis to "dominate and enslave the entire human race." The United States and the Allies would fight back to preserve freedom for all people.[6]

In 1940, that message rang hollow for many Black Americans. Writing for *The Crisis*, the NAACP magazine, editor Roy Wilkins openly wondered if Roosevelt's determination to fight for freedom applied to Black citizens in the United States. "A great many people in America are on the verge of hysteria about the threat to liberty and democracy from Hitler's onward-marching legions," he wrote. "We are being told from every printed page, from every radio loudspeaker, from every rostrum that this country must arise and defend by every means within its power the democracy we have set up here." But what did democracy really mean for Black people? It meant that if a white mob chose to "hunt down, shoot, hang, or burn alive a Negro, it can do so with serene knowledge that no sheriff, no grand jury, no judge—*nobody*—will do anything about it."[7]

Black people already knew the face of fascism. Denied full citizenship and equality under the law, they lived under the degradation of Jim Crow and the lurking threat of racial violence. Pervasive segregation in America's neighborhoods, schools, theaters, restaurants, railroad cars, buses, hotels, hospitals, churches, courtrooms, prisons, parks, and virtually every other public space reinforced an oppressive system. Law enforcement terrified Black folks. White people "were the judges, the jurors, the bailiffs, the court clerks, the stenographers, the arresting officers, and the jailers. Only the instruments of execution—the electric chair and gas chamber—were desegregated, used for whites and Negroes alike." In other words, mob rule was as likely to exist inside a courtroom as it did outside.[8]

In America, democracy did not exist for Black people any more than it did for Jews in Nazi Germany. Wilkins wrote, "The only essential difference between a Nazi in Central Europe and an American mob burning black men at the stake in Mississippi is that one is actually encouraged by its national government and the other is merely tolerated." And yet Uncle Sam expected Black citizens "to become fanatic in defense of American democracy" while government contractors denied them defense jobs and the War Department turned away Black volunteers willing to risk their lives on the battlefield.[9]

While Black citizens debated their role in the war and Congress deliberated the Selective Service Act, the first peacetime draft in the nation's history, President Roosevelt needed the support of prominent Americans who would enlist in the fight for freedom and oppose fascism. At that crucial moment, Joe Louis emerged as an important voice in America's intervention debate. The boxer announced that he would not hesitate to serve his country and protect America against a foreign invasion. In an exclusive interview with the *Pittsburgh Courier*, the same Black newspaper that lobbied for equal opportunity in the armed forces, Louis declared, "This is the best country I know of . . . And I'd gladly fight to defend it. Every colored man I've ever known has been 100 percent American and I'll always be loyal to my country and my race. I'd never let either down."[10]

Louis offered a message of gratitude that could only reassure white people that he did not harbor any resentment about the country's racial hypocrisies. Only in America, he said, could the son of a Black sharecropper rise and become the heavyweight champion of the world. At a time when white politicians and military leaders feared that training and arming Black soldiers would lead to racial unrest, Louis, with a little prodding from the *Courier*'s reporter Chester Washington, insisted that the FBI would not find any spies or subversives in Black America. Undoubtedly, publisher Robert Vann, an astute businessman who had proudly declared the *Courier* "*the* Joe Louis paper" in 1935, now wanted to use the champ as a model of Black patriotism in his campaign for abolishing the color line in the armed forces.[11]

"All my people stick by America," Louis said in an interview edited by Washington. "Even in the South where they are pretty tough on my race, sometimes, they're still loyal to America. They respect the Federal government and its flag and they have always been willing to fight for Roosevelt just like they did in the last World War." His statement sounded exactly like what America wanted from its patriotic champion, the cheerful and virtuous "Good Negro" who loved God and country, a fighter who would make an ideal soldier. Louis did not have a critical word to say about Roosevelt or the segregated army. Soon, though, the war would test his beliefs, and he would find himself jabbing the president and his party.

IN LATE SEPTEMBER 1940, A FEW WEEKS AFTER FRANKLIN ROOSEvelt signed the Selective Service Act, the president's advisers wanted to invite Joe Louis to the White House for a photo op. Edward J. Flynn, the chairman of the Democratic National Committee and Roosevelt's top campaign adviser, contacted Black attorney Julian Rainey, the head of the DNC's "Colored Division." Flynn asked Rainey to deliver Joe Louis to the Oval Office so that the heavyweight champion could "thank the President for increasing Negro participation in defense" and "offer his own services" to Roosevelt during the election.[12]

FDR liked the idea. He had met Joe Louis once before, in August 1935, two months after "the forthcoming champion of the world" whipped Primo Carnera. The Improved Benevolent and Protective

Order of Elks of the World, "the Negro Elks," had invited the two most famous Black athletes in America to the nation's capital for their fraternal convention. Louis and Jesse Owens, a blazing sprinter from Ohio State University and the owner of three world records in track and field, had become linked as young Black heroes whose athletic victories over white opponents challenged the racial order. Touring the Black neighborhoods of Washington, Owens stood in awe of Louis. The president was equally impressed with the strapping prizefighter when they met at the White House. After asking Louis to flex his bicep so he could feel his muscle, Roosevelt said, "Joe, you certainly are a fine-looking young man." In the coming years, that story, true in its basic facts, was told and retold until it became a myth that Louis met Roosevelt in the Oval Office on the eve of his rematch against Max Schmeling. According to legend, FDR said in 1938, "Joe, we need muscles like yours to beat Germany." Roosevelt never uttered that line. He would not have viewed the Nazis as a genuine enemy of the United States then. But by 1940 Roosevelt had every reason to invite Louis back to the White House.[13]

Four years earlier, Roosevelt won his reelection bid with overwhelming support from Black voters who broke the long-standing tradition of casting their ballots for Republicans. Since emancipation, the Grand Old Party, the party of Abraham Lincoln, had enjoyed the allegiance of most Black citizens. In contrast, for many Black Americans, the Democratic Party represented the party of discrimination and disfranchisement. But between 1932 and 1936 Black Americans moved decisively into the Democratic coalition—a shift that dramatically altered national politics. In the age of Herbert Hoover, Republicans had largely ignored the political and economic concerns of Black voters while pursuing support from white Southerners. That inattention to Black citizens created an opportunity for Roosevelt Democrats. After defeating Hoover,

Roosevelt succeeded with Black voters not because he confronted racial inequality but because his New Deal programs provided a modest amount of economic relief, jobs, education, housing, and health care.[14]

However, by 1940 Roosevelt's uninspiring record on civil rights made him politically vulnerable. In the eleventh year of the Great Depression, when more than 20 percent of Black folks remained on the dole, Black citizens complained that New Deal employment programs, particularly in the South, discriminated against them—and Roosevelt said nothing about it. Black journalists skewered him for catering to white Southern Democrats—the base of his party—by refusing to challenge segregation or advocate for an anti-lynching law.[15]

After Roosevelt signed the Selective Service Act in September, political commentators suggested that Black voters might leave the Democratic Party. The law allowed the War Department to maintain its long-standing policy of segregating military personnel based on race, an affront that made Black Americans question the president. Furthermore, Roosevelt had approved a War Department statement that maintained the US military would "not intermingle colored and white enlisted personnel" in the same regiments because segregation had "been proven satisfactory over a long period of years." Desegregating the US military, the War Department claimed, would prove "destructive to morale and detrimental to the preparations for national defense." In a bitter rebuke of FDR, the editor of the *Baltimore Afro-American* wrote, "In this regard, President Roosevelt not only forgot us but he neglected us, deserted us, and abandoned us to our enemies."[16]

Roosevelt's Republican opponent, corporate attorney Wendell Willkie, a charismatic Hoosier and ardent interventionist, promised not to forget Black Americans. Offering the strongest civil rights plank in the party's history, the Republicans promised Black

Americans "a square deal in the economic and political life of this nation." A firm believer in equal protection under the law, Willkie pledged to end racial discrimination in federal employment, the military, and the voting booth. And he called for an anti-lynching bill—an action Roosevelt refused to do. Willkie famously rejected the support of Father Charles Coughlin, the notoriously antisemitic "Radio Priest," and the endorsement "of anybody else who stands for any form of prejudice as to anybody's race or religion." In the fight against fascism at home and abroad, Willkie refused to be associated with bigots. "I don't have to be President of the United States," he said, "but I do have to live with myself."[17]

Competing with Willkie for the support of Black Americans, Roosevelt ran on a platform that made broad appeals to Black voters. Short on specific policy proposals that would change the structural racial conditions in America, the Democratic Party emphasized the benefits Black Americans received under the New Deal. The president's campaign offered only vague assurances that his administration would advocate for Black Americans in the future: "We shall continue to strive for complete legislative safeguards against discrimination in government service and benefits, and in the national defense forces." Black critics lamented that the Democratic platform fell "far short of the promises made to Negro voters by the Republican party."[18]

Courting Black voters, the Roosevelt campaign aimed to use racial symbols that would draw them to the polls. Campaign chairman Ed Flynn understood that there was no bigger symbol in Black America than Joe Louis. But if Flynn thought that the champ would visit the White House and endorse FDR, perhaps he was misled by erroneous reports during the previous presidential election that had Louis rooting for Roosevelt. In 1936, when the United Colored Democrats invited Louis to Jersey City to give a campaign speech, Joe stumbled, failing to mention Roosevelt's name or anything about the Democratic Party. The embarrassing public appearance only furthered the image of Louis as politically uninformed and incapable. One headline read, "JOE LOUIS FLOPS IN SPEECH FOR ROOSEVELT." John Roxborough rushed to his defense and explained that the young contender had been duped into appearing at the rally. He insisted that Louis had not endorsed any candidate or party and did not know that his hosts wanted him to give a campaign speech.[19]

Roxborough preferred that Louis concentrate on his training and avoid any distractions that might harm his chances of competing for the heavyweight title. "Joe is a boxer and while he is as interested in politics as any American youth, we feel that he would be stepping out of character to dabble actively in campaigning," he said. Of course, there was one exception. That year, Joe appeared at campaign events for Michigan's first Black state senator, Republican Charles Roxborough—John's older brother—who ran unsuccessfully for a seat in the US House of Representatives. Outside of Detroit's Black neighborhoods, however, no one thought much about Joe's presence at Roxborough's campaign events.[20]

Four years later, in the fall of 1940, Louis stunned fans and sportswriters across the country when he announced that he planned to hit the campaign trail and deliver a series of speeches for Wendell Willkie. Jack Miley, a columnist with the *New York Post*, a liberal newspaper published by Democrat Dorothy Schiff, a frequent visitor of Hyde Park, wrote that Louis was nothing more than a "stooge" for the Republicans. Miley claimed he had the inside scoop on how Louis became a spokesman for Willkie. "Joe was originally offered to the Democrats, but his asking price was too high," Miley charged. In other words, the Republicans outbid the Democrats and bought the heavyweight champion. His managers had contacted Ed Flynn and "suggested Louis might be willing to take the stump for . . . F.D.R., if he could be

The Campaign

formally presented to the president at the White House." According to Miley, Roosevelt declined the meeting with Louis because he was simply too busy, but correspondence from the president's secretary indicates that FDR had approved and planned to visit with Louis until the White House learned that the champ had ties to the GOP. John Roxborough, like his brother, a longtime Republican, insisted that the "New Dealers" courted Louis, not the other way around.[21]

Years later, Louis reflected on his decision to support Willkie over FDR. "Through the years, I had always supported Roosevelt," he said. "After all, I knew he was a big fan of mine, and thank God for the Welfare Relief programs that he had set up, not only helping my people but the whites, too." He recalled that in the early 1930s, before he turned professional, his mother stood in line every week waiting for a relief check that kept the family fed and sheltered. Louis believed that Roosevelt was a genuinely good person, but he grew frustrated when he heard stories about Black citizens being bumped from relief rolls to make room for white men. This was FDR's New Deal?[22]

Louis maintained that he had not been pressured by anyone in the Grand Old Party to campaign for Willkie, insisting that he had been a Republican and a Baptist his entire life—just like his mother. Unquestionably, though, he was influenced by the Roxborough brothers. Louis had never voted before, but he felt that now was the time "to use what I've got to help my people." In St. Louis, Joe addressed a crowd of Black voters and said that he was supporting Willkie because in eight years Roosevelt had failed to advance civil rights and deliver an anti-lynching law. The humble champion admitted he was no political scientist, but he recognized that he had a responsibility to use his position for advancing democracy and racial equality. "I'm just Joe Louis," he said. "I am a fighter, not a politician. This country has been good to me, has given me everything I have, and I want it to be good for you and give you everything you need. I am for Willkie because I think he will help my people. I figure my people ought to be for him, too."[23]

On the same day that Joe stumped for Willkie in St. Louis, Ed Flynn announced that Jesse Owens planned to campaign for President Roosevelt, a stunning development considering that the Olympic hero had endorsed FDR's Republican opponent, Alf Landon, in 1936. Now Owens claimed that Roosevelt had done more for Black people than any other president. Not only did Owens change political stripes, he also telegraphed Joe Louis and challenged him to a debate, as if they were running alongside the candidates for the Black vote. The *New York Daily Mirror* suggested that Flynn, "the Bronx Boss," was "rubbing his hands over the notion that he has checked the swing of Negro votes to the Republican nominee" by neutralizing Joe Louis's popularity with an equally popular Jesse Owens.[24]

The truth, however, was that the Brown Bomber had eclipsed the Buckeye Bullet in relevance and importance. In 1940, Louis was widely recognized as the "greatest Negro athlete in history," though that had not been the case four years earlier. In 1936, after losing to Max Schmeling, Joe had little confidence as an orator supporting a presidential candidate. Yet after winning four gold medals at the Berlin Olympics and returning home to a ticker-tape parade in New York City, Jesse Owens was courted by both parties, assuming an endorsement from him would influence Black voters. Massachusetts Republican congressman Joseph W. Martin arranged for an oil magnate to pay Owens to endorse Landon. During his campaign appearances, Owens emphasized that Landon would defend American freedom and capitalism against the "planned economy of Europe as offered by the Roosevelt New Deal Democrats."[25]

The Campaign

Appearing in thirty cities above the Mason–Dixon Line, adoring crowds turned out to hear Owens recount stories about his Olympic exploits. He praised the Germans as exceptionally efficient and said that Adolf Hitler was "a man of dignity." But Black audiences didn't want to hear that. They wanted to hear about the time that Hitler had snubbed him. During the Berlin Games, a story circulated in the Black press that the Nazi leader had refused to shake hands with Owens after he won the gold medal in the men's 100-meter race. Owens disputed the tale, insisting that he and Hitler waved to one another at Olympic Stadium. Eyewitness accounts confirmed that Hitler saluted Owens. "Hitler didn't snub me," Jesse said at Republican rallies. "It was our president who snubbed me. The president didn't even send me a telegram." In fact, Owens said, Alf Landon, the governor of Kansas, sent him a congratulatory message and that was why he had decided to support the Republican candidate—a dubious claim since no one had ever seen the telegram.[26]

After Roosevelt trounced Landon in the presidential election, the Republicans had no more work for Owens. Making matters more complicated, the president of the United States Olympic Committee, Avery Brundage, had suspended Owens from all Amateur Athletic Union (AAU) events when he refused to compete during an AAU fundraising tour across Europe. Exhausted from traveling and competing, Owens fumed that the AAU had exploited him. Once Brundage vanquished his amateur status, he eagerly turned professional, hoping to profit from his global fame. But after 1936, without a professional track circuit, Owens struggled making a living. Broken promises from publicists and promoters left him sprinting from job to job, searching for success in America.[27]

He dropped out of college to support his wife and children and began barnstorming with baseball teams in the Negro Leagues, where he performed various sprinting exhibitions between innings. At different venues, Owens raced trains, cars, motorcycles, dogs, and horses. "I sold myself into a new kind of slavery," Owens said years later. "I was no longer a proud man who had won four Olympic gold medals. I was a spectacle, a freak who made his living by competing . . . against dumb animals. I hated it." He recalled earning five cents of every dollar that people paid to watch him run against thoroughbreds. "It was degrading and humiliating."[28]

The painful story of Jesse Owens was all too typical of Black athletes during the 1930s. In 1938, Paul Gallico, one of the most prominent white sportswriters of the age, observed, "When the colored brother is capable in sports or athletics of any kind, he is usually too capable for his own good. It is written, or, rather, unwritten, in our land that he may give but not receive. When we need him for the track team or the boxing squad, for football or to take part in the Olympic Games, he is a full-fledged American citizen, our dearly beloved equal, and a true American." But outside the sports stadium, Gallico wrote, "he remains a plain nigger, and we'd rather he weren't around, because he represents a problem."[29]

The problem for Owens was that the world he longed for, the one where he was celebrated as a true American and an Olympic hero, no longer existed. By the summer of 1938, he had not run a meaningful race in nearly two years. After working as a bathroom attendant at a public pool in Cleveland and as a playground supervisor for the city's department of recreation, he was desperate to earn real money. The twenty-four-year-old sprinter accepted his role as "a sideshow artist, a gimmick runner selling his name to attract crowds." In Chicago, a few weeks after Joe Louis knocked out Max Schmeling, Negro League baseball promoters announced a major event at South Side Park: a race between the fastest man in the world and the heavyweight champion of the world. The competition was a total farce, a vaudeville performance that mocked

Jesse's past achievements as an Olympic athlete. Between games of a doubleheader, they lined up for a sixty-yard dash. At the sound of the starter's gun, Owens stumbled and fell while Louis flew past him, coasting to the finish line.[30]

Two years later, when Owens endorsed Roosevelt and challenged Louis to an election debate, he insisted that he would win and expose Joe's ignorance. "Joe is a nice fellow," Jesse said, "but he doesn't know the issues." It was a common refrain from Louis's critics. When Louis declined the invitation from Owens, Dan Parker, a white columnist with the *New York Daily Mirror*, imagined a satirical debate between the two friends. Relying on old racist tropes, Parker portrayed Louis as a stereotypical Southern "minstrel darky" speaking in the primitive dialect of Uncle Remus, a stark contrast with Owens's character, a sophisticated intellectual whose erudition confused Joe.

JOE—Ah'm fo' Mistah Willkie because Mistah Roxborough say he gonna be 'lected and he gonna get jobs for mah people.

JESS—I wish to emphatically contradict you. Such suppositions on your part are extraneous.

JOE—What you mean by such highfallutin' talk? Man, why don't talk words ah can understand. You know Roosevelt is makin' our people lazy wit' his $15 a week. They ain't no future in $15 a week.

JESS—Your comprehensions may be too stultified for such classical allusions, so I shall refrain from metaphors and polysyllabic words. Roosevelt has taken care of our people who can't get work. He is the 20th Century Emancipator.

JOE—'Mancipator? Don't talk like that. Ah don't tell nobody he shouldn't vote fo' Mistah Roosevelt, but ah tell them ah'm gonna vote for Mistah Willkie. He promise jobs fo' our race. He have our interests at heart.[31]

Parker's cruel depiction of Joe Louis as a dim-witted simpleton revealed that no matter what the heavyweight champion had accomplished in boxing, he was always liable to be painted as a buffoon, clueless about the world around him. "Joe rarely opens a book or magazine," wrote *New York Times* reporter Meyer Berger in 1936. Comparing him to Luther "Dummy" Taylor, a mute baseball player with the New York Giants, Berger suggested that the shy boxer could barely mumble when reporters questioned him. Joe enjoyed watching movies and listening to radio shows, but he had "no interest in current events, world history, or politics." And, Berger wrote, Louis showed no trace of a racial consciousness, as if he failed to recognize how his life had been shaped by his heritage and the history of the color line. While white reporters turned him into a menacing killer inside the ring, a bestial fighter no white man would want to meet in a dark alley, they also rendered him servile outside the gym, a harmless Black man who knew his place.[32]

Throughout his rise in the 1930s, Louis always resented the way white writers put words into his mouth and invented stories about him. As a regular newspaper reader, he knew how illustrators turned him into a cartoonish caricature, a "kinky-haired, thick-lipped" Sambo with skin as dark as coal. Louis recalled that when he first turned professional, his managers urged him to resist letting any white man from the press turn him into a cartoonish buffoon. One time, when he was training at Pompton Lakes before his fight with Primo Carnera, a white photographer asked him to pose with a giant watermelon, playing into stereotypes about poor

Black field hands' insatiable weakness for the fruit. Even without Roxborough or Jack Blackburn present, Louis knew the photographer wanted to make him look like Stepin Fetchit. Joe declined. Agitated, the photographer pressed him repeatedly until Louis snapped, "I don't like watermelon."[33]

Louis refused to let white men diminish him. He was not the "deadpan animal type who never thought or laughed," as the "Jim Crow scribes" made him out to be. "Anybody who's chatted with Louis after a fight or known him at all outside the ring knows that to be just a contemptible, conscious falsehood," Lester Rodney wrote in the *Daily Worker* in 1941. "Every boxing writer knows that Louis is quick, friendly, articulate and intelligent in the moments after a fight when a battery of writers are shooting all kinds of questions at him. Unusually so. He'll give the boys exactly what they want and need for the deadline with no aimless braggadocio, and with the same quick and thorough thinking that motivates his 'fastest punching.' And of course, he'll relax and laugh and exchange badinage with writers. They all know that."[34]

Although Louis didn't usually reveal his inner thoughts, it was not because he did not think about the world outside of boxing. For years, Joe struggled to overcome a childhood speech impediment, a stutter that made him so self-conscious that he avoided conversation. And even after he stopped stammering, Louis remained insecure, worried that he might mispronounce words or say something that might jeopardize his career.

Louis buried his anger and frustration over racism as a means of survival in a business that had outright refused to let any Black man compete for the heavyweight title for more than twenty years. It was a pragmatic choice, influenced as much by the times as by his managers. Outside his donations to the NAACP, Louis remained silent on civil rights, as did John Roxborough. The champion was no crusader challenging segregation. "Joe does what he is told," noted liberal journalist Heywood Broun in 1937. "Generally, he dodges questions such as those bearing on his attitude toward the Scottsboro case and other vital problems affecting the Negro." A year earlier, when a reporter from a communist magazine approached Louis about racial injustice and the Scottsboro Nine, Roxborough interjected and pulled the writer aside. "Don't think Joe isn't intelligent," he said, lowering his voice. "He feels those things keenly. But he's a prize fighter right now. He's got to think of the nation as a whole; and he can't afford to alienate anybody."[35]

But by 1940 much had changed for the boxer. Since beating Max Schmeling in 1938, he had grown more confident and mature, less concerned about how others perceived him, especially white people. Increasingly, after defeating the Nazi puppet, Louis came to see himself as more than a boxer, as someone who had a responsibility "to try to help America and my own people." Equally important, Charles Roxborough provided him with a political education, presenting the Republican program as an alternative to the New Deal. When Louis appeared with Roxborough on the congressional campaign trail in 1936 and 1938, he heard his manager's brother repeat how the Democratic Party was controlled by the Ku Klux Klan. He heard Roxborough accuse the Works Progress Administration (WPA) of intentionally keeping Black people dependent on government programs instead of helping them find meaningful work. Louis, noted *Detroit Tribune* columnist Alfred Cassey, "heard statistics read time and again showing the disproportionately large number of Negroes on relief and WPA jobs throughout the nation." During the Great Depression, while northern Black Americans gained a greater awareness that they could trade ballots for racial advancements, Louis developed stronger political views, an allegiance with Republicans, and a conviction that he needed to speak out against Democrats.[36]

The Campaign

With the election a week away, an incident in New York City reinforced Louis's conviction that FDR's administration didn't care about Black people. On October 28, 1940, after a day of strenuous campaigning throughout the five boroughs, Roosevelt's press secretary Stephen Early rushed to Penn Station to catch the presidential train back to the capital. As Early pushed through security lines, two policemen blocked him from boarding. A brief scuffle ensued, during which Early encountered James M. Sloan, a Black patrolman and decorated veteran who was recovering from hernia surgery. Early shoved Sloan and kicked him in the groin, shouting, "Get out of my way, nigger!" The next day, when the White House press corps questioned him, Early shrugged and admitted only that he had kneed Sloan in the groin.[37]

The story became front-page news in the Black press. The racism in FDR's White House now had a name and a face. Republicans moved quickly to exploit the story, and the GOP National Committee distributed a flyer with a picture of Sloan lying in a hospital bed alongside a warning to Black voters: "NEGROES—if you want your President to be surrounded by Southern influences of this kind, vote for Roosevelt. If you want to be treated with respect, vote for WENDELL WILLKIE." Joe Louis wired the news agencies: "If Mr. Steve Early kicked the colored policeman in New York, he pulled the foulest blow in boxing . . . I don't see how colored people could have any respect for Mr. Early after this."[38]

Roosevelt knew that he could no longer avoid the mounting pressure from Black America to address racism in the military. A week before the election, he promoted sixty-three-year-old Colonel Benjamin O. Davis Jr. to brigadier general, making him the first Black general in the US Army. Roosevelt also appointed William H. Hastie, dean of the Howard University law school, as civilian aide to Secretary of War Henry L. Stimson. These gestures were entirely symbolic—Hastie had to accept his position knowing that he could not publicly challenge the War Department's racist policies—and the Black press knew it. The *Pittsburgh Courier* declared, "the day has passed when colored Americans can be bribed by the appointment of two or three Negroes." Louis agreed. Promoting Davis, he said, was "just publicity for Mr. Roosevelt." It didn't change anything. Roosevelt "thinks that he can appoint one man and we'll forget the last eight years."[39]

A few days after Stephen Early assaulted James Sloan, Louis stumped for Willkie in New York City. Campaigning for twelve hours, he gave short speeches, posed for photographs, and signed autographs. The grueling day required him to smile and shake hands with every stranger he encountered. Crowds followed him everywhere: Grand Central Terminal, GOP campaign offices, schools, and lodges. When he visited Patrolman Sloan's home with reporters and a group of Republican politicos, Louis expected the officer to tell him that he was voting for Willkie. But when Sloan told him that he supported FDR, Louis could not hide his "disgust" and disappointment. Later that night, when Joe spoke at the Golden Gate Ballroom in the heart of Harlem, hecklers taunted him, but he countered without missing a beat. "Go ahead and boo," he told the Democrats in the crowd. "I'm used to boos—and I win anyway."[40]

Crisscrossing the Northeast and the Midwest during the campaign, Louis visited about a dozen cities and gave more than one hundred speeches. Just about everywhere he went, Black crowds cheered and listened intently to what he had to say. Even if they disagreed with his politics, he was their champion and he always would be. In Chicago, standing calmly before thousands of Black people across four events, Louis spoke directly and sincerely about the election. Why, he asked, would Black citizens flee Southern states controlled by Democrats only to vote for them after moving north? Every vote for the Democrats, he said, was a vote for Black voter suppression. "You can't vote in the South, and if Roosevelt is re-elected you may not be able to vote here in four years." On the eve of the election, he urged his fans not to forget his central message: A vote for Willkie "will mean freedom from the WPA and freedom for the Negro."[41]

Louis predicted that Willkie would beat Roosevelt "by a knockout." But not even the heavyweight champion could tip the scales in Willkie's favor. Roosevelt won by a substantial margin, with 54.7 percent of the popular vote to Willkie's 44.8 percent. FDR collected 449 Electoral College votes and Willkie received 82. Roosevelt's "broad and inclusive coalition—Blacks, ethnic minorities, Jews, immigrants, urban workers, organized labor, farmers, intellectuals, southerners, including white supremacists, and some independents" held up against Republicans, isolationists, and the anti-third-term Democrats. Historians estimate that Roosevelt maintained the support of approximately two-thirds of Black Americans, who were more convinced by his economic record than by Willkie's promises. Although those figures are difficult to verify, Joe Louis spoke before tens of thousands of Black voters, encouraging them to cast their ballots and exercise their political power. In that way, he claimed a new role for himself as a vocal champion for civil rights.[42]

The election marked a significant turning point for Louis. It signified his growing importance outside the ring and changed the way he viewed himself. Before Louis and Jesse Owens, presidential candidates never courted endorsements from Black athletes. But no other Black man could single-handedly attract an audience like Louis did—and that gave him an enormous opportunity to fight for democracy at home and abroad during the war. And although many sportswriters and fans, Black and white alike, disapproved of him entering politics, claiming that he didn't know anything about it, Louis had grown tired of letting others define him.

When Joe was younger, he was a follower. No more. Now, he was beginning to think of himself as a leader. Campaigning for Wendell Willkie, he grew more independent and discovered his voice in the fight for justice and racial equality, a voice that no one had heard publicly before 1940. On the campaign trail, Louis defied stereotype, proving that he was not some uncivilized "bushman" or "a wooden Indian." He was neither Dan Parker's Sambo or "Mike Jacobs's pet pickaninny." Joe Louis was nobody's boy. He was a man—a Race Man determined to define his own place.[43]

Chapter Three
AGAINST THE ROPES

Can NEGRO AMERICANS "take it"?
Frankly, I don't believe they can.
And if they can't take it, I'm preparing them right now for something—which might happen at any time . . .
If Joe keeps on fighting (and fighting is his business), there's a day of reckoning due.
IF . . . and when Joe Louis is defeated, show that you can "take it." Act in defeat as Joe Louis will do . . .
IF . . . and when he loses, Joe will take his defeat in his stride!
So will we!
And so must you!

—William G. Nunn, *Pittsburgh Courier*, June 19, 1941

JOE LOUIS NEEDED A KNOCKOUT. IF HE FAILED, HIS REIGN WOULD end. At the Polo Grounds, on June 18, 1941, the title he had successfully defended an unprecedented seventeen times looked lost. In the twelfth round Billy Conn pummeled his body and face with fifteen unanswered punches. Blood dripped from Joe's nose. His eyes looked like small puffed pillows; his lungs ached. In Joe's corner, his managers cringed, conferring in desperate whispers. John Roxborough turned to his business partner, Julian Black, and said,

"Oh my God, he's way behind. What's he going to do?" There was no answer to the question. What could he do? Conn was younger and faster, and was fighting the match of his life.[1]

After the twelfth round, bleeding from a cut over his right eye but saturated in sweat and confidence, Conn glanced from his corner across the ring at Louis slumped on his stool. The ever-cocky Pittsburgh fighter grinned. The title was as good as his.

Across the country millions of Black Americans suffered with Joe, hanging on the Mutual Broadcasting System's Don Dunphy's every word as he described the action. Louis was *their* champion, *their* Black Moses, *their* avenger for the sins of white oppressors. Black journalist Roi Ottley recalled that in the early rounds, with Conn battering Louis, Black Harlem feared the worst: This would be the moment a "Great White Hope" finally dethroned Louis. "As the fight progressed," Ottley wrote, "there were ominous grumblings, with some near hysteria. The cheers of fifty-five thousand white people in the Polo Grounds, which echoed down the streets of Harlem, heightened the distress."[2]

Listening to the broadcast in every corner of the country, Black Americans held their breath. In *I Know Why the Caged Bird Sings*, Maya Angelou recorded a poetic account of listening to Joe Louis's fights on the radio in her grandfather's general store in the tiny hamlet of Stamps, Arkansas. Back then, she wondered if the announcer knew that he was addressing "all the Negros around the world who sat sweating and praying, glued to their 'master's voice.'" His staccato cadence became most excited when some white challenger pushed Joe into a corner and whaled away at his body.[3]

For Maya and the other Black listeners, it was agony. "My race groaned," she wrote. "It was all our people falling. It was another lynching, yet another Black man hanging on a tree. One more woman ambushed and raped. A Black boy whipped and maimed.

It was hounds on the trail of a man running through slimy swamps. It was a white woman slapping her maid for being forgetful." Perhaps it was even worse: "It might be the end of the world. If Joe lost, we were back in slavery and beyond help. It would all be true, the accusations that we were lower types of human beings." It would be the evilest confirmation of unspeakable thoughts, she imagined.

Tuned into the Mutual Broadcasting System, Lena Horne agonized as she imagined Billy Conn ending Joe's reign. By that time, the songstress had fallen for the champ, and they had begun a torrid love affair. Over the past year, Lena and Joe had developed serious feelings for one another and found ways to meet without drawing attention from gossip columnists. Training for the Conn match in Greenwood Lake, New York, he frequently called Lena at Café Society, an interracial cabaret in Greenwich Village. On the night of Louis's fight against Conn, her friend John Hammond, a white record producer and board member of the NAACP, drove her "around and around" Central Park. In the tensest moments, he turned up the volume on the car radio. Lena was overcome with fear, hysterically crying and throwing punches at Hammond. The next day his right arm was black and blue from Lena's blows.[4]

Joe refused to let his wife, Marva, attend the fight. She had not seen Joe fight since 1936 when Max Schmeling bludgeoned him. For a long time, vivid nightmares from that match haunted her. She could still see Max pounding Joe's swollen face. Instead of sitting ringside for his fight against Billy Conn, Marva listened to the radio broadcast in her suite at the Hotel Theresa in Harlem. She resented that Joe wouldn't let her near him whenever he had a match. Like all boxers, Joe had rules about not having sex before a match. He would only let Marva visit his training camp on Sundays, and when they finished eating dinner she had to leave immediately. She fully understood why her husband trained so hard.

She knew what the title meant to him and her people. That's why listening to the Conn match left her as emotionally wrecked as it did Lena Horne. In her husband's desperate hour, she said a prayer that he would rise again.[5]

In Joe's corner, his seasoned trainer Jack Blackburn looked across the ring and saw Conn's crooked smile. He knew what it signified. Conn was underestimating Louis, as so many others had done throughout his life. Blackburn tapped Joe on the shoulder and shouted in his ear that Conn was going to try to knock him out. Watch for Conn's trademark power punch, a looping lead left, Blackburn said. If Joe could see Billy's left hook coming, he had to step inside and deliver a lethal straight right. That, the trainer thought, would wipe the grin off the challenger's face. Moments before the bell rang for the start of the thirteenth round, Blackburn urged Louis to finish the fight: "I'm tired of going up and down these steps. Go knock that son of a bitch out."[6]

BILLY CONN'S UNRESTRAINED CONFIDENCE STEMMED FROM A FIRM belief that he was too smart and too fast for Joe Louis. He thought that over the past year the champion had "softened up and started to slip." It seemed that the champ had started to slide into the descent of his career. In Conn's mind, Louis had a fatal flaw: He was Black and that meant he had an innate weakness. About a week before the fight, the brash "Little Irishman" told a group of reporters that Louis was "just a big, slow-thinking Negro. Nobody knows this better than Joe himself. He's a dangerous fighter because he can punch and because he's been taught well. But he's a mechanical fighter doing only what he's been told. He can't think under pressure in the ring, and he knows it." Conn's trainer Johnny Ray, a rummy who spoke with whiskey on his breath, nodded and said, "Louis is as slow on his feet as he is in his brains."[7]

Conn's racist taunts irritated Louis. When reporters asked him about Billy's slurs, Joe retorted, "That little Conn boy talks too much." Louis rarely revealed his anger in front of reporters, but there was no mistaking how he felt. "I hope I catch him with his mouth wide open," he said. But Conn just sneered. Quoted in his hometown newspaper, the *Pittsburgh Post-Gazette*, the challenger mocked the champion: "I'm laughing at you, Joe Louis. Can you hear me, old-timer? I'll be seeing you, Uncle Tom."[8]

Suddenly, writers found Louis training harder than before, refusing to cut back his sparring sessions despite Jack Blackburn's pleas. For the next week, reporters covering the match printed every brag, boast, and insult exchanged between the fighters. Compared to Conn, the "wrathful" twenty-three-year-old scrapper who gave up twenty-five pounds to the champ, Louis was described as "a tired and slowed-up old man at 27." Fight fans anticipated the championship bout becoming a good old-fashioned brawl, a bloody grudge match between "the Dark Destroyer" and "the Great White Hope."[9]

The hype around the fight pleased Mike Jacobs. It was all part of the plan that he had hatched in late 1940. Before the Conn fight, the promoter had Louis defend his title six times in six months, an unprecedented schedule considering that past heavyweight champions had typically defended the title only once or twice a year. Uncle Mike viewed the six title defenses as a lengthy and financially profitable prelude to a Louis–Conn match. To be sure, it was a gamble. Jacobs was betting that Louis would not fall victim to an unlucky knockout punch, a gushing cut from a head butt, or any other unforeseen accident that might befall a fighter. But always shrewd in matters of business, he had embarked boldly on the strategy.[10]

Jacobs understood that the European war presented opportunities as well as potential problems. On the positive side, the buildup of the US armed forces and the European demand for American goods stimulated the economy, an enormous benefit for the fight game. "The year 1941 is going to be a great one at the box office," he had told Dan Daniel back in January. "National defense means jobs. Jobs mean three shifts in the factories. Working factories mean that the fight lover will begin dishing it out again at the ticket window. And that means a big year for Uncle Mike."[11]

At the same time, the more aggressive stand by the Roosevelt administration increased the likelihood of the involvement of the United States in the war. It was only a matter of time until the national draft claimed Louis, a catastrophic blow to Jacobs's boxing empire. More than anything else, the fear of losing his meal ticket drove Jacobs into putting Louis into the ring far more than was healthy for the champion. In what became known as the "Bum of the Month Club," Louis risked his title more often than any other heavyweight champion, fighting opponents who ranged from the well-known to others hardly known at all.[12]

In March 1941, a few days after President Roosevelt signed the Lend-Lease Act that provided US military aid to the Allies, *New York Amsterdam News* writer Dan Burley reported that Jacobs had grown "openly worried about the Army getting his biggest moneymaker"—Joe Louis. Publicly, Joe had stated that he would not ask the military for special treatment, even though he had been classified 3A with a hardship deferment on account of claiming three dependents: his wife, mother, and sister. Still, Jacobs feared Louis's draft board would reclassify the champ and then Uncle Sam could call him up at a moment's notice. If Louis had to serve in the military and retire from boxing, then he would not be able to pay back the large advances Jacobs had loaned him against future earnings until after the war ended—whenever that might be.[13]

Jacobs exploited Louis's financial ignorance by keeping the cash-strapped prizefighter perpetually indebted to him. On the eve of his fight with Billy Conn, Louis desperately needed money. The Internal Revenue Service did not deduct taxes directly from the fighter's purse, and Joe had failed to set aside enough money to pay his tax bill. To meet an income tax payment with the IRS, he reportedly borrowed $42,000 from Jacobs. Most of his ring earnings were tied up in real estate, including apartments he owned in Chicago and in Harlem's exclusive Sugar Hill neighborhood, as well as a historic Spring Hill farm in Utica, Michigan, that once served as a haven along the Underground Railroad. Maintaining his lavish lifestyle, luxury automobiles, and sprawling 477-acre farm—replete with a lodge, restaurant, dance hall, stables, and his prized thoroughbreds, Flash and Jocko—cost Louis a fortune. Adding to his debts, he also owed John Roxborough a considerable sum.[14]

During his frantic fighting schedule, Louis realized that he would have to take all the money he earned from his matches and hand it over to Jacobs, Roxborough, and Uncle Sam. The problem for him was that each fight pushed his income to the point of diminishing returns. For each bout, Louis split his purse with his managers: He received half, and his two managers got 25 percent each. After counting his federal tax bill, he was left with much less money from his fights than the headlines suggested. Making matters worse, the purses from his first five bouts in 1941 totaled less than $120,000. He had made nearly three times as much in a single match when he'd beaten Max Schmeling three years earlier. The truth was that Louis was fighting for whatever crumbs he could get, barely maintaining his extravagant lifestyle and keeping Uncle Sam off his back.[15]

By the time Louis prepared for Conn, all the travel, training, sparring, and punching had taken its toll. Since he had knocked out Al McCoy in Boston the previous December, he had fought forty-two championship rounds over six months. Ringside observers thought that Louis was taking more and harder punches. He absorbed the worst blows against Max Baer's younger brother Buddy, a big rugged fighter who stood six foot six and weighed 237 pounds. During the first round in that brutal May contest in Washington, DC, Baer knocked the champion out of the ring, cut his left eye, and bloodied his face. Louis rallied and punished the challenger, pounding him with repeated left hooks and straight rights. In the sixth round, they traded punches until Louis landed a devastating right, knocking Baer to the canvas. Somehow Buddy struggled to his feet. As spectators screamed with excitement, Joe, one of the finest finishers in the history of boxing, pushed forward, landing another right cross that dropped his opponent for a final time. Unfortunately, the bell had already sounded, though neither the fighters nor referee Arthur Donovan had heard it. Baer's seconds dragged him to his corner but could not revive him sufficiently to continue. His cornermen argued with Donovan about the late punch, insisting that their man should win on a foul. When they refused to leave the ring, Donovan awarded the bout to Louis on a disqualification.[16]

Immediately after the match, Louis left Griffith Stadium for Freedmen's Hospital, the only federally funded health-care facility for Black Americans in the nation. A doctor examined his swollen face and stitched a gash above his left eye. Although he won, Louis had to hit Buddy Baer a hundred times before flooring him. *The Ring*'s Dan Daniel concluded that Joe's punching power had diminished. His colleague Nat Fleischer, editor of *The Ring*, disagreed. If Joe looked completely drained after the Baer fight, he said, it was because he was boxing too often. Fleischer argued that no fighter, not even a superman, could defend his title every month without his knees buckling. The champ needed a break.[17]

But five days after leaving the hospital, Joe had already started training again for his fight against Billy Conn. In the weeks leading up to the match, reporters wrote that as much as Jacobs favored Louis, Uncle Mike treated Conn like a beloved nephew. On those nights when Billy fought at Madison Square Garden, the promoter sat ringside, rooting for "his boy." The contender enjoyed lounging at Jacobs's estate on the Shrewsbury River in Rumson. And he often visited Jacobs at his plush apartment on Central Park West. Perhaps, the promoter thought, if Billy overcame the odds and beat Joe, the new champion could revive interest in a stale division victimized by Louis's dominant four-year reign.[18]

Nearly fifty-five thousand fans packed the Polo Grounds for what would be remembered as the last great heavyweight fight before Japan's attack on Pearl Harbor. On the morning of the bout, June 18, 1941, few Americans fully appreciated Imperial Japan's threat in the Pacific. The front page of *The New York Times* focused on the crisis across the Atlantic and the American government's growing alarm over Nazi espionage. Two days after President Roosevelt ordered all German consulate offices operating in the United States closed by July 10, breaking virtually all diplomatic relations with Hitler's government, FDR directed American customs and immigration officials to detain any German nationals seeking to leave the country. The Roosevelt administration had also taken steps to freeze all German and Italian assets in the United States while swarms of British fighter planes clashed with Nazi planes over the Strait of Dover, the narrowest part of the English Channel. The situation in Europe, the *Times* reported, convinced Secretary of War Henry Stimson that the United States must prepare for a long-lasting war. But in the sports section of the *Times*, there was no mention of the war; the headlines announced Joe DiMaggio had extended his hitting streak to thirty games (a New York Yankees record) and that gamblers favored Louis to win—four to one—in his showdown against Conn.[19]

THE FIGHT OF HIS LIFE

After Conn outboxed Louis for eleven rounds, the "Big Show" really began in the twelfth when the challenger unleashed a torrent of head shots that left the champ reeling. Joe didn't need his trainer to tell him that he was losing the match and behind on the officials' scorecards. He could tell that Billy wanted to finish him and suspected the contender might get impatient if he didn't land a quick knockout blow in the thirteenth round. Louis had been studying Conn's tendencies throughout the fight and he realized that he couldn't hit a moving target. Joe had to wait for the moment when Billy stopped circling the ring, planted his feet, and threw a long left hook. He knew that at some point Conn would stop running and would have nowhere to hide.[20]

When the bell rang, Conn rose from his stool as Johnny Ray implored him to adhere to a plan that was working. All Conn had to do was avoid danger for three more rounds. Ray reminded him: *Stay away from Louis. Stick and run. Stick and run!* But Conn had other ideas. As the frenzied spectators screamed themselves hoarse, anticipating Joe's defeat, Billy carelessly rushed the champion and tried to win a slugging match. He didn't want to box. He wanted to fight, and that proved a fatal mistake. Joe pounded Billy into the ropes with sharp jabs and uppercuts. Conn's "neck seemed to break with every hit that Louis scored," noted a ringside reporter from *The Boston Globe*. Badly cut, Billy covered his bloodied face and stumbled. He threw a flailing left hook and missed, exposing his chin. Louis hammered his jaw with a sharp right cross. Conn crumpled onto the canvas, unable to rise before the referee's ten count at 2:58. Had Louis landed the knockout blow two seconds later, Conn would have been saved by the bell and given a minute on his stool to recover. Instead, radio listeners heard Don Dunphy exclaim, "Conn is *out!* Joe Louis is *still* the champion of the *world!*"[21]

When it was over, Uncle Mike wrapped his arm around Billy and consoled him. Fighting back tears, Jacobs kissed Conn on the cheek. He told Billy that he was proud of him, knowing that the contender had come so close to fulfilling his dream. The irony of it all was that "the smart guy was outsmarted" by a man he had called a "slow-thinking Negro." Fighting the most remarkable round of his career, Joe Louis proved that he was not some shuffling "savage." Conn admitted that Louis had duped him into thinking he was on the verge of collapse after the twelfth round. But the champion's superb strategy of luring Billy into a brawl proved that "Joe was still the cool fighter he [had] always been."[22]

A day after the fight, while Mike Jacobs smiled counting the gate receipts, John Roxborough met with him at the offices of the Twentieth Century Sporting Club. Discussing the prospects for Louis's next match, Jacobs would ultimately settle on Lou Nova, who, unlike Conn, had a draft deferment, and that meant that the fight wouldn't be canceled by the Selective Service. During the meeting, Roxborough revealed that Joe's draft board in Chicago had requested that Marva visit their office to answer a few questions about her husband's deferment. It made everyone uneasy, though Roxborough told reporters that he was not too concerned about Joe losing his service deferment. Soon, however, Marva would give the manager a real reason to worry that Uncle Sam would call the champ's draft number.[23]

JOE'S VICTORY CELEBRATION DIDN'T LAST LONG BEFORE HIS WIFE slapped him with a divorce lawsuit that stunned him as much as his fans. In early July, while he was preparing to sink a four-foot putt on the ninth green of a golf course in suburban Detroit, a local reporter broke the news to him. In her Chicago court filing, Marva claimed that Louis had assaulted her twice "without provocation." First, she said that on January 2, 1941, Louis "struck her a violent blow on the mouth with his hand," and again on April 19, when he "hit her in the face with his hand and stepped on her ankle." Marva also stated that Joe's "extreme and repeated cruelty" was traumatic and forced her to seek constant attention from a physician. Joe could not believe it. "She say I hit her?" He paused, processing the gravity of the charge. "What I hit her for?" The reporter didn't have an answer. The court filing provided no other details about the alleged assaults. Joe acknowledged that he argued with Marva but denied striking her. Shaking his head, he suggested this was just the latest rumor about him splitting with his wife. There were frequent stories about him running off with some "chorus girl" or another woman. "Ain't nuthin to it," Louis said.[24]

He soon realized that Marva's suit—and her allegations of domestic abuse—threatened everything he had built in his life and career. Immediately, Roxborough, Joe's lawyers, and members of the Black press defended him against her charges. When she petitioned the court for Louis to pay her lawyers' fees and substantial alimony, critics questioned her motives and whether she ever really loved him. The Black reporters who knew Joe Louis could not imagine that he would harm a woman, let alone his wife. "Marva says Joe did his boxing against her," Carter Wesley wrote in the *Dallas Express*. "Frankly, we don't believe it." The *Norfolk Journal and Guide*'s Lem Graves Jr. feared that a nasty divorce trial would expose a disreputable side of Joe Louis, damaging his prestigious reputation and crushing the faith of millions of Black Americans.[25]

Several male sportswriters suggested that Marva was a materialistic ingrate who owed everything good in her life to Joe. "A few years back Marva was just another pretty but unidentified eyeful in Chicago's teeming Negro section whose aspirations probably did not transcend beyond the usual girl's yearning for a steady job, a little cottage of her own and a fur coat," wrote Black columnist Edgar T. Rouzeau. "Today, thanks to having been the wife of the world's most successful fighter, Marva owns a six-family apartment house in Chicago, several fur coats, oodles of jewelry, and many trunks of expensive clothing. And she has more money, more leisure and more freedom than she ever dreamed of." Yet Nell Dodson, "The Lady in the Press Box," one of the few Black women who covered sports, defended Marva against the attacks. "I doubt that the public has understood what her life has been," she wrote. Marva had "lived a goldfish existence, her every action scrutinized by the public."[26]

From the very beginning, the marriage had strained under the weight of Louis's celebrity and the fawning female fans who sought his attention. Being Mrs. Joe Louis—always introduced as "the champion's wife"—meant living in her husband's shadow. "Your life is just not your own," she lamented. They were hardly ever alone. Their home was filled with his staff—a secretary, publicist, maid, valet, and chauffeur who drove Marva everywhere. Frequently, Joe's friends showed up at their home unannounced. And whenever they appeared in public a bodyguard accompanied them. Crowds surrounded Joe and Marva when they went on dates. There was no escaping the reporters and photographers who hounded them. "People followed us everywhere we went," Joe recalled. "If we went to the movies, we'd have to leave before it was over; if we went to dinner, we'd have to leave before dessert." Countless women "were coming at me as if Marva wasn't there. They'd just push her aside."[27]

Marva wed into the boxing world—literally. In September 1935, when she was just nineteen years old, she married Joe only hours before he fought Max Baer. Rushing to marry her on the eve of the biggest fight of his career made little sense to boxing insiders. The day before the fight, Marva told a reporter that she was not sure whether they would wed before or after the match, but Joe simply could not wait any longer. He was not a planner, and he gave little thought to the future. He simply lived in the moment. In a Sugar Hill apartment in Harlem, around 7:45 p.m., Marva's brother, Reverend Walter C. Trotter, officiated the wedding, with John Roxborough, Julian Black, Jack Blackburn, and Mike Jacobs bearing witness. Then, a few minutes after eight, police officers cleared a path for Joe to make his way through a packed sidewalk crowd. He hurried into the back seat of a green car and headed for Yankee Stadium.[28]

Looking back on Joe's wedding night, *Afro-American* sportswriter I. F. Coles recalled how Louis "told a number of reporters, including myself, that he would never disgrace his race as Jack Johnson had done." Coles knew exactly what he meant. In the early twentieth century, Johnson, the first Black heavyweight champion, openly flaunted his sexuality, traveling with white prostitutes. Ignoring the color line and death threats, he married three white women. After losing the title in 1915, Johnson cast a shadow over Louis and every other Black boxer who aspired to win the heavyweight title. Louis recognized, as he suggested to Coles and the other writers, that he could not—and he would not—marry a white woman or even be seen with one.[29]

Joe's managers could not have been happier that he had married Marva. Julian Black, who had once employed Marva as a stenographer, strongly encouraged the wedding. He and Roxborough had grown increasingly alarmed about Louis becoming involved with the wrong woman. By the summer of 1935, after beating Primo Carnera, Louis was the most eligible bachelor in Black America and he entertained dancers, singers, secretaries, and showgirls. Most of them were fair-skinned Black women, but some were "flaming redheads, brunettes, blondes, chestnuts, and auburn-haired beauties." In July, rumors circulated in Detroit that Joe was engaged to Roxborough's vivacious niece Elsie, a bright college student who dreamed of becoming a director or playwright. "She was a lovely-looking girl, ivory-white of skin with dark eyes and raven hair like a Levantine," recalled her friend Langston Hughes. Elsie had such light skin that she passed as a white woman. Her relationship with Joe Louis, however, didn't last after she caught him flirting with another woman at a nightclub. Furious, Elsie hurled a red brick through the window of Joe's Buick. That story, plastered on the front page of the *Pittsburgh Courier*, must have embarrassed her uncle John and the entire Roxborough family.[30]

Less than two months later, in September, the Black press began publishing stories about Joe and Marva's engagement. Reporters speculated that Julian Black had grown fanatically concerned about protecting Joe's image—and his investment in him. Supposedly, he orchestrated the marriage. "Julian wanted control over Joe," his friend Truman Gibson explained, and the marriage "was one element of control." In many ways, Marva seemed to represent the ideal Black wife and that made her "an asset" for the boxer's career. She was "an old-fashioned girl, sweet, clean, modest, pretty," noted a correspondent from the American Negro Press. "She has intelligence, poise, common sense. She has personality and is a pleasant, friendly type who makes friends because she is cheerful and kindly." Most important, despite her light complexion, Marva, "the brown beauty," could not pass for a white woman or one of Jack Johnson's wives.[31]

Yet within a year of the Louis marriage, reporters wondered whether Marva had become a liability for Joe. In the summer of 1936, after he lost to Max Schmeling, "a whispering campaign" developed in Chicago that on the eve of the match, Joe and Marva had an argument when the young contender discovered a letter from his wife's old boyfriend. Outraged by the letter, the story went, Louis could not concentrate in the ring and left himself open to Schmeling's overhand right. The couple denied that the letter from Joe Gibbons Jr. had anything to do with Louis's loss, but the story did not end there. A Black private investigator named Sheridan Bruseaux learned that Gibbons, a taxi driver, had acquired a marriage license with Marva's name on it in 1934, more than a year before her engagement to Louis. Marva insisted that she had never been very serious about Gibbons and that he applied for the marriage license without her consent. Two months after the Louis wedding, Julian Black reportedly paid Gibbons $300 for the marriage license, concerned that the jilted lover might blackmail the boxer.[32]

After threatening to sue Joe Louis for slander and denying he had tried to shake him down, Gibbons told his mother that he feared for his life when Julian Black warned him to leave Chicago. Then, on October 5, 1936, a Black police officer shot and killed Gibbons under mysterious circumstances. South Side patrolman Earl Wilson had finished his shift at midnight and was taking a long walk home when he heard a woman scream near 5649 Indiana Avenue. According to police, for some unknown reason, Gibbons had hurled a pole through the window of Rufus Kennedy's home and fled down an alley. That's when Officer Wilson chased the unarmed Gibbons and shot him in the back. About a month later, after reports suggested that Kennedy, the lone witness, was involved with the same woman as Gibbons, burglars shot and killed Kennedy outside his house. Without Kennedy's testimony, prosecutors could not convince a grand jury to indict Wilson for manslaughter. Gibbons's mother remained convinced that Julian Black hired Earl Wilson to silence her son, though she could never prove the charge.[33]

For nearly five years, until Marva filed for divorce, that story stayed buried with the body of Joe Gibbons. Ozzie Nielson, a Chicago reporter who attended high school with Marva, suggested her old classmates were surprised that she had "gotten over her school day romance so suddenly" after meeting Joe Louis. Nielson had long believed that her marriage to the boxer had no chance of surviving since they had little in common and because Louis was never home. Training and defending his title kept him away from Chicago for weeks or months at a time. And when Joe did return, he didn't stay long. Louis was a road man who grew restless when he had nowhere to go. He would often wake up in the morning and tell Marva that he was going to run an errand or visit a friend and then he simply disappeared for days without so much as a phone call. When Joe finally walked through the front door, he came bearing gifts: diamonds, dresses, and mink coats.[34]

Traveling with his buddies, Louis usually retreated into the Black neighborhoods of his favorite cities: Chicago, Detroit, and New York. He could relax more easily in Black enclaves, because his people—the sycophants and reporters who wanted access to him—would protect the champ's anonymity *and* his activities with other women. Marva knew that Joe was a serial philanderer. His mysterious disappearances and extramarital affairs crushed her, leaving her feeling invisible and alone. For a long time, she tolerated Joe's betrayals, but in the summer of 1940, about a year after she suffered a miscarriage, Marva discovered a letter Lena Horne had written her husband. Threatening to leave Joe, she packed all his possessions into a moving van. But even that didn't stop Joe from seeing Lena.[35]

When Marva finally filed for divorce in July 1941, Joe denied her charges. He asked the Chicago Circuit Court to dismiss her suit, alleging that she had not been any more faithful or virtuous than he had been. Stunned, Marva said to a reporter, "Oh! That isn't true! I can't believe Joe said it. His managers must have drawn the answer for him." Claiming that she had been an adulterous wife precipitated "a real court battle," her attorney said. Joe's friend, John C. Dancy, the executive director of the Detroit Urban League, heard a rumor that Marva had been secretly involved with a prominent Washington, DC, doctor. Dancy also believed that

Joe was so hurt that Marva had accused him of hitting her that he would never reconcile the marriage.[36]

On August 18, Joe and Marva entered a tense Chicago courtroom for an alimony hearing. A reporter noted that Marva smiled when she looked at her husband, but Joe avoided eye contact. On the witness stand, Joe complained about Marva's extravagant spending. As a result, he explained that he had far less money than Marva claimed he did. She countered that Joe spent frivolously and irresponsibly, and she worried about their future. When Louis's attorney questioned Marva about the state of her finances, she gave evasive answers and struggled to prove that she did not have excess cash, though the couple shared a checking account and vault box. And she owned outright a Chicago apartment building that Joe had purchased for her.[37]

New York Daily Mirror columnist Dan Parker speculated that the divorce proceedings would expedite Louis's entrance into the military. Parker thought that the hearing undermined Louis's claim that he should receive a 3A deferment based on his three dependents. The columnist argued, "If Marva, the ex-stenographer, owns an apartment house, she's not a dependent." And if Joe had "$400,000 invested in real estate and $400,000 more in cash and bonds, as Marva, his loving helpmeet claims, his dependents, if any, are set for some time to come, whether or not Joe fights another lick." Therefore, Parker reasoned, Marva may have unintentionally given the Chicago draft board a reason to reclassify Louis 1A—eligible for service.[38]

A day after the first hearing, the couple stunned virtually everyone by ending their suits and emerging from a courthouse conference room with Joe smiling and carrying Marva in his arms. It seemed that all was forgiven—at least for the moment. Sweeping a giggling Marva off her feet, Joe announced, "Boy, this is like getting married all over again!"[39]

Joe had promised Marva that "he would do better" and spend more time with her. But he didn't. As his wife recalled, before she knew it the phone rang, and he had to leave to train for his next fight. His managers reminded him that he had work to do. After an unsuccessful "second honeymoon," Joe headed to his training camp in Greenwood Lake, where he embraced a chanteuse that he just couldn't quit.[40]

THE WAR WAS STEAMING TOWARD AMERICA'S SHORES. IN EARLY September an unidentified Nazi U-boat fired torpedoes at the USS *Greer* in the North Atlantic off the coast of Iceland. The American vessel suffered no damage and responded with a series of depth charges. This began a string of tit-for-tat Atlantic engagements that pushed the United States and Germany toward war. It also spurred draft boards to redouble their efforts. Only weeks later, Louis learned that his Chicago draft board had indeed reclassified him 1A. The news unnerved Mike Jacobs. But the chairman of Joe's draft board reassured him that the champ would not be inducted until after the Nova match. Selective Service officials refused to say whether Marva's lawsuit, which revealed her husband's earnings and assets, influenced the reclassification. But Joe did not blame Marva. "She had nothing to do with it," he said. Louis told reporters that he would not ask for a deferment or carry the heavyweight title into the army. He planned to beat Nova and retire from boxing as the heavyweight champion.[41]

None of that seemed to matter when Lena Horne smiled at him. At the time, the radiant singer from Café Society had become the darling of the Black press, described as the "sepia toast of Broadway's nite life circles." She likely first met Joe in 1935 at the Cotton Club when she was a young "chorus girl" or when her father, Edwin "Teddy" Horne Jr., a friend of John Roxborough and a small-time numbers dealer in Pittsburgh, brought her to Joe's training camp. That summer, five days before she turned eighteen years old, Lena attended Joe's fight against Primo Carnera. From that night on, she idolized Louis. In the coming years, they encountered one another at the New York nightclubs where she performed. According to Joe, sometime in 1940, when Lena was separated from her husband, Louis Jones, and working as the only Black performer in Charlie Barnet's jazz band, he connected with her in New York. "She was more beautiful than she'd ever been," Joe recalled in his memoir. "Nice and sweet, but Lord, she had a filthy mouth. Could cuss better than any sailor wished he could. We started talking and talking; next thing I knew, we were getting real serious. We were planning all kinds of places and ways we could see each other."[42]

In April 1941, when she was twenty-three years old, Horne sang with the Barnet band at the Paramount Theater on Broadway, capturing the attention of John Hammond, the liberal record producer known for "discovering" Black artists such as Billie Holiday and writing about American race relations in *The Nation* and *New Masses*. Hammond wanted to integrate the music industry and believed that Horne would play an important role. After traveling with Barnet for six months, enduring the indignities of being turned away from Jim Crow hotels and restaurants on the road, Horne had returned to New York. Engaged in a nasty divorce and custody battle, Lena missed her two young children, and she desperately needed a steady job. Hammond, a talent scout for Café Society, was impressed with her, more so for her looks than her voice. He called Barney Josephson, the nightclub's radical impresario, and suggested that he see her in person. Hammond believed that her beauty—and the presence of Joe Louis sitting near the stage—would draw large crowds to the club.[43]

Barney Josephson had opened Café Society because he wanted to end the rigid racial segregation that existed in New York nightclubs outside of Harlem. "I wanted a club where blacks and whites worked together behind the floodlights and sat together out front," he explained. He was unafraid of breaking racial boundaries, and his progressive politics defined Café Society, a cabaret that attracted white liberals, prominent Black artists and activists, and the scrutiny of FBI Director J. Edgar Hoover. "In his club," wrote Horne's biographer James Gavin, "Billie Holiday stood in a pin spot and introduced 'Strange Fruit,' a bloodcurdling lament for lynched Negroes down South. Paul Robeson, who sang there too, was photographed dancing on the Café Society floor with Julie Gibson, a white Warner Brothers starlet. Josh White, a country-blues guitarist and singer, detailed the hard-knock lives of rural blacks in his haunting story songs."[44]

In a matter of months, after Josephson hired her, Horne's fame grew, and she quickly became known as "the reigning queen of Café Society Downtown." But the club offered Lena something more than a platform for advancing her career; it provided a political education that changed the way she viewed herself. Influenced by her stage hero Paul Robeson and the Black artists and activists she met at the club, for the first time in her life, she seriously engaged in discussions about history, politics, and civil rights. When she told Robeson that she was exhausted from battling the racism that pervaded show business and the contempt she felt from Black folks accusing her of "trying to pass," he reminded Lena that she was a fighter who must rise above the forces trying to pin her down. Looking back, she said, it "was a time of awakening for me."[45]

Being with Joe Louis erased Lena's worries about her career and her family—for a moment, anyhow. And whenever possible, the two lovers carved out time to be together. One evening, Lena proudly showed Barney Josephson a stack of photographs of her with Joe. Years later, Josephson vividly recalled a picture of Joe and Lena in a rowboat. "Joe at one end, rowing. Lena at the other end, looking at him. And Joe Louis is beaming, this man who almost never had a picture taken with a smile." It wasn't quite like that—but it was close enough.[46]

Less than a month after patching up his marital problems with Marva, Joe had returned to his training camp at Greenwood Lake. Although it was twenty miles farther away from the Polo Grounds than his old training camp in Pompton Lakes, New Jersey, Greenwood Lake boasted a "society settlement" owned by a group of prominent Black families and promised a more convivial racial climate. A reporter for the *New York Amsterdam News* believed that the move permitted the champion to live "in an all-Negro community instead of the almost lily-white environs that prevailed at Pompton Lakes."[47]

Once again Marva remained primarily in the Midwest—at the apartment in Chicago or at their compound in Michigan. Lena Horne, however, was nearby, performing frequently at the downtown Café Society. On September 15, 1941, less than two weeks before Louis defended his title against Lou Nova, Lena visited Joe at Greenwood Lake for an unconventional rendezvous. At some point during her time with Joe, Carl Van Vechten, a Midwestern transplant in New York who dabbled in highbrow and lowbrow criticism, novels, and photography, snapped a series of pictures of Louis and Horne separately and of the couple together. Van Vechten had been a devoted fan of Louis since the Brown Bomber had arrived on the national scene and he had attended several of Joe's New York fights. Most likely, Lena arranged the photo shoot, which had the potential to harm both Joe's marriage and her own career.[48]

Few members of Harlem's literary life held neutral opinions about Van Vechten. Some regarded him as a stalwart champion of the Harlem Renaissance. Others thought him a racist. At cultural soirees in his apartment on West Fifty-Fifth Street, Black and white intellectuals mixed in a uniquely progressive manner. Always the perfect, if eccentric, host, the pink-faced, white-haired writer dressed in a flamboyant cerise-and-gold mandarin robe, looking strangely like "the Dowager Empress of China gone slightly berserk," and moved from guest to guest, complimenting each person. Few who attended such gatherings could forget them. Where else might sparkling conversation be punctuated by Paul Robeson singing "Ol' Man River" or George Gershwin playing *Rhapsody in Blue*? Robeson was a frequent visitor at Van Vechten's gatherings and counted the host as a dear friend, and poet Langston Hughes also enjoyed a long, fruitful relationship with Van Vechten, yet novelist Ralph Ellison believed that the critic "introduced a note of decadence into Afro-American literary matters which was not needed." Historian David Levering Lewis commented that Van Vechten's most infamous novel was a "colossal fraud." An instant bestseller, the controversial novel with its offensive title, *Nigger Heaven*, is filled with gross distortions and stereotypes of the lives of Harlem's Black residents.[49]

Undoubtedly Horne knew Van Vechten from the Cotton Club or Café Society. He wallowed in Harlem's nightlife and, like Baudelaire, evinced a strong nostalgie de la boue. In the 1930s and early 1940s, portrait photography gripped his attention, and by 1941 virtually every significant Black performer from any field had sat for Van Vechten. Joe Louis was the primary exception. Lena provided the ticket into Joe's world. Van Vechten snapped photos in color and black-and-white, some with the champion wearing a loose yellow linen shirt and others with him stripping it off and posing shirtless. In all the photographs Joe is relaxed but expressionless—not uncomfortable, just uninterested. Van Vechten also photographed Lena. Wearing a multicolored horizontally striped jersey, her uncombed hair slightly wet and pushed behind her ears, she looks like a doe-eyed ingenue.

The most provocative photographs show Joe and Lena together in a small rowboat. It is almost a stock scene of young, innocent love—a scene echoed across numerous novels, paintings, and films—but with a suggestive twist: Louis is only half dressed. In the unpublished photographs, Lena sits legs akimbo, gazing toward the sky, while Joe rows the boat, his powerful naked back pulling against the water. Taken together, they are not pictures of two people happily married to different spouses. They are pictures of two lovers paddling against the current. Stormy weather lay ahead.

Chapter Four

KING JOE

Been in Cleveland, St. Louis, Washington, and Chicago, too,
Been in Cleveland, St. Louis, Washington, and Chicago, too,
But the best is Harlem when a Joe Louis fight is through.

—Richard Wright, "King Joe," 1941

JOE LOUIS LAY ON HIS DRESSING ROOM RUBBING TABLE, "SERENE and drowsy," wearing a gray plaid robe. He could hear his managers and cornermen whispering. The calm bickering over strategy seemed no more intense than a small group of friends discussing the best Yankee infielder. The room smelled like a mixture of liniment and sweat, perhaps spiked with a dose of his managers' anxiety. From outside came the muffled sound of a gathering fight crowd preparing for the main event. The champion appeared detached from the concerns of his handlers, the mounting tensions of the spectators, and the fight itself. Instead, he focused on his conversation with sportswriter Jimmy Cannon.[1]

Sportswriters who knew the boxer insisted that something about him had changed since his 1938 knockout of Max Schmeling. He had found his voice. Now he was the kind of man who made after-dinner speeches, appeared on radio sports quiz shows, and campaigned for Wendell Willkie, making it known that he opposed Jim Crow and the Democrats. Now, he had something to say. In the patronizing words of Caswell Adams, "Joe can think. He thinks and feels deeply about the war and this country and his debt to this country." Where he had once spoken sparingly with Black reporters and hardly at all with white ones, now he talked openly with the few he trusted. And with Cannon, a man close to his own age with liberal racial views, he was comfortable.[2]

Stretching and wriggling his toes "the way a man does who lies on the beach in the sun," Joe talked about what everyone was discussing in late September of 1941—America's approaching war and his role in it. "The Army's all right," he said. "It's good for a lot of fellows. The kids. The kids from all around the country. No place to eat and no place to sleep and the army gives it to them. It'll be good in the Army." Glancing at his own feet, he added, "these feet will stand the marching." And he had no doubt that millions of other American feet would one day be marching toward Hitler's Berlin. Louis had no use for the German dictator. "Who say he the boss of the world?"

The discussion moved from Hitler, to golf, to whatever Louis wanted. Finally, trainer Jack Blackburn said, "Let's go, Chappy." Louis rose to his feet, smiling at Cannon. "I'll look better than you in that soldier suit. So long. I gotta go to work." Then he walked into the cold night air to face another challenger.[3]

This was not the kind of fight he wanted. He had been in the ring too much, absorbing too many punches. Although he had won every one of the "Bum of the Month Club" matches, each had exacted a price. Al McCoy, fighting from a crouch, had landed a series of punishing blows. Red Burman, a tricky contender from Baltimore, had sliced open Joe's eyelid. Six-foot-four-inch, 255-pound Abe Simon gave him a thirteen-round struggle. In the early part of another contest, Tony "Baby Tank" Musto gave better than he took. And the formidable Buddy Baer—winner of forty-five of fifty fights, many against leading contenders—knocked Louis through the ropes onto the ring apron in the first round and busted open his eye in the third. Even before his battle with Billy Conn, Arthur Donovan, a referee who had worked most of the champion's defenses, told reporters that Joe "had seen better days." And then there was Conn—his seventh defense in seven months. The champ was being chewed up and spit out.

But with Louis's army physical exam fast approaching, Mike Jacobs angled to squeeze in one additional payday before the end of the outdoor season. When his managers told him that they had signed an agreement with Jacobs for a September 19th defense against Lou Nova, a promising contender, for the first time in his career Joe balked. After the numbing series of defenses and months spent in training camps, hours devoted to punching and being hit by sparring partners, and thousands of miles logged in cars, trains, and planes, Joe said no. He was too young to feel so old and tired. In the month or so since battling Conn, Joe had enjoyed playing golf, attending ball games, riding horses, and spending time with Marva and his friends. He believed he deserved a real vacation.[4]

John Roxborough and Julian Black "were bewildered." This was a new Joe Louis, more independent and assertive. They argued, they cajoled, they pleaded. "Wait till next spring," Joe insisted. Getting nowhere, the managers summoned Uncle Mike. Louis depended on the promoter for the money that funded his celebrity lifestyle—in fact, he still owed Jacobs a considerable sum. After hearing Jacobs's plan, Louis asked for a compromise: "Can I have ten more days? Can I fight him on the twenty-ninth instead of the nineteenth?" Jacobs agreed. The Nova fight was set.

By the late summer of 1941, Nova, a tall well-built heavyweight, had become *The Ring*'s number one contender. Yet reporters considered him something of a flake. At a time when most boxers employed time-tested training techniques—including roadwork, light calisthenics, skipping rope, punching the speed and heavy bags, and sparring—Nova believed in the value of Hindu philosophy and Far Eastern metaphysics, including the teachings of yoga to "liberate the spiritual self." Yogi Dr. Pierre Bernard, known as "Oom the Omnipotent," had initiated Nova into the mystical search for enlightenment while the Californian was training for a match against Tony Galento—a brutal fight that saw "Two Ton" foul his way to a fourteenth round TKO victory. But Nova stuck with the Hindu program, convinced that "the development of mind and body simultaneously" was the wave of the future. He considered himself a "Man of Destiny," and even boasted that he had discovered a new punch. He dubbed it his "cosmic punch." It began in his "seventh vertebra, the center of balance," and when perfectly delivered would take out any opponent. The key to the blow was to deliver it "with the motion of the earth's surface thus obtaining the extra leverage which every fighter strives for." But for all the theory, the punch looked suspiciously like an earthbound right cross.[5]

As expected, the press filed miles of newspaper columns ridiculing Nova's philosophical meanderings and training practices. Not only did Nova boast a "cosmic punch," but he also crowed about his "dynamic stance," a sort of two left feet positioning that rendered him all but impossible to knock down. Taken together, it appeared that Louis would have to battle both Nova and the cosmos, a daunting task if one bought into the challenger's metaphysics. Louis, however, didn't, admitting that he "didn't like all that mysterious shit [Nova] was talking about." Instead of searching the universe for a better punch, he told reporters, "I'll stick to the old jabs, hooks, uppercuts and crosses."[6]

September 29 was a late date for an outdoor match. It was a chilly early fall evening. More than fifty-six thousand spectators, many wearing sweaters, overcoats, and gloves, moved through the turnstiles at the Polo Grounds. Early weather reports had predicted rain, a major concern for Jacobs. But it held off, and writer Jesse Abramson noted that the promoter's "symphonic teeth hit a faster beat as a courier arrived with the important news that standing room was being gobbled up at $3.50 a stand." Instead of rain, stars filled the near-cloudless sky. In both attendance and gate receipts, it was the most successful promotion since the 1938 Louis–Schmeling rematch. Some had turned out to see if Joe could survive Nova's "cosmic punch," and others to see whether he could beat Father Time. Like millions of Americans, President Roosevelt arranged his schedule so that he could stay close to a radio. He changed the departure time of the Presidential Special train from Hyde Park so that he could listen to the bout in the lounge on his way back to the White House.[7]

As it turned out, Nova never got his punches synced with the rotation of the earth, and Louis demonstrated that his rumored decline was badly exaggerated. In the early rounds, the two boxers slowly circled each other, cautiously waiting for the other to lead, pawing the empty space between them. Both seemed wary of the other's power. In the fourth and fifth rounds Louis moved closer to his opponent, landing several hard punches and cutting Nova's right eye. "There were no fireworks," wrote the *New York Herald Tribune*'s Richards Vidmer. "In fact, it could be called a dull, drab performance" until late in the sixth round. "Then suddenly it happened. Like a flash of lightning out of the darkness [Louis's] destructive right fist streaked." It crashed into Nova's jaw, and the challenger crumbled like a pedestrian who had been hit by a truck. In the locker room after the fight, Joe said that it was the hardest punch he had ever landed. With a three-month layoff between title defenses, Louis convincingly demonstrated that he remained in a class of his own.[8]

The Fourth Estate was well represented at the fight, due mostly to the opening World Series game between the New York Yankees and the Brooklyn Dodgers two days later. More than five hundred newsmen and photographers elbowed into the champ's dressing room. Jimmy Powers reported that if the electricity in the room were cut off, he still would have been able to read by the popping camera light flashes. His work complete, Louis was as relaxed after the match as a man lounging on a Central Park bench. Yet the war and his draft status loomed. "I'm taking my title into the army with me," he said. "It doesn't look as though I'll be fighting again for some time though I'd like to get some real fighting in the army. There's some to be done."[9]

Less than two miles from the Polo Grounds, the end of the fight sent Harlem residents into a predictable celebration. At the heart of the revelry, ten thousand celebrants gathered outside the Hotel Theresa, where Louis was staying. In the early morning hours of September 30, he slipped into a side entrance and used a service elevator to reach a microphone readied for the occasion. Police captain Walter Harding raised his hands, signaling for quiet. Joe had something to say. The cheering stopped. A throng of happy, smiling faces looked up to where the champion was standing. Never one to give a long-winded speech when a few sentences would do, Louis spoke into the microphone: "I want to thank all of you for pulling for me. I did my best. Thank you."[10]

No reporter noted—because none could have known—that it was the end of an era. The Joe Louis who had thrilled millions of Americans during the hardest times of the Depression, the young fighter who was such an inspiration for his race, had just fought his last defense before America went to war. Although he was not through with boxing, a war was looming. NAACP Executive Secretary Walter White recognized that the War Department would need Louis to do more than defend his title. Outside the ring, he would have to defend America.

King Joe

AS IF TO PUNCTUATE THE MOMENT, A SMALL GATHERING OF BLACK luminaries met on the morning of October 1, 1941, two days after the Nova match. Lena Horne's friend John Hammond arranged the meeting, inviting singer Paul Robeson, William "Count" Basie and his orchestra, writer Richard Wright, and civil rights leaders, including Walter White. They met at Liederkranz Hall on East Fifty-Eighth Street, a cavernous building with great acoustics that Columbia Records used as a recording studio. Hammond planned to commemorate Louis's nineteenth successful title defense and decision to enlist in the fight against Hitlerism with a song appropriately titled "King Joe." Wright wrote the lyrics, Basie and Lawrence Brown arranged the music, and Robeson sang.[11]

While Basie and Brown refined the traditional blues structure, Wright scribbled out a thirteen-stanza song. The writer had only recently become instantly famous when his 1940 novel *Native Son* was selected by the Book-of-the-Month Club and sold an astounding 215,000 copies in two weeks. He revered Louis. Since Wright had begun following Louis's rise in 1935, the boxer had inspired the writer. In Louis's fights, he recognized Black America's "pent-up folk consciousness," the "fleeting glimpse of the heart of the Negro, the heart that beats and suffers and hopes—for freedom." Writing the lyrics to "King Joe," he reflected on the past and what the champ had meant to his people.[12]

As he sat in the Columbia studio, attempting to carve out the essence of the Brown Bomber, he looked beyond the undecipherable granite face of the boxer. Except when Louis was especially comfortable with people around him, he wore a mask that was, depending on the observer, blank and devoid of emotions. Wright recognized that expression. It was one that many Black men—especially those born in the South—learned to wear during their youth. Its dominant feature was a nonthreatening indifference, a minding-my-own-business emotional distance. In one stanza of the song, Wright expressed his identification with the boxer. Studying Louis's deadpan expression, he observed how the fighter concealed his inner thoughts from white America, but Wright fully understood that Joe's powerful fists struck an undeniable blow against his people's oppressors.[13]

"King Joe" is a telling narrative and touching evocation of Joe Louis's life and what he meant to Black Americans. It begins with his childhood in Alabama and adolescence in Detroit, moves to his power in the ring, glories over his victories against white fighters, suggests his active love life, and ends with a two-stanza appreciation for all he had done to enrich the lives of his race. As far as Wright was concerned, "no man will ever wear [Joe's] crown," and Louis would forever reign as the king.

There is a sad lament to "King Joe," one given added gravity by Robeson's deep bass voice, and a growing sense that the champ's domination of the heavyweight division may have come to an end with the war escalating in Europe and Asia. By October 1941, Richard Wright had witnessed the cleansing power of Joe Louis—the flood of joy on Chicago's South Side after he defeated Max Baer, the jolt of electricity inside Yankee Stadium the night he knocked out Max Schmeling, the crazy lovefest in Harlem after each important victory. But Wright understood that Louis's career—his time as the King of Heavyweights—belonged to Depression America. Now the nation was lurching toward a different type of crisis, and for very specific reasons, Wright embraced it. To be sure, few Americans believed that in just over three months the United States would be engaged in a two-ocean war. But prominent officials inside and outside the Roosevelt administration were already discussing a new role for the Brown Bomber.

King Joe

AS LOUIS PREPARED TO FIGHT LOU NOVA, UNIDENTIFIED SOLdiers in army camps across the country were scrawling OHIO on field pieces, latrine walls, and any other place they could do so without getting caught. It had nothing to do with the Buckeye football team or pitching heroics of Cleveland Indians ace Bob Feller. In true army fashion, it was an acronym—Over the Hill In October. Its meaning: The army had a problem. Soldiers grumbled about a host of issues—the six-month extension of the draftees' service time, the pay, the lordly behavior of officers, the inhospitable treatment soldiers received in the towns near army camps, and the absence of women.[14]

A journalist interviewing hundreds of soldiers in New York City uncovered the hostility and contempt white GIs held for Black men in uniform. White soldiers' racial animosity had reached the boiling point. "They haven't just the normal anti-Negro prejudice which you find everywhere in the United States, in the North as well as the South," wrote reporter Harold Lavine. "They *hate* Negroes, and their hatred seems to be mounting to hysteria. They make sudden, irrelevant remarks: 'Say, I read where Joe Louis is going to join the army. I hope they send him down my way. First dark night I'll shoot the bastard.'"[15]

There was nothing rhetorical about the violence implicit in the complaints of white soldiers. Eruptions of tempers—fueled by an unpopular draft, a segregated army, the discomforts of life in the camps, and the summer heat—threatened the fragile social balance on posts throughout the South and North. A jostling on a bus, an angry racial slur, a punch thrown in response—the line between manageable animosity and full-scale rioting was as thin as a razor's edge. African American newspapers carefully documented the steady accumulation of such conflicts. While Louis demolished his Bum-of-the-Month contenders, Black soldiers on army bases confronted their own opponents. Screaming headlines in Black America's newspapers captured the relentless assaults on Black soldiers encamped in Southern outposts. "TERROR REIGN SWEEPS NATION'S ARMY CAMPS, NEGROES GO AWOL," reported the *New York Amsterdam News*. Unlike Joe Louis, Black soldiers under attack could not fight back without the threat of an armed white mob descending upon them.[16]

For Black soldiers, simply wearing an army uniform could provoke anger and violence. Widely publicized was the fate of Private Felix Hall, a nineteen-year-old Black soldier from Alabama who had enlisted in 1940 and was stationed in Fort Benning, Georgia. On February 12, 1941, he disappeared from his post. Vanished—without leave and without warning. He was last seen alive in a white quarter of the training complex. Six weeks later, his body, still in a tattered green uniform, was discovered hanging from a tree in a ravine near the Chattahoochee River. Hall's feet were bound in bailing wire and his hands tied behind his back; a noose cut into his neck.[17]

The death of Felix Hall was certainly the result of a lynching. The coroner agreed, ruling the death a homicide. Investigations by both the War Department and the FBI turned up ample evidence of murder, though neither demonstrated any inclination to track down the killers. Authorities at Fort Benning, however, were not so sure, offering without evidence that perhaps the private's death was a suicide. In the absence of what post commanders considered clear-cut evidence, they dropped the matter. The NAACP, Black newspaper editors, and concerned citizens demanded that President Roosevelt and Secretary of War Henry Stimson take all "action deemed necessary to discover and punish the perpetrators of [the] crime." But the government ignored their pleas. The case, like so many similar ones, died unsolved. Together they sent a clear message. As William Hastie, civilian aide to Secretary of War

Stimson on racial matters, wrote to his boss, "The War Department remains silent. The public interprets this silence as indicative of indifference."[18]

The irony of America preparing to battle Hitler by practicing racism in a Jim Crow Army was not lost on Black citizens. Roy Wilkins, editor of *The Crisis*, the official magazine of the NAACP, recognized the absurdity and expressed concern for Black men in uniform. "America is marching to war for the purpose of stopping brutalities overseas but apparently our own government does not choose to stop lynching within its own borders, even within the borders of army camps." It was enough to make Black Americans "throw their hats into the air at the very mention of 'defense of democracy.'"[19]

While Stimson remained silent about lynching in the army's camps and Roosevelt worried about losing the support of Southern Democratic senators, the military searched for a way to portray itself as concerned about racial matters. Walter White had a plan. He thought that it was a splendid idea for Louis to enlist in the army. If the War Department used Joe's talents properly, the boxer had the power to improve race relations, unifying Black and white troops. A week before the Louis–Nova title fight, White wrote First Lady Eleanor Roosevelt, suggesting that the champion should enlist immediately after the defense, and that after thirteen weeks of basic training, the army should promote him to the rank of first lieutenant and assign him to the Morale Branch. Not only would this lift the spirits of Black troops, but his selfless example would also have "a beneficial effect on white soldiers who hither may have been prejudiced against Negroes." He asked the First Lady to squeeze a few minutes out of her busy schedule to meet with him to discuss his plan.[20]

Even before he heard back from Mrs. Roosevelt, he went to work on his scheme. Writing Julian Black, John Roxborough, Joe Louis, and Truman Gibson—William Hastie's assistant—White explained that he might not get to the First Lady before the title fight, but he hoped she would be enthusiastic about his plan. Roosevelt's brother was "critically ill," and she had announced that she might have to cancel a luncheon with the Duke and Duchess of Windsor to rush to her brother's side. It went without saying that if she canceled a date with the former king, she was likely not to find time for White. But he hoped to meet with Eleanor soon.[21]

The First Lady did not have a face-to-face with White, nor did she publicly endorse his plan. But Brigadier General Frederick H. Osborn, chief of the US Army's Morale Branch, wrote to White on her behalf. Standing six feet, eight inches tall, raised in a wealthy banking family, and devoid of military training, Osborn was self-effacing and friendly, a talented businessman and accomplished scientist. He had inherited family money and made a fortune of his own in railroads and investment banking, retired at age forty, and turned to a career in the science of eugenics and demography. He wrote widely on heredity, the environment, and population problems. Osborn agreed that Louis's "fine character" would boost the morale of troops of both races. But he could not make any promises. He suggested that the champion enlist, complete his thirteen-week basic training program "without any special privileges," and then see where the army could best use his special talents. Although the letter has the tone of a polite brush-off, there is no doubt that Osborn was at least intrigued.[22]

A few days later Osborn met with White and embraced his plan—but for an unusual reason. Reporters had begun to write about Louis's finances, which in the context of the sacrifices being made by drafted GIs seemed obscene. Going into the army earlier than he would otherwise have to would end much of the negative publicity. In 1948, Louis told reporters that White and Eleanor Roosevelt "talked a lot about using me in the Army for morale."

There was even talk about a commission. But Louis did not want any special treatment. "I just wanted to be a GI." Probably, White worked out the details with Osborn and not Eleanor Roosevelt. But from the day Louis went into the army, he was slated for the Morale Branch.[23]

While White waited for the Roosevelt administration to move on their plans for Joe Louis, the champion began a voluntary one-week army tour at Camp Grant in Rockford, Illinois. Louis was accompanied by Julian Black, Joe's secretary and longtime friend Freddie Guinyard, golf pro Clyde Martin, and several sparring partners. His plans were simple: Box several rounds against his own sparring partners and give talented base and local boxers "the once-over." Between exhibitions, he hoped to "sock a few" golf balls and, at the end of the week, when he traveled to Michigan, get together with Detroit Tigers power hitter Hank Greenberg, who was now a soldier in the United States Army.[24]

The tour of military posts proved a fabulous success. Virtually all activities stopped when Louis arrived, and audiences of more than ten thousand troops, white and Black, watched him go through his paces with sparring partners and listened to him praise the nation's preparedness activities. Photographers posed him looking over the barrel of a 1905 field artillery piece, sitting at the controls of a bomber—an image that produced an obvious headline: "Bomber in a Bomber," of course—and even taking his preliminary army exam. At each stop on the junket, he told soldiers that it was a "joy" "doing his bit" for America. He left no doubt that if or when the war came, he would stand ready to defend the nation and perform his duty. He did not realize that the war was moving closer to home than almost all Americans thought.[25]

Chapter Five

ANCHORS AWEIGH

If America must forget me, if I must forget myself to remember America, if my nation cannot outlaw lynching, if the uniform [of the army] will not bring me the respect of the people that I serve, if the freedom of America will not protect me as a human being when I cry in the wilderness of ingratitude; then I declare before both GOD and man . . . TO HELL WITH PEARL HARBOR.

—James R. Stewart, editor, *New Negro World*, February 1942

BY MID-OCTOBER 1941, LOUIS HAD FINISHED TOURING TRAINing camps, and hoped to spend some time recovering at his farm in Utica as he awaited his call from the army. By the time he arrived, war with Germany appeared just a breath away. Eleven dead American sailors from the USS *Kearny*, a destroyer sent by President Roosevelt into the freezing waters off the coast of Iceland, had become the first of their country's casualties of the undeclared Atlantic war. At the time, Utica seemed in a different world than Reykjavik, and the dead sailors appeared to have no connection to Joe Louis. But within a few weeks, the naval tragedy and the heavyweight champion had merged into a critical national debate that hinged on a basic question: Was race or country most important to Black Americans? Or framed another way, what did Black citizens owe blatantly racist American institutions in a time of war?[1]

The origins of the assault on the *Kearny* date to an August 1941 meeting between FDR and Prime Minister Winston Churchill aboard a naval ship in Placentia Bay, off the coast of Newfoundland. Most famous for the promulgation of the Atlantic Charter, the face-to-face also played a critical role in Roosevelt's prewar military plans. Churchill had pressed for an American declaration of war against Germany. Judging that such a drastic action would receive neither a favorable vote from Congress nor the support of the American people, Roosevelt offered another strategy, one that would shift the onus of starting the war onto Adolf Hitler and Germany. According to Churchill, the American president promised that "he would wage war, but not declare it, and that he would become more and more provocative . . . Everything was to be done to force an 'incident.' . . . The President made it clear that he would look for an 'incident' which would justify him in opening hostilities."[2]

A minor incident occurred about three weeks after the rendezvous in Placentia Bay. The US destroyer *Greer* received a British alert that a U-boat had been spotted ten miles dead ahead of the American ship's course. The *Greer* then closed range and stalked the submarine, reporting its position to British pilots in the skies above. The *Greer* did not fire on the U-boat, but a British pilot did drop four depth charges. Clearly under attack, the submarine's captain fired two torpedoes. Though both missed their target, the *Greer* responded with its own series of depth charges. They also missed. With that, the U-boat slipped away and the American ship sailed to an Icelandic base.

As "incidents" go, it was clearly of the minor order. Yet Roosevelt made the most of it, distorting the facts and shifting all blame onto the U-boat commander. In a radio address, he labeled the German U-boats and commerce raiders "the rattlesnakes of the Atlantic" and announced a new "shoot-on-sight" policy. The *Kearny* incident in October gave FDR a fresh reason to heat up his rhetoric. Although his evidence was questionable, he accused Hitler of planning to divide South America into "vassal states." Furthermore, he said that the Nazi leader proposed abolishing all existing religions. In his "Navy Day" speech, the president claimed, "In the place of the churches of our civilization, there is to be set up an International Nazi Church—a church which will be served by orators sent out by the Nazi Government. In the place of the Bible, the words of *Mein Kampf* will be imposed and enforced as Holy Writ. And in place of the cross of Christ will be put two symbols—the swastika and the naked sword."[3]

The attacks on the *Greer* and the *Kearny*, however, paled next to the sinking of the USS *Reuben James*, a four-funnel post–World War I destroyer assigned to North Atlantic winter escort service. At daybreak on October 31, 1941, the convoy was about six hundred miles west of Ireland in dangerous waters and running fast. The ships were not zigzagging, and most, including the *Reuben James*, did not have radar. A torpedo fired by a U-552 slammed into the *Reuben James*'s port side, igniting the forward magazine and causing a massive explosion. An orange flame lit the night sky. "Ol' Rube," as the men called her, split in two. The front reared up and then just as quickly slid beneath the water. The aft part of the vessel lingered above the surface for about five minutes before going under. Minutes later, several unsecured depth charges exploded, killing some unfortunate sailors splashing about in the ocean. One hundred and fifteen crewmen, including every officer aboard the *Reuben James*, were lost with the ship; forty-five survivors were pulled out of the frigid waters, most of them covered with a thick layer of slick black oil.[4]

THE FIGHT OF HIS LIFE

The attack on the *Reuben James* made the dark side of America's undeclared war on the Atlantic visible. But not colorblind. Among the sailors who died were three Black messmen—Raymond Cook, from Warner, Virginia; Nebraska Dunston, from Spring Hope, North Carolina; and Joseph Johnson, from Elm City, North Carolina. They were probably preparing to serve breakfast when the magazine exploded. None had advanced beyond messmen duties, nor could they under the racial restrictions of the US Navy. Had their ship engaged the enemy in a firefight, they had not been trained to handle naval ordnance nor were they expected to assume combat roles. In the navy, skin color was destiny. As a *Pittsburgh Courier* editorial pointed out, "Nazi torpedoes make no distinction between admirals and messmen . . . Death drew no color line against them but the Navy does."[5]

Josh White, one of the era's leading Black bluesmen and song writers, spoke the truth in his song "Uncle Sam Says." Dubbed the "Joe Louis of the Blues Guitar," he voiced the rumbling discontent in Black America. With the peacetime draft slotting young men into segregated camps, "Uncle Sam Says" underscored the hypocrisy of battling Nazi racial ideology with a Jim Crow armed forces. It begins:

> *Well, airplanes flyin' 'cross the land and sea*
> *Everybody flyin' but a Negro like me*
> *Uncle Sam says, "Your place is on the ground*
> *When I fly my airplanes, don't want no Negro 'round"*
>
> *The same thing for the Navy when ships goes to sea*
> *All they got is a mess boy's job for me*
> *Uncle Sam says, "Keep on your apron, son*
> *You know I ain't gonna let you shoot my big Navy gun."*[6]

The implied emasculation in the lyrics is clear. The navy was not shy about its preference for whiteness in all things—from Teddy Roosevelt's White Fleet at the beginning of the century to its white dress uniform and white gloves. Between the wars, it had endeavored as a matter of policy to eliminate Black sailors from its ranks. As a result of the "problem" of "mixing the races," the navy had funneled Black servicemen into "mess boy" positions, and even in that role, they were being replaced by Filipinos, Chamorros (natives of Guam), and Japanese. By 1940 Black sailors composed a mere 2.3 percent of the force, and that number was declining, moving closer to the 0.0 percent in the US Marines. As for the chances of change, Secretary of the Navy Frank Knox assured President Roosevelt and a gathering of civil rights leaders that he would resign before the sun rose on that day. You see, he said, "men live in such intimacy aboard ship that we simply can't enlist Negros above the rank of messmen."[7]

Even on the open and democratic athletic fields, the navy discouraged any mixing of the races. In the spring of 1941, for instance, Harvard's lacrosse coach withheld his one Black player in deference to the Naval Academy's informal ban on interracial competitions. Football teams playing against Annapolis did the same. An editorialist in the *Cleveland Call and Post* believed that the message was clear: Race mattered desperately to the naval hierarchy. "Every Negro, who has ever been appointed to the Naval Academy, has never stayed at the school more than two weeks . . . and have left the school that trains officers of the Navy telling how rotten this school treated them."[8]

Promoter Mike Jacobs may not have been cognizant of the navy's draconian racial policies, but in the sinking of the *Reuben James* he saw an opportunity to enhance his and Louis's reputations as patriotic Americans while supporting his country. As early as October 31—the day the ship went down—sportswriters noted rumors that Jacobs planned to stage a Louis–Buddy Baer rematch for the benefit of the US Navy. The reports lacked specificity, and Jacobs quickly issued an equally nonspecific denial. The eve of a big football Saturday, he said, was no time to announce a heavyweight title bout, and all talk of such a fight, which may or may not happen, was premature. He blamed Baer's manager Ancil Hoffman for leaking what were no more than preliminary discussions.[9]

Although the premature announcement enraged Jacobs, he itched for the match. It appealed to his basic instincts. Though war with Germany seemed certain, there was no telling what the conflict would mean for professional sports. The Selective Service had no rooting interest in Major League Baseball. The entire roster of the New York Yankees might be wearing khaki uniforms before the next World Series. Or, in an effort to conserve rubber, gas, and other vital commodities, Roosevelt might suspend professional baseball for the duration of the war. The same logic applied to professional boxing. Reporters and predominantly white sports fans were already grumbling about the money Louis made in the ring. How would it look if he made $200,000 in a rematch against Billy Conn—a fight that was already marinating and seemed certain to attract a gate of nearly two million dollars—at the same time American GIs made less than fifty dollars a month? As far as Jacobs was concerned, staging a title fight for navy relief might earn him a chit that he could cash down the line.

But this business motive should not diminish the legitimacy of Jacobs's religious and patriotic concerns. Hitler's persecution of Jews inside the Reich was widely reported. It was a matter of state policy, and Der Führer made no secret of his plans for a "Jew-free Germany." Antisemitism, as much as the loss of lives on the Atlantic, motivated Jacobs. "My people are discriminated against as much as yours, so I'm against any such practices," the promoter told Billy

Rowe of the *Pittsburgh Courier*. The Louis–Baer fight "might help the Navy open its eyes." Of course, he had used essentially the same argument to battle Jewish and anti-Nazi groups that sought to prevent the 1938 Louis–Schmeling bout.[10]

For several reasons, Louis and his managers agreed. In part, managers John Roxborough and Julian Black did not want their fighter branded "un-American." Before he became heavyweight champion, Jack Dempsey had avoided the First World War, and reporters hounded him for it during much of his title reign in the 1920s. Louis's motives were less complex. He knew the navy's racist reputation. But when asked to participate in the benefit match, he did not hesitate. Once again, he had a chance to make a political statement in the ring. His complete obliteration of Max Schmeling in 1938 had sent a message around the world about the fallacy of Nazi racial ideology. A fight benefiting the navy—at a moment when it was at the center of the country's attention—would send an equally important message about racism and nationalism at home. It would focus a floodlight on the navy's Jim Crow policies as well as Black Americans' commitment to their country.[11]

Billy Rowe was with Louis when he accepted Jacobs's proposal. Surprised, Rowe looked at the boxer. Joe knew others would second-guess his decision to fight for the navy. Yet he showed no concern. In a few words, he had the ability to cut to the heart of a matter. "There's lots of things wrong," he told the reporter. "Anybody knows that. But Hitler ain't going to fix them."[12]

Although it took more than a week of negotiations, Jacobs finally unrolled the details of the Louis–Baer bout. It was set for Madison Square Garden on January 9, 1942. For a sport that normally exhibited the most ruthless form of dog-eat-dog capitalism, the match was virtually unique. Both Louis and Jacobs agreed to donate their entire shares of the bout's proceeds to the New York

THE FIGHT OF HIS LIFE

Auxiliary of the Navy Relief Society, a private fund that assisted dependents of killed or disabled naval officers and crewmen. Repeatedly, Rear Admiral Adolphus Andrews emphasized that the champion was risking his title for no remuneration, save modest training expenses. As an act of generosity, it was unprecedented in the annals of boxing. To reporters asking why he would take such a risk for nothing, Louis crafted a stock reply: "I'm not fighting for nothing—I'm fighting for my country."[13]

In the mainstream press, Louis's popularity soared. He was—and had been since he demolished Primo Carnera in his first Yankee Stadium fight—a model athlete who had "brought nothing but credit to his race and profession," Richards Vidmer wrote in the *New York Herald Tribune*. The champion "had never ducked an opponent," nor "given less than his best." And outside the ropes, there had never been "a breath of scandal." But his actions in the Navy Relief Society fight made him more admirable to white America. He was giving back to his country. Already he had toured fourteen army camps and navy yards, providing boxing exhibitions and visiting with troops—all on his own dime, paying for himself and his sparring partners. His willingness to fight for the widows of American sailors lifted him above other professional athletes and celebrities. "Never before has a champion been willing to put his title on the line without possible reward," commented Vidmer. "And I can't conceive of any other [professional athlete] doing it. Yet it is typical of Louis."[14]

This time, Black reporters did not shower the champion with praise. For probably the first time in his career, a portion of the African American press criticized him. Dan Burley, a polymath newspaper editor, journalist, boogie-woogie piano player, composer, actor, and author of the *Original Handbook of Harlem Jive*, epitomized the reporters who challenged Louis's decision to fuse his reputation to the navy's. Trim and neatly dressed in a conservative suit, Burley might have looked like a banker, but his columns in the *New York Amsterdam News* demonstrated that he understood the residents and mood of Harlem, and that he heard the rants percolating from the street corner soap boxers along 125th Street and Seventh Avenue.

Even before Jacobs announced the Navy Relief Society match, Burley was against it. Under the headline "HARLEM COLD ON LOUIS BOUT," he announced his opposition. The thought of the Black champion "taking part in such an affair for an institution that would probably see to it that he, himself, blackened boots, cooked dinner or waited on its officers" prompted many Harlem sports fans to decry the match. One person he interviewed remarked, "Negroes will stay away in droves . . . when they realize that the Jim Crow Navy will get the benefit." The navy, an observer commented, commissioned former white heavyweight champion Gene Tunney, but they would never elevate Louis to any officer rank.[15]

Throughout late November and early December, Burley pounded Louis for his decision to fight for the navy. "JOE LOUIS DEAD WRONG FIGHTING FOR THE JIM CROW NAVY" blared a November 22 headline in the *New York Amsterdam News*. "FANS ROUSED OVER LOUIS FIGHTING FOR JIM CROW NAVY" headlined another piece on November 29. And on December 6—the day before the Japanese attack on Pearl Harbor—Burley continued his assault on the champion. Pleading to be understood, he asserted that he had nothing but admiration for Louis. Like virtually every Black American, he was proud of their champion. "Proud of him as a man. Proud of his record and what he has done toward breaking down barriers of prejudice and discrimination. Make no mistake about it. Joe is a mighty influence for good." But his decision to fight for the Navy Relief Society was "dead wrong." The navy, whose approach to Black citizens wavered between indifferent paternalism and violent hostility, epitomized the core problem in the country. It was an institution, Burley believed, "hostile to all ideals of fair play and democratic treatment of ALL of this nation's citizens." But now it sought to use Joe Louis as some sort of minstrel performer—insisting that he "cringe, show his teeth and grin and come bouncing like the sorriest Uncle Tom to do its bidding—giving everything, receiving nothing." He begged the Bomber not to "sell out his race."[16]

Yet a far larger orchestra of support smothered Burley's drumbeat of criticism. Poll after poll in the African American press applauded Louis's decision. No one doubted the character of the US Navy. Its racist policies were indefensible. So much so that their contrast to Louis's benevolence became even more striking. The *Pittsburgh Courier* asked Black religious, educational, legal, business, and political leaders to add their voices to the debate. Some agreed with Burley, following the general argument of M. C. Clarke, president of Dunbar Mutual Life Insurance Company, who insisted, "I am just as much opposed to Hitlerism in our Navy as I am opposed to Hitlerism in Europe. Racial discrimination in our Navy is Hitlerism of the worst sort." For him, the fight resembled a form of racial appeasement, a policy that had utterly failed to alter Hitler's aggression. But even more of the Black leaders thought that Louis's actions would increase the pressure on the navy to amend its discriminatory policies. If appeasement did not work, embarrassment might. "Joe has proven himself far bigger than the Navy," wrote Walter White. "Let us hope his example may have some effect on the outfit which bars Joe's people except as menials." But even the normally hopeful White had his doubts, noting, "Having dealt with Secretary [of the Navy] Knox and the Navy which is filled with Southerners I very much doubt it will."[17]

All this time, Americans—Black and white—were looking east toward the Atlantic and Germany. News of the Nazis' blitz across Europe and the undeclared war on the Atlantic framed the Louis controversy. Japan's actions in China and Asia figured not at all. Then came December 7th. Flying out of the northwestern sky, more than 350 Japanese fighters, dive bombers, and torpedo bombers attacked American naval and air bases on Oahu. Most targeted the ships anchored along battleship row and the other vessels in the crowded harbor. Imperial Japan inflicted a considerable blow—including extensive damage to eight battleships, five destroyers, and 250 planes. Before the last enemy plane disappeared over the western horizon, some 2,300 Americans lay dead or dying and 1,100 more had been wounded.

On a tragic day of destruction and death, treachery and infamy, American heroism was not in short supply. Aboard the USS *West Virginia*, a battleship occupying an unenviable position between the heavily damaged USS *Oklahoma* and USS *Arizona*, Mess Attendant Second Class Doris "Dorie" Miller was picking up dirty laundry when he heard the commotion outside the ship. Perhaps some sort of drill, he thought, but hardly what a sailor would expect on a Sunday morning with half of the men still in their racks. A torpedo explosion near the ship's rudder announced the truth of the matter. Miller's battleship was in trouble, and as the heavyweight boxing champion of the *West Virginia*, Miller was not about to let her go under without a fight.[18]

That morning, he distinguished himself. After helping to carry his dying captain to shelter, he manned a .50-caliber antiaircraft machine gun, a venerable naval workhorse. Although he had only rudimentary knowledge of the weapon, he knew enough to jam ammunition into it and pull the trigger. He kept firing until encroaching flames forced him to abandon it. He thought he had brought down a Japanese plane, and later estimates credited him with five or six kills, but in the fire, smoke, noise, and confusion, no one knows for sure what successes he experienced. Eventually,

THE FIGHT OF HIS LIFE

on the dying captain's order to abandon ship, he climbed down a rope into the oily, flaming water and swam a quarter mile to shore. Dorie Miller, messman and boxer, went beyond the call of duty on one of his nation's most fateful days—though navy officials were slow to publicize it.

Suspiciously, for more than two months the navy withheld Miller's name from the press. In their reports of the battle, white columnists referred to him only as an "unknown Negro messman." Eventually, editors of the *Pittsburgh Courier* were able to identify Miller and piece together his story. An outstanding Waco, Texas, football player and navy boxer, he was from a family of four boys and had enlisted in the navy in 1938 at the age of nineteen. He began his naval career as a messman, and almost three years later was still a messman. That was all the navy regulations would permit. But as the *Courier* pointed out, regardless of his lowly rank, "it was natural for Dorie Miller to grab that machine gun and start its stuttering messages of death." Even if the navy hesitated in releasing his name, his actions were heroic.[19]

Unlike Dorie Miller, not all Black Americans rushed to take up arms to defend their country. An early and not very scientific survey indicated that about one in five believed that a Japanese victory would improve their lot. "The colored races as a whole would benefit if Japan should win the war," one man told a *Baltimore Afro-American* reporter. "This could be the first step in the darker races coming back into their own."[20]

Yet before the wreckage at Pearl Harbor was cleared, virtually every American, Black and white, condemned the attack and supported their country's war in the Pacific. In a press release, civil rights activist and founder of the National Council of Negro Women Mary McLeod Bethune called for unity: "I know that at a time like this, every Negro man, woman, and child will stand straight up without reservations to his responsibility to his country."

A front-page editorial in the *Pittsburgh Courier* agreed: "Colored America, among the most loyal segment of this heterogeneous population, which is America, stands solidly phalanxed, hands joined in this titanic struggle to defeat a common enemy." But perhaps it was Alfred Edgar Smith, better known for his popular *Chicago Defender* column "National Grapevine" as Charlie Cherokee, who best expressed the mood of his race. "'War is Hell,' said Sherman. Had he been colored he would have been more inclusive—so is peace! However, my chickadees, since we are up in this mess to our necks, let's smack the Axis down pronto so we can get back to the important business of fighting Jim Crow. All together!"[21]

Almost overnight, the public controversy over Louis's Navy Relief bout ended. Wendell Smith, an influential sportswriter for the *Pittsburgh Courier*, expressed the mood of the hour in his editorial "Louis, Navy Fight for Each Other—Nothing Else Matters." The battle lines had been drawn. Democracy was at stake. "For America," he wrote, "this is no time to quibble. And for the Negro this is no time to turn his back on the United States of America."[22]

For six weeks, Smith recounted, Black Americans had voiced their opinions about Louis fighting a benefit for "a part of the armed forces which discriminates against them." It was a meaningful debate, a healthy airing of legitimate grievances. "But now that war has come . . . the American Negro can no longer be divided on any issue. . . . There can be no question now . . . Joe Louis must fight Buddy Baer for the benefit of the Navy. The color question, discrimination and segregation now become secondary. There is only one thing that counts . . . America. And because we are part of it, we must agree that it comes first, last and always!" Smith finished his patriotic plea by repeating that Louis had an obligation to fight for the navy, "just as the Navy has an obligation to the people of this nation."

THE FIGHT OF HIS LIFE

It was the final words of Smith's editorial—"the Navy has an obligation to the people"—that struck a chord with Black citizens. To be sure, they condemned Japan's treachery and Hitler's racism, and they lined up with white Americans to enlist in the army and navy. They also hoped that their sacrifices would end the catalog of abuses they suffered in "the land of the free." A good starting point, Black leaders argued, was the elimination of a segregated military. On December 8—the same day President Roosevelt asked a joint session of Congress for a declaration of war against Japan—US Army spokesmen assured white Americans that Jim Crow would remain in uniform. Although Army Chief of Staff George Marshall told a group of Black newsmen that he was "not personally satisfied" with the progress against discrimination in the service, the official army position did not reflect Marshall's view. Only hours after Marshall had raised the reporters' hopes, Colonel Eugene R. Householder, the adjutant general's adviser on race matters, made the army's position painfully clear. Any attempt by the army to solve racial problems "would result in ultimate defeat." Echoing Henry Stimson, Householder said, "the Army is not a sociological laboratory."[23]

Householder's candor, his chilling acceptance of the brutal racial status quo, may have improved Roosevelt's declining popularity among Southern Democrats in Congress but it angered the gathering. One reporter wrote that the statement "the Army is not a sociological laboratory" was tantamount to announcing that "segregation is here to stay." Roy Wilkins, editor of *The Crisis*, delivered an urgent message to his readers: Now was the time to speak out against "the breaches of democracy." If America had embarked on a war to create a "new world which shall not contain a Hitler," it should also end Hitlerism, in all its masks. "To thirteen millions of American Negroes that means a fight for a world in which lynching, brutality, terror, humiliation, and degradation through segregation and discrimination, shall have no place—*either here or there*."[24]

In a matter of days and weeks, the assault on Pearl Harbor unified Americans against fascism, military aggression, and racist ideology. Yet entrenched racism at home compromised the nation's position. Since the president was unwilling to take meaningful action—passing an anti-lynching law, eliminating poll taxes, ending Jim Crow in the military—both the Roosevelt administration and cooperative white journalists combed the landscape for symbols of racial advancement, particularly Black leaders who had excelled in music, acting, athletics, writing, and education. Of a distinguished group, Joe Louis stood at the pinnacle. His athletic excellence was unquestioned, his public reputation appeared sterling, and he was already doing the job. Even before Pearl Harbor, Louis had become a one-man traveling advertisement for the country and the military, giving freely his time and money. He toured military camps, donated to patriotic causes, and, unlike other well-known professional athletes, made no effort to avoid or delay conscription. When asked why, he said, "I love this country like I love my people."[25]

Louis's words and actions inspired the nation. Celebrating the first Christmas of the war in his Greenwood Lake training camp, after his morning roadwork he attacked a seventeen-pound turkey and posed for pictures with neighborhood children. Then he thumbed through some of the 884 Christmas cards, letters, and telegrams he received. But there was not much of a holiday mood that season. A sense of uncertainty nagged the close-knit members of the camp. Joe's trusted manager, friend, and surrogate father John Roxborough was less than two weeks away from hearing his sentence for running an illegal numbers operation. Prison was not just a possibility. It was a certainty. And Joe's trainer and fight strategist, Jack Blackburn, suffering from a heart condition, was running out of time, slipping a bit each day.[26]

THE FIGHT OF HIS LIFE

Since Pearl Harbor it seemed all front-page news was bad. The month between the US declaration of war and the Louis–Baer match on January 9th unfolded like a tragic opera. While Japan steamed ahead on land and sea, the United States and Western Powers fumbled from one crisis to the next. From Guam and Wake Island to the Philippines, the string of defeats shocked America. It mixed with equally grim reports from British Hong Kong, Malaya, and Singapore; the Dutch East Indies; and French Indochina. If it were not for bad war news, there would have been no news at all. In this dire context, the magnanimity of Joe Louis shone like a candle in the night.[27]

The grim news seemed reflected in the harsh conditions of the camp on Greenwood Lake in the Ramapo Mountains. In the mornings Joe slogged seven miles in the snow, occasionally knee deep along the edge of the lake. In the afternoon, spectators, many in uniform, gathered to watch the champion train. They stood near the ring, chilled by the frozen January air, watching Louis batter his sparring partners to the canvas. The brutality of the sessions prompted sportswriter Caswell Adams to compare the ring to an "abattoir." The Bomber would not make a penny for the title defense, and given his age and the uncertainties of the draft and the war, he might not get a chance to fight again. He trained not only to win but to destroy Buddy Baer.[28]

In camp, Louis fielded the same question dozens of times: How did he feel about fighting for nothing? At first, he replied, "It's jus' history repeatin' itself. I fought for nothin' many times when I was a kid." Eventually, he gave a more considered answer, stressing that he was fighting for his country. But he was more consistent when asked how long he thought it would take to knock out Baer. Louis replied that he planned to discard the contender quickly. After all, he was fighting for free.[29]

On the night of the contest, Madison Square Garden was decked out for the occasion. Old Glory was present in all its splendor—everywhere. American flags hung limply from the rafters and were featured prominently in programs and printed tributes. Red, white, and blue bunting greeted the eye at every turn. Celebrities packed the ringside seats. Joe DiMaggio, Gene Tunney, and the usual New York sports and entertainment idols were there, of course. So were many of the nation's political and military power hitters. Assistant Secretary of the Navy Ralph Bard attended as the representative of Secretary Knox, who evidently had more pressing war business but did send a telegram. A fleet of admirals and assorted naval leaders flanked Bard like a convoy screen. Praise for the champion was the order of the day. Joe Louis was fighting for America, and it seemed that celebrities, as well as the roughly nineteen thousand people in the Garden, cheered for him alone.[30]

Standing in the center of the ring, Lucy Monroe, illuminated by a single white spotlight that knifed through the darkened arena, performed an emotional rendition of "The Star-Spangled Banner." Then Joe's favorite presidential candidate, Wendell Willkie, took the microphone. Willkie may have campaigned with Louis at his side, but he clearly did not know much about the fight game or the champ's career. He confused Buddy Baer with his brother Max, and pronounced Louis "Lou-ee," as if Joe were a descendant of a Bourbon king.

Nonetheless, Willkie knew how to work an audience. Standing in the ring, he remarked, "I took on a champion myself last year." A broad smile crossed his face as the Roosevelt crowd roared. "I lost but I had a lot of fun while the struggle lasted." But now "the conviction that American democracy shall rule the world" united him and his opponent. Finally, it came time to acknowledge the champion. "Joe Lou-ee, your magnificent example of risking for nothing your championship belt, won literally with toil and sweat and tears, prompts us to say, 'We thank you.' And in view of your attitude, it is impossible for me to see how any American can think of discrimination in terms of race, creed, color."[31]

In fact, Louis's contribution was substantial. It totaled $47,100, a significant donation. As for the title fight, it was shorter than Willkie's talk and about as exciting as Louis's rematch with Schmeling. Joe's right hand landed early and hard. After he knocked Baer down twice in the first round, he landed a devastating left hook–right uppercut combination just before the bell. Baer went down like he had been shot, his head bouncing off the canvas. For a few seconds he lay inert, then slowly struggled to one knee before crumbling over once again. The referee counted him out four seconds before the end of round one. Joe had promised that he would not fight long for free. And he didn't.

The Ring editor Nat Fleischer and a host of other sportswriters thought it was the best Louis had looked since his second match with Max Schmeling. "Joe had everything. He was magnificent. He was a whirlwind on attack, a master on the defense, a terror with his devastating punches." But Fleischer and the others could not separate the Brown Bomber's athletic performance from wartime realities. The basic truth that he donated his entire purse to the Navy Relief Society made him a national benefactor. Journalists now transformed Louis, long a symbol of race relations, into a metaphor for America at war. The champion, Fleischer wrote, "tackled his opponents as the Yankees will shortly do to the sneaky, slimy, yellow rats of Japan."[32] It was that malleable putty, that many-sided metaphoric quality that the Roosevelt administration's opinion makers glimpsed in Louis, that would make him so important to the war effort.

On January 10, the day after he knocked out Baer, the champion, accompanied by John Roxborough and Mike Jacobs, appeared at the Selective Service Headquarters at 331 Madison Avenue. Instead of waiting for a draft notice, he wanted to enlist in the army. "I'm ready," he said. "Give me that gun. I want to fight now. I can ride a horse and shoot a rifle and revolver." When informed that he had to weigh under two hundred pounds to qualify for the cavalry, he responded, "Well that lets me out. I'd be too weak if I weighed only 199."[33]

In their columns, sportswriters noted that Louis was enlisting ten days before his call-up by his Chicago draft board. He could have enjoyed another week and a half of "fried chicken and easy civilian life," wrote famed sportswriter Bob Considine. The journalist's glib racism suggested the scale of the challenge that Louis and other Black soldiers had to face daily.[34]

Now that he was in the military, the army had plans for Joe Louis. Colonel H. Clay Supplee told a group of reporters that the army had tracked Joe for the Morale Branch. It made no difference to the compliant boxer. "I'll be in there for whatever purpose they want." Hand-to-hand combat against Schmeling in no-man's-land, lead a cavalry charge against German panzers, or lift the morale of American troops—he was ready. His only hope was that he could do as well for Uncle Sam as he'd done for Uncle Mike.[35]

Chapter Six

GOD'S WAR

What's all this morale stuff, anyway?

—Joe Louis to a reporter, January 13, 1942

QUIET! QUIET, PLEASE! ARMY OFFICIALS SHOUTED THE ORDER repeatedly as a platoon of reporters, photographers, and cameramen followed Joe Louis during his medical examination at Fort Jay's First Army Headquarters. Joe's entire day on January 12, 1942, had been scripted—from his morning ferry ride departing Lower Manhattan to his arrival at Governors Island, directly across from the Statue of Liberty. Photographers snapped pictures of the champion aboard a ship on the Hudson River, waving farewell to the Battery onlookers with his brown felt hat in hand. They took more pictures of him arriving at the induction center. There were shots of Louis buying a war bond from Mike Jacobs. Later, wearing registration tag number 374, Joe sat down in an office, surrounded by burning klieg lights and fresh-faced inductees—almost of all of them young white men. Right before Private Abraham Taubman, a nervous clerk sitting at a typewriter, began questioning Louis, army officials again urged everyone within earshot to remain quiet. Then the newsreel cameras rolled:

THE FIGHT OF HIS LIFE

Taubman: What's your name, Joe?

Louis: My name is Joe Louis Barrow.

Taubman: What's your occupation?

Louis: Fighter. And let's get at them Japs.

LOOKING A BIT BORED, THE CHAMPION HAD TO REPEAT THOSE lines for the cameras several times. If Louis hadn't realized it before, it was now clear that when he joined Uncle Sam's Army, he had enlisted in a propaganda mission too.[1]

After Joe completed the questionnaire, the chief medical officer, Captain Manuel J. Scham, conducted his physical. Standing six foot two, shirtless, wearing trousers, shoes, and socks, Louis tipped the scale at 220 pounds. Allowing five pounds for his clothing, he weighed about ten pounds more than his usual fighting weight. His chest measured 43 inches expanded and his waist measured 33.5 inches. After taking X-rays, Scham pressed a stethoscope to Joe's chest and nodded for the newsreels, indicating the champ had a strong heart. Except for a deviated septum, there was hardly a scratch on him. Scham noted that Louis had "no significant medical history," a questionable conclusion considering how many blows he had taken to the head. Finally, a "civilian fingerprint expert" "took prints of Joe's murderous fingers." Like all inductees, his FBI military fingerprint card was sent to the adjutant general in Washington, DC. Typically, the entire exam process took about twelve to fifteen minutes. But Joe had to repeat the ordeal several times for the cameras. Two hours later, by the end of the "most ballyhooed examination" of the war, he looked exhausted.[2]

The following afternoon, Louis and Mike Jacobs delivered a check worth $89,082.01 to Rear Admiral Adolphus Andrews at his office at 90 Church Street. Surrounded by naval officers and photographers, Louis and Jacobs presented the single largest donation to the Naval Relief Fund in its thirty-eight-year history. Joe's share—$47,100.94—represented his entire purse from his fight against Buddy Baer. Jacobs contributed $37,229.96. During the ceremony, Andrews announced that since the Navy Relief fight had been so successful, he was now planning a navy benefit at Madison Square Garden that would involve show business stars—including Joe Louis.[3]

Later that night, after touring nightclubs in Harlem, the champ returned to the Hotel Theresa. Stacks of telegrams and phone messages—hundreds of them—filled his hotel room, wishing him good luck in the army. He thought he might see Marva before leaving for Camp Upton. She'd had no idea that her husband had suddenly decided to enter the military until reading about it in the newspaper. Marva packed her bags immediately and rushed from Chicago to join him. But Marva did not arrive at the hotel until the morning of Joe's departure—just minutes after his chauffeur George McArthur whisked him away, along with Mike Jacobs, Julian Black, and Freddie Guinyard.[4]

On a bitterly cold morning, Louis left the city behind for a desolate encampment on Long Island. Five miles northeast of Yaphank, a rural hamlet in Suffolk County, Camp Upton was surrounded by wilderness. There was nothing remarkable about Yaphank except that in the late 1930s, the German American Settlement League, an organization of Nazi sympathizers, convened there to establish Camp Siegfried, a summer destination modeled after Hitler's youth camps. In Yaphank, "Hitler's most visible American friends" organized Nazi rallies and built a community of tract homes with swastikas engraved into the bricks. Carrying rifles and Nazi flags, they paraded down a town street named after the Führer and conducted military maneuvers. But by the time Joe Louis passed through Yaphank, after the Germans declared war on the United States, the federal government had seized Camp Siegfried and interned dozens of the group's Nazi allies at Camp Upton.[5]

Shortly before noon, Louis stepped out of the car wearing a brown overcoat and hat, squinting in the glare of the sun. He met two MPs who escorted him across a muddy street to the reception center "warehouse." While a military band struck up a patriotic tune, a train pulled into the ramshackle post station and unloaded "another cargo of raw material for Uncle Sam's war machine, and the various groups surging across the street merged into one in front of the building." The *New York Daily Mirror*'s Dan Parker described the draftees as "dejected and bewildered as they came out, tagged like immigrants and loaded down with handbags and bundles." Swallowed by a small crowd of admiring draftees, Louis "got routed across the avenue to a company of white recruits," noted a writer from *The New York Times*. At that moment, a uniformed man yelled to Joe that he didn't belong in the queue with white soldiers. Louis didn't say a word. He simply ambled over to the segregated line of young Black men attached to L Company of the Second Battalion. After registering at the reception center, he sat down for lunch with his fellow soldiers in L Company at the "Negro" mess hall and ate his first army lunch: pork chops and bean soup.[6]

Later that afternoon, Joe experienced the standard screening process for enlisted men. After meeting the camp commander, he was fingerprinted, vaccinated, and sworn into the army. Then he completed the Army General Classification Test (AGCT), an aptitude exam used to determine where soldiers should be assigned. Although the War Department denied that the AGCT measured innate intelligence, army officials ignored the fact that exam results strongly correlated with educational achievement and pointed to the lower test scores of Black soldiers as proof that they were incapable of serving in combat units and leadership positions. Whatever Joe scored on the AGCT mattered little since his future in the army's Morale Branch was all but certain. It took him about an hour to complete the exam and then he received basic orientation in military customs, hygiene and morality, and the Articles of War.[7]

During his first week at Camp Upton, *Baltimore Afro-American* writer Ollie Stewart, the first Black reporter credentialed by the War Department, visited Louis. He found a secluded champion, isolated from his friends and family in a segregated camp where the "colored company" took orders from white officers. Marching around the perimeter of the camp in the brutal cold, a sergeant shouted at Louis and the other members of his squad to "get in step." For the heavyweight champion of the world, a wealthy man, it was a humbling experience, to say the least, digging foxholes and conducting gas mask drills. He had moved from the best suite in Harlem with his own bedroom and bathroom to a drafty barracks with nearly two dozen bunkmates. When he wasn't policing the mess kitchen, Louis pushed a mop and polished his size twelve boots. He learned how to make his bed and sew a button. Outside the mess hall, he had to pick up trash and cigarette butts. After MPs counted hundreds of cars approaching the camp gate, the passengers hoping for a glimpse of the champion in uniform, the commandant confined Joe to his quarters and prohibited family members from visiting him. Louis was trying to make the best of army life, but he had never been lonelier.[8]

When another writer from the *Pittsburgh Courier* visited Joe, the champion assured him that "army life is great." His bunkmates found him a friendly "regular guy" who enjoyed playing cards and swapping stories. Joe went so far as to say that being in the army would make him a better fighter. It all sounded good. But Ollie Stewart reported that the segregated conditions in the New York camp were as bad as any in the Jim Crow South. The barracks occupied by Black troops were in the back of the post and the small two-room recreation center assigned to them had virtually no furnishings. A Black soldier told Stewart about a time when a group from L Company departed for the station theater and "a white soldier pushed them and demanded, 'Where you n—s think you're going?'" Although many white soldiers from New York did not agree with the segregated camp conditions, white officers discouraged them from fraternizing with Black troops. Before a unit of white men prepared to travel to Camp Croft, South Carolina, a white officer reminded them not to drink with Black soldiers or even shake their hands. Writing to *PM*, New York's liberal newspaper, a white soldier described the cruel conditions at Camp Upton: "It looks, smells, and tastes like Fascism; it is Fascism in practice."[9]

At a time when Black newspapers published daily accounts about the harassment Black soldiers faced in America's military camps, the Roosevelt administration struggled to comprehend why many Black citizens lacked enthusiasm for the country's war efforts. The stories published in the Black press demonstrated the hypocrisy of America's professed war aim of fighting for democracy while Black soldiers "were treated like convict labor." Nonetheless, government officials blamed Black journalists for "misleading the Negroes" about camp conditions and exacerbating racial tensions. *New York Amsterdam News* reporter Roi Ottley recalled Archibald MacLeish, the director of the Office of Facts and Figures, organizing a meeting with "Negro editors" and urging them "to lay off the rough racial stuff—for the duration of the war, at least." Convinced that the Black press was disseminating propaganda that could be used by the Axis Powers, FBI Director J. Edgar Hoover coordinated a censorship campaign where his agents interrogated and intimidated Black editors whom he suspected of violating the Espionage Act, a draconian law from the

First World War that criminalized free speech. At one point, the Justice Department threatened to shut down Black publications if they didn't soften their coverage of the military, though Attorney General Francis Biddle never actually took that drastic step.[10]

In 1942, the Office of War Information (OWI), the government's wartime propaganda agency and successor to the Office of Facts and Figures, investigated the question of "Negro morale" and devised a strategy for mobilizing wider support for the war effort among Black Americans. OWI adviser Milton Starr, a wealthy white businessman who owned a chain of forty-nine "Negro theaters" throughout the South, wrote an influential report recommending the government address the "Negro problem," not through policies or structural changes that would end discrimination. Instead, he suggested the government downplay racial conflict and promote America's democratic ideals by staging propaganda events and elevating race heroes like Joe Louis. Lamenting the militant leadership of Black activists and journalists who called for civil rights protests, Starr believed that they could be neutralized if OWI exerted greater influence over the Black press and demonstrated in pictures, posters, and pamphlets how Black citizens were contributing to the war effort.[11]

Starr recommended OWI build its propaganda campaign around "prominent Negro names" and faces. Before the Second World War, the US government had never celebrated Black soldiers as war heroes. But there had never been a universally beloved Black hero like Louis, let alone one who served in the military. "The Army and the government have a tremendous propaganda asset in Joe Louis," Starr wrote. "To a great majority of the Negroes, he appears almost as a god. The possibilities for using him are almost unlimited." Joe's overt patriotism, his calls for national unity, and his mild demeanor outside the ring made him an ideal figure for OWI. Despite the fact that Louis made speeches denouncing Jim

Crow and Black voter suppression during the 1940 presidential election, most white Americans didn't think of him as political or confrontational, someone demanding racial equality.[12]

Starr envisioned OWI employing Louis in a variety of ways: on tour with a boxing troupe, visiting military camps throughout the country, promoting war bond drives, and appearing on radio shows and in newsreels, perhaps in a short called "A Day with Joe Louis." Staged photos and moving pictures had the power to convince people of all races that the Joe Louis story represented something larger than the rise of a boxer. In a time of war against fascism, it evoked celebrations of the American way of life and the country's democratic ideals of freedom and equality, framing Louis, the patriotic champion in uniform, as a unifying force—even though he could not sit with white troops for a meal of pork chops and bean soup.[13]

RARELY, IF EVER, HAD SO MANY WHITE MEN GATHERED TO PROfess their admiration for a Black man. On January 22, 1942, about a week after the heavyweight champion began training at Camp Upton, "the biggest men in New York's public life told Joe Louis how much they thought of him and all he had done for his people, his profession, boxing . . . and his country." During the Boxing Writers' Association annual banquet, the organization awarded Louis the Edward J. Neil Memorial Award, given to the person who had contributed the most to boxing the previous year, and *The Ring* magazine named him Fighter of the Year. Inside the oak-paneled Knickerbocker Tap Room of the old Rupert Brewery on Third Avenue, the smell of lager and cigar smoke filled the air as reporters, statesmen, and military officers imbibed around square tables and a long polished bar. Several prominent speakers honored Louis, including former heavyweight champion Gene Tunney, a lieutenant commander in the navy; Abe Greene, president of the National Boxing Association; General John J. Phelan, chairman of the New York State Boxing Commission; Nat Fleischer, editor of *The Ring* magazine; and James A. Farley, the former postmaster general. Even J. Edgar Hoover, the chief G-man who had long scrutinized "Negro activities" in his weekly intelligence reports under the suspicion that virtually every Black activist was subversive, hailed Louis as "a great hero" and "a great American."[14]

That night the most memorable speech from the white power brokers came from James J. "Jimmy" Walker, New York City's former mayor, who, as a state senator, had successfully campaigned for the passage of a 1920 law that legalized prizefighting and subsequently made the Empire City the mecca of boxing. As the father of the Walker boxing law, he proclaimed pugilism an honorable sport that had offered Louis a rare opportunity to rise above the country's racial barriers. Walker praised Joe as an "American gentleman." Louis never forgot his roots or his people "even though a million dollars jingled in his pockets." Reflecting on the champ's recent fight against Buddy Baer for the Navy Relief Society, Walker recognized Louis as a patriot who had risked his title and his future for his country. "Joe . . . that night . . . you laid a rose on Abraham Lincoln's grave!" At that moment, noted a writer from the *Pittsburgh Courier*, "a hush fell on the nation's most hard-boiled audience." Then 250 men rose from their seats, clapping and cheering for the modest champion who sat before them in his khaki uniform.[15]

When he stood to face the audience, only the sound of clinking glasses could be heard. Filled with emotion, Louis paused and took a deep breath. In a soft, low voice, he said, "Gentlemen . . . I never thought I would ever feel as good as the night I won the championship . . . But tonight, I feel better than I have ever felt in my life." The congregation cheered. Joe continued, thanking Mike

Jacobs, General Phelan, and everyone present: "You cannot imagine how grateful I am to you."[16]

After Louis returned to Camp Upton for his basic training, in late February Mike Jacobs announced that the heavyweight champion would once again defend his title and donate his entire purse, only this time he would do it against Abe Simon at Madison Square Garden for the Army Emergency Relief Fund. The news came at a time when Americans debated whether sporting events should continue. Some sports fans questioned whether they should spend money on entertainment that did not directly contribute to the war effort, while others no longer experienced the same thrill cheering for a boxer or a ballplayer as they had before the Japanese attack on Pearl Harbor. Quite simply, American views of sports—and the country's priorities—had changed. "There are no more heroes in the world of sports," Richards Vidmer wrote. "Not these days, for their deeds, no matter how dramatic, are dwarfed by comparison with the achievements of those in more important fields."[17]

Yet Vidmer and countless other columnists argued that Americans should continue enjoying sporting events during the war. More than ever, Nat Fleischer wrote in *The Ring*, Americans, especially the soldiers defending democracy, needed diversions from the international crisis. And boxing and baseball provided relief "from the more serious work of blasting the Japs and their slimy allies off the map." President Roosevelt agreed. In January, FDR wrote his famous "green light letter" to Major League Baseball commissioner Kenesaw Mountain Landis, expressing approval for baseball's continuation. For the duration of the war, Roosevelt replied, "there will be fewer people unemployed and everybody will work longer hours and harder than ever before. And that means that they ought to have a chance for recreation and for taking their minds off their work even more than before."[18]

Jacobs interpreted Roosevelt's message as a sign that professional boxing should play as much of a role in boosting the morale of the country as Major League Baseball. But since the attack on Pearl Harbor, Jacobs had grown increasingly concerned about his business. In the months ahead, most boxing clubs would cease their operations, while Jacobs's Twentieth Century Sporting Club curbed its schedule considerably. With Joe Louis and most professional boxers in the service, fight fans had little reason to buy tickets to commercial bouts. In the two months since the attack on Pearl Harbor, Jacobs had already noticed trouble at the gate. Compared to the previous December and January, he reported that attendance for Madison Square Garden matches had declined by one-third. If he was going to sustain any interest in boxing, the promoter would have to wrap the events in the American flag.[19]

After Uncle Mike's announcement, the army agreed to transfer Louis to Fort Dix, New Jersey, so that he could train at the camp's new sports gym. Military brass invited journalists to Fort Dix so that they could publicize the champ training. Reporters described Louis visiting with one regiment or another, shaking hands and signing autographs until he could no longer make a fist. Photographers posed Joe with his gloves raised in front of an integrated group of Black and white soldiers packing the gymnasium bleachers. In one photo, he is shown jogging past camp tents with a group of white troops trotting behind him, as if a Black soldier could lead white servicemen in Uncle Sam's Army. And in another picture, Joe can be seen jumping rope, again surrounded by pale-faced admirers. Viewed together, the photos suggested that Louis, the great Black morale builder, promoted racial harmony in the US Army. Yet outside the frame of the cameras, the racial tensions at Fort Dix had grown so intense that there were "frequent fist fights among white and Negro troops"—a development that went unreported until two white MPs shot and killed two Black privates and wounded five others in a confrontation a week after Louis left the post.[20]

On March 10, a few days after he started training for his bout against Simon, Louis appeared at Madison Square Garden for a Navy Relief Society fundraiser. Syndicated columnist Walter Winchell, one of the evening's hosts, introduced Private Louis to "a storm of applause that stopped the show." Twenty thousand Americans cheered and whistled when Joe appeared beneath a spotlight. When he stepped toward the microphone, a deep hush came over the crowd. Louis briefly thanked Winchell for recognizing his contributions to the Navy Relief Society and delivered a "soul-touching" speech. "I'm only doing what any red-blooded American would do," he said. Joe paused and declared, "We're gonna do our part and we'll win 'cause we are on God's side." That simple line turned the Garden into a deafening madhouse of civilians and soldiers shouting and stomping their feet as if Louis had just leveled Adolf Hitler himself.[21]

Later that evening, *Pittsburgh Courier* reporter Billy Rowe, a friend of Joe's, visited the champ at his hotel. Louis asked him, "How'd I do?" Rowe said, "You dummy. You made a big mistake," explaining that Joe should have said, "God's on our side." Louis shrugged. "Well, I guess I blew it." But the following day, when Billy showed up at his hotel room, Louis opened the door and threw the morning papers in his face. "Who's the dummy now?" he asked with a grin. New York's columnists had universally praised him for his sincerity and dedication to the country.[22]

Joe's line, "We are on God's side," instantly became a popular war slogan. The US government transformed his message into an American crusade against evil, immortalizing Louis in a widely circulated poster that redefined the image of the Black soldier, not as a messman but as a warrior enlisted in "God's War." Careful not to offend white Americans, the Office of War Information and the country's white-owned newspapers rarely published images of armed Black men in combat, but the Louis poster—reprinted in newspapers read by Americans of all races—showed him glowering at an invisible enemy and jabbing a bayoneted rifle with an inscription that reads: "Pvt. Joe Louis says—'We're going to do our part . . . and we'll win because we're on God's side.'"[23]

That poster answered a crucial question posed by an editorial in the *Pittsburgh Courier*: "Where are our Negro soldiers?" The newspaper's Black readers were "anxious to know and their morale would be immensely improved if the Army would tell them." The government's publicity campaign around Louis made it possible for the Roosevelt administration to refute those complaints and demonstrate Black participation in the war effort without antagonizing white people who disapproved. The War Department and the Office of War Information made sure that Americans could read human-interest stories about white soldiers, but mostly ignored the contributions of Black troops, who were rendered all but invisible—except for Private Louis. Failing to publicize the activities of Black soldiers, however, further advanced the argument from Black critics that this was "a 'white man's war,' and that Negroes had nothing to fight for."[24]

Claudia Jones, a Black journalist and editor of the Young Communist League magazine *Weekly Review*, wrote that it was "ridiculous" and "dangerous" to call the global conflict a "white man's war." In her pamphlet, "Lift Every Voice for Victory," featuring a photograph of Louis on the cover, she insisted, "This is our war. Joe's war. Your war and mine. It is a people's war to preserve the integrity and independence of our nation . . . a war for freedom of all mankind so that men can once again think and breathe freely the whole world over." Equating Jim Crowism with fascism, Jones believed that if the Nazis conquered Europe, Hitlerism

THE FIGHT OF HIS LIFE

would come to the United States, the Ku Klux Klan would run the government, and the law of the "slave master" would preside. In that horrific scenario, Paul Robeson would be silenced, Richard Wright's books would be banned, and "Joe Louis would not be able to give the lie to 'Aryan' supremacy."[25]

The champion agreed that Black Americans had every reason to join the fight against totalitarian rule. "We Negroes have a big stake in this war," he said. "Lincoln freed the slaves and we want to be sure that Mr. Hitler doesn't change any of that. Sure the Negro has a lot of beefs, but Hitler and Hirohito aren't going to help them any."[26]

"The fighting spirit of Joe Louis" may have strengthened the nation's resolve against the intertwined forces of fascism and racism, but the War Department had no intention of letting him anywhere near the battlefield—or civil rights rallies, for that matter. The only real combat he would experience during the war occurred in the ring.

After training at Fort Dix, on March 27, 1942, for the second time in eleven weeks, Louis defended his title and donated his entire purse to the war effort. "From the white cliffs of Dover to the foxholes of Bataan, from the snow-swirled shores of Iceland to the sun-washed Halls of Montezuma," soldiers and civilians listened to the fight on the radio, as did Jack Blackburn from his Chicago hospital bed. Before Joe's match against Abe Simon began at the Garden, radio broadcasters told listeners that Louis had purchased thousands of dollars' worth of tickets for his fellow soldiers, a patriotic gesture from America's champion. And after the ringside announcer introduced Robert F. Patterson, the undersecretary of war, he paid tribute to Louis, not as a credit to his race, as so many white journalists did, but as "a credit to the ring and a credit to the Army."[27]

In the opening rounds, Louis dominated Simon. Then, "for 16 torrid seconds in the sixth round, Private Joe Louis released a barrage of anti-aircraft ammunition on the granite chin of towering Abe Simon," Wendell Smith wrote in the *Pittsburgh Courier*. And, Smith reminded readers, Louis knocked him out "free of charge!" Joe had promised Jack Blackburn that he would knock out Simon in the third round. Fighting cautiously, seemingly unsure of himself, he struggled with timing his punches. He threw too many wild shots that failed to connect, perhaps, Nat Fleischer suggested, because he wanted to keep his word to Blackburn. Undoubtedly, training for a heavyweight fight in a bustling army camp proved unsuitable. The fight was unspectacular, but Louis fulfilled his mission, raising nearly $65,000 for the Army Emergency Relief Fund.[28]

Increasingly, a pattern of praise coming from white people had emerged since Joe enlisted in the service and donated his purses to the army and navy relief organizations. White writers and public officials celebrated Louis as "a great citizen," less a representative of his race than of his country. They made every effort to present him as an exceptional "Negro," as if the champion occupied a world apart from Black America. Of course, it was only possible for white folks to celebrate him as a model American if he didn't complain about the color line. The evolution of his image in the white mind can be found in the writing of Paul Gallico, who once described Louis as "a magnificent animal" untouched by civilization. But now "Louis had found his soul" and proven himself "a good American," earning the admiration of Gallico and countless white fans, who finally recognized the humanity of a Black man so long denied.[29]

IN LATE APRIL, ABOUT A MONTH AFTER THE SIMON FIGHT, WHILE Louis was standing in the "ready line" with the men from L Company on the Camp Upton firing range, a corporal delivered devastating news: Joe's longtime trainer Jack Blackburn had died. Stunned, Joe nearly dropped his rifle. Blackburn had suffered a heart attack and collapsed in his home. When Louis last saw Blackburn, the doctors told him that Jack would recover from a bout of pneumonia. "This is the worst news—the worst shock I ever got in my life," he said. Then it was his turn to shoot the target. Visibly shaken, he raised the rifle and fired ten rapid shots. With Blackburn gone it was hard to think about being a soldier.[30]

More than anyone, Blackburn had molded Louis into a devastating knockout puncher. The old trainer's methods and his bitterness about life were shaped by years of hard living and the cruelty of Jim Crow America.

In the early twentieth century, Charles Henry "Jack" Blackburn, the son of a minister, had been among the toughest and most feared fighters. A tall wiry lightweight, he fought all comers, regardless of size. He once sparred with Jack Johnson in a Philadelphia gym and bloodied the heavyweight champion's nose. "Blackburn stabbed Johnson repeatedly in the mouth with his left, and the latter did not relish it at all," observed a reporter. Seething, Johnson would never forget that Blackburn had embarrassed him in the ring.[31]

Blackburn inhabited a volatile world, searching for an outlet to unleash the pain he carried into every barroom, brothel, and boxing gym. A hot-tempered alcoholic enraged by the racism that circumscribed his life, Jack could snap easily and turn completely homicidal—"wholly unnatural," in the words of Truman Gibson. In January 1909, Blackburn and Maude Pillion, a white madam and his common-law wife, took a taxi ride to the Philadelphia home of Alonzo Polk. According to news reports, Maude knocked on Polk's door while Blackburn, intoxicated, waited in the cab. At the time, Jack was still recovering from a brutal fight with his brother Fred. A few weeks earlier, Fred had insulted Maude, and when Jack erupted, Fred slashed his left cheek with a razor, leaving a jagged scar that ran from the corner of his mouth to his ear. Now, sitting outside Polk's home, Blackburn watched a violent argument ensue between Maude and Alonzo's wife, Mattie. Rushing to Mattie's defense, Alonzo brandished a gun. Blackburn unloaded his own revolver, piercing Alonzo with three deadly bullets—two in the neck and one in the gut. Maude and Mattie both suffered wounds of their own but recovered. Detained and jailed by police, Blackburn survived a reported suicide attempt after swallowing poison in his cell. One news article suggested that Maude smuggled him a vial during a visit—a story prison officials denied. After his lawyer blamed the entire provocation on Maude, Blackburn pleaded guilty to second-degree murder and was sentenced to fifteen years behind bars. When Blackburn asked Jack Johnson to visit him in prison and help raise funds for an appeal, the champion supposedly sneered, "Let the son of a bitch stay in jail."[32]

After being paroled for good behavior in 1914, Blackburn returned to the sporting life embittered, having lost more than four years of his prime to the penitentiary. He continued boxing, but his best years in the ring were behind him, and eventually he became a trainer, working almost exclusively with white boxers. In 1934, when John Roxborough and Julian Black approached him about training Joe Louis, Blackburn hesitated to take on a Black heavyweight. When Joe's managers pressed him further, the trainer explained that Black heavyweights had no chance of succeeding since Jack Johnson acted like he "owned the world," fooling around with white women. Perhaps he was thinking about how his own turbulent relationship with a white woman derailed his career as much as he was thinking about Johnson. Besides, he said, if a Black boxer wouldn't take a dive in fixed matches, then no promoter would sign him. The odds were stacked against Louis. But Blackburn needed money, and he accepted the offer from Joe's managers. At the onset of training, Blackburn preached that for a

Black man to have any success as a boxer, he had to be "very good outside the ring and very bad inside." To Joe, he said, "You've got to be a killer, otherwise I'm getting too old to waste any time on you." Louis listened closely and replied, "I ain't gonna waste any of your time."[33]

Blackburn taught Louis how to become a lethal puncher. The trainer worked with Joe on his balance so that he fought from a flat-footed stance, not bounding all over the ring on his toes. He trained Louis to throw a stream of punches without falling forward and clinching, which would only give Joe's opponents a chance to recuperate. Blackburn wanted to turn Louis into a stalking fighter who could crowd an opponent, cut off the ring, and batter the other fighter with short snapping punches. Once Louis had his man on the ropes, Blackburn instructed, he could not let the referee or the judges decide the outcome. He knew all too well that Black fighters rarely won decisions. "You gotta knock 'em out and keep knocking 'em out," he implored. Blackburn raised Joe's taped right hand and said, "Let your right fist be the referee. Don't ever forget that. Let that right fist there be your referee!"[34]

Blackburn may have been an outstanding boxer and a great trainer, but he was no marksman. In October 1935, about a month after Louis knocked out Max Baer, Blackburn again found himself reaching for a gun to settle a dispute. On the South Side of Chicago, Jack exchanged gunfire with a man named John Bowman. The reported origins of the shoot-out were tangled. It seemed to have something to do with a real estate deal gone bad. Years later, however, Truman Gibson, one of Blackburn's defense attorneys, revealed that the shooting began after Jack caught Bowman cheating at craps. Enraged, Blackburn stumbled home, retrieved a pistol, and returned, firing wildly on the streets of Chicago. The shooting resulted in the death of Enoch Houser, a sixty-nine-year-old man, and the maiming of Lucy Cannon, a nine-year-old girl.[35]

In his inquest, deputy coroner Benjamin Grant exonerated Blackburn after declaring that there were no witnesses, and, besides, Houser died "from pneumonia superinduced by gun shot wounds fired by unknown parties." It was a curious finding, to say the least. In his memoir, Gibson implied the coroner had been bought. Nonetheless, prosecutors filed manslaughter charges against Blackburn. However, after a trial jury acquitted Blackburn, Lucy Cannon's parents filed a civil suit against him. Roxborough and Julian Black paid a settlement to protect the trainer and the rising career of Joe Louis.[36]

During Blackburn's trial Louis sat beside him. They were inseparable, as close as father and son. They called each other "Chappie," and formed a bond that profoundly shaped Joe's life and career. Jack provided guidance and reassurance. He instilled confidence in the young fighter. Blackburn could be seen in Joe's corner of the ring, "hovering over him like a halo," whispering words of encouragement and patting him on the shoulder. And when Joe won a match, Jack beamed, saying, "Boy, ain't he sumpin'!"[37]

Chappie's influence over Joe extended beyond the ring. Simmering with resentment over a lifetime of slights inflicted by white men, Blackburn railed against Jim Crow. His repeated sermons on the wicked ways that white promoters and managers exploited Black boxers made an impression on Joe. The fight racket offered a larger lesson about America's racial order: Only in the ring could a Black man defend himself and strike a white man with impunity. Although Louis recalled that he had not encountered many instances of overt racism growing up in rural Alabama and Detroit, Blackburn reminded him that he could never escape the harsh reality that even as the heavyweight champion of the world, the color of his skin still determined his place in America.[38]

When Louis returned to Chicago to pay his respects and say goodbye to his old friend, he thought about everything Chappie had taught him and all the glory that they had achieved together. On the day of the funeral, thousands of people gathered at the First Pilgrim Baptist Church. Police estimated that somewhere between twenty-five and thirty thousand mourners paid tribute to a man whom no one remembered as a murderer. For hours, people passed the bronze casket. Joe sat solemnly in the front row between John Roxborough and Julian Black. Reverend J. C. Austin delivered the eulogy, reminding Joe—and everyone who thought of him as their Black Moses—that his mentor would always be in his corner. "Think not for one moment that Jack Blackburn has left the ring," he preached. "Think not that he has been hammered down by the clenched fist of death to take the count of ten. Think not that he has deserted the man who was the best work of his genius, mind and soul. He still lives and will be at the next fight, climbing through the ropes as a second to his protégé and will lean forward in his usual style saying to him: 'Fear not, Chappie, keep up the shuffle I taught you. Remember the black boy starts out with two strikes on him. Make good with your last strike and don't let it be a foul.'"[39]

When the pallbearers lowered Blackburn into the ground, Louis did not completely realize it yet, but his managers were starting to fade from his life. In early January, after a jury found Roxborough guilty of criminal conspiracy and racketeering charges, a Detroit judge sentenced him to prison for two and a half to five years, though he remained free on appeal. Then, later that month in Chicago, a Cook County grand jury indicted Julian Black on similar charges, though he was never convicted. Blackburn's death, the criminal cases against Joe's managers, and the war portended a transformative period in the champ's life.

Serving in the army with his boxing career on hold, Louis matured and grew more independent. "Army life changed me," he said after the war. "It took me away from Mr. Roxborough and Julian Black and Chappie. When I didn't have them around to think for me . . . I had to figure things out myself. I grew up in the Army."[40]

Chapter Seven

WAR BOXING, INC.

> I sincerely believe it was his worth and understanding, plus his conduct in the ring, that paved the way for the black man in professional sports. . . . My love for Joe Louis goes much beyond what he did in the ring, or even his desire to right an injustice.
>
> —Jackie Robinson and Wendell Smith,
> *My Own Story*

THE TIME HAD COME: UNCLE MIKE NEEDED A FIGHT JUST AS badly as the heavyweight champion did. On May 16, 1942, Jacobs wrote the Army Emergency Relief office, proposing a heavyweight title match for June or July. He promised the match would generate "a substantial sum of money" for the Army Emergency Relief Fund and the federal government's tax coffers. Offering to promote the bout and cover all costs, Jacobs suggested Army Relief would receive a percentage of the gross ticket receipts and a percentage of the profits derived from the fight's film and broadcasting rights. Additionally, the champ and his opponent would each donate 5 percent of their purses to the Relief Fund. Not only would the match guarantee the army charity $150,000, it would also earn Louis enough money to wipe out his $117,000 federal income tax debt. Left unstated in his letter was that Joe also needed the fight to pay debts to Jacobs for nearly $60,000 and to John Roxborough for more than $40,000.¹

The War Department hesitated. When Louis had donated his entire purse to the Emergency Relief Fund from his fight against Abe Simon, army officials had eagerly accepted his generous donation. According to Dan Parker, when Louis consigned his entire earnings from both relief bouts, "he was assured by proper authorities that permission would be granted him to fight some time this summer to earn his income tax money." But now military representatives recognized that Louis and Jacobs would profit from the match, and questioned whether they should. "The Army," Jimmy Powers reported, "is afraid other business men in the service might request permission to carry on their private businesses by making a deal guaranteeing the army a slice of their profits if they, too, are 'let out' from time to time." In other words, granting Louis a furlough so he could enrich himself would set a dangerous precedent.²

While Jacobs campaigned for another Army Relief fight, thousands of US soldiers, the biggest contingent of troops yet, began landing in Northern Ireland. There were so many Americans pouring into the countryside that the Irish towns began to look like the United States. The streets were suddenly filled with American infantry units marching alongside tanks, trucks, and jeeps. Six months into the war, however, Jacobs recognized that America had only begun to fight. The Allies were still on the defensive and nowhere near ready to open a second front in northwest Europe. Jacobs believed that if Louis did not fight a match in the summer of 1942, he would not fight again until the war ended.³

The promoter's allies in the Hearst newspapers pressured the army to let Louis box for his own benefit. "Our Government needs money badly to pursue the war," Parker wrote in the *Daily Mirror*. "The only favor good citizen and good soldier Joseph Louis Barrow asks is the privilege of earning a considerable sum for his

Government, to help preserve the way of life that has been so good to him—and to which he has been so good. Can there be any answer to this humble plea but 'Yes!'?"[4]

Syndicated Hearst writer Henry McLemore understood the War Department's resistance to approving a furlough just so that a soldier could reconcile his tax bill, but he also believed the public would support an exception for the "most popular athlete in this country." The War Department should "know that the public is on Joe's side . . . You could knock on all the doors from [New York] to Walla Walla and back without finding a half dozen citizens who didn't feel that the army owes Joe this chance to square himself."[5]

In late May, Louis and Jacobs met with Joseph T. Higgins, the collector of internal revenue. Louis explained that without fighting for another purse he could not pay his enormous balance with the IRS. In his charitable fights against Buddy Baer and Abe Simon, he had made a grave financial error: Instead of waiving his end of the purse, Louis had accepted both checks and then endorsed them over to the relief agencies. That meant that he owed taxes on the income from those charity bouts. Joe should have refused the checks altogether to avoid tax liability. That mistake cost him dearly. Higgins sympathized with Louis and gave him an extension until July 15. If the champ could not pay his bill, like all GIs, he could apply for an interest-free tax deferment that would extend the due date until six months after his service ended. But he would receive the deferment only if he could prove his military service had "materially impaired" his ability to pay income taxes.[6]

Army officials maintained that Louis needed to focus on being a soldier. Since he had enlisted thirteen weeks earlier, though it was no fault of his own, he had fallen behind in his basic training. Traveling to various camps to perform boxing exhibitions had set him back. Of course, he did so under the orders of the army. Nonetheless, the army promoted him to corporal at the end of

May. But after conferring with military officials in Washington, DC, Jacobs received word from Major General Alexander D. Surles, director of the army's Bureau of Public Relations: "Inquiry at the War Department develops the fact that no authority has been given to anyone to assign Joe Louis to a commercial fight." Dejected, Jacobs had all but given up on staging another heavyweight title bout during the war.[7]

Yet the War Department still planned on letting Louis raise money for its relief funds. On June 14, he staged a four-round boxing exhibition at the Polo Grounds for the Army and Navy Relief Societies in an "All-Sports Carnival." For six hours, more than twelve thousand fans watched eighteen events, including a five-inning baseball game featuring Cleveland Indians star pitcher Bob Feller, a mixed doubles tennis match pairing Don Budge with Alice Marbles, and a variety of competitions in golf, soccer, track, and lacrosse. "With rain threatening all day," noted sportswriter Joe Bostic, "you couldn't help but feel that, but for the Bomber, there would have been naught but a vast expanse of empty seats." After sparring with George Nicholson, Louis had little to say when a reporter asked him about a rumor that he would fight Billy Conn in September, with the army staging the match and a committee of sportswriters handling the publicity.[8]

A few days after the sports carnival, Secretary of War Henry Stimson announced that Louis had been ordered to report to the Cavalry Replacement Training Center at Fort Riley, Kansas. Until Louis completed his basic training, Stimson declared, "his public appearances, except those for the armed forces, will be discontinued." The army controlled Joe's fate, but Stimson had left open the possibility that he could return to the ring after finishing his basic training.[9]

Departing Grand Central Station on June 22, 1942, at 6 p.m., Louis slung his army bag over his shoulder and boarded the

In Joe Louis's first major New York fight, a sensational knockout of former champion Primo Carnera in 1935, he leaped into the center of the American sporting scene. For the next sixteen years reporters chronicled his rise and fall. Getty Images.

Louis seemed virtually unbeatable in the ring, losing only once before becoming heavyweight champion in 1937 and going undefeated during his title reign until 1949. Outside the ring his life was a soap opera. Here he strolls down a Harlem avenue arm-in-arm with his wife Marva, much to the delight of local residents. International News Photo Collection, Chicago History Museum.

After Max Schmeling's long-shot knockout of Louis in 1936, he became the darling of Nazi Germany, a visible example of the regime's strength and determination. Even Adolf Hitler extolled the boxer's virtues. Getty Images.

The 1938 Louis-Schmeling rematch was perhaps the most consequential sporting event of the twentieth century. As this Burris Jenkins Jr., cartoon suggests, that night the eyes of the world focused on the ring in Yankee Stadium. *New York Journal-American* Archives.

Behind Louis were two visionary managers and a crafty promoter. Standing are managers John Roxborough (left) and Julian Black (right). Presenting a check to Louis is matchmaker Mike Jacobs. Associated Press.

Trainer Jack Blackburn lived a checkered life that included a successful boxing career and a stretch in prison for manslaughter. A trainer in his later life, he refined Louis's fighting style and became the champion's chief strategist. Getty Images.

During the 1940 presidential election, Joe Louis campaigned on behalf of Republican candidate Wendell Willkie. At a Harlem rally, Louis declared, "There is no future on relief and the WPA." *New York World-Telegram and Sun* Newspaper Photograph Collection, Library of Congress.

On June 18, 1941, at the Polo Grounds in New York, Joe Louis battled Billy Conn in the last great heavyweight title fight before the United States entered the war. After knocking out Conn in the thirteenth round, the champ towered over the challenger. *New York World-Telegram and Sun* Newspaper Photograph Collection, Library of Congress.

Joe Louis and Lena Horne had much in common. They were both celebrities: He was the heavyweight champion; she was a Hollywood starlet. But more than that they were symbols of Black advancement. Before and during World War II, they were lovers. Long after the war ended, they remained friends. Getty Images.

On January 13, 1942, Joe Louis began his basic training at Camp Upton, New York. When he arrived, Louis attracted a crowd of Black soldiers who were eager to meet their hero. International News Photo Collection, Chicago History Museum.

During World War II, the United States government rarely disseminated images of armed Black soldiers. But the Office of War Information immortalized Louis as a crusader fighting "God's War." United Sates Office of Facts and Figures, Library of Congress.

This Is the Army (1943) was famed composer Irving Berlin's World War II tribute to the American fighting forces. The US Army sent Louis to Hollywood to play a central part in the film in an effort to persuade Black Americans that they had a role in a war where "free people" were "fighting to be free." Getty Images.

During the war, Joe Louis and future welterweight and middleweight champion "Sugar" Ray Robinson headlined "the world's greatest boxing show," an exhibition tour that brought them to more than 100 stateside military camps. In Southern military posts they endured racism and hostility. But when the Louis troupe set sail for Europe, Robinson did not board the ship. Getty Images.

In peacetime and war, Black Americans had always supported their country. Or at least that was the message of the film *The Negro Soldier* (1944). Produced under the loose supervision of famed Hollywood director Frank Capra, the film satisfied the War Department's desire to present a common racial front in the nation's war effort with Joe Louis serving as a unifying symbol.

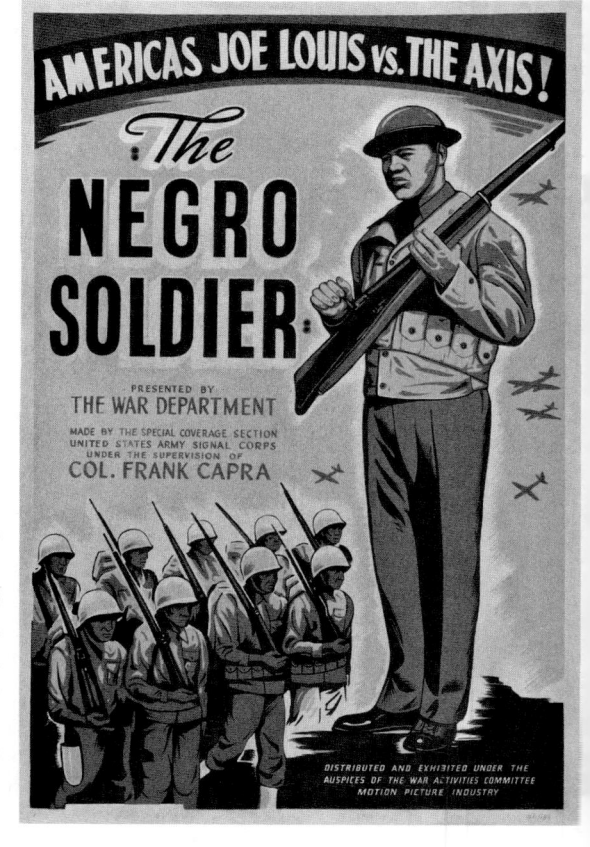

On September 9, 1944, Joe Louis addressed a crowd of soldiers during a boxing exhibition that he put on as part of the Salerno Day show held at Fifth Army Headquarters to commemorate the Allied invasion of Italy. U.S. Army Signal Corps photograph, William F. Caddell Collection, National World War II Museum.

After the war ended, Joe Louis served as the Honorary National Commander of the United Negro and Allied Veterans of America. In this advertisement published in the July 1946 issue of *Our World* magazine, Louis called on veterans of all races to organize and fight for democracy at home, especially for the civil rights of Black Americans.

In June 1942, Jackie Robinson and Joe Louis began training together at Fort Riley, Kansas. Four years later, while Robinson was playing with the Montreal Royals, the minor league affiliate of the Brooklyn Dodgers, the friends reconnected at Joe's training camp in Pompton Lakes, New Jersey, where the champ prepared to defend his title for the first time since the end of the war. Getty Images.

On August 9, 1946, Joe Louis [left] and Neil Scott [right], guided blinded veteran Isaac Woodard up the stairs at the Hotel Theresa in Harlem. They met to plan a benefit for Woodard sponsored by Louis after South Carolina police had beaten and blinded Woodard, provoking outrage among Americans *New York Daily News* collection Getty Images.

Twentieth Century Limited headed for Chicago's La Salle Street Station. Traveling alone, he planned to visit Marva before continuing his journey westward to Fort Riley. Standing in the train doorway, Louis answered a few questions from reporters. Joe said he would not fight anyone but Billy Conn. "No sense fighting anyone else," he explained. Only a title rematch against Conn could draw a sellout crowd at Yankee Stadium. Was he worried about his overdue tax bill? Not really, he answered. The IRS was "going to let it ride until after the war."[10]

Then the conductor waved a lantern, and as Joe bid farewell to the crowd, the passenger train slowly rolled away. His trainer, Mannie Seamon, the man who had replaced Jack Blackburn, waved and said, "Good luck, Joe. God bless you."

WHEN JOE LOUIS ARRIVED AT FORT RILEY, HE JOINED THE ONLY all-Black cavalry regiment in the United States military. During the second half of the nineteenth century, Fort Riley had served as a frontier outpost for troops protecting the wagon trains of white settlers traveling along the Overland Trail and for guarding the railroad lines being built across Kansas. At various times between the end of the Civil War and the First World War, "Buffalo soldiers," the Black cavalry regiments nicknamed by the American Plains Indians, quartered at Fort Riley. By World War II, the Ninth and Tenth Cavalry Regiments had become part of the Second Cavalry Division, and Fort Riley functioned as the only cavalry school in the US Army. It seemed an ideal assignment. Since he had purchased a Michigan farm, Joe enjoyed riding and training horses.

At Fort Riley, he formed a lifelong friendship with Jack Roosevelt Robinson, a talented Black athlete from Pasadena, California. Jack idolized Joe. After meeting him, Robinson praised the heavyweight champion "as a soldier, as a gentleman and a race man." When they weren't training and riding together, they chatted about sports. Inside the boxing ring, Joe taught him a few lessons in the sweet science. They also enjoyed playing cards and golf. Robinson recalled one occasion when he had received his monthly $21 check from the army but he owed the local golf course $14. He said, "Joe just put his big hand over my hand with the money in it and pushed it back into my pocket." Then Louis "pulled out a roll of bills and paid for everything." Robinson never forgot Louis's largesse and how he encouraged him. "Jackie," he said, "be yourself, man."[11]

Joe Louis and Jackie Robinson were more than just the two most famous and influential Black athletes of the 1940s. They were proud Black men who fought two wars, Robinson said, "one against the foreign enemy, the other against prejudice at home." Invoking the Double Victory campaign promoted by the *Pittsburgh Courier*, Robinson found inspiration in Louis at a time when Jim Crow tested his patriotism and resolve. When they met in 1942, the number of Black soldiers in the army was swelling. Between the attack on Pearl Harbor and December 1942, Black enlistments had grown fivefold to nearly 470,000. The navy and the coast guard began accepting Black recruits for general service and the marine corps ended its ban on Black enlistments. But the rapid expansion of Black men in the armed forces exacerbated racial friction with white servicemen who resented their presence. At Fort Riley, Black troops endured countless humiliations, and they looked to Louis for leadership. The champion's arrival, said Robinson's wife, Rachel, "brought much-needed power to the Black soldiers and gave Jack an opportunity to form an alliance and work with his longtime hero."[12]

Before he met Louis in the army, Robinson had been a sensational four-sport athlete at UCLA. Known as "the greatest ball carrier in the nation," he could have played running back in the National Football League, but in 1941, the league's owners maintained lily-white rosters. In March 1942, five years before he broke Major League Baseball's color barrier with the Brooklyn Dodgers, Robinson practiced with the Chicago White Sox in Pasadena, hoping he might get a shot at playing in the big leagues. Although he impressed Sox manager Jimmy Dykes, the liberal skipper said he was powerless to sign "Negro players" unless Commissioner Landis and the club owners ended segregation. Discouraged, Robinson could not envision a future in professional sports. Five days after the Sox tryout, he received a notice from his local draft board to report for duty in the army. Despite his reticence about training for combat in a segregated camp, Robinson reported to Fort Riley with aspirations of becoming an officer. As an intelligent, college-educated soldier, he was certainly qualified for officer candidate school (OCS). When Jack applied, however, he was "advised unofficially that Negroes were not permitted in OCS at Fort Riley."[13]

Robinson fumed. Nothing angered him more than being treated like a second-class citizen. Listening to him complain about the army's racist restrictions, Louis shared his outrage. "It's bad enough to have a segregated Army," Joe thought, but "at least some Blacks should be officers over their own people." Years later, he recalled telephoning his friend Truman Gibson, who by that time had left his law practice to serve as an assistant to William Hastie, the Black civilian aide to Secretary of War Stimson. Gibson flew to Fort Riley to investigate the conditions in the camp. He met with Louis, Robinson, and other Black soldiers who had been denied admission to OCS. The reported details are vague, but, according to Louis, after the summit with Fort Riley's Black troops, he and Gibson met with the post's commanding officer, Brigadier General Donald Robinson. That conversation convinced the commander to desegregate OCS.[14]

However, Gibson denied playing a central role in the story. The army, he said, had already established a policy against segregated officer training schools. According to one historian, by the spring of 1942, there were so many protests about racial restrictions in OCS that "President Roosevelt intervened, and, in turn, Secretary Stimson ordered that more Negro officers must be provided for the Army." Ultimately, a few months after meeting with Louis and Gibson, Jackie Robinson was admitted to OCS. It was a significant turning point in the war for Black soldiers. For the first time in the segregated camp, Black and white officers in training studied, worked, and ate together. Whatever doubts Gibson had about his own influence at Fort Riley, Robinson respected Louis for using his political clout to challenge institutional racism.[15]

Yet Joe Louis's many biographers have exaggerated his influence over Jackie Robinson's army career. In Louis's memoir, written in 1974 with Edna Rust and Art Rust Jr., he claimed that he told Brigadier General Robinson that Jackie had been denied an opportunity to play for the camp's baseball team and football team on account of his skin color. When Joe told the commanding officer that Jackie had been a star athlete at UCLA, the brigadier general authorized him to play on both teams. "After some back and forth talk between me and the Brigadier," Joe told the Rusts, "Jackie wound up the champion baseball and football player at Fort Riley. Not only that, it opened the door over many parts of the country for integrated Army Camps."[16]

There's just one problem with the story: Jackie Robinson never played for Fort Riley's baseball team or football team. During basic training, he wanted to join the camp baseball lineup, but the squad's captain barred Black soldiers from the field. However, a colonel at the post who wanted to build a winning football team was willing to let Robinson play on one condition: He could not suit up against the team's first opponent, the University of Missouri. Knowing the Tigers football team refused to take the field against Black players, the army offered Robinson a two-week leave so he could skip the game against Mizzou. When Robinson returned from his furlough, he received orders to pick up his football gear. But Jack informed the colonel that he had decided against playing football since he could not compete in every game. Incensed, the colonel threatened to force him to play under official orders. Robinson didn't flinch. "You wouldn't want me playing on your team, knowing that my heart wasn't in it," he replied.[17]

In another widely accepted tale told by Truman Gibson, Robinson would not have finished OCS if Joe Louis had not rescued him from self-destruction. According to Gibson, Robinson was on a drill field when he heard a white officer denigrate a Black soldier as a "stupid nigger son of a bitch." Robinson interceded and confronted the white officer: "You shouldn't address a soldier in those terms." The white officer retaliated, "Oh, fuck you. Screw you, nigger." Again, according to Gibson, Robinson erupted and "knocked all of the officer's teeth out." Jack "almost killed the guy," Gibson said. When Louis learned that Robinson had assaulted a white officer, he called Gibson in a panic, fearing what might happen to his friend. After Louis bribed the brigadier general with "very expensive gifts"—a Piaget watch and a case of champagne—Fort Riley's commanding officer forgot the incident and let Robinson complete OCS.[18]

Decades after the war ended, Truman Gibson told this story to Joe's biographer, Chris Mead, and several other interviewers. Subsequently, writers have repeated Gibson's version of events, but it's highly unlikely this incident ever occurred. In his memoir, Gibson wrote that after Robinson struck the white officer, he "faced court-martial, prison, and . . . possibly even death." But there is no record in Robinson's extensive military file that he assaulted a white officer. Later, he faced a court-martial when he was stationed at Camp Good, Texas, charged with disrespecting and disobeying his superior officer. The prosecution would have certainly uncovered evidence of a volatile confrontation at Fort Riley. Furthermore, in his own memoirs, newspaper columns, and interviews, Robinson never mentioned slugging a white officer at Fort Riley. If he had assaulted a white officer, eyewitnesses would have come forward and verified Gibson's account.[19]

The legend of Joe Louis grew under the claim he had "saved" Jackie Robinson—his successor as Black America's next great hero, a freedom fighter on and off the field—from imprisonment or death. During the Great Depression and World War II, there were numerous folktales about Louis, the Black Moses, saving the day or answering a prayer. At the height of his fame, he received thousands of letters from Black men and women who needed his help with a job, a train ticket, or rent money. Fathers, field hands, and factory workers asked him for "touches"—small loans to help them get over a difficult time. In Oklahoma, a Black inmate wrote Louis, asking for "a sawbuck." When Joe sent the prisoner ten dollars, other Black inmates in the penitentiary wrote asking for a touch of their own.[20]

The most desperate pleas came from helpless Black men on death row, illustrated in the apocryphal tale involving Allen Foster, a nineteen-year-old inmate who was sentenced to the gas chamber in 1935 after being convicted of assaulting and raping a white woman in rural North Carolina. Foster was only one of many Black men accused of defiling a white woman. Alice Capps testified that Foster had entered her farmhouse and threatened her at knifepoint, demanding money, before striking her in the head with a bottle. Although a medical examiner found evidence of forced sexual intercourse, according to police, Foster denied "completion" of the act. On the eve of his execution, however, he told a reporter that he had never seen Alice Capps and that deputies had bludgeoned him into confessing. Upon his conviction, Foster's distraught mother petitioned the governor, urging him to consider her only son's mental impairment. In his prison photograph, Foster smiled, as if he had no idea that he had been sentenced to the gas chamber. "Please save him from that Gas please," his mother begged. "I taught him all I could and all I knowed about the white people law."[21]

On a cold January morning, the state proceeded with its first execution by gas asphyxiation. The night before his death, Foster appeared "openly terrified." He told United Press correspondent John Parris Jr., "The soul can be ready, but the flesh ain't, and I'm worried." During an interview with Parris, the condemned inmate said he had sparred with Joe Louis as a boy growing up in Birmingham, an unlikely event since Louis did not start boxing until his family had moved to Detroit. Draped in a blanket and shivering, Foster entered the freezing chamber wearing only boxing shorts. Before being strapped to an oak chair, he clenched his fist and threw an uppercut as he said, "I fought Joe Louis . . . Tell my mother good-bye." Then as the chamber doors shut, he shouted, "I'm innocent!"[22]

Then a dense gray vapor fogged the chamber, filling his lungs with gas until his eyes rolled. For more than ten minutes, his limp body convulsed and lurched violently, "as though he was trying to leave the chair." Foster suffered a gruesome death. Horrified eyewitnesses could hardly watch the prolonged torture. Newspaper reports of his execution provoked a public outcry throughout the South. Perhaps the most sensational account came from the *Daily Worker*'s Ted Benson, who described Foster praying as the executioner turned on the gas valve. "Slowly strangulation sets in, his breath comes in staccato gasps. And those who listen to the ghastly performance hear him cry: 'Save me . . . Joe Louis . . . save me . . . Joe Louis . . . Joe . . . save . . . Joe!'"[23]

In the coming years, Foster's desperate plea took on greater significance in Black folk culture. Without using the inmate's name or mentioning his alleged crime, Martin Luther King Jr. evoked Foster's execution as an allegory for explicating the meaning of Joe Louis. King claimed, "a microphone was placed inside the sealed death chamber so that scientific observers might hear the words of the dying prisoner," but that was not true. No one could hear Foster's cries inside the glass compartment, as Ted Benson had originally claimed. King insisted, however, that as the potassium cyanide pellet dropped into the sulfuric acid container, "and the gas curled upward, through the microphone came these words: 'Save me, Joe Louis! Save me, Joe Louis! Save me, Joe Louis.'"[24]

Those heartbreaking words spoke to "the helplessness, the loneliness, and the profound despair of Negroes in that period," King wrote in 1963. "The condemned young Negro, groping for someone who might care for him, and had the power enough to rescue him, found only the heavyweight champion of the world." King continued, "Joe Louis would care because he was a Negro. Joe Louis could do something because he was a fighter." Foster's mythic last words revealed the powerlessness and desperation in Black America, and the yearning for a Black Messiah. "Not God, not government, not charitably-minded white men, but a Negro who was the world's most expert fighter, in this last extremity, was the last hope."[25]

The truth was that Joe Louis could not rescue a man from the gas chamber any more than he could protect Jackie Robinson from a court-martial. By the summer of 1942, the heavyweight champion couldn't even save his own boxing career. His professional future depended entirely on whether War Department officials would sanction an Army Relief bout.

Truman Gibson paid him a visit on September 2, 1942, at Fort Riley delivering good news: The War Department had approved an army benefit with Louis defending his title against Billy Conn on Columbus Day. Although initial reports indicated that the War Department authorized the match on the condition that Louis would donate his entire purse to the Army Emergency Relief Fund, Louis balked at the proposal, insisting he would not fight for free—not again. Supposedly, Gibson then promised Louis that if he fought Conn, the champ would earn enough money to pay off his debts to Uncle Sam and Uncle Mike. And that's when the deal got complicated.[26]

ABOUT A WEEK AFTER GIBSON MET WITH THE CHAMP AT FORT Riley, the War Department issued an official announcement that Corporal Louis and Private Conn would meet in the ring on October 12 "with every penny of the receipts going to the Army Emergency Relief, and with the two gladiators getting nothing more than their regular [army] pay." Breaking Gibson's arrangement with Louis, the War Department made clear that "no private interests would receive any financial benefit" from the bout. Under the agreement, Mike Jacobs would serve as chief promoter and War Boxing, Inc., a committee of sportswriters—basically, a "dummy management" group—chaired by Grantland Rice, would stage the match. Acting on behalf of the War Department, Major General Alexander D. Surles, director of the army's Bureau of Public Relations, would serve as an adviser to the committee. After being promoted to sergeant, Louis, looking slightly overweight, received an emergency furlough to train at Greenwood Lake, while Conn prepared to train at Jacobs's quarters in Rumson, New Jersey.[27]

A meeting took place in New York City on September 15 involving Surles, Jacobs, and the sportswriters' committee. According to *The Sun*'s sports editor Wilbur Wood, a member of War Boxing, Inc., Surles informed the committee that he had learned that

Truman Gibson had promised Louis that he would be allowed to pay his debts to Jacobs, Roxborough, and the IRS from his purse. Someone at the War Department had promised Conn that he could earn enough from the match to pay his debts to Jacobs too. Apparently, Surles knew nothing about Gibson's agreement with Louis. Initially, Surles thought the total amount the fighters owed Jacobs was insignificant, but he then learned that Louis owed the promoter $59,000 and Conn owed him approximately $35,000, not to mention Joe's $41,000 debt to John Roxborough. Surles suggested the War Department could allow $50,000 to be taken out of the receipts so that Louis and Conn could reduce their personal debts to Jacobs's Twentieth Century Sporting Club, but Joe refused to fight "unless the promises made to him were fulfilled." Once Surles relented, the committee voted to let Louis and Conn pay off about $135,000 in total debt to Jacobs and Roxborough, but the committee made no concessions for Joe to reconcile his IRS bill. When the committee agreed to compensate the fighters, Grantland Rice wanted to call off the contest. Opposing the committee's position, he resigned as chairman, replaced by *New York Times* columnist John Kieran.[28]

Louis and Conn appeared at the New York State Athletic Commission office on September 22 to sign contracts for a fifteen-round match at Yankee Stadium. During the signing, Jacobs, standing between Louis and Conn, raised his arms to the heavens, smiling as if divine intervention had brought them together. In *YANK*, the army newspaper, editor Joe McCarthy praised Jacobs for his patriotism. "This is a great service Mike is doing for the Army, a fitting and eloquent answer to those who have always pictured his kind of sport financier as a grasping avaricious shell game operator more concerned with the size of the house than the improvement of the breed of athletes." After the Louis–Conn rematch, McCarthy reported, the War Department planned to hire Jacobs as a civilian promoting an overseas "sports circus" with a troupe of boxers entertaining American soldiers in Ireland, Iceland, and Australia.[29]

Jacobs had secured his future for the duration of the war—or so it seemed. A day after the contract signing, New York congressman Donald O'Toole denounced Jacobs as greedy and exploitative, accusing him of "making a mockery of this war" by pressuring the War Department into letting Louis and Conn fight for his own financial benefit. From the House floor, the Democratic representative from Brooklyn urged Congress to launch an investigation to determine whether Louis and Conn had received favorable treatment from the War Department. Calling for an end to all War Department sporting events, O'Toole exclaimed, "The United States Army is being used for the first time to guarantee obligations that are owed to a fight promoter!"[30]

The following day, fearing a congressional investigation would embarrass the Roosevelt administration, Secretary of War Stimson told reporters that he was shocked to learn about the financial arrangements of the army charity bout. Expressing outrage, he promised to personally investigate the matter, insisting that he had only learned about the contractual details earlier that morning. Defending himself against O'Toole's charges, Jacobs insisted that he welcomed an investigation from Stimson and denied that he had demanded Louis and Conn repay him from the Army Relief fight purses. "Louis mentioned the debt he owed me and asked to be allowed to pay it off," Jacobs said. Then, switching to passive voice, he added, "permission was granted, and that's all I know."[31]

It's hard to believe that Mike Jacobs, a lifelong hustler who made sure he benefited from every contractual advantage possible, suddenly embraced casual business practices. According to Truman Gibson, Jacobs demanded complete control of the first twenty rows of seats. Monopolizing the fight racket, working as a promoter and a ticket broker on the side, Jacobs made a fortune setting prices for every major New York bout and then selling choice seats at inflated prices. In the case of the Louis–Conn rematch, he anticipated a sellout crowd at Yankee Stadium, and he scaled ticket prices accordingly. By late September, he had already sold more than $300,000 worth of tickets. He now predicted that the match would generate at least $500,000 for the Army Relief Fund, but Henry Stimson did not care. Once he learned that Jacobs and the fighters stood to benefit from the scheme, Stimson recoiled with sanctimonious righteousness. Three days after his seventy-fifth birthday, the secretary wrote in his diary, "This is the most ill-smelling and flamboyant result of the attempt to promote collections for the A.E.R. by ballyhoo and artificial stimulus."[32]

"The Louis Conn Fight Scandal," as Stimson called it, proved a great annoyance to the secretary at a time when some Americans had begun questioning the leadership of President Roosevelt and his cabinet. After building the US armed forces, despite a few successes in the Pacific, especially the Battle of Midway, Americans were restless with the seeming stalemate in the European theater. Looking ahead to the November midterms, Roosevelt and the Democrats believed that a winning election season required taking the fight directly to the Germans. Throughout the summer, a vigorous strategic debate between President Roosevelt and Prime Minister Churchill took shape. Roosevelt, Stimson, and General George C. Marshall, the army chief of staff, favored Operation Roundup, an ambitious cross-channel invasion of northern France. Churchill and the British chiefs of staff, however, were skeptical that inexperienced American troops were prepared for a complicated cross-channel landing. Instead, Churchill urged Operation Torch, an Allied attack of French North Africa, arguing that it would draw Axis forces away from Soviet attacks on the Eastern Front and allow the Allies to gain control of the

Mediterranean. Stimson adamantly opposed Torch, favoring a direct invasion of Europe from Great Britain. Recognizing that a cross-channel invasion was logistically unrealistic that fall, Roosevelt ordered a safer invasion of Morocco and Algeria, America's first land operation against Germany—an invasion that would not begin until November 8, five days after the Democrats suffered heavy election losses in the House and Senate.[33]

Writing in his diary in late September, while the Allies planned Operation Torch, Stimson criticized Churchill's strategy and complained about the "dirty" arrangements for the Louis–Conn fight. A wealthy patrician, Stimson was an establishment insider who ignored the sports pages and showed no interest in boxing. The secretary of war, noted columnist Hugh Fullerton, "probably wouldn't know what to do with a pair of padded mittens." Educated at Andover, Yale, and Harvard Law, Stimson espoused the values of the noblesse oblige, praised by his admirers for "his elevated standards of integrity and decency . . . in everything he says or does." Like most white Anglo-Saxon Protestants of his time, however, he adhered to "a hierarchical view of the world's nations and peoples." Although he considered himself "an old abolitionist," he did not believe in racial equality or that Black soldiers had the ability to do anything more than serve in support units. Referring to Judge William Hastie as his "colored aide," as if he were the hired help, Stimson lamented that although the army might be able to address some "grievances of [Hastie's] race," he showed no interest in addressing segregation in the armed forces.[34]

When he reviewed the contract for the Louis–Conn rematch, Stimson blamed Hastie for pressuring Undersecretary of War Robert Patterson to approve it. Patterson admired Louis and was sympathetic to the cause of Black soldiers. After Stimson recalled Alexander Surles from California, the major general flew back to Washington overnight and met with the secretary. Surles told

Stimson "that he had made up his mind to quash the [fight] proposal early, but Judge Hastie, who [was] anxious to have turned it into an exploitation of the features of the colored troops, got hold of Judge Patterson and persuaded him that it would be all right." According to Surles, Jacobs had misled him about the debts owed by Louis and Conn. First Jacobs said that the debt amounted to $15,000, but when it came time to sign the contract, he "pulled out a claim for over $130,000." The deal smacked of corruption, Stimson thought. As a result, he called John Kieran, chairman of War Boxing, Inc., and informed him that the War Department no longer sanctioned the match.[35]

Stimson released a statement on September 25 announcing the cancellation of the Army Relief bout. He ordered Louis and Conn to return immediately to their military duties. Recognizing Joe's past charitable contributions to the armed forces, the secretary made clear that the fighters should remain blameless in the whole affair. Sparing criticism for the sportswriters' committee, he inferred that Jacobs's greed had tainted the fight and violated Stimson's personal code of honor—a code that he could not separate from the army's. "The standards of the army," he declared, "do not permit the proposed contest to be carried out."[36]

At Greenwood Lake, Louis took Stimson's order stoically. "I'm terribly sorry about it," he said. "It's too bad that all that money can't go to the widows and orphans. I'm ready to fight for nothing if it can be done." Joe did not complain or protest, but his offer to fight for free came too late. Attempting to clear his name, Jacobs made a final plea to Stimson, offering to bankroll the Army Relief fight, with all proceeds going to the charity. But the secretary refused to reconsider. Stimson wanted nothing to do with Mike Jacobs.[37]

"The only real victim of the unfortunate mess," Dan Parker lamented in the *Daily Mirror*, "is Joe Louis, as fine an American as lives." Certainly, he added, the Army Emergency Relief Fund lost a considerable contribution from the canceled bout. Unfortunately, Billy Conn missed an opportunity at redemption and his second shot at the heavyweight title. And although Jacobs forfeited thousands of dollars he spent on promotions and printing tickets, he wouldn't miss the money. Out of all the actors involved, Parker said, Louis suffered the most. The "honorable" champion's career was now tarnished because critics questioned his motives for seeking compensation in the Conn rematch. Joe was "utterly blameless," Parker maintained. "He is a victim of a situation that wasn't of his making and which he was powerless to alter." Ultimately, what began as a noble benefit "wound up in the War Department's garbage can because selfish interests were put ahead of the nation's."[38]

When the fight was officially canceled, Louis told a reporter from the Associated Press, "My fightin' days are over." Surrounded by a gaggle of reporters and autograph hounds in Omaha, Nebraska, he spoke after serving as the color-bearer for the Fort Riley drill team at Creighton University Stadium. Waiting for a car to pick him up after the Creighton–Fort Riley football game, Louis said, "I'm in the Army now, and they're taking care of my plans, but by the time this war will be over, I'll be in my 30s, and that's too old for a fighter." Then, he admitted that he had lost his desire to return to the ring. Although he was only twenty-eight years old, he had defended his title more often than the previous nine heavyweight champions combined. Besides, he said, "I'm too old for it now."[39]

When the story came across the wire, Mike Jacobs scrambled to reach him by phone. Everyone in the fight game seemed stunned by the news. Jacobs had not heard from Joe recently, and John Roxborough knew nothing about a retirement announcement either. When Jacobs spoke to Louis, the champ explained that the

AP reporter had misunderstood him. Joe did not mean that he had permanently retired or surrendered his heavyweight title. He simply meant that he would not fight again until the war ended. "I want to fight again," Louis told Jacobs. "I can use the money."[40]

The truth was that Joe needed more than money. He needed an escape. Turmoil and commotion defined his life. Everywhere he went, reporters and photographers crowded around him, demanding something from him—a pose, a smile, a quote. Joe's hectic schedule hardly gave him a moment to think about what he wanted outside of life in the army. And he missed Marva. Pregnant with their first child, she had moved near Fort Riley to be closer to Joe, but Marva could not see him as often as she liked. The lonely soldier's wife returned to Chicago to be near her family and friends, hoping Joe could join her when the baby was born.

In October, when Joe received a fifteen-day furlough, he boarded a Kansas City plane bound for Los Angeles. If Marva wanted to see him, she would have to wait. Officially, his commanding officer said, it was a private business trip. In Hollywood, a reporter noted from a set of Metro-Goldwyn-Mayer (MGM) that Joe had made it his business to keep "an eye on blues-singing Lena Horne." The curious writer suspected that there was more to the story.[41]

Chapter Eight

STORMY WEATHER

> The easiest way to inject a propaganda idea into most people's minds is to let it go through the medium of an entertainment picture when they do not realize that they are being propagandized.
>
> —Elmer Davis, director of the Office of War Information, January 27, 1943

IT WAS JUST A FEW LINES IN J. CULLEN FENTRESS'S SPORTS COLumn "Down in Front" in *The California Eagle*. "[Sergeant] Joe Louis was met at his plane last week by actress-singer Lena Horne [and] visited her a day or so later on the 'Cabin in the Sky' set at MGM." Nothing scandalous. No mention of the ongoing problems in Lena's marriage or that Joe's wife was five months pregnant. America's most famous athlete was visiting Los Angeles, so it was perfectly natural for a notice of his activities to get a mention in the local news. For folks who scrutinized the private lives of celebrities, however, the notice was enough to fuel speculation.[1]

Joe Louis surely didn't think he was doing anything out of the ordinary. After several months of basic training in the heat of Fort Riley and army goodwill appearances at other posts, Joe was ready to kick the prairie dust off his boots and treat himself to some rest and relaxation in LA. The city bustled during wartime, as thousands of Americans arrived weekly to take well-paying jobs in the expanding defense industries and military installations. Still, Hollywood remained the world capital of cinema. Working day and night, the players and pawns in the industry churned out more than 350 motion pictures each year, tallying over eighty million admissions a week. That amounted to two out of every three Americans visiting a movie house weekly. The great studio factories in Hollywood had become so streamlined and efficient that they might as well have been assembly lines spitting out sausage links. Even so, in ornate movie palaces and barebone country theaters around the nation, they were delivering "the stuff dreams are made of."[2]

There was nowhere else Lena Horne would rather be. Long before Lena became a movie star, she'd dreamed about being famous. Even as a young Black girl who had only ever seen white starlets on celluloid, she knew, deep down, that there were no Black Cinderellas in Hollywood. In early 1942, after Horne signed her long-term contract with MGM, the first of its kind for a Black actress, she answered a questionnaire for the studio's publicity office that revealed her distrust of an entertainment industry that had either erased Black people from the big screen or reduced them to stereotypical roles as buffoons, servants, and cowardly characters. "Never hope too hard," she wrote. "Never pans out."[3]

Joe Louis could relate. When sportswriter Barney Nagler asked him if he ever imagined being rich and famous while growing up in Jim Crow Alabama, he replied, "I couldn't dream that big . . . It seems like people expect you to dream that way, but I'm not cut out like that." If you were a Black man when Joe was young, you didn't dream of winning the heavyweight title, earning millions of dollars, and becoming a symbol of American democracy. If you were a Black woman maturing in a broken family, shifted from relative to relative, you didn't dream of signing a Hollywood contract, becoming a leading lady, and seeing your name on the Palace marquee. Joe and Lena might just as well have dreamed of becoming president of the United States of America.[4]

Instead of dreams, Joe and Lena had the present—those moments alone, those days in Hollywood. And they made the most of their hours together in the make-believe capital of the world. He became a regular visitor on the set of *Cabin in the Sky*, a musical comedy with an all-Black cast that had finally started production after several delays, and the champion was impossible to overlook. Between takes, studio officials, tourists, and movie stars of both races surrounded him, peppering him with questions and requests for autographs and photographs. Joe patiently answered, signed, and posed, but his real interest was Lena.[5]

WHEN LENA HORNE MOVED TO LOS ANGELES WITH HER DAUGHter Gail and cousin Edwina, she was too realistic to hope she would be discovered by some casting director. She planned to continue her cabaret singing career. In the fall of 1941, she boarded the Twentieth Century Limited at New York's Grand Central Station and transferred to the Super Chief in Chicago. As the train pulled into Los Angeles's Union Station, she was singing a full-throated "California, Here I Come" with her daughter. For Gail, the trip was a glorious adventure. She loved sleeper cars, the chill of starched linen sheets, and especially the hours spent with her mother. Just as comforting were the Pullman porters in their "snowy white jackets."[6]

The odds against Lena becoming a romantic leading lady were impossibly long. She had seen enough movies to understand that Black actors were doomed to play crude stereotypes. One of the era's most progressive screenwriters, Dalton Trumbo, summed up the situation at a 1943 conference, arguing that Hollywood made "tarts of the Negro's daughter, crap shooters of his sons, obsequious Uncle Toms of his fathers, superstitious and grotesque crones of his mothers, strutting peacocks of his successful men, palm-singing mountebanks of his priests, and Barnum and Bailey side-shows of his religion." If Hollywood's white audience conjured any image of Black performers at all, it was likely Bill "Bojangles" Robinson dancing a soft-shoe with Shirley Temple, Stepin Fetchit taking orders from Will Rogers, or Hattie McDaniel as Mammy speaking her mind to Vivien Leigh's Scarlett O'Hara. Hollywood filmmakers presented Black people as gifted at singing and dancing but not fit for much more. White Americans largely accepted the gross misconceptions that the merchants of white popular culture peddled.[7]

Lena immediately disliked Los Angeles. She had never learned to drive and missed New York and her friends who lived there. But once she got on stage at a new cabaret dubbed the Little Troc, she became a headliner. It was January 1942, a little over a month after Pearl Harbor, and the cramped nightclub and small stage were perfect for Lena. Even her somber stage presence, the fact that she seldom smiled or talked between songs—her "take me as I am or go home" attitude—seemed to fit the mood of the day. Performing without a microphone, she sang "The Man I Love," "Stormy Weather," and other torch songs that touched the nerve of a nation at war. Caught, as she had been all her life, between two Americas and two cultures—Black and white, bluesy and show tune standards, bohemian and bourgeois—Lena Horne was unique, and those who watched her on stage knew it.[8]

She challenged every stereotype and threatened the long-held beliefs that white Americans entertained about Black female performers. In the words of her biographer, "she wasn't a mammy or a whore; she didn't growl the blues or speak in Negro dialect. Instead, she sounded like an educated, well-bred young lady, one whom a few white families might even welcome in their homes." In short, like Joe Louis, she had that certain undefinable "it" that Hollywood scouts recognized and craved.[9]

But Lena understood who was at the top and who was at the bottom of the film industry. White studio moguls, producers, and a few bankers controlled the industry and decided which stories became movies and which actors became stars. Then white directors with white crews of camera operators, makeup artists, clothes designers, and assorted technicians combined with a catalog of stars, character actors, and bit players to make the product that the industry sold. Black performers were all but invisible except for minor comedic roles that conformed to well-established stereotypes or parts that called for them to sing and dance. Yet Lena was poised to become the exception.

Although she would later plead that she wasn't interested in working in the industry, didn't like Hollywood, and found nothing comfortable about the place, even before the start of the war, several prominent Black and white men had singled her out as a potential groundbreaker. And of these men, NAACP Secretary Walter White was the most dogged.

Wendell Willkie, the Republican candidate in the 1940 presidential election, introduced White to the Hollywood power brokers. Although White had refused to support the Hoosier lawyer, after the election they enjoyed a dinner together. Quickly they became warm friends, sharing a common interest in improving race relations and the motion picture industry. Willkie's influence in Hollywood was significant. As chief counsel for the industry, in 1941, he had outmaneuvered and outargued attempts by a Senate subcommittee led by isolationist Gerald P. Nye to muzzle Hollywood producers. Nye, the Republican senator from North Dakota, alleged that movies had become increasingly propagandist and interventionist, driving Americans toward war with Germany.

Willkie responded that in the case of Hitler's Germany, the industry trafficked in irrefutable truths. If anything, Hollywood films underplayed the brutal crimes of the Nazi regime. At a moment when Germany was marauding through the Soviet Union, Willkie carried the day, keeping the isolationist politicians out of Hollywood's business.[10]

White's interests in Hollywood involved propaganda of a different sort. He explained to Willkie that "the most widely circulated medium yet devised to reach the minds and emotions of people all over America and the world was perpetuating and spreading dangerous and harmful stereotypes of the Negro." With remarkable alacrity Willkie made the calls, arranging for White to meet with many of the leaders of the industry, including liberals Walter Wanger and Darryl Zanuck of Twentieth Century-Fox.[11]

Initially, however, White's foray into the boardroom and backroom politics of the Hollywood studio system were remarkably modest. He asked only that every Black performer in a movie, from a face in a crowd scene to a highly paid star, be pictured as a "normal human being instead of as a monstrosity." It seemed a simple enough request. Yet in repeated visits to Los Angeles in 1942 and 1943, White was rebuffed by leading liberal producers, directors, and actors, heads of studios and union bosses alike. The motion picture industry was a business, they protested, no different than any other major industry, and a business could not afford to alienate its customers. Simply put: Millions of white Southerners bought movie tickets each week. They supported grand movie palaces in Memphis, Atlanta, and New Orleans, as well as modest theaters in thousands of midsized towns and tiny backwater hamlets. And throughout the South, state and local censors insisted that they would not approve any film that treated Black Americans "as normal human beings." Hollywood studio chiefs imbued the censors with far-reaching, almost magical power and catered to their Lost

Cause views of race relations. The guardians of Dixie sensibilities tolerated stock minstrel characters, ranging from bossy mammies to toadying Toms, but humanized and "integral" Black Americans seldom appeared in the Hollywood films they sanctioned.[12]

White wasn't about to give up on his vision of a new Hollywood. He hoped to see a Black star on the silver screen with the cultural power of Joe Louis—and Lena Horne, he thought, was the model candidate for the role. An admirer and friend of Lena's grandmother—who had once been a political force in New York's African American community—the NAACP leader had known Lena for years. He had heard her praised by Paul Robeson and other race leaders, and he had seen her mesmerizing performances. With regal composure, physical beauty, and a sultry voice, she seemed ideal for the role of Black trailblazer. And when she was still singing at the Café Society, he advised her to move to California. Furthermore, White could hardly have been unaware that Lena was as light-skinned as he was, lending her an added familiarity to white audiences. His only fear was that while she waited for the perfect role, producers would cast her in imperfect ones. He had no desire to see her talents wasted onscreen playing a maid or an exotic African queen.[13]

Other men inside the motion picture industry also had their eyes on Lena. Roger Edens, an astute musician and song arranger who worked for Arthur Freed's musical production unit at MGM, had heard Lena sing at Café Society and the Little Troc. Impressed by her stage presence and voice, Edens encouraged Freed to see her perform. It was a wise decision because Freed had an almost unerring eye and ear for musical talent.[14]

In January 1942, while fears of a Japanese attack against California ran high, Lena visited MGM to sing for Freed. One song and Freed was sold. Next, he wanted her to sing another—this time for Louis B. Mayer, the head of the studio.

THE FIGHT OF HIS LIFE

During the 1930s, Mayer occupied a position in Hollywood akin to the pope in Rome—that is, if the pope were Jewish. No mogul professed a greater love for his adopted country than did Mayer. At some point in his fabulous career, he either forgot his birth date, or decided to invent one more fitting his imagined status. He chose the Fourth of July, suited perfectly to overly elaborate celebrations of America's birthday and his own. During the reign of King Louis I, MGM became the Dom Pérignon of studios. Everything and everyone were the best—the women more beautiful, the men more manly, the films more entertaining. Their salaries were the highest, budgets the top in the industry, and workers the most skilled. Mayer did not give the people what they wanted; he gave them something better. Perhaps Ann Rutherford, a top supporting actress, said it best: "From the time you were signed by MGM you just felt you were in God's hands."[15]

The short, heavyset boss knew talent when he saw it, and while Lena sang, Mayer beamed. What Lena did not know then, but soon learned, was that MGM had recently bought the rights to *Cabin in the Sky*, an all-Black musical with a leading part perfect for her. It was not yet near the production stage, but that posed no problem. Part of the studio's success was its willingness to allow properties to marinate. This was particularly true in Freed's musical unit. Mayer's hesitation—and it was slight—was what to do with Lena until *Cabin in the Sky* went into production. But like Scarlett O'Hara said in MGM's blockbuster *Gone with the Wind*, that was a problem he would "think about tomorrow."[16]

Distrustful of studio executives, Lena discussed her worries with Walter White and her father, Teddy. Both men raised concerns about her image. At the time, she was known to a relatively small group of people in New York and Los Angeles as a singer. MGM's publicity department could change that based on the role the executives assigned to her. The first few roles Lena received were critical. White emphasized that she should not accept any demeaning parts. Teddy expressed similar concerns, coated with a father's love and desire to protect his daughter.[17]

The studio planned to make her a star, and not in the tradition of Hattie McDaniel or Butterfly McQueen. When the negotiations concluded, Lena signed a landmark long-term contract. The seven-year deal included yearly salary raises, as well as more individualized clauses that addressed her lucrative nightclub career and a 122-pound cap on her weight. At a time when most Black actors received only picture-to-picture deals, the phrase "long-term contract" put Lena in a class by herself.[18]

Horne's signing appeared to open a sliver of a crack in the Hollywood racial status quo. Mayer himself seemed to signal as much soon after Lena arrived at his enormous "family studio" in Culver City. It was a high-quality, one-stop-shopping campus that had everything. From its property and costume departments to its swimming pool and offices, it was the tops. Especially its commissary. But when Lena and the all-Black cast of *Cabin in the Sky* began work on the film, they were refused service. Outraged and undoubtedly embarrassed, Mayer invited them to lunch in his private dining room. The next day he sent a memo to all department heads: "All colored performers and other employees of MGM will, in the future, have the same access as white performers and employees to all the facilities of this studio."[19]

Like Joe Louis, Lena Horne carried the hopes and dreams of Black America. She knew she had to be more than a brilliant actress or a great singer. As a test case, she would have to navigate the color line and prove that she was "The One," the first crossover screen star who could appeal to white audiences without reminding them that she was *too* Black. Walter White stressed that she could not lose herself in the glamour of Tinseltown. "Remember your position," he urged. How could she ever forget? "If it is within my power," she told a reporter at *The Chicago Defender*, "there'll be many more Negro girls getting similar breaks in the movies."[20]

JOE AND LENA WERE IN MOST RESPECTS A MATCHING PAIR SHARing similar experiences and following similar paths. Although Joe was beginning to decline as a boxer and Lena was still ascending as a singer, both were entertainers near the heights of their powers. Between boxing and army training camps, personal appearances, and travels with friends, Joe had spent little time with Marva, contributing significantly to the recent rupture in their marriage. Lena's marriage to Louis Jones was even rockier. They lived apart, he in Pittsburgh and she mostly in New York and Los Angeles, and when they were together, her steely independence and his "dyed-in-the-wool male chauvinism" guaranteed fireworks. Jones could be "almost medieval," demanding subservience from his wife, but Lena refused to abide abuse from any man.[21]

When reporters asked Horne about her love life, assuming she had permanently split from her husband, Lena insisted that she did not have "time to think of new romance or even of activities outside the studio or stage." MGM's "glamour girl" received fifteen hundred to two thousand letters each week, many of them from GIs requesting autographed pinup pictures or dinner dates when the war ended. But in the fall of 1942, she had her eye on only one soldier: Sergeant Joe Louis.[22]

Away from the MGM set, the two spent hours together, talking and enjoying each other's company. Even in the spotlight that had become her life, Lena was lonely, unsure of whom she could trust and who were her real friends. She confided in Joe. He was a "kind, gentle man," she thought. Looking back on their time together, she said in 1980, "I would say that he was the best and closest friend that I had at the time. He was very supportive. He was the only man I was seeing at that time."[23]

In a town as celebrity conscious as Hollywood, eyes would have naturally followed either Joe or Lena. The attention they received when they were together heightened speculation and rumors. They looked so striking together, appeared so happy visiting a Los Angeles nightspot, that they had to be in love. In mid-November the press confirmed the gossip. Billy Rowe, a *Pittsburgh Courier* columnist who covered the West Coast scene and a longtime friend of Joe and Lena's, reported "radio and street corner rumors" that "they were planning a merger." It had all been decided during Joe's fifteen-day furlough.[24]

The news created headlines, but the two quickly squashed talk of impending nuptials. "People are always talking about things they know nothing about," Louis told Rowe. "I think that Lena is a grand person, on and off the screen, but that doesn't mean I want to marry her." Lena also denied any plans of becoming the next "Mrs. Joe Louis." "I'm in the dark about these rumors, and I don't mean because of the new blackout regulations that have come to this tinsel city," she said. Certainly, she admired Joe as "a symbol of greatness," but that didn't mean she was bouncing off to the altar.[25]

Meanwhile, Joe's wife, Marva, complained that in eight years of marriage, she had spent less than one year with her husband. "Just having your husband at home and being able to call him your own can mean so much. I was never able to do that with Joe," she said. Cleo Hayes had a fling with Louis in 1942 and would have liked to have said that "he was [her] fella." But she understood that the champion, though "a funny guy, a sweetheart, just as nice as he could be," belonged to no one woman. "There was no one person that could put her name on that and say,

'Oh, that's mine!'" That certainly went for the former Cotton Club chorus line dancer Cleo, the singer and actress Lena, and his wife, Marva.[26]

While Joe courted Lena with bouquets of flowers and an expensive mink coat, Marva was fuming in Chicago, carrying Joe's first child. During his fifteen-day furlough, Joe could have visited his wife. Instead, he stocked the headlines of gossip columnists, appearing with Lena. By February 8, 1943, when his daughter Jacqueline was born in Chicago at the Provident Hospital, Louis had returned to Fort Riley. For Marva, the baby "was a blessing." Jacqueline filled an emptiness in her life. "It takes a family to make a home, and even though Joe was gone a lot I could still be happy doing and caring for 'Jackie.'" Joe received a furlough to meet his baby girl, but he couldn't stay in Chicago very long. Hollywood beckoned again. The War Department needed him to deliver an important message about American unity on camera.[27]

THE WEEK AFTER HIS DAUGHTER WAS BORN, LOUIS RECEIVED orders from the War Department's Bureau of Public Relations to report to Los Angeles. There was a part in the film version of Irving Berlin's *This Is the Army* waiting for him. Berlin's gift to his adopted and beloved homeland, the production began as a musical revue, a mixture of minstrel and vaudeville song and dance numbers replete with comedians, jugglers, acrobats, and a magician. Army chief of staff General George C. Marshall gave his full and enthusiastic support to the project, and Berlin insisted that all the proceeds went to the Army Emergency Relief Fund. The songwriter had produced a similar revue during the Great War, and *Yip! Yip! Yaphank* was so successful that he used several of its songs in his new production, including "Oh, How I Hate to Get Up in the Morning," which he insisted on singing himself.[28]

Stormy Weather

Since writing the celebrated 1911 song "Alexander's Ragtime Band," Berlin had become a one-man assembly line for turning out hits—"Always," "Blue Skies," "Puttin' On the Ritz," "Easter Parade," "Cheek to Cheek," "Let's Face the Music and Dance," "God Bless America," "There's No Business Like Show Business,"—and on and on. Had he only written "White Christmas," he would be remembered as the composer of the most popular song ever. But his oeuvre includes more than fifteen hundred tunes in virtually every genre. He worked fast and obsessively, driven by fears so deep-seated that to fully understand his need for acceptance, one would have to be a Serbian Jew driven out of his Russian village by vicious pogroms and dropped in America to succeed or fail on his own wits and the fickle whim of popular tastes. As evidence of his work ethic and single-mindedness, for *This Is the Army*, he wrote twenty songs in three weeks—a song a day. Irving Berlin was not a man who missed deadlines.

The timing of *This Is the Army* could not have been better for Berlin, precisely because it was so bad for America. He wrote the songs, put together a production team, and selected performers from military and civilian ranks during America's season of discontent, the spring of 1942. He aimed to deliver a morale-building patriotic play for a nation whose morale desperately needed reconstruction. The Japanese bombing of Pearl Harbor had dealt a blow to the reputation of America's military leadership. Both the United States and its Pacific allies suffered a series of defeats. Japanese forces overran smaller American units in Guam, Wake Island, and the Philippines. During the same agonizing months, the Imperial Japanese raised the Rising Sun above the British colonies of Hong Kong, Malaya, and Singapore, as well as the Dutch East Indies.

On Saturday, July 4, 1942, *This Is the Army* opened at the Broadway Theatre in New York. It was a spectacular production, boasting a cast and crew of more than 350, including several dozen

Black soldiers, who performed "What the Well-Dressed Man in Harlem Will Wear," a lavish song and dance number. The inclusion of Black troops made Berlin's company the first integrated unit in the US Army. Although the songwriter also included white soldiers in blackface and other minstrel overtures, he could hardly white out the Black musicians or Black culture that was central to his success as a composer.[29]

A critical and commercial smash, *This Is the Army* exceeded all expectations. It was scheduled for a four-week Broadway run but was extended to a twelve-week engagement—113 full-house performances. In the process, the show raised over two million dollars for the Army Emergency Relief Fund. And there was more to come. A national tour followed, and even before that run had ended, Jack Warner, head of the solidly pro-Roosevelt Warner Brothers studio, bought the film rights for the hefty sum of $250,000. Seemingly overnight, screenwriters Claude Binyon and Casey Robinson pasted a plot onto the revue, and director Michael Curtiz—whose 1942 hit *Casablanca* was still in the theaters—began work.

The theme of the film emphasized that the Allies were fighting a "People's War," a conflict that engaged men and women, soldiers and workers. The United States was destined to lead the Allies to victory because of the inherent strength of its democracy and its pluralism. A nation of citizen soldiers on the battlefield and the home front, united and committed, would win the final victory and secure a just peace.

These lessons are dramatized in the relationship between the show's manager, Johnny Jones (Ronald Reagan), and his fiancée, Eileen Dibble (Joan Leslie). She wants a quick wartime marriage; he fears that if they wed, she might end up as a war widow. Throughout the film, bracketed between jugglers and singers, comedians and dancers, men in drag and others in blackface, she argues her case, threatens to break the engagement, and finally elevates her demand to the level of national mandate. Dragging a minister with her to the show's final performance—before President Roosevelt in Washington, DC—she demonstrates that she is as obstinate and determined as her nation at war. "You don't know what this war is about," she accuses. It concerns "a free people fighting to be free," and all Americans have a stake in the outcome. More to the point, she concludes, "this is a free United States, and if we want to get married, god darn it, we should get married." Just before baritone Robert Shanley brings down the curtain with a rousing rendition of "This Is the Last Time"—a patriotic promise that this war, unlike the last, will be contested to the bitter end—*This Is the Army* ends with a marriage and a resolution to get on with the job.[30]

Joe Louis's role in the film was straightforward. He was there to endorse the government's war aims and affirm that Black Americans understood that they had a vital role to play in the struggle between democratic and fascist nations. His most important scene begins when Jerry Jones (George Murphy), veteran of the Great War, asks Joe if he was nervous to go on stage. In a flat, awkward delivery, Louis answers, "Mr. Jones, I stopped worryin' the day I got into uniform. All I know is that I'm in Uncle Sam's Army and we are on God's side." Jones responds, "Well that's a fine way to feel. And I don't know anyone who could say it better than you, Sergeant." "And we're right behind you, Joe," another Black soldier adds, pledging that all Black citizens in the army share the boxer's patriotism.

Louis's speaking scene is followed by an elaborate song and dance performance of "What the Well-Dressed Man in Harlem Will Wear." It was a song that Irving Berlin had labored over, insisting that he wanted something "with a real Harlem beat," a wartime answer to "Puttin' On the Ritz." Finally, he hit upon the answer. "What the Well-Dressed Man in Harlem Will Wear" has almost the same tempo as "Puttin' On the Ritz," but an entirely different melody. It suggests that "sun tan, shade of green / Or an olive drab color scheme" had replaced "top hat, white tie and tails." If there was any doubt about it, just "take a look at Brown Bomber Joe."[31]

Punching the speed bag to the beat of the song, Louis, dressed in a crisp "sun tan" uniform, looked every bit the Hollywood star. The final image in the production is of him saluting the audience. All this was to the liking of the Bureau of Motion Pictures (BMP), a division of the Office of War Information (OWI), the federal government's propaganda agency. But the production also trafficked in crude stereotyping. The set design included huge paintings of Sambo-ish hipsters in zoot suits and the appearance of a tap-dancing Black man in drag. In 1942, when the BMP issued the "Government Information Manual for the Motion Picture Industry," it aimed to ensure that every film enhanced the image and reputation of the United States around the world. It also asserted that the Bureau wanted to eliminate racial stereotypes from films. A year later, the promises were largely unfulfilled. Some negative portrayals had been softened, but more often this came at the expense of eliminating Black roles entirely. Rather than writing sympathetic parts for Black actors, Hollywood producers mostly ceased employing leading Black talent. There is no mention of race in the BMP review of the script and film. Reviewer Eleanor Berneis thought it was "a magnificent presentation of the spirit of the American Fighting Forces."[32]

The set of *This Is the Army* illustrated that racism was inescapable in Hollywood. Director Michael Curtiz, a Hungarian Jew who came to Hollywood in 1926 at the invitation of the front office of Warner Brothers, was one of the premier directors of the industry's golden age. He was thirty-nine years old when he arrived on American soil. He may have learned English imperfectly, but he mastered it well enough to express the prejudices of the day. George Murphy, one of the film's two leading men, recalled Curtiz positioning singers and dancers. "Bring on the white soldiers!" he bellowed. Once they were on the stage, he shouted, "Bring on the nigger troops!" Murphy stopped the action. He explained to Curtiz the indignity of the word, suggesting using "colored" instead. Insisting he meant no offense, Curtiz tried again. "Bring on the white soldiers!" Then, after they were in place, "Bring on the colored niggers."[33]

Louis did not thrive on the set. Frederick C. Othman, a reporter who visited him on a Warner Brothers sound stage, found the champion "badly frightened." "This is the first time I've ever been scared in my life," he muttered. He only had a few lines but pounding a speed bag to the beat of "What the Well-Dressed Man in Harlem Will Wear" proved challenging. It took days of practice, rehearsals, takes, and retakes. Exasperated, at one point he hit the bag like it was Max Schmeling's head. The leather bag exploded. "Kind of scared me," remarked dance director LeRoy Prinz. "It's funny what the camera does to him," Prinz added. "Off with his friends he is a bright and witty man. He can laugh and smile and crack jokes. Then we get him on the stage. And look at him. Trembling like a leaf."[34]

Louis's problems delivering a few lines or pounding a speed bag to the beat of tap-dancing soldiers passed unnoticed by movie reviewers. Released in August 1943, *This Is the Army* won critical acclaim. "It's democracy in action to the hilt," wrote an enthusiastic *Variety* reviewer. "It's showmanship and patriotism combined to a super-duper Yankee Doodle degree." More importantly, it was the box office sensation of the year, surpassing such other hits as *For Whom the Bell Tolls*, *The Song of Bernadette*, and *Casablanca* by millions of dollars. Its income from domestic rentals exceeded every film since *Gone with the Wind* (1939) and led all movies made during World War II. Like the play, all proceeds went to the Army Emergency Relief Fund—more than eight and a half million dollars.[35]

Several reviewers singled out Joe Louis and the Black performers in "What the Well-Dressed Man in Harlem Will Wear." In *The Commonweal*, Philip T. Hartung gushed that Joe and company "almost steal the show." On talent alone that may have been the case. Nevertheless, critics in the Black press charged that Hollywood's treatment of Black performers had not significantly changed since the days of *Birth of a Nation*. At the Southern premiere of the film in Atlanta, Black columnist William A. Fowlkes lamented that the motion picture industry "merely continued its policy of 'grin and jive' for Negro actors, even while directing them in a military show." Walter White's optimism aside, the promises of the Office of War Information and Hollywood moguls languished unfulfilled. The problems that Truman Gibson recognized in the War Department and that White spotted in the film industry appeared immutable.[36]

Lena Horne's career threw a spotlight on the predicament. Booked into small venues, aided by some of the finest arrangers in the business, her nightclub act thrived. In mid-July, while Joe was finishing his work on *This Is the Army* and Lena was waiting to begin filming *Cabin in the Sky*, she sang at the Mocambo. Located in West Hollywood on the Sunset Strip, the place oozed exoticism. Glass cages adorned the walls, housing parrots, cockatoos, macaws, and other birds. Although it had only opened at the beginning of 1941, it had already become popular with Hollywood stars. On any given night, Humphrey Bogart, Lauren Bacall, Lana Turner, Marlene Dietrich, or some other movie star would be seated at one of the premier tables.

Ted Le Berthon, a Los Angeles *Daily News* reporter, described the atmosphere when Lena performed. "Cops have had to shove back crowds made up of screen stars—on one night a friend of mine counted 62 big names in a mob of several hundred niftily habilimented people—who had tried futilely to get into the Mocambo to see and hear Lena Horne." For readers unfamiliar with the singer, the journalist described her as an "exquisite olive skinned" Black woman "whom anyone might mistake for an aristocratic and exciting Latin American senorita, with inkily dark eyes." Le Berthon swooned over her talent, the way she commanded the audience with a smile and a gesture, claiming that she was "the greatest artist in her field in our time in history." If she were white, he mused, "she'd go beyond Bette Davis, Colbert, Shearer, Garbo, Crawford, and all the rest. She has a bigger presence."[37]

Perhaps to conceal her race, in 1942, studio chiefs stuck her in as a café singer in *Panama Hattie*, where many viewers—as well as reviewers—assumed she was a Latin American actress. "What a beautiful woman. She can't be black," commented a man in a Hollywood theater. But Lena was already well known among Black audiences. The father of historian Delilah Jackson saw the film in the Harlem Opera House. Everyone was enchanted with Lena. As Jackson recalled her father's story, "It was like, Lena's our sister. Our daughter. She's *us*."[38]

IN 1943 HORNE STARRED IN TWO MAJOR FILMS, MGM's *CABIN IN the Sky* and, as a loan-out, in Twentieth Century-Fox's *Stormy Weather*. Both were musicals. The first, produced by Arthur Freed and directed by Vincente Minnelli, has an elaborate and fanciful Faustian plot. The second film had virtually no plot. More of a singing and dancing revue, it delivered a string of spectacular numbers by such headliners as Bill "Bojangles" Robinson, Fats Waller, Cab Calloway, Katherine Dunham, and the Nicholas Brothers.

Lena Horne performed brilliantly in both films. Her commanding presence and her stunning voice received exceptional reviews.

Talent, then, was not the problem with either *Cabin in the Sky* or *Stormy Weather*. The primary issue, Roosevelt's watchdog in Hollywood explained, was that neither movie furthered their self-proclaimed war aims. The OWI and the BMP labored to show America as a unified people, democratic and free from the racial, ethnic, and religious schisms of Nazi Germany. But the casts of both films were entirely Black. The BMP's script review of *Stormy Weather* cautioned that the production "fails to illustrate constructively the stake of the Negro in the war, or his proper place in the American way of life." Showing the world an America where white and Black countrymen exist in two separate spheres underscored the nation's failures, not its successes, and did "a disservice to the war effort." Nor were the BMP censors pleased with the final film. Again, they criticized the producers for showing a segregated America, with Black citizens scarcely aware that there was a war.[39]

The BMP harbored even deeper concerns about *Cabin in the Sky*. Not only did the exclusively Black cast smack of a segregated society, but the characters in the movie also pandered to vile stereotypes. Three BMP reviewers previewed the production and judged it "a detriment to national unity at this time." Although a few of the characters in *Cabin in the Sky* were presented as "responsible citizens," the majority came across as "simple, ignorant, superstitious folk, incapable of anything but the most menial labour." Little Joe, the lead character, was especially craven: "totally irresponsible when he acquires money, he returns to his former life of gambling and dissipation upon slightest provocation." At a time when Black Americans were "contributing their full share to the war effort . . . dying side by side with other Americans on the battlefield," their depiction in the film seems to render them "unfit for the responsibilities of citizenship." Only harm, the reviewer suggested, could result from such a movie.[40]

The fate of Lena Horne's wartime Hollywood venture highlighted the modest hopes and dismal failures of the film industry. MGM signed her to a long-term contract. She had the makings of a star. But the studio executives proved too timid to cast her as the lead in an integrated film. Instead, they gave her self-contained singing roles that Southern censors could cut without doing any damage to the plot. Louis B. Mayer promised Lena that he would not remake her in the image of Hattie McDaniel, and for the most part he kept his promise. Perhaps he did something worse. "They didn't make me into a maid," she said years later about MGM producers, "but they didn't make me into anything else, either. I became a butterfly pinned to a column, singing away in Movieland."[41]

Off and on in 1943, that year of fragile hopes and unfulfilled dreams, that year when she learned how the star industry worked and her rigidly circumscribed place in it, Lena's path crossed with Joe's. She was lonely, missing her New York friends and wary of the feuding and backstabbing that pervaded Hollywood. For a brief time, Joe provided an escape and the affection that she had long desired.

Years later Cleo Hayes, a friend of Lena's from her Cotton Club days who had also moved to California, recalled the time when Louis came to Hollywood. Hayes said that at one point Lena thought she might marry Joe. The champ had other ideas. After entering one unhappy marriage, he was not about to double down. Alice Key, friend of Lena and Joe's from the war years, once asked Louis what happened between Lena and him. "She thinks she's too cute," Joe answered. Key disagreed, arguing that Lena was "one of the least affected women" she knew. "And if she does think she's cute, she has a right to; she's a movie star! She's beautiful!"

Joe answered, "There's a whole lot of movie stars, Alice, but there's only one heavyweight champion of the world!"[42]

No matter what the gossip columnists wrote, though, any thoughts that Lena and Joe would each get divorced and marry each other were fanciful. Struggling to balance nightclub engagements and a film career with the demands of USO appearances and raising her daughter, she had no time for a lasting commitment to Joe. And the champion, who was about to embark on an equally hectic travel schedule with the US Army, had never enjoyed monogamy anyway. It was, after all, 1943, midpoint of World War II, a better time for flings than marriages.[43]

In *Panama Hattie*, Lena sings a Cole Porter song that might have been written about her affair with Joe, a fling simply too hot not to cool. The tune was "Just One of Those Things." Set in a smoky saloon, oozing a wartime mise-en-scène, Lena sings about a torrid love affair, doomed from the start but not regretted in the least. Like many fleeting romances during the war, it ended in a friendship that contained no hard feelings. In the end, it was "great fun," a fine time, but "just one of those things." Like in the song, Lena and Joe were too much alike—passionate, impulsive, and independent—for anything beyond a transitory affair.

Chapter Nine

THE AMERICAN GESTAPO

> The domestic scene, as you listen to the radio and read the papers today, is anything but encouraging, and one would like not to think about it, because it gives one a feeling that, as a whole, we are not really prepared for democracy.
>
> —First Lady Eleanor Roosevelt, June 22, 1943

On a sweltering Sunday night in June 1943, Hitlerism came to Joe Louis's hometown. A packed crowd leaving Belle Isle Park trekked across a congested bridge above the Detroit River, heading downtown. Seeking relief from the heat, a crush of civilians and sailors, squeezing shoulder to shoulder, gathered at the city's amusement center, an oasis of forests, beaches, and gardens. While a stream of cars crept along the bridge, Black and white pedestrians bustled on sidewalks, eyeing each other with trepidation after a day of racial skirmishes. Nobody really knows who threw the first punch, but around 10:30 p.m., fifty police officers were called to the bridge because, according to the *Detroit Free Press*, "several youths had been stabbed in a fight between Negroes and whites." More than two hundred white sailors from the Brodhead Naval Armory joined the fracas, attacking Black men and

THE FIGHT OF HIS LIFE

their families. In a matter of minutes, a knot of Black and white bodies became entangled in a bloody brawl.[1]

Rumors spread across the city, sparking waves of violence. At the Forest Club, a popular cabaret on Hastings Street in the heart of Paradise Valley, a Black neighborhood where Joe Louis once lived, a young Black man named Leo Tipton rushed the stage and grabbed a microphone to make an urgent announcement. He claimed that a melee had erupted at Belle Isle and a mob of white sailors had killed a Black woman and her baby and dumped their bodies into the river. The story was false, but the crowd was outraged, and a group of Black men surged toward the bridge. Seeking vengeance, they looted stores owned by white proprietors and hurled stones at cars with white drivers. Later that night, after an unfounded but horrific tale circulated that a gang of Black men had raped a white woman on the bridge, an armed white mob clustered outside the Roxy Theater on Woodward Avenue, Detroit's busiest thoroughfare. When Black patrons spilled out of the theater, completely unaware of the raging riot, white marauders pummeled them with baseball bats and metal pipes.[2]

The *Detroit Free Press* reported "an endless series of attacks by white rioters upon Negroes who had wandered unknowingly into the danger zone." Throughout downtown, swarms of white troublemakers dragged Black passengers off streetcars and buses, stomping, "stabbing, and shooting Negroes." Several cars owned by Black motorists were overturned and set ablaze. Whether they were outnumbered or merely indifferent, the city's overwhelmingly white police force did little to disperse white mobs, which only emboldened them further. Some cops hid in their squad cars, while others unleashed nightsticks and revolvers upon unarmed Black bystanders and looters—making no distinction between them. Writing about "The Gestapo in Detroit," NAACP attorney

Thurgood Marshall noted that the police killed seventeen Black citizens, but did not kill a single white person.³

On June 21, "Bloody Monday," air raid whistles screeched, alerting terrified citizens to stay home. The alarm signaled that Detroit was "at war with itself." Mayor Edward J. Jeffries ordered city schools and businesses closed while wartime factories remained locked down. That evening, as hospital emergency rooms filled with hundreds of wounded casualties, Michigan's governor, Harry Kelly, declared martial law and called President Roosevelt, pleading for federal forces. At midnight, FDR signed a proclamation mobilizing more than 3,500 armored troops. By Tuesday morning, after three days of urban warfare and eighteen hundred arrests, US troops had emptied the streets. In the worst race riot since the Tulsa massacre of 1921, thirty-four people died, twenty-five of them Black citizens.⁴

The roots of the riot stemmed from escalating racial friction sparked by the war. A city of defense factories, the "arsenal of democracy" had attracted more than fifty thousand Southern Black migrants and hundreds of thousands of Southern white job seekers. The growing demands for labor and housing mixed with deep-seated racial resentments provoked countless fights over jobs, neighborhoods, and schools. Three weeks before the riot, twenty-five thousand white workers at the Packard plant, some of them members of the Ku Klux Klan, walked out during a "hate strike," refusing to assemble bomber engines alongside Black men. In its aftermath, a reporter from the *Detroit Free Press* wrote, "It did not take a prophet to know the riot was coming."⁵

A week after the riots began, the War Department ordered Joe Louis to his hometown in the hopes that he could quiet the tensions in the city. While he was there, Joe checked on his mother, Lillie. In 1934, he'd purchased a ten-room house for her and his stepfather at 2100 McDougall Street, about two miles away from Belle

Isle bridge. During his visit, federal troops were still patrolling the city in army jeeps loaded with machine guns and tear gas canisters. On Hastings Street, where thousands of Black fans had once celebrated his victories, the homes and stores looked "as if they had been bombed from the air with block busters." Although Louis had fans of all races, some white Detroiters despised him and what his victories represented. On the night of his fights, noted a local reporter, "a white man was not safe in Paradise Valley." Since Louis defeated Primo Carnera in 1935, police in several cities, including Detroit, reported violent clashes between Black men and white men whenever he fought—and beat—a white opponent. While the Office of War Information produced propaganda promoting Louis as a force for racial unity in America's military camps, there was nothing he could say or do to extinguish the smoldering rage among Detroiters.[6]

When a Black reporter from the *Detroit Tribune* interviewed Joe, the champ refused to talk about the riots. Nor would he discuss the discrimination he witnessed at Fort Riley. The War Department censors wouldn't allow it, especially since the government had propped him up as a symbol of democracy at a time when there were increasing reports about "unchecked, unpunished, and often unrebuked shooting, maiming, and insulting of Negro troops, especially in the Southern states." Still, he had strong feelings about the gross mistreatment of Black troops and the growing discontent in Black America. Knowing that army authorities would never let him speak about those issues publicly, he told the reporter that he wanted to tour America's military camps with a troupe of boxers, hoping to boost the morale of his fellow Black soldiers. But War Department officials worried about sending him into the South, "where he would be put through the paces by the crackers," noted the writer. If the government sent him to Dixie on such a mission, the reporter warned prophetically, the heavyweight champion "could not escape the indignities that are heaped on Negroes."[7]

THREE WEEKS BEFORE THE DETROIT RIOTS ERUPTED, SHORTLY after Joe Louis finished filming *This Is the Army*, Mary McLeod Bethune speculated about the heavyweight champion's future. As vice president of the NAACP, she was one of a few women working in President Roosevelt's "Black Cabinet," an informal group of advisers serving in the Federal Council on Colored Affairs. Since 1936, when Roosevelt appointed her Director of Negro Affairs in the National Youth Administration, Bethune had become a close friend of the First Lady and had gained unprecedented access to the White House. Despite her frustration with a president who showed no interest in addressing the nation's racial dilemma, Bethune remained a tireless advocate for civil rights. She firmly believed that Black America was fighting for democracy at home and abroad. And she viewed Joe Louis as a central figure in that struggle.

Writing General Frederick Osborn, Bethune proposed an ambitious plan involving Louis and a troupe of Black boxers and entertainers, who would tour American military camps in the United States and overseas. The proposal was built around Louis and his friend "Sugar" Ray Robinson, a young welterweight boxing prodigy, and a theatrical company of famous Black actors and singers, including Paul Robeson and Lena Horne. "This unit could go to every place in the world, no matter what the dangers may be," she wrote, "and put on a show for our fighting men. Can you picture the reaction a soldier would have to see Joe Louis and other great fighters fly across thousands of miles of enemy infested lands and waters, just to put on a show for them? Just picture the feeling it would give a man to see Joe Louis in action anywhere or under any conditions."[8]

Osborn agreed that a publicity tour featuring Louis would advance the Roosevelt administration's propaganda aims. In August, the War Department announced that the Brown Bomber would embark on a grand excursion across the United States and overseas. Although Robeson and Horne did not join the tour, Ray Robinson, Joe's old sparring partner George Nicholson, and George "California Jackie" Wilson, a highly ranked welterweight who had won a silver medal at the 1936 Berlin Olympics, would travel with the heavyweight champion. It was an unprecedented arrangement. Never had the War Department treated a group of Black soldiers as representatives of America's Army. At a time when white celebrities such as Jimmy Stewart and Clark Gable served in the military, "there were no Negro Hollywood stars for the War Department to woo," noted Robinson's biographer Wil Haygood. "No figure from the Negro community in Tinseltown whose weekly movements were followed and marveled at by the larger public, giving them an aura of celebrity and creating a public relations boon. Having no one in Hollywood to turn to, the War Department reached into the 'Negro world of sports.' And that meant Joe Louis and Sugar Ray Robinson."[9]

By the time the War Department began planning the tour, Robinson had an established reputation as a boxing phenom, a future champion who drew comparisons to his hero, Joe Louis. Born Walker Smith Jr., he grew up in Detroit's Black Bottom district, not far from where young Joseph Barrow lived. Looking back on his childhood, Robinson liked to tell stories about how he followed Joe around the neighborhood, carrying his gym bag to the Brewster Recreation Center. "Whenever Joe was in the gym," he said, "so was I. He was my idol and still is." Robinson's mother, Leila Smith, could not help but dispel that "convenient bit of fiction." Perhaps young Walker Smith had crossed paths with Joe Barrow, an unaccomplished seventeen-year-old novice who was just beginning to learn how to hit the heavy bag. But in 1932, a few years after Walker's parents had separated, Leila moved to Harlem with her three children.[10]

Crafting his life story, Ray Robinson embellished certain myths and excluded uncomfortable truths. In his memoir, the famous boxer revealed that his parents fought frequently, especially when his father came home drunk. When Leila scolded her husband for blowing his paycheck at local speakeasies, "Pop" would "have his say because mom liked to drink, too." But what Robinson did not disclose in his book was that his father's eruptions quickly turned violent. Sometimes his father hit him. On more than one occasion, Junior witnessed his dad brutally attack his mom. In a fit of rage, Walker Sr. stabbed Leila in the breast, a traumatizing event seared in the boy's memory. It's not surprising that Junior grew up an anxious child, compulsively biting his nails and wetting his pants at school—an embarrassment that troubled him until he was about seven years old. Even though he grew up without his father, several pictures of Walker Sr. could be seen in his childhood home. Pop remained a shadow in his life even when they were not together.[11]

If his father's name once defined him, his mother, a tough and resilient woman, taught him how to survive hardships in Harlem. She urged him to defend himself against neighborhood bullies. When he wasn't shining shoes or selling newspapers, Junior fought "street urchins for pennies from corner idlers." He learned the sweet science in the basement of Salem Methodist Episcopal Church where ministers had established a boxing club. One night in 1936 in Kingston, New York, on the Amateur Athletic Union circuit, the event organizer wanted to match two flyweights. Smith pleaded with his trainer to let him fight, but George Gainford did not have an AAU registration card proving Walker's amateur status. Gainford thought for a moment before handing him a card with the name of one of his old fighters: Ray Robinson. The name stuck. He quit school and began fighting under his new alias.[12]

In 1939, he traveled with Gainford and the Salem boxing team for a tournament in Waterford, New York. At Starbuck Arena, a local sportswriter named Jack Case watched Robinson hammer Dom Perfetti. After the fight, Case greeted Robinson and Gainford. "That's a sweet fighter you've got there, a real sweet fighter," Case said to the trainer. A woman sitting near the ring overheard the conversation and added, "As sweet as sugar." Later that night, when Case typed his column, the woman's words echoed in his mind. Case called the clever fighter from Harlem "Raymond Sugar Robinson." Soon, ringside announcers began introducing him as "Sugar" Ray Robinson, a moniker made for the marquee.[13]

After winning every one of his eighty-five amateur matches and capturing Golden Gloves titles in the featherweight and lightweight divisions, in 1940, Robinson turned pro. Two years later, after knocking out twenty of twenty-five professional opponents, the "Colored Welterweight Champion of the World" appeared on the cover of *The Ring* magazine. Although he had not actually won a title yet, he was the undisputed top welterweight contender. Robinson displayed remarkable gifts inside the ropes: inexhaustible energy, dazzling hand speed, superb timing, and a powerful punch that stung "like the kick of a misanthropic mule." Before losing to Jake LaMotta at Detroit's Olympia Stadium in early February 1943, Robinson had won his first forty professional fights. Knowing, however, that he would be inducted into the army by the end of the month, he wanted to earn as much money as possible. Two weeks after losing to LaMotta, he agreed to fight Jackie Wilson at Madison Square Garden, a bout promoted by Mike Jacobs, who usually avoided matching two Black fighters in the main event. After easily beating Wilson, on February 23, Robinson was inducted into the army. Granted a furlough, four days after his induction, Robinson returned to Olympia Stadium, where he avenged his loss to LaMotta in a close decision. The following week, Walker Smith Jr. reported to Fort Dix for active duty.[14]

A few months after Robinson's induction, Joe Louis invited him to join a tour that would change their lives. In late August 1943, "the world's greatest boxing show" debuted near Boston at Fort Devens. Followed by a trail of photographers from Army Signal Corps and *Life* magazine, Louis and Robinson toured the base, shaking hands with soldiers and signing autographs on the plastered arm casts of injured GIs, many of them wounded in the North Africa campaign. During a brief press conference, Louis delivered a short speech about the importance of physical fitness, reminding the enlisted men that "a soldier's best weapons are his hands." Out of the seven thousand soldiers who packed the camp sports arena, none were more excited to see him in the ring than the men in the 366th Regiment, an all-Black unit. Seeing Louis tangle with George Nicholson for three exhibition rounds, swapping stories with the champ over dinner, and reminiscing about his greatest fights, the men in the 366th Regiment swelled with pride. But the story in *Life* magazine was how Louis made "a good impression" on "hundreds of white soldiers, officers and men," who were "proud to shake his hand." The Louis–Robinson tour, *Life* concluded, had already succeeded as "a quiet parable in racial good will"—a powerful myth that served the War Department well.[15]

After visiting several camps in the Northeast, the Louis–Robinson caravan ventured below the Mason–Dixon Line, entertaining troops at military bases named after Confederate ghosts. The American South remained haunted by the Lost Cause, a war that had never really ended. Stationed in the segregated South, Black soldiers were constantly reminded that they had to obey

Jim Crow laws and follow the region's segregationist customs. Making matters worse, the army brass typically assigned Southern white officers to lead Black units, convinced that Confederate grandsons were uniquely suited to command Black troops. In reality, though, Black soldiers resented Southern white officers, who inflicted punishment like abusive overseers. For example, forty miles west of Savannah, at Camp Stewart, one of the posts on the Louis–Robinson tour, white officers kicked and cursed "sick colored soldiers" and refused to give them medicine. In Virginia, at Camp Lee, another fort Louis and Robinson visited, white officers routinely assaulted and threatened to kill Black GIs, denigrating them daily with racial epithets. "We are treated like dogs," complained a Black enlistee. The situation was so bad at Camp Lee, he wrote, that all the Black soldiers wanted was to get "out of the Army and back to our homes."[16]

For Black troops, especially those from northern cities like Louis and Robinson, navigating the rigidly segregated South proved daunting. The lives and careers of both boxers, for instance, were shaped by Detroit, New York, and Chicago. The famous prizefighters moved freely through those cities, enjoying an eminence reserved for royalty. "Up North," noted *New York Amsterdam News* columnist Dan Burley, "these fighters are kings. They have won their way to a sort of Promised Land and rule it as is their privilege." Before entering the army, they had each fought only once below the Mason–Dixon Line (Joe in Washington, DC; Ray in Savannah, Georgia). Their managers understood that they could not schedule matches with white opponents in the South. It posed too many risks. Besides, interracial sports competitions of all kinds were barred by Southern state legislatures and municipalities. Nonetheless, given his experience fighting before racially integrated crowds, Louis expected that when he boxed on a US military base all troops could sit where they pleased.[17]

But when he reached the outdoor boxing ring at Fort Monroe, Virginia, Joe realized that Black troops had been barred from ringside seats. The first five rows were reserved for white officers and their wives; all the folding chairs from the officers' section to the bleachers were arranged for white enlisted men; and the bleachers, farthest from the ring, were designated for Black personnel. Infuriated, Louis did not want to box. He resented Black men being treated as second-class citizens in the US Army, telling his commanding officer, Captain Carroll Fitzgerald, "You can order me to fight but I won't get in that ring." According to Fitzgerald, the champ maintained "that the tour was not for any one race group." Louis was not there just to entertain white men and their wives. Under protest, he agreed to continue with the show, but Joe demanded equal accommodations for Black troops in future exhibitions. The next day, when his troupe arrived at Fort Henry, large groups of Black soldiers sat ringside. During the war Louis did not deliver speeches about racial oppression, but life in the Jim Crow Army was turning him into "a race leader" taking an important stand for his people.[18]

Confronted with similar circumstances during her USO tour of Southern camps, Lena Horne also rejected the degrading conditions imposed upon Black soldiers. In December 1944, when she visited Camp Robinson in Little Rock, Arkansas, Horne performed at the post theater before white soldiers. During her previous stops at Southern bases, she had entertained interracial audiences, but there were no Black troops present at the Camp Robinson theater. The next day, after discovering that Black soldiers were not informed of her appearance, she insisted on performing for them at the Black soldiers' mess hall. When she was singing on stage, she noticed German prisoners of war entering the hall. She later said that she had never been more outraged in her life. In her memoir, she recalled stepping offstage, turning her back on the Nazis, and singing a few more tunes for "the Negro guys in the back of the hall." But by the third or fourth song, she was too upset to continue. According to a War Department memorandum, the camp's commanding officer asked her to sing for German POWs, but she flatly refused and left in protest. She immediately wired the Hollywood USO branch and informed them that she had quit the tour.[19]

This was not the first time German POWs received preferential treatment at the expense of Black American GIs. At several Southern bases, German prisoners were allowed to sit in the same camp theaters and cafeterias as white American troops, but Black soldiers were prohibited from entering. A few months before Horne visited Camp Robinson, Corporal Rupert Trimmingham, a Black electrician serving in the Army Corps of Engineers, wrote a letter to the editor of *YANK*, explaining how he and a group of Black soldiers traveling by train through Louisiana could not find a diner that would serve them. Eventually, they found a lunchroom at a rural railroad station that offered to feed them as long as they ate in the kitchen. When about two dozen German POWs entered the depot with American guards, the Germans "sat at the tables, had their meals served, talked, smoked, in fact had quite a swell time." The scene provoked him to ask American GIs reading *YANK*, "Are these men"—Hitler's soldiers—"sworn enemies of this country? Are we not American soldiers, sworn to fight for and die if need be for this country? Then why are they treated better than we are?" He could not help but wonder, "If we are to die for our country, then why does the Government allow such things to go on?"[20]

AFTER FIVE MONTHS OF TOURING, LOUIS AND ROBINSON HAD visited more than one hundred military sites, performing for more than six hundred thousand troops. The grueling schedule took them from coast to coast. Joe wrote infrequent letters to Marva and called her on the phone, but it wasn't enough to hold together a fractured relationship. During the tour he often visited two or three camps each day. Rushing from one post to the next, his troupe struggled to catch planes, trains, and a good night's sleep.[21]

In early 1944, Joe admitted to reporters that a divorce was inevitable after the war. Initially, Marva said that she was not mad at him; she just accepted that they were not meant to be married. Separated for months, she rarely saw Joe and began imagining a life raising their daughter, Jacqueline, alone. In Chicago, she sang at the city's USO Centers and urged Americans to buy war bonds. After receiving rave reviews for her performances, Marva aspired to become a famous chanteuse. Without Joe's boxing income, though, Marva needed money to provide for her daughter and pay the family bills. She hired an agent and took voice lessons before starting a national tour. In January 1944, Joe attended one of her New York concerts, expressing support for her career, but he insisted they would not reconcile. His public comments sparked an old rumor: The champ planned to marry Lena Horne. But Marva refused to believe it.[22]

She still seemed to be competing with Lena and all the other women vying for Joe's attention. Marva just could not give up on her marriage—at least not yet. She convinced herself that if she could be a stage star like Lena, then maybe Joe would stay with her. "Why should Joe and I get a divorce?" she asked a reporter after performing on stage in Philadelphia. "He has no one he wants to marry and I have no one, and we both have Jacqueline. I've just one aim—to be good at [singing]. Maybe if I'm good Joe will think me the most glamorous woman he's ever met when he comes home from the war."[23]

Like Joe and every other GI, Ray Robinson rarely saw his wife—or the son he had during his first marriage. Army life made him lonely and miserable. He appeared depressed, constantly complaining about fatigue, dizziness, and severe headaches. He showed no interest in drills or any other military work. And things were getting worse.

In February 1944, the Louis–Robinson convoy arrived at Camp Sibert, Alabama, a massive chemical warfare center sitting on thirty-six thousand acres. The camp's primary purpose was to provide basic military training and instruction about how to use chemical weapons. By the time he reached Camp Sibert, Robinson's headaches had grown so severe that Joe removed him from boxing exhibitions, concerned that something was seriously wrong with his friend. On the rifle range Ray complained that the explosive sound of gunfire caused unbearable ringing in his head. The headaches were so bad that he could hardly sleep. During a visit at the camp clinic, Robinson explained that he had experienced terrible headaches since childhood, and they had grown worse since he began basic training at Mitchel Field in March of 1943. The headaches were so debilitating that he had to be hospitalized for a few weeks before joining Joe's boxing troupe. He feared he had become "punch-drunk," a colloquial term used in boxing for fighters suffering from brain trauma because of recurring blows to the head. Absorbing even one more punch, he thought, might kill him.[24]

Yet Captain Fred Maly, a former sportswriter turned Selective Service officer in charge of the tour, questioned his claims. Maly told the camp psychiatrist, Lieutenant Colonel Soll Goodman, that Robinson was "bucking for a discharge," desperate to return to his professional boxing career. But after examining his patient's X-rays, Goodman diagnosed Robinson with "probable intracranial pathology," noting irregular markings in the "inner table of his skull." Scheduled to embark overseas from New York in a few weeks, Robinson argued with Maly about crossing the Atlantic.

Maly insisted that he could travel with the group and entertain soldiers overseas even if he did not box. Nonetheless, Goodman recommended that Maly take Robinson to a New York hospital, where physicians could perform an electroencephalogram (EEG) for further brain study. "The doctors at Camp Sibert," Robinson said in a sworn statement, "advised me to give up boxing."[25]

While Robinson agonized about his health, alarming news swept Camp Sibert: On March 11, 1944, Raymond McMurray, a twenty-year-old Black soldier from Chicago, had been shot and killed by civilian police not far from the camp under suspicious circumstances. The headline in the *Gadsden Times* stunned readers: "Negro Rapist Killed by Gadsden Officers as He Attempts Escape After Identification." The newspaper's tale, based entirely on the officers' accounts, sounded contrived. The story began about a month earlier, when McMurray supposedly went AWOL from Camp Sibert. In the evening of February 18, police alleged, McMurray brutally attacked and raped a forty-year-old white woman, leaving her unconscious in a culvert near a Gadsden school. On the run, after allegedly stealing a car in Birmingham, on March 8, McMurray was apprehended by authorities in Chattanooga, Tennessee, and shortly thereafter brought to the Etowah County jail in Gadsden. After McMurray was transferred to the Calhoun County jail in Anniston, a local reporter described a theatrical scene that would have made D. W. Griffith blush. The Gadsden woman studied a lineup of seven Black soldiers, pointed at McMurray, and cried, "That's him! I would know him anywhere!" Then she fainted and crumpled to the floor.[26]

Fearing a mob would storm the Etowah County jail, Sheriff Osmond P. Reagan decided to transport McMurray to the Jefferson County jail in Birmingham. Reagan drove a squad car with Gadsden Police Chief Fay Boman sitting next to him, and McMurray, handcuffed, sat in the rear with Gadsden Detective Captain

Jack Fisher. According to police, on the way to Birmingham, a few miles east of Pell City, "the suspect suddenly lunged forward and seized Sheriff Reagan about the head, breaking his spectacles and scratching his face." Reagan lost control of the wheel and drove the car into a ditch. "The Negro then grabbed for the pistol that Captain Fisher was drawing, but both Fisher and Boman opened fire." Seven bullets pierced McMurray through the chest. Yet the officers never explained how during this alleged struggle they were able to face McMurray at close range and shoot him in the chest. Most likely, they removed the unarmed prisoner from the car and executed him on an open road. Whatever doubts existed about the officers' account, an all-white coroner's jury hastily exonerated all three lawmen, calling McMurray's death a justifiable homicide.[27]

Emory O. Jackson did not believe the story. As editor of the *Birmingham World* and the city's NAACP branch secretary, he began investigating the case. Jackson learned that a day after the alleged rape, Camp Sibert officials strip-searched Black and white soldiers looking for any evidence of a fight with a woman, namely scratches on a soldier's face and "a plug bitten out of one hand." Writing Roy Wilkins, then the acting secretary of the NAACP, Jackson explained that the only soldier bearing these marks was a white GI, who confessed to camp authorities "that he had been going with this woman who was married and that the husband found it out." Furthermore, a Black soldier who stood with McMurray in the police lineup reported that the Gadsden woman could not identify her attacker until the officers pulled her aside for a word. Only after an officer whispered in her ear and pointed toward McMurray, did she seem to recognize him. "Reliable sources at Camp Sibert" informed Jackson that McMurray "was beaten to death and then shot." Based on the evidence he collected, Jackson concluded that McMurray's death "was a well-plotted police lynching."[28]

In the wake of McMurray's killing, racial tensions crackled across the camp. On March 22, 1944, eleven days after McMurray died, Louis and Robinson ran afoul of white military policemen who demanded they adhere to Jim Crow customs. A confrontation began when Joe and Ray were waiting for a bus to take them into Attalla, a small town near Gadsden. Camp Sibert had assigned two buses for white soldiers and one for Black soldiers. That disparity forced Black troops to wait much longer for transportation. Growing impatient, Louis decided to call a cab, but the only phone booth was on the white side of the depot waiting area. The two boxers strolled over to the empty phone booth. After dialing a cab company, Joe sat on an empty bench with Ray until a white MP demanded they return to the "colored" waiting section behind the station building.[29]

Joe glared at him and refused to move.

"Soldier," the MP urged, "your color belongs in the other bus station."

Indignant, Joe retorted, "What's my color got to do with it? I'm wearing a uniform like you."

"Down here," the guard drawled, "you do as you're told."

Robinson recalled, "I never saw Joe so angry. His big body looked as if it would explode at that MP." According to Robinson, the MP raised his club, preparing to strike Louis, but Robinson reacted instinctively and tackled him to the ground. A group of MPs rushed to separate them. Black soldiers encircled them, shouting, "That's Joe Louis! That's Joe Louis!"[30]

When a lieutenant arrived on the scene, Louis explained to him that he refused to listen to the MP's orders because he believed Black soldiers were protected from the state's Jim Crow restrictions. "I said, 'I'm on a Government reservation and I am not in the State. I know about the segregation law in Alabama, but I'm on the reservation, and it is not state law, so I am entitled to everything a soldier is entitled to on the reservation.'"[31]

After listening to Louis, the lieutenant ordered the MPs to take him and Robinson into custody. Accounts differ as to whether they were under arrest or simply escorted to the post jailhouse until the provost marshal could determine what to do with them. Robinson later said that he thought he would face charges for assaulting an officer. After a jeep carrying Louis and Robinson drove them away, a rumor spread across camp that MPs had beaten them with nightsticks and hauled them to jail.[32]

The provost marshal, Captain Walter Buck, scolded Louis. "When an MP tells you to do something, you do it, or you'll get in trouble," he fumed. Joe replied he would not stand for discrimination on the base. He refused to remain silent. "I'm on a regulation post and I'm entitled to sit where I want to," he said. Louis knew that if he had been an ordinary Black solider, he would have faced formal charges. But he was *Joe Louis*, heavyweight champion of the world. The War Department would not print posters of him behind bars.[33]

Captain Buck insisted that the camp's Jim Crow regulations were established by the post commander, Brigadier General Haig Shekerjian. When Louis asked the general about segregation, Shekerjian denied authorizing any such policies, insisting that discrimination would not be tolerated at the base. The general also told Louis that he could use any military bus. Before dismissing Joe and Ray, Shekerjian, clearly concerned that a scandal could tarnish his reputation or the War Department, urged, "Don't say anything about this. Don't mention it to anybody."[34]

When Louis and Robinson stepped outside the camp headquarters, a bus stopped for them. A private serving as a bus "doorman" told them that they could sit up front, but Joe and Ray elected to sit somewhere in the middle, effectively desegregating the bus system at Camp Sibert. There were no photographers or newsreel cameras present to capture the historic moment. But Joe's protest against racism, a profound civil rights demonstration widely circulated in the Black press, added pressure on the War Department to end discriminatory practices on military bases and inspired Black soldiers to follow his lead.

A few months later, Jackie Robinson refused to move to the back of a camp bus at Camp Hood, Texas, when a white driver ordered him to the rear. Citing Joe and Ray's stand at Camp Sibert, Robinson objected to the driver's demand. Writing the NAACP, Lieutenant Robinson also explained that he refused to budge because he "recalled a letter from Washington which states that there is to be no segregation on army posts." It's not exactly clear which government document Lieutenant Robinson read, but two days after his bus protest, on July 8, 1944, the War Department issued a formal directive prohibiting discrimination in military transportation. "Restricting personnel to certain sections of such transportation because of race," the order stated, "will not be permitted either on or off a post, camp, or station, regardless of local civilian custom." The War Department also banned racial discrimination in camp recreational facilities, theaters, and post exchanges, though many officers ignored the order.[35]

Jackie Robinson's protest ultimately led to a court-martial, where he faced charges of insubordination, disturbing the peace, and refusing to obey the lawful orders of a superior officer. Although he was found not guilty of all charges, his defense attorneys argued that countless other Black soldiers endured similar harassment from white officers, venting "their bigotry on a Negro they considered 'uppity' because he had the audacity to exercise rights that belonged to him as an American and a soldier." The daily harassment and constant threats could drive a man mad.[36]

SUGAR RAY ROBINSON HAD ENDURED ENOUGH OF THE JIM CROW Army. He wanted out. From Camp Sibert, he telephoned Truman

Gibson and complained about the racist conditions. When the War Department sent an undercover investigator to Camp Sibert, a lieutenant told the agent that Robinson was "attempting to get out of the army in order to resume his boxing career." The investigator also believed that Ray planned to enter Walter Reed Hospital "with the hope of being discharged from the United States Army." If he could get out of the army, the agent reported, Robinson's promoters would pay him $10,000.[37]

On March 30, a few days after leaving Camp Sibert, Joe and Ray were scheduled to depart New York's Port of Embarkation and sail across the Atlantic, as more than three million other soldiers did throughout the war. The War Department had planned for them to entertain Allied troops in the European theater. On March 26, their unit, the First Casual Battalion, arrived at Fort Hamilton on the southern tip of Brooklyn. As they prepared to depart for England, General Dwight D. Eisenhower, supreme commander of the Allied Expeditionary Force, was making plans for Operation Overlord: the long-anticipated, cross-channel invasion of northern France, a risky plan for breaching Hitler's Atlantic Wall. For some men, the very thought of crossing the ocean and entering the unknown proved frightful. When Robinson was later asked about boarding a transport headed for the UK, he offered contradictory statements about how he felt. Ray said he was "thrilled about going over and seeing what it was like over there," but later admitted that he was "quite nervous about going overseas" and that he was "very much afraid of submarines"—a legitimate fear since German U-boats had sunk dozens of US ships crossing the Atlantic, killing thousands of American seamen and passengers.[38]

A day after arriving at Fort Hamilton, the boxers, flat broke, visited Uncle Mike "to put the touch on him," asking for advances on their next fights. Jacobs never turned them down, and he filled their pockets with cash. The following morning, March 28, a sergeant informed Robinson that he would not receive any more leave passes. Ray would be stuck on the base until he boarded a ship bound for England. That same day, still complaining about persistent headaches and insomnia, Robinson received a medical examination at the Fort Jay Station Hospital to determine his fitness for overseas duty. The doctors interpreted his EEG as "abnormal and consistent with a post-traumatic cerebral disturbance." Nonetheless, on March 29, a day before Ray and Joe were scheduled to depart, Lieutenant Lindsay J. Crawford, now the commanding officer of the boxing troupe, informed Robinson that he had passed his medical exam and that the army had deemed him physically fit for service. According to Crawford, Robinson replied, "They'll never put me on the boat."[39]

Crawford clearly believed Robinson meant every word. The lieutenant read him Article of War number 28, explaining that if he did not board the transport, then he would face formal desertion charges and possible imprisonment. Crawford reported the exchange to his superior officer, who considered forcing Robinson aboard the ship immediately or placing him under guard until embarkation. Fearing either scenario would threaten the Joe Louis tour, the commander afforded Robinson the opportunity to fall in line and step forward when his name was called at the pier the next day.[40]

A few hours before his detachment was supposed to board, Ray missed roll call. Crawford could not find him anywhere, and informed Captain Stockbridge H. Barker, the author of an infantry manual titled *So You're Going Overseas!*, that Robinson had failed to report. Barker immediately organized a search of Ray's barracks, the camp theater, and the service club. But no one could find him. Joe Louis called Robinson's Harlem home, but the phone rang without an answer. Military policemen were directed to question "all colored soldiers" about Robinson's whereabouts and use force if necessary to bring him back to the base. The captain scratched Robinson's name from the ship's passenger list and determined that he had gone AWOL.[41]

It seemed that Robinson just disappeared. Where was he? Someone at the base must have seen him. According to a War Department investigation, on the day of embarkation, around 4 p.m., Private Edward F. Flaherty spotted Robinson near a bus station just outside the post gates. At first, Flaherty confused Robinson with Joe Louis. But after introducing himself, Robinson told Flaherty that he was going overseas since doctors had cleared him despite his persistent headaches. Ray also said that a friend was coming to pick him up in a car, but Flaherty never saw any driver approach Robinson. When they reached the corner of Cropsey Avenue and Bay Seventh Street, Flaherty boarded a bus and never saw Robinson again.[42]

What happened to Ray in the coming hours remains a complete mystery. But in the middle of the night on April 1, a stranger, perhaps a white man, found Robinson on a Bronx street and brought him into the Veterans Hospital on Kingsbridge Road. His clothes were torn, and he was acting strangely, unable to identify himself. A few hours later, he was transferred to the Fort Jay Station Hospital on Governor's Island. Medical records indicate that he appeared "confused, disoriented and unable to give any information about his past life or the events leading up to his hospitalization," though he showed no external evidence of a recent head injury. When George Gainford visited the hospital, the trainer told doctors that Robinson had complained about headaches for years and he had used them as an excuse to avoid training and to cancel scheduled fights. When Ray's wife, Edna Mae, unexpectedly appeared at his bedside, a doctor standing behind a curtain observed that Robinson did not recognize her. Surely, the Fort Jay doctors thought, the patient "was a victim of amnesia and that his condition was not feigned."[43]

On the morning of April 4, Robinson was admitted to Halloran General Hospital, where the chief neurologist, Captain Robert L. Craig, examined him closely. When Ray first awakened at Halloran, he seemed completely bewildered, asking the same questions repeatedly. He did not understand how he'd wound up in a hospital bed. Panicked, he kept asking for Joe until a nurse explained that he had suffered a case of amnesia. The last thing Robinson remembered, he said, was that on the night of Friday, March 29 (*again, the evening before embarkation*), he had been playing poker with Joe and the other boxers in the troupe. After losing a hand to Joe, he left the card table to use the latrine. When he reached the head of the stairs, he tripped and tumbled down the steps. He told Dr. Craig that he could not remember what happened after his fall. No one in the boxer's troupe was available to confirm the story since the battalion was already on a ship somewhere in the Atlantic. Regardless, the chronology didn't add up, since Private Edward Flaherty had seen Robinson *the day after* he supposedly fell down the stairs, only hours before embarkation. And when Flaherty met him, Robinson seemed completely coherent, talking about going overseas with Joe Louis.[44]

After Captain Craig ordered Robinson to receive an injection of sodium amytal, "the truth serum," Ray became "hyper-emotional, alternating between laughter and depression," talking about his childhood and how his father beat his mother and how she became distressed, drinking heavily. Ray confessed that when he suffered severe headaches as a kid, he would pull his hair, punch his head with his fists, and slam his head against a wall. But repeated attempts to get him to reconstruct what had happened between the time he left Fort Hamilton and when he was admitted to the hospital "failed completely." Craig speculated that Robinson was either afraid that admitting his actions would result in desertion charges or that he had suffered amnesia because of a concussion. He doubted Ray fell down a flight of stairs, but whatever caused Robinson's "hysterical amnesia," Craig concluded, the sergeant was "not mentally responsible for his actions at the time he deserted his post." At the time, Craig believed that Robinson was fully capable of being rehabilitated for duty within the United States.[45]

Soon thereafter, however, Ray's commanding officer at Fort Hamilton requested the sergeant return to base to stand trial for a court-martial on charges of desertion "with an intent to avoid hazardous duty." Yet testimony from psychiatrists who believed Robinson really had amnesia made it impossible for a general court-martial to obtain a conviction beyond a reasonable doubt—even though Lieutenant Lindsay Crawford stated that Robinson had proclaimed he would not travel overseas. Ultimately, the desertion charges were dropped and Robinson returned to Halloran Hospital for further supervision.[46]

Over the next month, Robinson acted like "a psychopath," completely "uncooperative and theatrical," Craig wrote. He complained frequently about headaches but refused to accept medication or have his temperature taken. And he insisted on taking "a blue capsule" every night before bed, which turned out to be nothing more than a placebo. Curiously, Robinson began walking with a cane, wearing a pained expression on his face. When asked why he needed a cane, Robinson said that he had seen other patients using them. His behavior made no sense—unless he was putting on an act, as Craig now believed. "In my opinion," the doctor wrote, Robinson "is totally useless as a soldier and should be discharged."[47]

A medical board at Halloran Hospital agreed with Craig's recommendation. In late May, Halloran physicians declared that Robinson suffered from a "constitutional psychopathic state" and "inadequate personality." Furthermore, the doctors said, he possessed the "mental deficiency" of an illiterate ten-year-old "moron." Therefore, the medical board endorsed his release from the hospital. Then, on June 3, 1944, three days before D-Day, a military panel at Fort Hamilton granted him an honorable discharge for "inaptitude."[48]

A few months after being discharged from the army, Robinson announced that he would donate 20 percent of his purse from a series of matches to the Hearst newspapers' Disabled Veterans' Fund, a scheme undoubtedly organized by Mike Jacobs to quiet the critics who accused the boxer of being a slacker. Without knowing all the facts about his case, writers suspected that Robinson had simply gone AWOL at Fort Hamilton. MPs arrested him, and then quarterlies restrained him at a hospital. That story lingered for years, casting a pall over the career of the champion who, by 1950, was largely considered "the best fist fighter in the world—the best, pound-for pound, the ring has seen in a quarter century."[49]

In 1952, when Robinson first considered writing a memoir, he approached W. C. Heinz, a distinguished sportswriter known for exploring what it meant to be a fighter inside and outside the ring. Before Heinz would consider helping Robinson write the book, he needed to know the truth about the champ's military record. The veteran war correspondent still carried vivid memories from D-Day and the trauma of hunkering down among frightened, shivering men on the USS *Nevada* as German shells rained from the sky. When they spoke, Robinson denied all charges of desertion, but Heinz remained unconvinced, pressing him for a detailed explanation of his discharge. Robinson simply could not provide satisfactory answers to his questions.[50]

"I'm sorry, but I just can't do the book," Heinz said.

"That's all right, old buddy," Robinson replied. "I understand."

THE FIGHT OF HIS LIFE

Looking back on his time covering Sugar Ray, Heinz reflected, "He was a guy you'd like to have as a friend. But you couldn't trust him. He was a great con man."[51]

FROM THE MOMENT HE WAS DISCHARGED FROM THE UNITED States Army, a cloud of suspicion followed Sugar Ray Robinson. Yet Joe Louis never questioned him, at least not publicly. During their army tour together, Louis believed that Robinson had suffered from debilitating headaches, and he had no reason to doubt his friend's pain. By the time Louis boarded a transporter bound for the United Kingdom, on March 30, 1944, he had no idea what had happened to Robinson or of his friend's whereabouts. But Joe was never a man who looked back over his shoulder. At that moment he had more urgent concerns. His ship was hastening toward the coast of England, where German torpedo boats lurked.

Chapter Ten

OVER THERE

The young Negro fighter pilots . . . who were among those shooting down Nazi planes in the fierce fighting over the Anzio beachhead are not risking their lives to intrench further the way of life . . . in their home towns. The Negro Marines in the South Pacific, the black engineers, the colored quartermaster units getting the supplies through the mud and heat and cold of the battle-fronts, are not working for the status quo . . . Nor will they take kindly . . . to surly suggestions as to their "place." Bullets, or threats of bullets, are not likely to cause them to bow and scrape once they are home.

—Roy Wilkins, "The Negro Wants Full Equality" (1944)

IN JUNE 1944, SHORTLY AFTER D-DAY, WHILE AMERICAN FORCES were struggling to break out of the Normandy pocket, Joe Louis visited a makeshift hospital near Dover, England. The day was so beautiful, sunny, and clear, one journalist wrote that the wounded troops could see the faint outlines of France. One exception was an infantry man from Tennessee, who saw nothing at all. Bandages covered the severe head wounds he had suffered in an explosion. Layers of gauze protected his eyes, keeping him in darkness as he healed.[1]

He stirred to the sound of cheers. What was happening? When he learned that Staff Sergeant Joe Louis had arrived at the hospital, the Tennessean insisted that his bandages be removed so that he could glimpse the heavyweight champion. "It's strictly against orders," an attendant told him. "No," his doctor flatly added. "It might cost you your sight, son."

"Just let me have a look at him," the soldier pleaded. "I'll take my chances on my eyesight."

By then Louis was beside the man's bed. The physician relented, carefully removing the bandages, putting some ointment into his eyes, and carefully opening them so he could see the Brown Bomber. The Tennessean and the champ smiled at each other. Joe held the patient's hand. "This is the happiest moment of my life," the soldier said.

According to Private Tom Ephrem, the encounter moved Louis to tears. "You'll be OK, pal. We've got good doctors, and they'll make you well," Joe said, barely above a whisper. Accompanying Louis on the overseas tour, Captain Fred Maly, a former sports editor for the *San Antonio News Express*, wrote his superiors in the Special Services Division that the champ had genuinely lifted the spirits of wounded men. Countless times, injured soldiers asked him to recount his greatest fights round by round. Hearing Joe's old fight stories temporarily eased their pain and suffering. In those moments, visiting dying soldiers, Maly said, Joe's heart nearly broke, but the hospital visits gave him purpose and helped him find meaning in the tour.[2]

During his seven-month tour overseas, Louis performed about seventy-five boxing exhibitions across England, Italy, and North Africa. Excitement followed him from camp to camp. "No movie star has been greeted by our fighting men with more enthusiasm than that displayed when the Brown Bomber got into action," wrote a journalist. "Louis's exhibitions in the various theatres visited shattered existing attendance records, over and beyond any combination of two or three visits from cinema, theatre, radio and sports personalities previously used under the entertainment policy invoked by the War Department," Maly added.[3]

And yet there was a great irony that Louis could never escape: The world's most celebrated fighter did no actual fighting. Instead, he spent the war *entertaining* the soldiers who faced enemy fire in combat. To be sure, he was undoubtedly more valuable to the War Department on a stage than in a foxhole. And Louis understood that reality. But still it silently gnawed at him. Max Schmeling had parachuted into Crete during the German invasion. Joe was whacking George Nicholson and visiting hospitals. Occasionally reporters commented on his feelings. Lieutenant Lindsay Crawford, another officer on the tour, said this of the champion: "[He] seems to feel that anyone who is able to win the heavyweight championship of the world ought to be up front doing some real fighting. He feels pretty apologetic about the role he has been assigned."[4]

By the time Louis arrived in England in the spring of 1944, the Allies had virtually won the Battle of the Atlantic. Between decoded Enigma transmits, Leigh Lights, Hedgehog multiple mortar projectors, centimetric radar, and improved air and convoy tactics, Great Britain and the United States had all but ended the once-crippling threat of Adolf Hitler's and Grand Admiral Karl Dönitz's dreaded wolf packs. Still, U-boats occasionally picked off enemy ships, and the Allies carefully guarded their manifest lists. Therefore, although there were newspaper reports that Joe was awaiting orders for his departure to the European theater, the public did not know when or where he would arrive. Suddenly, on April 8, the Associated Press announced he had reached England—not in London yet, but at some undisclosed location.[5]

The news aroused the Brits' sporting instincts. Even though spring offenses were about to start, Englishmen were keen to match Louis against Freddie Mills, the current British Empire light heavyweight title holder, who in 1948 would win the world light

THE FIGHT OF HIS LIFE

heavyweight crown. But the War Department had not shipped Joe overseas to fight Mills or, for that matter, Max Schmeling or any other German. Louis had crossed the Atlantic for an important assignment: Calm the roiling racial waters. Summarizing the junket for his superiors, Captain Maly wrote, "The Joe Louis tour was in England at a time when racial relations between colored and white American soldiers were strained and sometimes fractured . . . The primary purpose of sending the Louis tour first to England was to assist in developing a better understanding between the two races in the American Army."[6]

Maly maintained that Louis had indeed helped soldiers of both races better appreciate "the American Way"—those democratic values, rights, and freedoms that the nation fought to preserve for all. He reassured the Special Services director that there were no racial conflicts on the European tour and that "thousands of white soldiers drew a fairer and better evaluation of the Negro soldier upon seeing and talking with Louis." If only it were that simple. If only Joe Louis, "America's No. 1 American," could step into the ring, erase the color line, and defuse the racial tension permeating US military camps. That would make a great American story, a triumphant chapter in Studs Terkel's *"The Good War."* In England, Joe Louis discovered that the War Department could take Black soldiers out of Jim Crow America, but it would not take Jim Crow out of the army. During his extended overseas tour, while American troops battled across Europe, Louis confronted racism in the army that made him reconsider the limits of his mission. But as long as he wore the drab olive uniform, he continued to deliver the War Department's message.[7]

By the time he reached London, Louis had developed what he described as "a beautiful cold," and depending on which journalist one read, his mood was somber and childlike or cheerful and urbane. A reporter from Manchester labeled him "a simple, home-loving, Bible-reading negro"—standard patronizing fare in America—yet a writer for the *Guardian* found his "neat, bright turn of phrase" refreshing. Expecting a laconic athlete, James Butler of the London *Daily Herald* saw Joe at the American Red Cross Club and was won over by the boxer's charm and wit. The champ was far from "the silent sleepy boy presented by pre-war publicity." Rather he was "merry-eyed, wise-cracking and slamming back answers with all the old speed of his punching."[8]

Early in the tour, Louis proved adept at staying on message. He parried standard boxing questions. He did not expect to defend his crown until the war was won, but he remained in fine fighting shape, a fact that his sparring partner George Nicholson readily confirmed. He put all talk about a title defense this way: "We're all in the biggest heavyweight match of all time. That's enough of a challenge for me until Uncle Sam wins the big fight." He gave more complete answers about his role in the war, making it clear that he was prepared to follow orders. "I hoped to get a chance to fight with a gun when I entered the Army," he explained. "Maybe I'll still get that chance. I'm a soldier. I've got my orders, and I follow orders." Until he had the opportunity to fight on the front lines, he would entertain the troops. "Maybe they'll let me put on an exhibition in Berlin someday. I'd like that," he commented.[9]

London became Louis's home base during his exhibition tour. The days were gloomy and rain-soaked, the nights rendered inhospitable by bombings, blackouts, and curfews. The great imperial city was a mess. German bombers had destroyed several hundred thousand buildings and houses. The builders and craftsmen who were needed to repair the damage were off fighting, and even if they had been available, there were insufficient bricks and mortar to even begin the job. Appalling human carnage compounded the physical destruction. By the end of 1944, the Blitz followed by the V1 and V2 bomb attacks had killed more than thirty thousand Londoners. Of course, deep underground tube facilities offered some safety, but cramming three hundred or so people into a small, claustrophobic space with only a couple of latrines produced its own unpleasantness.

Joe did not see as many bombed buildings as he expected, but he did not spend time in the East End and docks, where the German attacks had flattened whole sections of neighborhoods and hampered shipping facilities along the Thames. But he did get a Cook's tour of the city, visiting Westminster Abbey, St. Paul's Cathedral, Scotland Yard, and other historic landmarks in the largest city in the world. Impressed by the Londoners' stoic ability to muddle through the bombings and wartime privations, he told reporters, "These people sure can take it. After being floored they've gotten off the floor to win the final round."[10]

Joe was less impressed with London than the English were with him. He missed the United States, especially New York and Chicago, and everywhere he went reminded him that he was not home. But the appearance of Joe on English soil was treated as a grand event for the British. Crowds of curious onlookers gathered to gawk at the great heavyweight champion who had knocked out Max Schmeling and Billy Conn and bested British heavyweight Tommy Farr. The security surrounding Louis's movements gave the encounters between him and the public a serendipitous feel, as if Clark Gable or Frank Sinatra had suddenly appeared on some puddled street corner. On one Sunday night in April, when he arrived at the Fleece Hotel in Cheltenham, a multitude of several hundred residents—who somehow "got wind" of his arrival—circled him with cheers and questions. A contingent of military policemen were needed to escort the boxer into the hotel.[11]

While his movements were confidential, Louis remained singularly focused on his mission to inspire American fighting forces, particularly Black servicemen. It was a herculean assignment. The simple truth was that a Black soldier in England in 1943 and 1944 was, in most cases, not appreciably better off than he had been in Mississippi or Alabama in 1942. The British government, like the American government, resisted the employment of Black American troops in the Allies' campaign. Fearing that their country would be flooded with as many as a hundred thousand Black GIs, some British leaders worked to limit the numbers. Harry Hopkins, President Roosevelt's friend and adviser, scoffed at that figure, assuring a British representative that the estimate was "fantastic," though in the end, that was roughly the number.[12]

More racially tolerant than the Churchill War Cabinet were the English people, who had no more experience with Black Americans than the soldiers had with them. Instead of following the official government recommendation that "it was desirable that the people of this country should avoid becoming too friendly with coloured American troops," most Britons welcomed the Black soldiers as warmly as they did the white GIs—perhaps even more so. There was a sense among many British soldiers and civilians that white US troops were a touch arrogant, that their accomplishments in the time before D-Day did not warrant their swagger and boasts. "Overpaid, overfed, oversexed and over here"—the familiar complaint was not mere hyperbole. The average GI was paid about two-thirds more than his Tommy counterpart, was bigger and heavier, and unquestionably thought he was more sexually virile. In contrast, Black soldiers, especially those from the South, tended to be more reserved around the British, and they earned only about half as much as their white counterparts. Weighing in on the subject, writer George Orwell opined, "The general consensus of opinion seems to be that the only American soldiers with decent manners are the Negroes."[13]

Orwell undoubtedly exaggerated. But even a small adjustment to the racial order did not sit well with many white soldiers. There were no accepted norms for relations between the races. In Great Britain, Jim Crow might just as well have been the name of the latest dance craze, or even Joe Louis's sparring partner. In village pubs or dance halls in larger towns, English women mixed comfortably with white and Black American GIs, a practice that bred hostility and often ended in violence. Some publicans attempted to mitigate the conflicts by designating "white nights" or "coloured nights." But it was not a uniform requirement, and it was at best haphazardly enforced. The result proved as combustible as a dry fuse.

Roi Ottley, the first Black war correspondent, watched appalled as race relations in Britain unraveled. The blame rested entirely with the attempt by white officers and soldiers to transplant Jim Crow into Britain. "The noose of prejudice is slowly tightening around the necks of American Negro soldiers, and tending to cut off their recreation and associations with the British people," he observed. White officers employed a range of tactics to accomplish their mission. They restricted Black people from the best cafes, restaurants, theaters, and hotels. If the proprietor complained, they declared the establishment "Out of Bounds"—indicating a place neither white nor Black soldiers could frequent. And if restricting Black soldiers with curfews to places they could enter, and other fiats that in theory the army had banned, there was always the threat and use of violence. Ottley believed that in Southern officers' minds lurked the fear that if they relaxed Jim Crow restrictions and unwritten racial codes, there would be hell to pay in Dixie when the war ended.[14]

In the year before D-Day, as roughly one million white and one hundred thousand Black soldiers arrived in Britain, the US supreme commander, Lieutenant General Dwight D. Eisenhower, showed little interest in solving the military's "race problem." Officially, he said, "It is the desire of this headquarters that discrimination against the Negro be sedulously avoided." If pressed, his standard response was to issue a vague "separate but equal" statement and shift to some war issue he considered more important. With minimal guidance from above, conflicts were increasingly settled by a .45's bullet, a knife's blade, or an MP's baton. Between late 1943 and early 1944, authorities reported fifty-six racial clashes across Britain, an average of more than four each week.[15]

A bloody gunfight in Bamber Bridge, a village in Lancashire in northwestern England, demonstrated how quickly the fuse could burn. On the night of June 24, 1943, only two days after the conclusion of the Detroit Race Riot, Black soldiers from the 1511th Quartermaster Truck Regiment were peacefully drinking in Ye Olde Hob Inn, one of two pubs in the village that ignored the American color line. The watering hole served as a sanctuary from segregation, a space where Black soldiers mingled with friendly British locals. Shortly before the 10 p.m. closing time, two white military policemen entered, apparently with instructions to arrest any "soldier out of camp without a pass, or disorderly, or not in a class-A uniform." The MPs found one Black soldier wearing a field jacket, technically an improper uniform but more comfortable in wet, blustery weather. The military police officers escorted the GI outside. It seemed such a trivial offense that the needless harassment of a Black soldier drew the attention of a crowd of British soldiers and civilians, as well as ten or twelve Black GIs who had moved outside muttering about the biased treatment. Outnumbered, after a tense argument with Black soldiers, the MPs decided to leave, but someone in the crowd threw a bottle at them. It crashed against their jeep's windshield and sprayed the military policemen with beer.[16]

For the next five hours rumors spread more rapidly than truths, especially after a Black soldier took a bullet in the back and died. Heavily armed MPs, all of whom were white, rushed to the side of their comrades and jerry-rigged an armored car, replete with a large machine gun. Alarmed by the rumor that MPs were shooting to kill, Black GIs broke into an armory and armed themselves with rifles. Firefights erupted across Station Street, Bamber Bridge's main thoroughfare, while local villagers hid behind locked doors. Finally, around 4 a.m., Lieutenant Edwin D. Jones, the unit's only Black officer, convinced the men of the 1511th to stand down and return their weapons. After the shooting ceased, several servicemen lay wounded. A few months later, a US Army court-martial convicted twenty-eight Black soldiers of staging a mutiny against their officers and the MPs, though the sentences were largely commuted or reduced, and fifteen of the men returned to duty. None of the white MPs faced charges.[17]

War Department censors muted published American newspaper reports about a "clash" between white MPs and "Negro troops" at an unnamed English town. Relying on an Associated Press report out of London, the papers downplayed the severity of the violence that had occurred at Bamber Bridge, quoting a local commander who said "the situation was never out of control." Despite the censored press reports about "the Battle at Bamber Bridge," the Black soldiers who defended themselves against a volley of gunfire never forgot that one of their brothers died with a bullet in his back. Nor did they forget the fleeting moments of freedom they enjoyed in the English pubs. Embittered with resentment, those Black soldiers would return to the United States resolved to fight for their freedom at home.[18]

AFTER THE WAR ENDED, JOE LOUIS REFLECTED THAT IN England, insidious racial prejudice "[popped] up in the most unexpected places." For instance, problems surfaced in Manchester at a private dinner held in a Red Cross club to honor the champion. Stationed at the door, checking reservations, was Corporal Eddie Green, a Black friend of Joe's. All was well, the meal was about to be served, and Joe was preparing "to do some serious eating," when there was a loud commotion at the door. An army colonel, accompanied by a woman and another man, had forced his way into the building, demanding to see Louis immediately. Green told him it was a private affair. The officer attempted stoutly to pull rank. "I'm an officer in the United States Army and I can go any place where there are American soldiers," he blustered.[19]

The officer said he did not give a damn if the dinner was private or who had approved it—*he* demanded to see the boxer. "You just tell Joe Louis that a U.S. colonel wants to see him. And tell him to come over here in a hurry." Green refused to back down, explaining that Joe had worked twelve hours that day and was on free time. Finally, the officer left, saying, "I can hardly wait till I get back to my home town in Mississippi. There we know what to do with niggers like you and Joe. We'd tar and feather you for not obeying a white man."[20]

There was nothing unique about the encounter. During his time overseas, Louis heard the demeaning word repeatedly—in the line of duty and off. He witnessed pubs, public spaces, and sometimes entire towns that were "off limits" to Black troops. Once, as he arrived at a base for a boxing exhibition, he noticed that the seating was Jim Crowed. Through all the hurled insults, wanton violations of military codes of behavior, even slights with no intended harm behind them, Louis accepted his role as a racial ambassador, approaching his job with dignity, treating everyone he met with a consistent graciousness, and striving for at least incremental change. He later said that he recalled the words of his manager and friend John Roxborough: "Joe, a colored fighter has to be a gentleman at all times if he expects to win respect." Louis acted accordingly, even when life seemed rigged.[21]

Journalists for the London edition of *Stars and Stripes* dutifully followed Louis as he crisscrossed England, Scotland, and Wales, although their stories were scrubbed of any war-sensitive details. For instance, Joe Fleming reported that the month before D-Day, the champion entertained two Black battalions of aviation engineers. The 320th Barrage Balloon Battalion was almost certainly one of the units. Crossing the English Channel with the first waves of soldiers, they launched and manned the large hydrogen-filled barrage balloons, tethered to ships or ground fortifications, that helped protect ships and landing forces from low-altitude Luftwaffe strafing and bombing assaults. In effect, the men of the 320th mined the sky above Omaha and Utah beaches—dangerous work but essential for protection during and after the landings.[22]

Medic Waverly Woodson Jr. of the 320th rendered distinguished service in action during the D-Day operation. The landing craft that carried him to the waters off Omaha Beach scraped a mine and was hit by a German artillery shell, sending shards of shrapnel flying. The man beside him was blown to bits, and shrapnel sliced into Woodson. Bandaged, he jumped into the surf, waded through the blood-soaked water to shore, and went to work saving lives. During the next thirty hours, he administered to more than two hundred men. "He patched wounds, removed bullets, and dispensed blood plasma," wrote historian Matthew F. Delmont. "He amputated a soldier's foot and saved three men from drowning." The army awarded him the Bronze Star. A general thought Woodson deserved the Medal of Honor. By the end of the war, Congress had approved 432 recommendations for the nation's highest decoration for valor. Not one of them was the same color as Woodson. Ironically, that was the exact same number of Black soldiers in the German army awarded an Iron Cross.[23]

Although Congress chose not to single out the contributions of Black soldiers, the Special Services Division in the War Department recognized the political importance of promoting the many achievements of Black Americans. Chief of Staff George C. Marshall understood that the army's racial problems could not be healed by a Joe Louis appearance. Besides, the champion could not visit every army garrison or outpost. Convinced of the propaganda value of motion pictures and aware of the success of Major Frank Capra's *Why We Fight* series of documentaries, Marshall asked the director to make a film about racial tolerance that could be shown to soldiers everywhere and to civilians on the home front. Although Capra turned the day-to-day work on *The Negro Soldier* over to Stuart Heisler, a young director, the finished product had "the Capra Touch," that rare ability to entertain, educate, and send the message that all Americans shared the same faith in the country and its people.[24]

In a film that become mandatory viewing for almost all Black and white trainees, *The Negro Soldier* was unprecedented as a piece of US propaganda that glorified Black troops. Released to theaters across America in 1944, the film appeared at a time when Black Americans charged that their contributions in the war effort had been erased by the mainstream press. "The role of the Negro soldier, sailor, and Marine on foreign soil is cloaked in mystery," lamented the *New York Amsterdam News*. "Most of America will never know we were in the war." After reviewing Hollywood movies produced between late 1942 and early 1943, the Office of War Information (OWI) confirmed that Black people appeared in less than a quarter of films, mostly playing stereotypical roles.

But officials in the War Department and OWI believed that *The Negro Soldier*—a triumphant picture that captured the history of Black American soldiers fighting for freedom since the American Revolution—could build racial unity inside the US military and bolster the morale of Black soldiers in combat zones.[25]

The film's central message—that Black soldiers and civilians were essential in the war against fascism—served as a powerful counternarrative to that produced by so many other Hollywood pictures. At the same time, *The Negro Soldier* made no mention of slavery, segregation, lynching, nor the ongoing racial violence on American military bases. Nonetheless, the film served the modest needs of the War Department and satisfied the NAACP.

The Negro Soldier presented a story of Black heroism and patriotism through the rise of Joe Louis. Carlton Moss, a Black playwright and screenwriter who cowrote Lena Horne's first memoir, drafted the script. The forty-three-minute film unfolds like an inspiring Sunday sermon. Set in a Gothic stone church packed with a Black congregation of uniformed soldiers and civilians wearing their Sunday best, the opening scene unfolds with a Black minister, played by Moss, preaching about the Louis–Schmeling rematch—an allegory for the war. "In one minute and forty-nine seconds, an American fist won a victory," the preacher declared as the film cut to newsreel footage from the fight. "But it wasn't the final victory. No, that victory's going to take a little longer, and a whole lot more American fists." It wasn't lost on the audience that the minister referred to Louis as an *American* champion, not a *"Negro"* champion. Perhaps Moss wrote those lines thinking about white Americans who admired the Brown Bomber. The screenwriter had long believed that if white people could see the humanity and heroism of Black Americans in the flesh, as they did when they witnessed Louis pummeling Schmeling, then they would embrace racial equality.[26]

"Now," the minister preached, "those two men who were matched in the ring that night are matched again. This time in a far greater arena—and for much greater stakes." The minister spoke over images of Louis and Schmeling in military uniforms, training for a war that would "determine which way of life will survive." Moss framed Louis as the ideal soldier, who "believes in this country," a role model for Black men to emulate. Citing the heroic contributions of "Negro soldiers" in previous wars, the minister reminded the congregation that they had helped build the United States, and now they must rise to defend their country and defeat the Nazis. "The movie," wrote a reviewer in the *New York Amsterdam News*, "succeeds in proving that this is the Negro's war. He is too deeply rooted in the making of this country—he has as much at stake in its destiny as any other waver of the red, white, and blue."[27]

Joe Louis agreed. In late August Roi Ottley and the champ attended a showing of *The Negro Soldier* in London. The correspondent was more interested in Joe's reactions than the film itself. "He was manifestly proud of the picture and the role of the Negroes in it," Ottley wrote in his diary. When the film ended, Joe praised the effort. "Anybody who says that ain't a good picture, is crazy," he commented. Given Hollywood's treatment of African Americans in movies, the boxer proved an astute film critic.[28]

SERGEANT GEORGE NICHOLSON HAD THE MOST DANGEROUS assignment on the Joe Louis tour. As Joe's sparring partner and straight man in exhibitions, his job demanded a unique skill set, including a hardy constitution, a pleasant disposition, and a keen sense of self-preservation. Three times a week, he pulled on heavily padded headgear, climbed through the ropes, and tried to remain upright for three rounds. The champion never intentionally tried to hurt or humiliate Nicholson, but being on the receiving end of

Joe's punches was a painful proposition. A Liverpool sportswriter commented that Nicholson needed as much head protection as possible, "otherwise he would have been cut to ribbons by Louis' left hand, which flashed in and out, and Nicholson appeared to have no guard for it." To the untrained eye, the champion looked slow, but a seasoned observer noticed something else: "he punches fast, sees an opening quickly, and moves out of the way with great speed." There was a reason he had only a single blemish on his professional record.[29]

Fred Maly observed the toll that the "exhibition matches" exacted on Joe. He later reported to his superiors in the War Department that Louis "boxed so frequently that he suffered occasional fist injuries of such a nature that to continue boxing endangered his entire boxing future, valued at millions; yet he risked all willingly rather than disappoint soldiers who frantically stormed by thousands to the scene of his exhibitions." Louis's hand injuries, of course, were the product of punching Nicholson in the head and face. Today, we know that repeated blows to the head are likely to result in chronic traumatic encephalopathy, a severe form of brain damage. In 1944, the science was far less sophisticated, but the basic cause and effect had been adequately studied and was widely known in boxing circles. Sixteen years earlier, Dr. Harrison S. Martland, chairman of the New York Pathological Association, who earned a distinguished medical reputation, published the pathbreaking paper "Punch Drunk" in the *Journal of the American Medical Association*, establishing the causal link between boxing and what he labeled "punch-drunk syndrome." The term had long been used in boxing to describe a fighter who moved unsteadily, slurred words, suffered memory loss, and occasionally had a dangerous "twinkle of TNT in their eyes."[30]

Soon after the end of Louis's tour through bases in Great Britain, Nicholson was through sparring, hospitalized with a damaged eardrum. Had Louis been in training for a title defense, he would have employed a team of sparring partners to help prepare for the match. In August 1944, as he began his tour of Italy and North Africa, he needed new heads to pummel, and there were not many George Nicholsons in the Italian Theater who wanted to trade punches three times a week with Joe Louis. The solution demanded that Joe box a different sparring partner in each camp. Amateur boxers who had competed in Golden Gloves, AAU, or army tournaments could be found at virtually any base, and a chance to climb into the ring with the heavyweight champion of the world—with the promise that he would not destroy them like he had Max Schmeling—was a near-irresistible proposition.[31]

It worked beautifully, especially when an officer volunteered to fight Louis. In one of his gags, the champion smartly saluted the officer when he entered the ring, then proceeded to playfully embarrass him once the bell sounded to fight. The reversal of rank represented by a Black sergeant spanking a white captain or major sent the GIs into spasms of laughter. Watching Louis box—and, for an afternoon, level the racial divide—prompted *Pittsburgh Courier* war correspondent Ollie Harrington to suggest that Walter White should "put Joe under contract. The champ is the only one over here who can do anything in that direction."[32]

The warm and enthusiastic reception Louis received from Black and white GIs encouraged him about the possibility of significant racial progress. Working and fighting together, Louis thought idealistically, convinced soldiers of both races that "a lot of stuff they have been taught before is not right." "I think that these fellows overseas know now that the world is not meant to be ruled by color," he told a Black reporter. "They know that is why we are beating Hitler. When the boys from the South go back home, they are going to carry a different feeling toward our race." After the war, however, the realities on the home front would challenge his optimism.[33]

THE FIGHT OF HIS LIFE

By October 1944, Louis's mood mirrored the war in Italy. After brutal fighting in the hills and mountains around Cassino and along the Gustav Line, the Allies finally had broken through, and Lieutenant General Mark Clark had "liberated" the open city of Rome—an accomplishment that attracted headlines around the globe but had little impact on the war. Germany had responded by pulling back to the Gothic Line, a fortified position in the rugged northern section of the Apennine Mountains and continuing its defense. The fighting was slow, brutal, and costly. Louis's tour also suffered from mounting injuries and lingering ennui. Boxing three days a week, visiting hospitals the rest of the days, meeting generals, traveling to front lines and back, listening to the legitimate complaints of Black troops—the steady grind appeared to have no end. Worst of all, like millions of other GIs, Joe missed home.[34]

One evening in Corsica he met Sergeant Sid Weiss, a New York reporter for *Radio Daily*. The two chatted late into the night about the city. The newspaperman had never seen the fighter more talkative. They traded stories about the Zanzibar, Café Society Uptown, and other late-night haunts; the doings of John Hammond, Duke Ellington, Hazel Scott, Lena Horne, and other friends; the activity of columnists Hype Igoe, Dan Parker, Bill Corum, Ed Sullivan, and the rest. Joe discussed opening an exclusive nightclub in New York. His major concern, however, was getting the latest baseball scores. His Detroit Tigers were engaged in a struggle with the St. Louis Browns for the American League pennant. In the rain and mud of Italy in autumn, home was still alive in his imagination.[35]

A DAY AFTER THE ST. LOUIS CARDINALS DEFEATED THE ST. LOUIS Browns in the World Series, Staff Sergeant Joe Louis arrived back in New York via a nonstop flight from Casablanca, "a little older, a little heavier but a lot funnier and more loquacious than ever before." Reporters quizzed him with questions at the army's Special Services Division headquarters. But not before Captain Fred Maly praised the Brown Bomber's contributions to the war effort. The numbers spoke for themselves. In the United States and abroad, Joe traveled more than thirty thousand miles and participated in more than two hundred exhibitions before more than two million troops, logging almost one thousand rounds. As Louis sat embarrassed, his eyes studying the ground, Maly estimated that Joe had also probably signed more autographs than anyone else in history. Occasionally, when the praise became too fulsome, Joe patted Maly on the knee, signaling that he had said enough.[36]

Columnist Al Laney noticed the absence of the nervousness that had once tortured Louis. Yet "the qualities [of] dignity and goodness and taste" beamed as brightly as ever. "In all the years he has been standing under the spotlight in a profession that, to say the least, is smelly, he has never once failed to make the proper gesture or to find the correct words, even in the days when he was, strictly speaking, inarticulate." As a boxer, the columnist noted, Louis understood his role as a representative of his race; now in olive drab, he demonstrated just as sincerely his awareness that he also represented America. He recounted his trips to front lines in Italy and his frequent visits to military hospitals. "You don't talk much about them things," he said. "But you fellows always write about courage of prizefightings. You don't know about courage. I know about it now. Those fellows got it."[37]

Journalists filed stories about the new, mature Joe Louis, but the old Joe had not disappeared somewhere in Europe. When the War Department gave him a twenty-one-day furlough, he returned to his peripatetic lifestyle rather than spending the time with Marva and his daughter. Shortly after the champion's furlough began, Dan Burley, his friend at the *New York Amsterdam News*, enjoyed a breakfast of liver, onions, and biscuits washed down with what Joe called "a spot of tea." As they ate in the Hotel Theresa, Louis told the journalist to call Sugar Ray Robinson. The boxers exchanged friendly verbal jabs, mixed with stories of traveling across the South and returning to the ring. What Joe really wanted, though, was to get his hands on the keys to Robinson's Buick. "Ray called somebody," Burley reported, "and the car was on its way without further ado to the champion and remained at his disposal as long as he was in town."[38]

Joe had a fine Detroit automobile, but there wasn't much else in his life that was then in fine working order. Less than two months after the champion stepped on American soil, John Roxborough finally entered Michigan State Prison in Jackson to begin serving a potential five-year sentence for running a numbers game. Louis's manager had appealed his conviction based on the deliberate exclusion of qualified Black citizens from the trial jury. The prosecuting attorney admitted as much, commenting that every Black person in Detroit participated in the numbers and policy racket and therefore was unfit to serve on the jury. Ultimately the US Supreme Court refused to review the conviction. Since Louis was a teenage amateur, Roxborough had served as a father figure and role model, instructing Joe on how to dress and act, behave and speak. Without Roxy it is difficult to imagine Joe becoming heavyweight champion of the world; in fact, it is doubtful he would have become Joe Louis.[39]

In lean financial times, Roxborough had acted as a source of funds as well as wisdom. When Joe needed money to carry him over to his next big payday, when he required cash to pay the bills of his softball team, nightclub, or some other drag on his finances, Roxy was second only to Mike Jacobs as a provider of short-term loans. And at no time in his professional life had Joe been so short of money. As a staff sergeant in the army, his basic pay scarcely topped one hundred dollars a month, not even daily pocket change for Louis on the eve of the war. He needed advances on anticipated future bonanzas—such as a rematch with Billy Conn—just to keep Marva and his daughter, Jacqueline, comfortable.

There was an "out of sight, out of mind" quality to Louis's behavior, and money for his family, when it arrived, did so slowly and inconsistently. Marva recalled, "Joe wasn't earning anything as a soldier. I was proud of him for volunteering, but we had grown accustomed to a pretty high standard of living." She had once sung in a church choir, and believed she could "do all right on the stage." To support her family, Marva followed the path of Lena Horne and became a nightclub performer. She appeared at the Zanzibar on Broadway as part of a revue that included the Mills Brothers and other top acts. She sang at the Club Three Sixes in Detroit, and other clubs on the East Coast and in the Midwest. She was prominently billed as "the wife of champion Joe Louis," but her career lacked the glamour and rapid ascendancy of Lena Horne's. She received some harsh reviews—and some generous ones. But for Marva, it was less a career than a job.[40]

Joe never belonged to Marva, or so she complained. Whenever they went out on the town, they were never truly alone. Someone always hovered nearby, waiting for an opening to ask a question or request an autograph, driving a wedge between the husband and wife. It was all part of the devil's deal Louis had made with celebrity. In the first act of his career, during the Great Depression, he belonged to Black America—to Richard Wright, Lena Horne, Walter White, young Maya Angelou, and the millions of other members of his race who saw in the beautiful, powerful champion some stirring of their own greatness. Then in his career's second act, during the Second World War, he belonged to all Americans, Black and white, who battled for the triumph of democracy over fascism, due process over mob rule, and equality over the gross disparities of Jim Crow.

By early 1945, Marva accepted the inevitable, recognizing that she could never enjoy a "normal" life with Joe. Several years later she mused that she could have been happy with him "if we could have had a life together as any other happily-married couple." But, she explained, "We simply couldn't call our lives our own." Finally, Marva realized that she would never convert Joe to her ideal of marital bliss, and in March 1945 she sued for divorce on the grounds of desertion. The two met in court for the brief proceedings. Marva admitted that Joe had been a good husband "when he was at home." Louis did not contest the action, agreeing to pay $200 a month for the support of his daughter, Jacqueline, and to establish an educational trust fund for her. In an out-of-court settlement, he additionally consented to pay Marva a much larger amount from future title fights.[41]

Divorce did not change Louis's behavior. Rumors were the bullets in celebrities' lives, and he attracted as much fire as Hollywood stars. Even before the end of his marriage, columnists periodically dropped hints that he would eventually marry Lena Horne, but when famed Hollywood scribe Louella Parsons asked Lena's friends about the talk, they flatly denied it. Lena's "affections [were] elsewhere," Parsons learned. But not wanting to disappoint her readers, in her June 15, 1945, column she announced that she "just heard that Marva, divorced wife of Heavyweight Champion Joe Louis, will remarry him as soon as he is out of the army."[42]

The war, however, had altered his sense of freedom and his means of living. The collapse of German forces after Hitler's suicide and the surrender of Japan after the United States dropped atomic bombs on Hiroshima and Nagasaki ended World War II. Millions of American soldiers, sailors, and marines clamored to get out of government issue and into civilian clothes. They had contributed to the war effort, and were weary of uniforms, K rations, foxholes, jungles, long stretches of blue water, and anything else that smacked of military life. Dreaming of white Christmases and wives and sweethearts who would be so nice to come home to, they craved a better life and a peaceful future. Louis was part of this army that served their country. Until the end of the war, he avoided questions about future matches. "Let's get the war over first," he told reporters. Except for exhibition bouts, he had not engaged in a meaningful fight since he knocked out Abe Simon in March 1942. For more than three years, he had missed out on title defenses at Yankee Stadium and the Polo Grounds and perhaps a million dollars or more in income. Though he had not fought on the front lines, he had sacrificed much for America.[43]

After V-J Day, Mike Jacobs worked every angle to get Louis discharged. According to Truman Gibson, Joe's friend in the War Department, Jacobs even floated the idea of a bribe. It was worth ten thousand dollars to the promoter if Gibson could get the champion out of the army. Gibson refused. The problem was that Louis had not engaged in actual combat, and the first soldiers mustered out were the ones with the most combat service points. As a result, fourteen points short of what he needed for a discharge, the champion waited, assigned to work as a physical conditioning instructor at the massive Camp Shanks in New York's Hudson Valley. There he trained a new crop of GIs who would never earn combat points in World War II. About thirty to forty miles from Pompton Lakes and Greenwood Lake, where he trained to battle Schmeling and Conn, Joe remained frozen out of the premiere dates for outdoor fights in Yankee Stadium and other ballparks in New York, Philadelphia, Detroit, and Chicago. Estimating his gross potential lost income, he was undoubtedly the highest paid PE instructor in world history.[44]

As the leaves began to turn shades of red and gold in the hills above the Hudson Valley, Joe's time in the army drew to an honorable end. Working official army channels, Fred Maly and other officers in the War Department's Special Services Division argued that Louis's service to America deserved special recognition. Maly insisted that the boxer had jeopardized his career and lost millions of dollars to entertain and console some two million troops in lands from Great Britain, North Africa, and Italy to all parts of the United States, Canada, Alaska, and Attu, one of the Aleutian islands attacked by Japan. His impact on the nation's soldiers was incalculable, wrote Maly, and his presence acted as a salve for inflamed race relations. Finally, and significantly, he had risked his title and sacrificed his purses in bouts to raise money for navy and army relief funds. For all this, Maly believed, Louis deserved the Legion of Merit, "the highest noncombat medal awarded military personnel."[45]

On September 23, 1945, three weeks after Japan unconditionally surrendered aboard the USS *Missouri*, Sergeant Joe Louis received the Legion of Merit. Before an audience of one thousand people at Fort Hamilton and many more listening to the *Army Hour* radio hookup, General Clarence H. Kells recounted Joe's contributions to the war effort. "Sir, I am sincerely grateful," Louis replied. But the medal meant less than what his government conferred on him a week later—discharge from the army. Now he could enjoy the fruits of peace. First on his list was a 7 a.m. train to Detroit. The Tigers were in the World Series, and he told reporters, "I'm going to see every game." Of course, there would also be time to talk to Mike Jacobs about a fight with a boxer named Billy Conn. "I sure hope we'll draw a $3,000,000 gate," he added. Finally, he mentioned plans to train in California for two or three months. Two things were certain: First, he had no plans to settle down; second, after collecting $1,422.59 for one year's back pay, he desperately needed money.[46]

The excitement of a World Series, the talk of a Louis–Conn rematch—for millions of Americans, that signified the war had concluded. In mid-October *New York Times* columnist Arthur Daley wrote, "The war definitely is over . . . What makes the termination of hostilities absolutely and unqualifiedly official is that Uncle Mike Jacobs not only has signed Joe Louis to defend his world heavyweight championship next June but airily talks about a three-million-dollar gate." Jacobs envisioned counting stacks of cash from the fight's ticket sales and the profits from broadcasting the match on radio and television. The sound of the promoter's "store teeth clattering contentedly" inside the Twentieth Century Sporting Club, talking deals and gazing "dreamily into the air," and imagining how much money he would make from the match was a sure signal that many Americans had turned the last page on the war for freedom and democracy. Millions of Black Americans, however, knew that the war at home remained unfinished. Their fight was only half completed. The world they fought for was still as unrealized as Jacobs's millions.[47]

Chapter Eleven

HOMECOMING

The [Black] veteran from Okinawa may well be lynched on the streets of a Georgia town if he does not step off the sidewalk when a white woman or man passes. He had better not wear his uniform or battle ribbons in certain towns in Mississippi. He will be patted on the back in large cities in the North by victory-flushed white Americans and then knifed for the job of his desire by the same whites who are seeking to continue the age-old policy of "last to be hired, first to be fired" where the Negro is concerned.

—Dan Burley, *New York Amsterdam News*, August 18, 1945

THE UNITED STATES WAS NO LONGER AT WAR—BUT JOE LOUIS knew that his fight wasn't over. In the summer of 1946, about a year after V-J Day, white lynch mobs attacked and sometimes killed Black veterans. It was the worst summer of racial violence since 1919, when race riots erupted in more than twenty cities and white vigilantes murdered dozens of Black Americans, many of them veterans. After the Second World War, Black men dressed in military uniforms were again seen as a threat to the racial caste system. Proud, patriotic Black GIs returned home victorious, determined to claim their rights as full American citizens. Yet armed white posses unleashed "a well-organized campaign of terrorism," Walter White wrote, torturing Black servicemen "with savagery equaled only at Buchenwald." Horrified by the brutal headlines published in Black newspapers, the heavyweight boxing champion fumed, "It's the same kind of thing Hitler did, the same. We went over there, and our boys fought and died to stop Hitler [from] doing this. And we come back and see the same thing here. It's a doggone shame, that's what it is."[1]

That summer the Black press published weekly stories about Black servicemen being attacked and murdered by white mobs. A rattled Black vet from Georgia told NAACP investigator Ollie Harrington, "They're exterminating us. They're killing negro veterans, and we don't have nothing to fight back with but our bare hands." That July, after Maceo Snipes, a thirty-seven-year-old veteran, became the first and only Black person to vote in a Democratic primary in Taylor County, Georgia, four Ku Klux Klansmen confronted him outside his family's farmhouse. Snipes had defied the Klan's threats against voting, and he paid for it with his life. An all-white coroner's jury exonerated the gunman who shot Snipes in the back and killed him. A few days later, on the outskirts of Monroe, Georgia, at Moore's Ford Bridge, a mob of about two dozen white men lynched a Black veteran named George Dorsey, his pregnant wife, Mae, and their friends Roger and Dorothy Malcolm. Roger had been arrested after allegedly stabbing a white man, but after he was released on bail, the mob abducted the two Black couples from a pickup truck on the bridge above the Apalachee River. The killers unloaded sixty bullets into their bodies at close range and then hung them from a tree. Despite national outrage and an investigation by the FBI, no one was ever charged in the murders.[2]

The lynchings across the South inspired Black veterans to stand up and speak out against injustice and mob violence. Increasingly, they joined the NAACP and other civil rights groups, organizing protests against segregation and lynching.

Homecoming

"The uprising of 1946" spurred the beginning of the modern civil rights movement. After learning about the lynchings in rural Georgia, a seventeen-year-old Morehouse College student named Martin Luther King Jr. wrote a letter to the editor of *The Atlanta Constitution*, insisting, "We want and are entitled to the basic rights and opportunities as American citizens," including "the right to vote" and "equality before the law."[3]

The violent assaults on Black veterans deeply troubled Louis. It sickened him to learn that decorated Army Sergeant Isaac Woodard had been attacked and blinded by a white police chief in Batesburg, South Carolina. After serving in the Pacific for fifteen months, Woodard was discharged from Camp Gordon, Georgia, on February 12, 1946. Later that night, wearing his uniform, he boarded a Greyhound bus bound for Winnsboro, South Carolina. About an hour into the trip, the driver stopped the bus outside a drugstore, and Woodard asked him for permission to use a restroom. An argument ensued between them, though the white driver ultimately relented. But when the bus reached Batesburg, the driver summoned local police, claiming that a Black soldier had caused a disturbance on the bus. When Woodard tried to explain himself, a white officer cracked him across the head with a blackjack. After dragging him to jail, two officers proceeded to beat him unconscious, gouging his eyes out of the sockets with their nightsticks. Woodard awoke the next morning lying in a bunk, covered in blood, permanently blinded by Sheriff Lynwood Shull. In the coming months, Woodard bravely told his story to reporters and members of the NAACP, calling on fellow veterans to fight for their civil rights. "Negro veterans that fought in this war don't realize that the real battle has just begun in America," he said. "They went overseas and did their duty and now they're home and have to fight another struggle, that I think outweighs the war."[4]

Later that summer, Joe listened intently when he met Woodard in Harlem at the Hotel Theresa. Seeing him in the flesh, scarred and hobbled, his eyelids swollen shut, Louis visualized the savage beating the sergeant had endured at the hands of his tormentors. As the honorary chairman of the United Negro and Allied Veterans, Louis committed to fighting for the rights of Black servicemen. He understood that they were counting on him in the battle against white supremacy. Black veterans were at the center of a revolution rooted in a war that made racial inequality and mob violence more unbearable than ever before. Disillusioned by lynchings, police brutality, and voter suppression, "a burning core of resistance" emerged among Black citizens. Veterans like Louis, noted *Ebony*, were "not the same Negroes who put on uniforms after Pearl Harbor. The war has been an education . . . Travel, better health and living conditions, even higher income made the Negro younger generation the most aware, most articulate, most militant in all U.S. history."[5]

Louis's experience in the war—building on his work campaigning for Wendell Willkie during the 1940 presidential election—made him think more about his "responsibility to his people and to his country," he said. Touring military bases in Europe and the United States, hearing desperate pleas from Black GIs, convinced Louis that he had a larger purpose beyond the ring. He was filled with anger over racial violence, and the blinding of Isaac Woodard stoked his activism. Louis sponsored an August benefit for Woodard at New York City's Lewisohn Stadium, a concert featuring Nat "King" Cole, Billie Holiday, Cab Calloway, Josh White, Count Basie, Woody Guthrie, and several other artists.[6]

On the eve of the benefit, Louis met with a reporter from *PM* at his Pompton Lakes training camp. Sitting on the porch of the colonial stone house, dressed in a blue suit, he gazed across the yard at a wishing well, contemplating the writer's questions. The reporter asked him how Americans could end mob attacks against Black people. Calling for racial cooperation and nonviolence, Louis said, "It's got to be like an army," a united front of people peacefully advocating for equality. "One color cannot do it," he maintained. "We got to do it together. Like I said, an army—not guns, men."[7]

Joe talked about the letters he received from veterans of all races who despised discrimination. He believed that they were the ones who had the power to change America, but it would take generations to cleanse the country of the deep prejudice that poisoned so many minds. Although young white people gave him a glimmer of hope for improving race relations, too many of them listened to their parents, he said, living in fear of Black men. That fear ensnared the country like a noose around the neck.

During the war army censors had prohibited Louis from speaking out against racism. Protesting the abuse of Black soldiers during the war carried severe risks—punishment from white officers or, worse, violent retribution. Relieved after being discharged, Louis said he was glad to be "out from army orders." When a publicist promoting the Woodard fundraiser handed him a speech for the *PM* interview, Louis brushed it aside. "You don't have to tell me what to say about Woodard. You don't have to tell me what I think about lynching."[8] Now, at last, he was free to speak his mind.

IN JUNE, TWO MONTHS BEFORE NEW YORK CITY HOSTED THE ISAAC Woodard benefit, Joe Louis finally defended his heavyweight title against Billy Conn at Yankee Stadium. The champ had not fought professionally in more than four and a half years. Despite sparring on a regular basis during his forty-five months in the army, he had gained about twenty pounds and lost his edge in the ring. In May, Joe turned thirty-two years old, well past his athletic prime.

His reflexes in the ring had already started to deteriorate. "When I came out of the army, I wasn't the fighter I was before I went in," he admitted. "Nobody can lay off that long and come back as good as he was."[9]

Reporters questioned whether he still had the desire or the ability to dominate the sport the way he had before the war. Louis had been fighting professionally for twelve years, training regularly and defending his title more often than any heavyweight champion before him. After a prolonged layoff, he had to find the motivation to wake up every day at 5 or 6 a.m., pound the pavement for a few hours, and then abuse the heavy bag and speed bag, shadowbox, and spar until he couldn't lift his arms. Plus, he had to do it without Jack Blackburn exhorting him. His new trainer, Mannie Seamon, a "jovial, rosy-cheeked" white man who had replaced Chappie, was no taskmaster, "more of a conditioner than a boxing coach." In the weeks before the fight, several boxing writers observed Seamon training Louis at Pompton Lakes and concluded that the champ "looked slow and almost completely indifferent most of the time." One reporter suggested he was "shot," a shell of himself. By contrast, Billy Conn appeared to be in much better fighting shape—at least that was the word according to the sporting press.[10]

Yet there was another group of writers who believed that Louis was putting on an act when reporters watched him train. One conspiracy theorist said, "Don't you know that it was Mike Jacobs' idea to build up Conn and play down Louis for the gate receipts?" Supposedly, Louis did his real training out of the public eye. These writers suggested that if fight fans were convinced that Conn could knock off the defending champion, then one hundred thousand people would pack Yankee Stadium, further enriching Uncle Mike. In the aftermath of the war, Jacobs was certain that Americans were eager to attend a major outdoor heavyweight title fight. "The Big Fight" would become something more than a sporting event, he calculated. Like baseball's World Series, it would be "a sort of national festival," a celebration of American life in peacetime. Charging $100 for ringside seats—an unprecedented figure—Jacobs boasted that the match would draw a $3 million gate, exceeding the $2.6 million record set when Jack Dempsey fought Gene Tunney at Chicago's Soldier Field in 1927.[11]

For all the concern about the champ's age and his declining skills, Louis didn't seem worried about beating Billy Conn. When Joe wasn't training, he relaxed with friends, especially Sugar Ray Robinson, a frequent visitor at Pompton Lakes. He enjoyed canoeing, listening to records, playing card games, and reading newspapers. Joe eagerly opened the daily sports section to see how Jackie Robinson was playing with the Montreal Royals—the Brooklyn Dodgers' top minor league ball club. If Robinson performed well, there was a good chance that Dodgers president Branch Rickey would bring him to Brooklyn. Joe was thrilled for Jackie, but he wondered why it took so long for a Black ballplayer to get a shot at the Major Leagues when he had been heavyweight champion for nine years.[12]

Undoubtedly, the war had galvanized the movement for integrating Major League Baseball, and Joe Louis played an important role in Robinson's breakthrough. During the global crisis, Black journalists, liberal white columnists, labor organizers, and civil rights activists campaigned for the sport's integration, arguing that segregation contradicted the nation's egalitarian war aims. *New York Post* columnist Jimmy Cannon could not reconcile "having Jim Crow as an umpire in organized baseball" since Louis had proven himself "a fine champion." Furthermore, as a symbol of the United States, baseball was seen by many Americans as a "democratic game." Yet Major League executives denied opportunities to Black players. An editorial in *The New York Times* condemned the hypocrisy: "If we are willing to let Negroes as soldiers fight wars on our team, we should not ask questions about color in the great American game." Major League Commissioner Albert "Happy" Chandler agreed. In 1945, he told reporters from the *Pittsburgh Courier*, "If a black boy can make it on Okinawa and Guadalcanal, hell, he can make it in baseball."[13]

After Rickey signed Robinson in October 1945, the press and the public debated the "great experiment." If Robinson took the field with white players, doomsday predictors thought racial violence would erupt in the stands and the streets. Those same detractors had disapproved of letting Joe Louis fight for the heavyweight title against a white champion. But they were proven wrong in 1937, and those same critics would be proven wrong again, suggested *Chicago Defender* columnist Frank Young. Louis had won over many white fans, and if Robinson thrived on the ball field, he would too. Surveying Southern writers about the great experiment, Young received a letter from former army Captain Fred Maly, the sports director of the *San Antonio News*. "A star is a star no matter what his race and I am not apprehensive over the consequences of the signing of Robinson by a major league club," he wrote. "I was Joe Louis' Army manager for more than a year. Lived with him and several other Negro fighters in our journeys overseas. I have grown to realize that a good man achieves friendship, respect and admiration from others regardless of color."[14]

Carrying the hopes and dreams of millions of Black Americans, Robinson vowed to follow the example of Joe Louis, knowing that he would be under immense scrutiny. If he was going to succeed—and gain respect from white America—Robinson would have to demonstrate "superior conduct and spotless behavior" just as Louis did, noted *Pittsburgh Courier* columnist Joseph Bibb. Although Black writers began comparing "the two most celebrated Negro athletic heroes of the decade," they never saw themselves as rivals competing for attention. Since they served together at Fort Riley, the two friends had supported one another. It was no surprise that five days before Joe's fight against Billy Conn, Jackie spent the day with him at Pompton Lakes. Jack knew that without Joe, Branch Rickey would have never signed him to a contract. "I certainly feel that the path for me and others to the big leagues was made easier by the performance and conduct of Joe Louis both in and out of the ring," he said in 1954, seven years after he broke the color barrier with the Brooklyn Dodgers.[15]

On the afternoon of the fight, Jackie Robinson, Sugar Ray Robinson, Lena Horne, and his ex-wife Marva Louis (though they were soon to be remarried), along with dozens of other celebrities, were scheduled to appear on the balcony of the Hotel Theresa during Harlem's "Joe Louis Day" festival. Teeming with fans from all over the country, Harlem overflowed with streams of people pouring out of apartments and taverns. Reporters estimated that 250,000 citizens filled the streets to pay tribute to their hero. In a two-hour motorcade procession, ten thousand cars, some from as far away as Texas and Georgia, crawled alongside parade floats on Lenox Avenue. Knots of men, women, and children dressed in their Sunday best, as if it were an official holiday, stood elbow to elbow on packed sidewalks. Crowds congregated on rooftops, fire escapes, and stoops as marching bands celebrated Joe's homecoming. It didn't seem to matter that he remained hidden inside his suite at the Theresa, preparing for the match. The din outside his hotel room probably scared him from opening the door. "The lobby was bedlam," noted one reporter. "The entrance was jam packed and you had to fight to get in and out of the place." Outside the hotel, street vendors sold Joe Louis pennants and buttons. One "slow-witted hawker" shouted, "I've got Conn buttons, too," and "he barely escaped with his life."[16]

Ever since the night of June 18, 1941, when Joe Louis dropped Billy Conn in the thirteenth round, the Pittsburgh Kid hadn't stopped thinking about a rematch. Stationed in Europe during the war, Conn brooded about it, plotting his revenge. He hated being in the army. He compared it to being in jail—"doing a bit in the can." Conn told Jimmy Cannon that the draft was "a plot schemed to swindle him out of the fortune he was certain to make in the ring." Obsessing over his return to professional boxing, he constantly thought and talked about "one subject," noted Whitney Martin, a reporter from the Associated Press. "On countless long, tedious airplane flights; in innumerable exhibition bouts . . . on flesh-punishing jeep rides through the mangled terrain of France and Germany; when he was cold and wet and hungry—no matter the circumstances or conditions his spirits were buoyed by the conviction that some day he would get the chance to win the title which he felt he once had within his grasp."[17]

And now that day had come.

On a cool, pleasant summer night, standing beneath a cloudless sky, Louis and Conn faced one another in the middle of the ring, enveloped by more than forty-five thousand people. Mike Jacobs was sorely disappointed that the Yankee Stadium crowd had nine thousand fewer customers than the first Louis–Conn bout. Although the rematch generated nearly $2 million, it was far off his $3 million expectation. While the most expensive infield chairs and the cheapest bleacher seats sold well, tickets in the lower deck were sparsely filled. Many fight fans simply could not afford a ticket.

In the aftermath of the war, the government canceled thousands of manufacturing contracts for military supplies and equipment, leaving workers frustrated with suppressed wages and surging inflation. Workers struggled to purchase necessities while overtime pay disappeared and veterans struggled to find work. In response, during 1946, the United States experienced the largest wave of labor strikes in history: more than 4,600 work stoppages involving some five million employees. Leading up to the fight, hundreds of thousands of workers across various industries walked out on the job, disrupting virtually every sector of the economy. Two hours before the Louis–Conn match began, engineers and technicians at NBC threatened to go on strike too, jeopardizing the first heavyweight championship match broadcast on television. Fortunately for Jacobs, he managed to settle the labor dispute before Louis and Conn touched gloves.[18]

New York Times columnist James P. Dawson believed that the television broadcast hurt ticket sales. As it was broadcast via coaxial cable in seven states and the nation's capital, an estimated one hundred thousand fight fans watched the match. Gathering around television sets in taverns, hotel bars, and living rooms, viewers saw the fight through the lens of five cameras stationed around the stadium. The black-and-white pictures on the screen came through clearly, but the fighters looked tiny, like Lilliputians, complained one reviewer. Watching the match on television, viewers missed "the smack of the leather and the grunts and groans that can be heard at ringside," but it was better than listening to it on the radio and trying to imagine the action based on the ringside announcer's description. The Louis–Conn rematch marked the beginning of a new era in broadcasting, an age where boxing, and sports more generally, became the greatest incentive for owning a television.[19]

Sadly, the fight itself was a dull affair, lacking any real drama or suspense. Covering it reminded Jimmy Cannon of a long dreadful night, "the way the slow hours" passed "for reporters sitting on a stoop waiting for a man to die." It was evident early on that Conn's only advantage in the first fight—his speed—was missing in action. Louis noticed it immediately. Conn moved much more slowly, constantly circling the ring and retreating. At times Joe looked bored stalking and chasing him. Remarkably, on two occasions—in the fourth and sixth rounds—Conn slipped and stumbled, exposing his chin to a kill shot. Joe could have chopped him unmercifully, but instead stepped back and allowed Billy to rise unharmed. Reporters marveled at Joe's sportsmanship, "his inherent sense of decency and fairness."[20]

Finally, in the eighth round, Louis unleashed a flurry of punches, staggering Conn with a devastating combination. Louis socked him with a straight right to the jaw, followed by a hard right uppercut that knocked Conn back on his heels, setting him up for a sharp left hook that knocked Billy to the canvas. Blood gushed from the challenger's nose, mouth, and a cut below the left eye. When it was over, Conn was in such bad shape that he announced his immediate retirement from the ring. "I should reenlist in the Army," he said, "I was lousy tonight."[21]

In Joe's dressing room, a group of reporters and photographers gathered around the champ as he stood on a bench, smiling, declaring proudly, "Everybody seemed to be wondering whether I would still be as good as I used to be. Seems as if I am, don't it?" Perhaps he had proven something, but Conn hadn't exactly tested him. Expecting a large purse from the fight, a reporter asked him how he planned to spend the money. "Pay some taxes," he replied with a grin. But not before Uncle Mike got his cut first.[22]

THE MONEY WAS ALREADY GONE BEFORE JOE COULD CASH THE check. He had earned the most profitable purse of his career—nearly $600,000—but he had accrued such enormous debts that there was hardly any money left by the time Jacobs was finished calculating his earnings. When Louis fought Conn, he reportedly owed the promoter somewhere between $140,000 and $150,000, plus another $30,000 or so he had borrowed from John Roxborough before the war, and additional debts to golfing buddies. Furthermore, he still owed the IRS about $115,000 in back taxes and the State of New York immediately deducted approximately $30,000 from his purse. After the Conn match, he remunerated his managers $140,000 and paid Marva thousands of dollars in alimony. But the greatest problem for Louis was that he could hardly manage his debts since he was taxed at the highest federal income rate: 91 percent. That meant that after Louis paid Jacobs, Roxborough, Marva, and his prewar IRS bill, he did not have enough money left over to cover the federal income taxes on the purse from the Conn fight. In other words, he had paid up with Uncle Mike, but he still owed Uncle Sam.[23]

Joe's new manager, Marshall Davis Miles, an old friend of John Roxborough, believed that Mike Jacobs had worsened the champ's financial problems by loaning him money during the war. Jacobs had permitted Louis to live beyond his means, he said, knowing that Joe would be unable to pay his personal debts and his deferred tax bill. Yet Joe dismissed the idea that Jacobs exploited or manipulated him by opening his checkbook. "Uncle Mike didn't give me the money to keep me under his control," Louis later told sportswriter Ed Linn. "Mike gave me the money whenever I asked for it, and he gave it to me without a question. He gave it to me because he was like a father to me. If anybody was getting hooked, it was Mike. Nobody knew how long the war was going to last in those days. I could have been an old man when I got out. I could have been killed."[24]

After the Conn fight, Louis insisted on repaying Jacobs—not because the promoter asked for the money, but because Joe believed it was the right thing to do. Yet Miles questioned Jacobs's motives. He expressed concern about Joe's dire finances and Jacobs's matchmaking for the champ. Although Roxborough maintained financial ties with Louis, he could offer little counsel from a Michigan State Prison cell. Therefore, in early 1946, Miles, "a melancholy little man," became Joe's manager of record, though he was "more

Louis's companion than Nestor," noted a close observer. A sharply dressed real estate investor, horseplayer, and numbers operator out of Buffalo, he had managed only one professional boxer before Joe. But that did not matter since he had the trust of Roxborough and had known Louis for years.[25]

In July, Jacobs arranged for Louis to fight once more in 1946 against Tami Mauriello, a powerful knockout puncher. Miles convinced Roxborough that they should waive their manager fees so that Louis could keep the entire purse from the Mauriello fight and pay down his IRS bill. In September, after knocking out Mauriello in the first round at Yankee Stadium, Louis earned about $100,000 from the gate, but it hardly helped him erase his income tax debt.[26]

About a month after Louis toppled Mauriello, he returned home to Detroit, celebrating Roxborough's release from prison. After serving nearly two years in the state pen, Roxy returned home to his apartment where his wife Wilhelmina, Joe, Marva, Marshall Miles, and several other friends greeted him. When Joe first saw "Uncle John," the champ smiled widely and threw his arm around him. "This is what I have been waiting for!" he exclaimed. Louis told a reporter from the *Pittsburgh Courier* that he no longer needed Miles's managing services. "John is my manager from now on."[27]

Critics charged that Marshall Miles was never really Joe's manager anyway. That title belonged to Mike Jacobs. The truth was that Jacobs not only controlled Louis, but he also ran the entire boxing industry. For years, he operated a monopoly, reigning over New York City—the mecca of boxing—staging the biggest outdoor fights at Yankee Stadium and the major indoor matches at Madison Square Garden. Any fighter who wanted a shot at a title and the big money that came with it had to work with him. Jacobs became the personal bank for rising prospects. When a contender moved his way up the ranks, the promoter willingly, and sometimes eagerly, purchased his future by offering loans to the fighter and his managers with a guaranteed return. He also dictated "terms to referees, politicians and rival promoters," reported two writers from *Life* magazine.[28]

By 1946, however, there were signs that Jacobs had ceded control over the boxing business to Paul John Carbo, aka "Frankie Carbo," a longtime soldier in the Lucchese crime family and notorious triggerman for Murder, Inc., an organization of mob assassins operating out of Brooklyn. "Mike Jacobs is frequently pictured as the czar of the fight game in the East, but this is only partially true," Lee Dunbar wrote in his *Oakland Tribune* column. Although Jacobs's fingerprints could be found on every major promotion in the sport, Dunbar wrote, "it is not stretching the truth to say that Frankie Carbo . . . is the real power behind the throne in New York." Informants cooperating with FBI agents investigating Carbo concurred. In July 1946, a source told the Bureau that Carbo "controlled the entire boxing game in New York City, even Mike Jacobs."[29]

Since the Great Depression, Carbo had controlled dozens of fighters across multiple weight divisions. During the 1930s, especially after the repeal of Prohibition, mobsters treated boxing—an unregulated sport—as a full-fledged racket that could bolster their shrinking incomes. Even before Carbo's rise as the "underworld commissioner," gangsters "ran fighters, promoted fights, fixed fights, and bet on fights," noted David Remnick. Intimidating fighters into signing ironclad contracts, Carbo owned a stable of boxers. He bought and sold them like racehorses. And he was always looking for fresh meat. Increasingly, during the Second World War, while the federal government diverted its resources away from investigating organized crime, Carbo strengthened his ties to "every important manager, matchmaker, and promoter," including Mike Jacobs.[30]

THE FIGHT OF HIS LIFE

Carbo, also known as "Mr. Gray," was a sophisticated, somberly dressed bravo with dark eye circles. He trusted no one and often directed his henchmen with orders in rambling, circular sentences, giving "the impression of uncertainty." Operating without a license as an undercover manager, violating New York state law, Carbo held court in smoky saloons and Stillman's, a notoriously rank gym that reeked of sweat and cigars. "The joint always smells wrong," A. J. Liebling wrote. When Carbo and his cronies weren't muscling fighters and managers at Stillman's, he dined at the Forrest Hotel on Forty-Ninth Street, just down the block from Madison Square Garden. Long before Angelo Dundee became Muhammad Ali's trainer, he worked at Stillman's as an errand runner for his older brother Chris, a promoter. One time, after delivering a package or a letter to Chris at the Forrest Hotel, Angelo boarded an elevator when "a debonair man of small stature wearing a well-fitted gray silk suit" and "an oyster gray fedora" joined him. Dundee recognized the ominous man's picture from the newspaper but couldn't recall his name. Perhaps that was because Carbo had used several aliases: Frank Fortunato, Frank Marlow, Frank Martin, Frank Tucker, Dago Frank, and Jimmy the Wop. Curious, Angelo turned to him and said, "I know you." Mr. Gray met his gaze with cold, dark eyes and said in a quiet but forbidding voice, "No you don't."[31]

In 1946, there were very few sportswriters on the East Coast who dared to use Carbo's name in print. Most boxing reporters avoided him. But in his *Look* magazine profile of Jacobs, Dan Parker wrote that Carbo could frequently be seen in Uncle Mike's office. An informant told the FBI that Jacobs would have preferred not to deal with Carbo, but the promoter couldn't evade the mobster since he lorded over the best middleweights and some very talented lightweights and heavyweights. Quite simply, Jacobs needed Carbo's fighters on his card, and Carbo could demand just about anything he wanted from him. Carbo liked to brag that he did everything for Uncle Mike except sign the fight contracts.[32]

Their relationship grew out of mutual necessity. But "not even Jacobs was immune from Carbo's wrath if he thought he'd been crossed," Dan Parker wrote. The reporter recounted a story that could have come straight out of the pages of Budd Schulberg's novel *The Harder They Fall*. After some undisclosed dispute, Carbo appeared in Uncle Mike's office "with murder in his eyes," his jaw clenched, demanding to see the promoter. Jacobs's secretary, Rose Cohen, trembled when Carbo laid a pistol on her desk and covered it with a handkerchief. Fearing for her life, she phoned a barbershop where she knew Frank Costello, the boss of the Luciano crime family, took his morning shave. Costello's relationship with Jacobs has never been documented, but it's likely that the city's gambling czar, a man who bet on virtually every sporting event at the Garden, knew the promoter quite well. Soon after Rose dialed the barbershop, Costello rushed into Jacobs's office, "his face still streaked with lather," shouting at Carbo in Italian. Rose did not know what Costello said, but he convinced Carbo to leave without firing his gun.[33]

Mr. Gray didn't have to bludgeon Mike Jacobs to snatch the keys to the Garden. The promoter had a series of health crises. In November 1946, he suffered a stroke that left his face partially paralyzed and his speech impaired. Then, on December 3, he was visiting a friend at the Capitol Theatre Building on Broadway when his knees buckled. Jacobs collapsed into his friend's arms. Suffering a cerebral hemorrhage, the sixty-six-year-old diabetic lay in a hospital bed in a coma for three days. When Jacobs regained consciousness a few days later, he suffered a heart attack. As he was fighting for his life, rumors swirled across "Jacobs Beach," the stretch of pavement on West Forty-Ninth Street between Broadway and Eighth Avenue. In his *New York Daily News* gossip column, Ed Sullivan wrote, "Friends say Mike Jacobs' heart attack was caused by his inability to fight off mobster demands."[34]

About a week after Jacobs entered Saint Clare's Hospital, Joe Louis visited him. No matter what critics said about the promoter, the champ considered Jacobs one of his best friends. He knew that the sport's future—and his own—remained in grave doubt, teetering on the brink with Uncle Mike's every labored breath. There were no legitimate heavyweight contenders who could challenge him, certainly none who could inspire a major payday. No one knew whether Jacobs would fully recover or who would run the show in his place, though Frankie Carbo certainly had his own ideas.[35]

WHILE MIKE JACOBS LANGUISHED IN A NEW YORK HOSPITAL BED, Joe Louis prepared to give the most important civil rights speech of his life. On December 16, 1946, the Southern Conference for Human Welfare, an interracial organization of New Dealers aiming "to restore democracy below the Mason-Dixon Line," held an honorary dinner for him at the Waldorf Astoria on Park Avenue.[36]

After the lynchings of several Black veterans, Louis joined the Southern Conference's campaign for a "New Dixie," calling for an end to racial violence. Although he remembered little about growing up in a windowless shack on the edge of an Alabama cotton patch, touring military bases during the war he experienced the misery Black folks endured in the Deep South. Working with the Southern Conference, Joe said "he wanted to do something for a better South." He believed in the liberal organization's postwar goals: eliminating the poll tax and expanding voting rights for Black citizens, establishing a permanent Fair Employment Practices Committee, desegregating the US Army, and passing a federal anti-lynching law. He donated his time to the campaign, recorded radio announcements, posed for publicity pictures, and appeared at rallies, urging his fans to march in the fight for freedom and donate money to the "Lend-a-Hand-to-Dixieland" fund drive.[37]

At the honorary banquet held on the Waldorf's Starlight Roof, toastmaster Frank Sinatra paid tribute to his good friend, "a great fighter, a great American, and a great humanitarian." Standing before an interracial audience of activists, veterans, journalists, and entertainers, Louis delivered a powerful speech. Reflecting on his experience in a segregated army and the countless slights he endured because of the color of his skin, he declared, "I hate Jim Crow. I hate disease. I hate the poll tax. I hate seeing people kept down because they are colored. I am not going to let this hate stay in my system, but I am going to help people fight Jim Crow and try to make this a better America. I am going to try to keep my punch in the ring as well as out of the ring."[38]

That night he thought about his fellow Black veterans and the horrific violence inflicted upon Isaac Woodard and the two Black couples lynched in Georgia at Moore's Ford Bridge. Louis urged Black Americans to fight for voting rights and demand full citizenship. When critics tried to stuff him back into his place—*stick to sports, champ*—Louis replied, "Lots of people think that I'm doing all right as a fighter and that I should stick to my business. They mean all right, but they don't understand that fighting prejudice, disease, and second-class citizenship is my business too."[39]

For years, Louis dreaded public speaking. Self-conscious about his childhood stammer and his Southern drawl, during the early years of his career he was reluctant to voice his views on civil rights. Insecure about saying the wrong thing in front of more educated people, Louis didn't trust white writers, who often quoted him in dialect and made him sound ignorant. His silence around civil rights during the 1930s later provoked unfair charges that he was an accommodationist—or worse, an Uncle Tom. However, although he was not known for joining civil rights marches or public protests, Louis meaningfully contributed to the Black Freedom Movement. Immediately after the war, he urged Black Americans—and white ones, as well—to support the NAACP, the Southern Conference, and the United Negro and Allied Veterans of America. He raised money for all those organizations so that they could fight injustice and inequality.

Equally important, before any other prominent Black athlete, Louis demonstrated how they could use their fame to advance the civil rights movement. Writing in *The People's Voice*, a Harlem newspaper aimed at Black readers, sportswriter Rick Hurt recognized that the champ's activism marked a new day for Black athletes becoming more politically outspoken. "The days when athletes were pure athletes who had neither the time nor inclination to speak out against social problems is gone," he wrote. "For a good example of an athlete who is using his great prestige and position to further the cause of the American Negro in the relentless fight toward full democracy[,] some of our head-in-the-sand [athletes] might give a look to Joe Louis, American."[40]

Yet, Joe's political activities with leftist groups during the late 1940s convinced the FBI that he supported communists—a blatantly false accusation. When the Cold War began, FBI director J. Edgar Hoover, a boxing fan who had once proclaimed Louis a great patriot, firmly believed that Black activists were "dupes of the Communist Party." Furthermore, during the Second Red Scare, the House Un-American Activities Committee, through its hearings and published reports, popularized the idea that civil rights organizations were fronts for the Communist Party. Against that backdrop, Joe's involvement with the Southern Conference and the United Negro and Allied Veterans of America—both identified as communist front organizations by the Justice Department—raised suspicions at the Bureau about his political motives. Furthermore, his personal admiration for and his public appearances with Paul

Robeson, a vocal supporter of the Soviet Union and one of the most outspoken Black men in the country, indicated to the FBI, if not to anyone who really knew Joe Louis, that the boxer had aligned himself with disloyal subversives.[41]

Paul Robeson, however, recognized that the real Joe Louis was a great patriot, a loyal American who defended his country and sincerely believed in its democratic ideals even when the government failed to defend the Black men and women who fought for freedom abroad and at home. During World War II, Louis appeared with Robeson at rallies before thousands of people in Detroit and Chicago, calling for interracial goodwill and urging Black citizens to support the Allies by purchasing war bonds. Time and time again, during the war, Louis reminded the public how much Black folks loved America, how they were willing to bleed and die, if necessary, for their freedoms and the freedoms of subjugated people overseas. For Robeson, there wasn't any question that Louis was a real hero, the people's champion. "Our Joe," Robeson wrote, was "of the Negro people and has shown awareness of their problems and struggles. He is of labor, for he worked in the cotton fields of Alabama and in the auto industry in Detroit. But more important than this," he concluded, "he is of America."[42]

Epilogue

THE FINAL ROUND

> Joe Louis is a living tribute to the democratic ideal.
>
> —Frank Sinatra, May 1947

THE PHONE KEPT RINGING, BUT JOE DIDN'T ANSWER. HE WAS slumped in a cushioned parlor chair, numbed with shame. Nothing could make him move. On a cold, blustery day in December 1947, Louis hid inside his eighth-floor apartment on Edgecombe Avenue in Harlem, mourning the loss of his invincibility. His face ached, disfigured by puffed lips, a lacerated left cheek, and a swollen left eyelid. A few nights earlier, after slugging it out with Joe Walcott for fifteen rounds at the Garden, the champ returned to his dressing room victorious, though he felt defeated, his pride bruised worse than his purple cheekbones.[1]

No one, especially Louis, believed that Walcott, a ten-to-one underdog, could beat him. In his long, unremarkable career, the thirty-three-year-old challenger's greatest claim to fame was that he had supposedly knocked down Louis during a 1936 sparring session—but the truth was that Louis had decked Walcott. The former middleweight journeyman who had all but quit boxing during the war, save for a few small-time bouts, entered the match against Louis with a mediocre record that included thirteen losses.

THE FIGHT OF HIS LIFE

In 1945, Felix Bocchicchio, a corrupt manager with ties to Frankie Carbo, lured Walcott out of a shipyard job, resurrecting him from the "scrap heap" of professional boxers. Two years later, on the eve of his fight with Louis, reporters fashioned the unknown contender into a "Brown Cinderella Man" making a dramatic comeback from the depths of the Great Depression and World War II.[2]

From the opening bell it appeared that Walcott had a shot at one of the greatest upsets in boxing history. Louis looked bored, lethargic, and uninspired, moving "slower than a peg legged man crossing a swamp," John McNulty wrote. In the first round, Walcott stunned Louis with a right to the jaw that knocked him down. Walcott leveled him again in the fourth. As the fight continued, Walcott landed more punches while Louis struggled to strike back. "Louis never looked worse in his entire ring career," Grantland Rice lamented. Convinced he had the match won on points, in the final rounds Walcott avoided the champ. After the final bell rang, Louis began exiting the ring in disgust, certain he had lost until his cornermen stopped him. If he left before the decision was announced, he would be automatically disqualified. When the scorecards were read and the crowd learned that Louis had retained the title on a split decision, fight fans booed the ringside judges, shouting that Walcott had been robbed. Standing in the middle of the ring, Louis told Walcott, "I'm sorry, Joe." Later, when reporters asked him about apologizing to his opponent, he explained, "I meant that I was sorry for him because he thought he had won."[3]

Over the next few days, Louis stayed in his apartment, refusing all phone calls. But the phone kept ringing and ringing until Joe finally answered a call. He picked up the receiver and said, "I ain't seein' nobody."

Undeterred, Barney Nagler, a diminutive, owlish-looking reporter for the *Bronx Home News*, insisted, "It won't take long."

The Final Round

"I'm tired." Louis sighed.

"I'll be right up," Nagler urged.

Louis told him to come alone. "Don't bring any of them other fellows."

A half hour later, sitting across from Nagler in a darkened room, Louis avoided eye contact with him. He hadn't bothered to shave his sore, stubbled face for days, and he was still wearing a striped black-and-white robe over his pajamas. The scarred champion appeared pensive and broken, contemplating his future and the doubts that weighed on him like a loaded rucksack.

Nagler asked him about Walcott. With the false bravado of an old fighter trying to convince himself that he still had the magic, Louis told Nagler that he wasn't finished in the ring—at least not yet. Joe added, "Next time, I'll knock him out." Then he stunned the reporter. "I'll beat him and retire."

"You're kidding, Joe."

"I mean it. I'm through after Walcott. It'll be my last fight."

"When did you decide that?"

"Just now, sitting here alone, I come to think of it."

When Nagler pressed him further, Louis maintained that he would not change his mind. A long silence followed. Nagler peered at the door, knowing that he had a scoop that he couldn't protect for very long. The reporter rose from his chair and shook Louis's hand, eager to return to the Bronx newsroom. He picked up his coat and hat, looked over his shoulder, and bid Joe farewell.

Later that day, the *Bronx Home News* printed Nagler's story under a banner headline: "LOUIS SAYS HE'LL RETIRE AFTER JUNE FIGHT."[4]

The champion had something to prove. Determined to end his reign in triumph, King Joe was as certain as Richard Wright that no man would ever wear his crown.[5]

THE FIGHT OF HIS LIFE

"I THOUGHT I HAD HIM," THE CHALLENGER SIGHED AFTER THE rematch. On a sultry June night in 1948, after needling and hammering the champion, Joe Walcott ran into the King's fist. In the early rounds, the contender "feinted, slapped, cuffed and jabbed Louis dizzy." Walcott clobbered him to the canvas in the third, but Louis quickly rose to his feet. Ahead on points, Walcott coasted in the middle rounds, boring a restless Yankee Stadium crowd that grew tired of watching the combatants throw light jabs like two novices. Several times during the dull bout, referee Frank Fullum urged them to fight like it mattered. Finally, late in the eleventh round, Louis came alive, staggering Walcott with a right to the jaw. For twenty seconds, the champ looked young again. Louis pinned his opponent against the ropes and unleashed a destructive torrent of head shots that floored Walcott. Dazed, Jersey Joe crawled across the canvas and "began to grope like a man suddenly blinded," unable to rise before Fullum counted him out. After successfully defending his title once again, Joe stood in the center of the ring, his right arm raised in glory as "the undisputed Monarch of Fistiana."[6]

Around midnight, after Yankee Stadium emptied, Bill Nunn, the managing editor of the *Pittsburgh Courier*, began punching the keys of his typewriter in a haze of cigar smoke, drafting a sentimental open letter to the champ. A longtime friend of Joe Louis, Nunn credited him for bringing "honor and dignity" to a sports racket that had "degenerated into a tank-town act for Negro fighters." As a source of inspiration for Black Americans, Louis became "a symbol of better days to come." Before his ascendance, Black folks "had little to cheer for. But you gave them the courage" and "the feeling of belonging."[7]

Reflecting on the champion's legacy beyond the ring, Nunn wrote that during World War II, Louis emerged as a "shining example of a REAL AMERICAN" hero who changed the way white people viewed Black citizens. "You made white America realize that Negroes were Americans, too. You let them see that Negroes had feelings . . . had patriotism . . . had loyalty . . . had decency . . . had a sense of honor." Nunn added, "You shamed White America into realizing that they had to do better by their 'forgotten tenth.'" Throughout his career, despite being taunted and insulted by white opponents who denigrated him for being Black, Louis remained composed, unwilling to let hatred poison his heart. Instead of retaliating before or after a match, he "turned the other cheek" and "returned good for evil." But that didn't stop him from fighting for equality outside the ring.[8]

IN THE SPRING OF 1948, A FEW MONTHS BEFORE LOUIS FOUGHT Walcott in their rematch, the heavyweight champion joined the growing movement for ending racial segregation in the United States military. While Congress debated legislation involving peacetime conscription and universal military training, union organizer and civil rights leader A. Philip Randolph encouraged Black Americans to join him in nonviolent protests against the military's racist policies. Testifying before the Senate Armed Services Committee, Randolph declared that he would lead Black Americans who dared to resist the draft rather than serve in a segregated army. Backing Randolph's call for civil disobedience, Louis issued a public statement criticizing the army's systematic discrimination against Black servicemen and service women. His telegram, provided to the Senate committee by Randolph himself, read, "It is time that we veterans who suffered while in uniform the humiliations of jimcrow Army barracks, and even jimcrow telephone booths," as Louis experienced in Alabama, "rise up in every corner of the land and say, in one massive voice, 'This shall not happen to our younger brothers.'" Furthermore, Louis urged "every member of Congress to insist upon a full program of civil rights to be included in any draft law so that Negroes in uniform of the United States may be protected from mob violence, police brutality, and indignities."[9]

Publicizing the endorsement from Louis, the most famous Black veteran, added greater weight to the pressure civil rights activists exerted on President Harry Truman to end racial segregation in the armed services. Although Truman, the grandson of slave owners, was raised in Independence, Missouri, a Confederate town that abhorred abolitionism, Abraham Lincoln, and Reconstruction, mob attacks on Black World War II veterans moved him to act, knowing it would cost him support among white Southern Democrats. "My stomach turned over when I learned that Negro soldiers, just back from overseas, were being dumped out of army trucks in Mississippi and beaten," Truman said. "Whatever my inclinations as a native of Missouri might have been, as president I know this is bad. I shall fight to end evils like this."[10]

In response to the lynchings of Black GIs, in 1946 Truman formed the President's Committee on Civil Rights to investigate racial violence and develop legislative proposals for strengthening the rights of Black citizens. A year later, he became the first president to address the NAACP. Standing in the shadow of the Lincoln Memorial, he voiced support for federal action against lynching, ending the poll tax, and eradicating racial discrimination in employment and education. "It is my deep conviction that we have reached a turning point in the long history of our country's efforts to guarantee freedom and equality to all our citizens," he declared.[11]

Convinced that adopting a progressive civil rights platform was a moral imperative that would garner crucial support from Black voters in his reelection bid, on July 26, 1948, he issued Executive Order 9981. Although the order is often remembered for effectively ending segregation in the US military, it did not explicitly state that the armed services would desegregate or integrate. Rather, the president's vaguely worded directive stated: "For all those who serve in our country's defense . . . there shall be equality of treatment and opportunity for all persons in the armed services without regard to race, color, religion or national origin." When questioned about the order, however, President Truman made clear that he expected the armed forces to end racial segregation, though he never provided a concrete timeline for the process. He established the President's Committee on Equality of Treatment and Opportunity in the armed services to recommend revisions for the military to implement the policy. It would take six years for the United States military to fully dissolve all segregated units.[12]

AFTER FIGHTING PROFESSIONALLY FOR NEARLY TWELVE YEARS AND successfully defending his title an unprecedented twenty-five times, Joe Louis knew the time had come to hang up the gloves. On March 1, 1949, the thirty-four-year-old champion retired. He planned to work for the International Boxing Club (IBC), a newly formed promotional organization established by sports magnates James D. Norris and Arthur Wirtz. For months, Louis and Truman Gibson, who now worked as Joe's attorney, considered how they could profit from the sale and promotion of the heavyweight title. Harry Mendel, a press agent working with Louis, suggested that they pitch Norris, whose family properties included major boxing venues in the Midwest (Chicago Stadium, Detroit's Olympia Stadium, and the St. Louis Arena). Norris and Wirtz also held a sizable interest in Madison Square Garden. After a series of meetings, Louis and Gibson struck a deal with Norris and Wirtz that fundamentally changed the business of boxing. Under the agreement, the champion would obtain exclusive promotional contracts with the top four heavyweight contenders. Then Louis would formally vacate the heavyweight title and assign control of the exclusive contracts to the IBC. In exchange, Norris and Wirtz paid Louis $150,000 cash and an annual salary of $15,000—plus shares in IBC stock. In the coming months, Norris and Wirtz acquired the rights to promote boxing matches at Yankee Stadium and the Polo Grounds in New York. With full control over the heavyweight title and several major sports arenas, the IBC now owned the most valuable assets in boxing.[13]

Joe's announcement stunned Mike Jacobs. His deal with the IBC pushed Uncle Mike out of business. "I'm through with promoting," Jacobs told a reporter in Miami. "I guess it looks like I'll have to retire." Since suffering a cerebral hemorrhage that left him hospitalized for sixty days, rendering him "a semi-invalid," Jacobs had no choice but to turn over the daily operations of the Twentieth Century Sporting Club to his cousin Sol Strauss, an attorney who had worked alongside him for years. But once Louis sold the promotional rights of the heavyweight title, Jacobs knew he could not compete with the IBC. After Norris and Wirtz increased their holdings in Madison Square Garden, they bought out Jacobs's Twentieth Century Sporting Club and his exclusive contract with Sugar Ray Robinson. In return, Jacobs agreed not to promote any more boxing matches. Four years later, in January 1953, after spending the day at a Florida racetrack, Jacobs suffered a heart attack and died. The promoter bitterly complained that he had made no friends in the boxing business. But after he passed away, Louis mourned the loss of "his closest friend." Jacobs "did more for me than any man in the world," he said.[14]

Although Louis was supposed to help the IBC promote matches, he showed virtually no interest in the job. Yet Norris treated him like a valuable business partner despite Louis offering no real value to the organization, other than his name. While Joe struggled to pay his bills, the IBC's founding partner kept him on the payroll.

Norris was "about the only man who has given Joe anything more than sympathy, and one of the few men who has given to him rather than taken from him," Ed Linn wrote in *Sport* magazine.[15]

As much as Norris enjoyed the prestige that came with being seen with Joe Louis, he was equally attracted to mobsters, and especially Frankie Carbo. The alliance between Norris and Carbo developed out of mutual interest. They had known each other for years, crossing paths at racetracks and sporting arenas. As the proprietor of several stadiums, Norris relied on Carbo to arrange matches. Carbo delivered a steady stream of compliant fighters who didn't dare cross him. If the fighters—and their managers— refused to cooperate with the IBC, then Carbo forced their hand. By the early 1950s, the Norris–Wirtz–Carbo triumvirate had firmly established a monopoly over professional boxing, holding exclusive contracts with virtually every champion and contender above the bantamweight division. And it was all made possible when Joe Louis sold the one piece of himself that no one man could take away from him in the ring: the heavyweight title.[16]

A FEW WEEKS BEFORE JOE ANNOUNCED HIS RETIREMENT FROM boxing, he signed divorce papers for a second time. He and Marva had remarried in July 1946, but his ongoing affairs and his frequent disappearances from their home made it impossible for Marva to remain married to him. Worse, she said, he hardly spent any time with their two young children. "He seemed to prefer a hotel suite to home and would drop by to see me as if I was his girlfriend and we were courting. Half the time I didn't hardly know where he was—only what I'd read in the papers," she said.[17]

Marva was as tired of reading about his rumored romances as much as Lena Horne detested gossip columnists intimating that they would now get back together. In June 1949, four months after the Louis divorce, an Acme News Agency photographer snapped a picture of Joe and Lena sitting close together and smiling on a piano bench at Chicago's Blackstone Hotel. Married to MGM musical director Lennie Hayton, Lena firmly dismissed reports that she was having another fling with Joe. Despite the rumors, Joe and Lena would remain friends. Since Joe was unattached, *Ebony* magazine proclaimed the former champion "Negro America's most eligible bachelor, with everything a woman wants—money, fame, and virile manhood." Undoubtedly Joe possessed fame and virility, but his money was all gone.[18]

In 1950 his financial problems deepened after an IRS audit concluded with a bill for nearly $250,000 in back taxes. After reviewing his past returns, the agency disallowed wartime deductions for expenses Louis had claimed related to his profession. Making matters worse, he mismanaged funds he was supposed to shelter under Joe Louis Enterprises, Inc., a dummy corporation set up in December 1947. The purpose of the corporation, explained his accountant Theodore Jones, was to administer various sources of income and "assist in liquidating the liabilities of Joe Louis." However, Louis not only incorporated himself, but he also borrowed more than his salary from the corporation. For years, Joe spent far more money than he made, and he invested in several failed business ventures, including a Harlem restaurant, a Chicago nightclub, a Detroit chicken shack, and a soft drink called Joe Louis Punch. By the mid-1950s, after calculating interest and penalties, the IRS determined that he owed the federal government more than $1 million, an enormous debt for a man with no meaningful employment to help erase it.[19]

Convinced that returning to the ring was the only way he could settle his tax debt, Louis announced his comeback in the summer of 1950. He began training immediately for a fight against Ezzard Charles, the twenty-nine-year-old heavyweight champion who had

The Final Round

defeated Joe Walcott in the elimination tournament. Fighting for the first time in more than two years, Louis took a severe beating in front of a paltry Yankee Stadium crowd. "There was old Joe," Gene Ward wrote in the *New York Daily News*, "his face splattered with the gore from his bashed-in nose . . . his left eye shut . . . his knees buckling. He looked like a stricken, confused bull." Humiliated in the second loss of his career, Louis wept in the ring after the judges returned a unanimous decision for Charles.[20]

When it was over, Joe returned to his dressing room, where he soaked his left hand in an ice bucket. Pressing ice bags against his battered jaw, he mumbled short answers when reporters questioned him. Sugar Ray Robinson recalled the pain on Joe's disfigured face that night. "In his dressing room . . . blood seeped from cuts above each of his eyes. One of his eyes was swollen shut. I was in there with him but it was like trying to console an old blind man." Joe's body ached so much that he could hardly dress himself. "I bent down and worked his feet into his big shoes and tied the laces," Robinson said. When Louis left the ballpark, he vowed that he would never step into the ring again.[21]

Drowning in debt, he could not keep his promise. And he couldn't relinquish his dream of beating Ezzard Charles and recapturing the heavyweight title. In 1951, he fought eight times, despite warnings from his doctor that he risked severe brain damage every time he stepped into the ring. Nonetheless, after Charles lost the title to Joe Walcott in July, Louis agreed to a match with the IBC's top heavyweight contender: Rocky Marciano. The Italian-American slugger hailed from Brockton, a rough-and-tumble blue-collar town in Massachusetts. In a sport dominated by Black heavyweights, he became enormously popular especially with white working-class fans, who admired the blunt force of his punches and his ability to take a blow on the chin. The Rock had a "fearless, unbridled instinct for the attack."[22]

THE FIGHT OF HIS LIFE

Although Louis entered the match at Madison Square Garden a modest betting favorite, veteran sportswriters doubted that "a deteriorating fighter" who was ten years older than Marciano could withstand the Rock's raw power. Louis started the fight strong, but in the middle rounds Marciano began to punish him. In the eighth Rocky floored him with a devastating left hook. Two seconds before the referee reached a ten count, Joe rose to his feet, dazed and staggered. Marciano pressed him against the ropes and clubbed him with a series of lefts before cutting him down with an overhand right that sent Louis toppling backward like "a big jack pine." Marciano's right knocked him through the ropes onto the ring apron. Joe crumpled; he lay on the canvas with his right leg dangling on the bottom rope. It was all over. On October 26, 1951, at precisely 10:36 p.m., his career ended.[23]

Whatever thrill or power Joe Louis once felt in the ring was long gone. He was once the greatest heavyweight champion who had ever lived, but he could no longer hold onto the glories of the past. Nor could the people who loved him. His family, friends, and longtime fans could not stand to watch him suffer as another man bludgeoned him over a paycheck. He could still fight for money, Jimmy Cannon thought, but it had always seemed that Louis fought for something more—that he stood for something more. "That's why you affected people so," Cannon wrote. "You can't help it if a whole lot of people feel lousy every time you fight. But they do. They do."[24]

A FEW MONTHS AFTER EXITING THE BOXING RING FOR THE LAST time, Joe Louis began what he called "the biggest fight of [his] life." In January 1952, a local Chevrolet sponsor of the San Diego Open invited Joe to play as an amateur in a Professional Golfers' Association (PGA) tournament. But when Louis arrived for the tournament, PGA officials informed him that only members of "the Caucasian race" could compete. Outraged, Louis told reporters that he had never experienced such blatant racial discrimination in sports. He urged local officials to call off the event unless Black golfers could participate. Using language most sportswriters had not heard from him before, he attacked PGA president Horton Smith, calling him "another Hitler." "Horton Smith believes in the white race like Hitler believed in the super-race," Louis fumed.[25]

An avid golfer with a two handicap, he had grown obsessed with the game. "There is nothing in sports right now that I love more than playing golf," he told a reporter. For years, whenever he wasn't training, Louis had swung his clubs from sunrise to sunset. Popularizing the sport, in August 1941, he sponsored the Joe Louis Open in Detroit, an event disrupted by the war. On furloughs, Joe often played golf, as did many Black servicemen. "During and after the war," noted golf historian George Kirsch, "black soldiers and sailors enjoyed more access to courses on military bases, while black middle-class citizens joined a growing number of private (although still segregated) clubs." In the aftermath of the war, Black golfers increasingly campaigned for access to municipal courses across the South and pressed the PGA for opportunities to compete in professional tournaments. This history contributed to Louis's stand. When the PGA drew the color line against him in San Diego, he decided that he would expose the officials who sanctioned segregation and force them to justify their racist decision.[26]

While Black and white soldiers fought together in the Korean War, Joe and his allies in the press framed the PGA's segregationist policy as wholly un-American. Louis called syndicated columnist Walter Winchell, who blasted the PGA on his enormously popular national radio show. Winchell told his listeners, "If Joe Louis could carry a gun in the U.S. Army he could carry a golf club in San Diego." Citing Joe's patriotic service record during the Second World War, *Washington Post* columnist Shirley Povich praised Louis for challenging the PGA's "Caucasians only" policy. It was absurd, Povich added, that the PGA would maintain the color line when it had been erased across most professional sports, including the US Lawn Tennis Association, which had allowed Althea Gibson to compete in the National Championships at Forrest Hills in 1950.[27]

Joe's friend Jimmy Cannon bristled, "I'm burned up good about Louis getting humiliated out in San Diego." The syndicated columnist denounced the hypocrisy of the PGA, an American sports organization that denied Louis and other Black men the opportunity to play "a silly game like golf," after the US Army had relied on Joe, "a soldier," during the Second World War. Cannon tried to imagine the frustration Louis felt as a Black man in a segregated country. "What must Louis and [other Black citizens] think when they see the flag and know what it stands for doesn't go for them and they got to go in the back door and plead for what most of us take for granted." Cannon continued, "If I was a Negro and I found out what [the PGA] did to Joe Louis I'd have to believe I'm an outcast in my homeland." Furthermore, he wrote, "the Louis story will get bigger play in Russia than it does here. Why shouldn't it? They're our enemies and it makes us a pack of liars when we brag about freedom for all."[28]

Just as he planned, Joe's protest sparked national outrage against the PGA. The tournament received an "avalanche of telegrams and letters" objecting to his exclusion from the San Diego Open. Hoping to defuse the situation, Horton Smith flew to San Diego and announced that the PGA's executive committee had agreed to provide Louis an exemption as an amateur guest of the tournament's sponsors. However, Bill Spiller, the only Black pro who qualified for the tournament, was not permitted to play. Smith explained that Spiller was rejected because the PGA's bylaws did not permit Black members. In other words, the PGA had no intention of changing its rules for Spiller or any other Black professional. But since Joe Louis was *Joe Louis* and an amateur, the PGA could make an exception since he was invited by the co-sponsoring committee.[29]

Louis did not hesitate to play the San Diego Open. He even shook hands with Horton Smith. Despite Black critics charging that he had surrendered to the all-white PGA by playing without Spiller, Louis believed that breaking the color line in professional golf would add greater pressure on the organization to change its rules. He argued that being the first Black golfer to play in a PGA event would "open the tournament doors to other qualified Negro golfers," knowing that this was just the opening round in an ongoing fight. Although the PGA did not repeal its Caucasian-only clause until 1961, Joe's battle for equality in San Diego forced the organization to grant him and three Black pros the opportunity to play a week later in the Phoenix Open. His efforts led to more exemptions for Black golfers seeking admission to PGA tournaments in the coming years.[30]

Pittsburgh Courier columnist Wendell Smith wrote that white sportswriters "expressed great surprise when [Louis] took such a militant stand" against the PGA. But Smith and other Black journalists had known since the Second World War that Louis did not waver whenever he was confronted with bigotry. "He has always been a fighter for racial equality," Smith wrote. "He has always been an ardent advocate for equal rights in this country." Louis did not go looking for trouble, but when he found it, he "put up his dukes and fought back in no uncertain manner."[31]

Smith explained that although many Americans did not see Louis as a rebel or an activist, he had defended the dignity of Black soldiers during the Second World War on numerous occasions, though his actions rarely received publicity. Joe said that he never viewed himself as "a spokesman for the whole Negro race," but his exalted position in Black America—and his prominent role in the US Army—compelled him to challenge the mistreatment of Black servicemen. His experience in the war convinced him that the country could not accept racism in any form, whether it was in the US Army or in American sports.[32]

In his column about Joe's battle against the PGA, Smith traced his stand to World War II. He told a story that Louis had shared with him, but hardly anyone knew about it except the Black soldiers who had seen the champ in England. One time, during his exhibition tour in Great Britain, Louis arrived early at a stadium where he was scheduled to appear. Joe noticed hundreds of white soldiers entering the arena while a group of Black GIs stood outside. When he asked the Black GIs if they had tickets, one of them answered, "We can't go in. This is supposed to be off limits for Negro soldiers. We were just standing here so we could get a look at you when you arrived."[33]

Infuriated, Louis told the Black soldiers not to leave. He had a plan.

Thirty minutes passed and Joe still had not entered the ring. The white servicemen sitting inside the stadium were growing impatient, clapping and shouting, "We want Louis! We want Louis!"

Searching for the champ, a special service officer found him sitting in the dressing room still wearing his army uniform. "Come on, Joe," he urged, "get dressed. It's time for you to go on."

Joe told him that he would not enter the ring until the Black soldiers outside the arena were admitted. Fearing an explosive situation, the officer left and returned with the commanding officer, a general, who ordered Joe to put on his boxing trunks and get in the ring.

The Final Round

Sergeant Louis refused.

The general could see that Joe was adamant about his position. The champ wasn't going to smile and shuffle for a bunch of white soldiers while his Black brethren were denigrated and denied admission.

Anxious to avoid an ugly confrontation, the general gave another order: "Admit the Negro soldiers."

Louis dressed and marched to the ring with his head held high. The crowd erupted when the great patriot appeared. America's champion had won again.

ACKNOWLEDGMENTS

Occasionally, writing a book feels as if one is stranded on an island. Most of the time we work alone, traveling to archives, thumbing through documents no one has read in decades (if ever), sitting in front of a computer laboring to write exactly what we mean. But there are times when a larger group of collaborators—agents, publishers, editors, archivists, librarians, colleagues, and friends—come to the rescue. Melissa Chinchillo of the United Talent Agency, our longtime advocate, found a splendid publisher for our book. This is our fourth collaboration published by Basic Books, and we have enjoyed our time with the dedicated people who work there. Lara Heimert remains a jewel, encouraging, supportive, and always there when you need her, even when she is out of the country. Editor Brandon Proia, who does the delicate work of telling us when we are not saying what we mean to say—or not saying it well enough—accomplished his duties with grace and tact. The rest of the team at Basic Books, especially Kristen Kim, performed with thoughtful professionalism and did so with a smile that radiated across a phone or in an email. Many thanks to Melissa Veronesi, who always kept us organized and on task throughout the production process.

We are especially grateful for the many people who assisted us with our research. Our graduate students Brett Russler and Eric Steagall helped us investigate various newspaper archives. At the Library of Congress, librarian Amber Paranick once again helped us access reels of newspapers on microfilm. The outstanding staff at the National Archives, especially Eric Van Slander, Theresa Fitzgerald, and Katherine Terry, helped us track down various military records. We appreciate the archivists and librarians who answered our questions and copied primary source material on our behalf at the following institutions: the Library of Congress Manuscript Division; the Beinecke Rare Book and Manuscript Library at Yale University; the Bentley Historical Library at the University of Michigan; the Franklin D. Roosevelt Library and Museum in Hyde Park, New York; the Schomburg Center for Research in Black Culture; the National World War II Museum; and the Chicago History Museum.

We consulted dozens of books in our research, but none proved more indispensable than Matthew Delmont's *Half American: The Epic Story of African Americans Fighting World War II at Home and Abroad*. Matt's research and insights about the experiences of Black Americans during the war years helped us better understand the world of Joe Louis and his role in the military.

We also wish to thank our favorite reader Aram Goudsouzian for providing constructive feedback on the manuscript. Aram is always reliable, enthusiastic, and encouraging.

Our home universities have provided great support for our research and writing. Purdue University, Randy Roberts's home for more than thirty-five years, remains an ideal place to write and teach history. David Reingold, dean of liberal arts, is a pillar of support, helpful in every way. Similarly, history department head Frederick Rowe Davis has ensured that Randy has the time to travel and write. Finally, he wishes to thank the provost's office for providing funds through his 150th Anniversary Professorship.

At Georgia Tech, the School of History and Sociology funded research for Johnny Smith. He is especially thankful to Kaye Husbands Fealing, dean of Ivan Allen College of Liberal Arts, for making it possible for the Tech library to acquire the ProQuest

Acknowledgments

Historical Black Newspapers database, an essential source for writing this book. Johnny is grateful for the tireless effort of Glenna Barney and the interlibrary loan staff. He also wishes to thank the family of Bud Shaw for endowing a professorship in the history of sports.

Our two families bring constant joy. Randy's daughters, Kelly and Alison, and his son-in-law, Corey Chambliss, all voracious readers, made him smile when they occasionally asked about the book. His wife, Marjie, supports him in every way possible, and he loves her more than she will ever know. And although the world's greatest dog Coco is gone, his presence is still keenly felt.

Johnny's daughter Madison is just beginning to learn how to read, but she appreciates a good story and asks lots of questions about Muhammad Ali and Joe Louis. She often tells her dad, "someday you are going to be a famous writer." That may be doubtful, but her belief in her father heartens him. Johnny's wife, Rebecca, inspires him with her kindness, generosity, and boundless love. Her unshakable faith in him means everything.

NOTES

Abbreviations

ADW	*Atlanta Daily World*	NYA	*New York Age*
BAA	*Baltimore Afro-American*	NYAN	*New York Amsterdam News*
BD	*Black Dispatch* (Oklahoma City)	NYDM	*New York Daily Mirror*
		NYDN	*New York Daily News*
BE	*Brooklyn Eagle*	NYHT	*New York Herald Tribune*
BG	*Boston Globe*		
BN	*Buffalo News*	NYP	*New York Post*
CD	*Chicago Defender*	NYT	*New York Times*
CDN	*Chicago Daily News*	NYWT	*New York World-Telegram*
CE	*California Eagle*		
CHA	*Chicago Herald American*	NJG	*Norfolk Journal and Guide*
CT	*Chicago Tribune*	PC	*Pittsburgh Courier*
DW	*Daily Worker*	PI	*Philadelphia Inquirer*
DFP	*Detroit Free Press*	PP	*Pittsburgh Press*
DT	*Detroit Tribune*	PT	*Philadelphia Tribune*
LAT	*Los Angeles Times*	SI	*Sports Illustrated*
MC	*Michigan Chronicle*	WES	*Washington Evening Star*
NARA	National Archives and Records Administration, College Park, Maryland	WP	*Washington Post*

Preface: A Silent Revolutionary

1. Francis X. Clines, "At Arlington, Final Tribute to an American Fighter," *NYT*, April 22, 1981; Barry Lorge and Donald Huff, "Joe Louis: The Champ Rests with U.S. Heroes," *WP*, April 22, 1981.

2. "Louis Burial at Arlington," *NYT*, April 16, 1981; "Statement on the Death of Former World Heavyweight Boxing Champion Joe Louis," April 13, 1981, Ronald Reagan Presidential Library and Museum.

3. "'And Still Heavyweight Champion of the World,'" *DFP*, April 13, 1981.

4. Stephen Tuck, "'You Can Sing and Punch . . . But You Can't Be a Soldier or a Man': African American Struggles for a New Place in Popular Culture," in *Fog Of War: The Second World War and the Civil Rights Movement*, ed. Kevin M. Kruse and Stephen Tuck (Oxford University Press, 2012), 108.

5. Don Deleighbur, "Joe Louis Symbol of Power to Negro GI's," *NJG*, April 20, 1944.

6. W. E. B. Du Bois, *The Souls of Black Folk* (A. C. McClurg & Co., 1903; repr. Dover Publications, 1994), 2.

7. Lorge and Huff, "Joe Louis: The Champ Rests with U.S. Heroes."

8. Gunnar Myrdal, *An American Dilemma: The Negro Problem and Modern Democracy* (Harper and Brothers, 1944); Bob Addie, "Joe Louis, Boxing's 'Brown Bomber,' Dies at 66," *WP*, April 13, 1981; George Puscas, "Joe Louis: He Was More than a Champion," *DFP*, April 13, 1981; George Vecsey, "A Final Ring for Joe Louis," *NYT*, April 17, 1981.

9. Chris Mead, *Joe Louis: Black Champion in White America* (Scribner, 1985; repr. Dover Publications, 2010), 291–292; Matthew Delmont, *Half American: The Epic Story of African Americans Fighting World War II at Home and Abroad* (Viking, 2022), 62–63.

10. Robert L. Miller, "Letter from the Publisher," *SI*, September 16, 1985, 4 (emphasis ours).

Prologue: He Belongs to Us

1. For the report of the death of Max Schmeling, see Max Schmeling, *Max Schmeling: An Autobiography*, trans. George B. von der Lippe (Verlag Ullstein GmbH, 1977; repr. Bonus Books, 1998), 165–168; "Max Schmeling Reported Killed Fleeing Captors," *NYHT*, May 29, 1941.

2. "Max Schmeling Reported Killed Fleeing Captors."

3. "Max Schmeling: Rome Pays Tribute Though Berlin Denies Death," *Corriere Della Sera*, May 29, 1941; "Former Heavyweight Champion Reported Killed in Crete," *Times of India*, May 30, 1941; "Max Schmeling Dead," *South China Morning Post*, May 31, 1941; "'I Hate War,' Baer Says," *NYT*, May 29, 1941.

4. "Louis Shocked by Report of Max Schmeling's Death," *BAA*, June 7, 1941.

5. Margery Miller, *Joe Louis: American* (Current Books/A. A. Wyn, 1945).

6. Richard Wright, "Joe Louis Uncovers Dynamite," *New Masses*, October 8, 1935, 18–19.

7. Chris Mead, *Joe Louis: Black Champion in White America* (Scribner, 1985; repr. Dover Publications, 2010), 100–101.

8. "'Did It Hurt His Nose?' Shouts Worried Marva," *BN*, June 20, 1936.

9. David Margolick, *Beyond Glory: Joe Louis vs. Max Schmeling and a World on the Brink* (Vintage, 2006), 160–161; Langston Hughes, *The Collected Works of Langston Hughes*, vol. 14: *I Wonder as I Wander* (University of Missouri Press, 2001), 307.

10. Lena Horne and Richard Schickel, *Lena* (Doubleday, 1965), 75.

11. Margolick, *Beyond Glory*, 5.

12. Edgar T. Rouzeau, "Rouzeau Gives Glowing Account of Joe's Victory," *PC*, June 25, 1938; "Louis Victory Revives World War Scenes in Hilarious Harlem," *PC*, July 2, 1938.

13. Richard Wright, "High Tide in Harlem: Joe Louis as a Symbol of Freedom," *New Masses*, July 5, 1938, 18.

14. Margolick, *Beyond Glory*, 308.

15. "Max Schmeling Is Alive," *The Star* (Guernsey, Channel Islands), June 5, 1941; "Schmeling Alive, Berlin Announces," *NYT*, May 30, 1941; "Crete Battle 'Tough,' Schmeling Declares," *NYT*, May 31, 1941.

16. Franklin D. Roosevelt, May 27, 1941: Fireside Chat 17: "On an Unlimited National Emergency," transcript, Miller Center, University of Virginia.

17. George B. Murphy Jr. to Henry L. Stimson, Secretary of War, October 6, 1941, letter from Joe Louis military personnel file, Record Group 319, Records of the Army Staff, NARA.

18. "Along the N.A.A.C.P. Battlefront," *The Crisis*, April 1944, 115; Matthew F. Delmont, *Half American: The Epic Story of African Americans Fighting World War II at Home and Abroad* (Viking, 2022), 26–28; John Morton Blum, *V Was for Victory: Politics and American Culture During World War II* (Harcourt Brace Jovanovich, 1976), 184–185.

19. Maggi M. Morehouse, *Fighting in the Jim Crow Army: Black Men and Women Remember World War II* (Rowman & Littlefield, 2000), 3.

20. Joe Louis Barrow Jr. and Barbara Munder, *Joe Louis: 50 Years an American Hero* (McGraw-Hill, 1988), 135.

One: Black Moses

1. Earl Brown, "Joe Louis: The Champion, Idol of His Race, Sets a Good Example of Conduct," *Life*, June 17, 1940, 49, 50; "Sport: Black Moses," *Time*, September 29, 1941, 60–64.

2. Mark Whitaker, *Smoketown: The Untold Story of the Other Black Renaissance* (Simon & Schuster, 2019), 8.

3. Stephen Eschenbach, "Earl Brown: Brief Life of Harvard's Latest Major League Baseball Players," *Harvard Magazine*, March–April 2022, www

Notes to Chapter One

.harvardmagazine.com/2022/02/features-vita-earl-brown; Ebeneezer Ray, "Dottings," *NYA*, June 29, 1940; "Trouble in Harlem," *NYA*, July 20, 1940.

4. "Sport: Black Moses," 60–64.

5. John R. Williams, "Writer of 'Insult Story' on Joe Louis Fired by N.Y. Paper," *PC*, June 29, 1940; "Hits and Bits," *ADW*, July 6, 1940; Lucius "Melancholy" Jones, "Slant on Sports," *ADW*, July 8, 1940.

6. Edward Van Every, *Joe Louis: Man and Super-Fighter* (Frederick A. Stokes, 1936), 1–2.

7. Brown, "Joe Louis," 52, 50.

8. Brown, "Joe Louis," 52, 55.

9. Brown, "Joe Louis," 50–53.

10. Sid Thompson, "Harlem Sketches," *ADW*, July 8, 1940; Jones, "Slant on Sports"; Roi Ottley, *New World A-Coming': Inside Black America* (Houghton Mifflin, 1943), 189.

11. Ebeneezer Ray, "Dottings"; "Trouble in Harlem."

12. Walter White to Earl Brown, June 19, 1940, Box II A405, Folder 3, National Association for the Advancement of Colored People Papers, Library of Congress, Manuscript Division (hereafter NAACP papers).

13. Walter White to Editor, *Life*, June 18, 1940, NAACP papers.

14. John R. Williams, "Article in White Magazine Stirs Champ's Manager," *PC*, June 22, 1940; Russ J. Cowans, "Ridicule of Joe Louis Stirs Manager's Ire," *DT*, June 22, 1940.

15. Joe Louis as told to Meyer Berger and Barney Nagler, "My Story—Joe Louis," *Life*, November 8, 1948, 127.

16. For the MacDonald–McBride saga see, Felicia Bridget George, "Numbers and Neighborhoods: Seeking and Selling the American Dream in Detroit One Bet at a Time" (PhD diss., Wayne State University, 2015), 130–135.

17. George, "Numbers and Neighborhoods," 148–149.

18. Jimmy Powers, "The Power House," *NYDN*, April 25, 1940; Roy Wilkins, "Watchtower," *NYAN*, May 4, 1940.

19. Wendell Smith, "Smitty's Sport Spurts," *PC*, May 11, 1940; W. W. Edgar, "Roxborough the Brains of Joe Louis' Management," *DFP*, April 25, 1940.

20. Gerald Astor, "... *And a Credit to His Race": The Hard Life and Times of Joe Louis Barrow, a.k.a. Joe Louis* (Saturday Review Press/E. P. Dutton, 1974), 32–38; Edgar, "Roxborough the Brains."

21. Edgar Rouzeau, "Roxborough Keeps Joe's Linen Clean," *NJG*, May 11, 1940.

22. George Dixon, "Did the Ring Worms Turn?," *NYDN*, April 8, 1940; "Mike Jacobs Victim of Hold-Up in Home," *NYT*, April 8, 1940.

23. Dan Daniel, interview by Randy Roberts.

24. Daniel M. Daniel, *The Mike Jacobs Story* (The Ring Book Shop, 1950), 28–39; Nat Fleischer, "I Knew Jacobs," *The Ring*, April 1953, 32–34, 49; *The Ring*, May 1953, 32–34; *The Ring*, June 1953, 32–34, 37.

25. David Margolick, *Beyond Glory: Joe Louis vs. Max Schmeling, and a World on the Brink* (Alfred A. Knopf, 2005), 29.

26. Margolick, *Beyond Glory*, 204–213.

27. Art Carter, "Braddock Suit Ends Mystery of 'Cut,'" *BAA*, March 16, 1940; "'Cinderella Man' Does Not Own Part of Joe Louis, Suit Against Mike Jacobs Reveals," *PC*, March 16, 1940; "Mike Says 20G Payment Ended Gould Contract," *NYDN*, March 28, 1940; "Mike Jacobs Sues Joe Gould," *LAT*, March 28, 1940; Harry Grayson, "Jimmy Braddock Was Given Part of Mike Jacobs, Not Joe Louis, as Fight Share," *Iowa Press Citizen*, March 29, 1940; Regis M. Welsh, "Frenzied Finances," *PP*, March 31, 1940; "Joe Gould Halts Suit Against Mike Jacobs," *NYDN*, May 19, 1940; Margolick, *Beyond Glory*, 214.

28. Carter, "Braddock Suit"; "'Cinderella Man'"; "Mike Says"; "Mike Jacobs Sues"; Grayson, "Jimmy Braddock"; Welsh, "Frenzied Finances"; "Joe Gould Halts Suit."

29. Art Carter, "What Does New Year Hold for Champion Joe Louis?," *BAA*, January 6, 1940; Lester Rodney, "A Few Thoughts on Joe Louis' Fight Friday," *DW*, February 5, 1940.

30. Jimmy Powers, "Louis Outpoints Godoy," *NYDN*, February 10, 1940.

31. Caswell Adams, "'No Go Home Now,' Says Godoy, 'I Win Championship Some Day,'" *NYHT*, February 11, 1940; Nat Fleischer, "Godoy Brings Out Joe Louis' Faults," *The Ring*, April 1940, 3–6; "Ratings for the Month," *The Ring*, March 1940, 51; "Ratings for the Month," *The Ring*, April 1940, 49.

32. Richards Vidmer, "Down In Front," *NYHT*, February 11, 1940.

33. Adams, "'No Go Home'"; "Southern Writer Charges Joe 'Carried' Godoy as Build Up for Future Title Bouts," *PC*, February 24, 1940.

34. Ed Harris, "Lonely Joe," *PT*, April 4, 1940.

35. Bob Considine, "Writers Say Joe Has Done All He Can," *PT*, April 11, 1941.

36. Joseph C. Nichols, "Godoy's Stand Acts as Spur to Division," *NYT*, February 11, 1940.

37. Joseph C. Nichols, "Louis Knocks Out Paychek in Second Round at Garden to Keep World Title," *NYT*, March 30, 1940; Nat Fleischer, "The Case of Johnny Paychek," *The Ring*, June 1940, 5; Richard Bak, *Joe Louis: The Great Black Hope* (Da Capo Press, 1998), 180–182.

38. Jack Mahon, "Louis Stops Godoy in 8th," *NYDN*, June 21, 1940; "Louis Pays Tribute to Foe's Courage," *NYT*, June 21, 1940; Sid Feder, "Louis Scores Technical Kayo over Godoy in Eighth Round," *St. Louis Globe-Democrat*, June 21, 1940.

Two: The Campaign

1. "The Presidency: Tenth of June," *Time*, June 17, 1940.
2. Doris Kearns Goodwin, *No Ordinary Time: Franklin and Eleanor Roosevelt: The Home Front in World War II* (Simon & Schuster, 1994), 67; Susan Dunn, *1940: FDR, Willkie, Lindbergh, Hitler—the Election amid the Storm* (Yale University Press, 2013), 39, 45.
3. "Sidelights on Roosevelt's Talk," *WP*, June 11, 1940; "The Presidency: Tenth of June."
4. Hadley Cantril, "Impact of the War on the Nation's Viewpoint," *NYT*, June 2, 1940; "The Text of President Roosevelt's Address at Charlottesville," *NYT*, June 11, 1940.
5. Goodwin, *No Ordinary Time*, 47; Dunn, *1940*, 46–47, 62–63; "Lindbergh Charges War Designs Here," *NYT*, June 16, 1940.
6. Dunn, *1940*, 40–41.
7. "Lynching and Liberty," *The Crisis*, July 1940, 209.
8. Gene Roberts and Hank Klibanoff, *The Race Beat: The Press, The Civil Rights Struggle, and the Awakening of a Nation* (Vintage Books, 2007), 9.
9. "Lynching and Liberty," 209.
10. Joe Louis as told to Ches Washington, "'I'll Be Ready When My Country Calls'—Louis," *PC*, August 24, 1940.
11. Italics ours. See Mark Whitaker, *Smoketown: The Untold Story of the Other Black Renaissance* (Simon & Schuster, 2019), 8, 21–22.
12. Telegram to Roberta Barrows from H.K. [Henry Kannee, White House stenographer], September 23, 1940, Box 13, Official File 300, Franklin D. Roosevelt Papers, Roosevelt Library, Hyde Park, New York (hereafter, FDR Papers).
13. Edwin M. Watson, Secretary to the President, to Julian Rainey, September 25, 1940, Box 13, Official File 300, FDR Papers; David Margolick, *Beyond Glory: Joe Louis vs. Max Schmeling, and a World on the Brink* (Vintage Books, 2005), 97–98; "Joe Louis and Jesse Owens," *The Crisis*, August 1935, 241; "Joe Louis Visits President F.D.R.," *NYAN*, August 31, 1935; "President Felt Joe Louis's Muscle, Told Him He's a Fine-Looking Young Man," *BAA*, September 7, 1935. It appears that the origins of the myth that Louis met FDR on the eve of his fight against Schmeling in 1938 can be traced to an interview Louis gave to Meyer Berger and Barney Nagler for *Life* magazine. See "Joe Louis' Story," as told to Berger and Nagler, *Life*, November 15, 1948, 133.
14. Nancy J. Weiss, *Farewell to the Party of Lincoln: Black Politics in the Age of FDR* (Princeton University Press, 1983), 3–8, 180–235.
15. "The Roosevelt Record," *The Crisis*, November 1940, 343; Leah Wright Rigueur, *The Loneliness of Black Republicans: Pragmatic Politics and the Pursuit of Power* (Princeton University Press, 2015), 13–16.

16. Bernard C. Nalty, *Strength for the Fight: A History of Black Americans in the Military* (The Free Press, 1986), 138–139; Weiss, *Farewell to the Party of Lincoln*, 277; Richard M. Dalfiume, "Military Segregation and the 1940 Presidential Election," *Phylon* 30, no. 1 (1969): 48–52.

17. Weiss, *Farewell to the Party of Lincoln*, 270; Harvard Sitkoff, *Toward Freedom Land: The Long Struggle for Racial Equality in America* (University Press of Kentucky, 2010), 132–133.

18. Weiss, *Farewell to the Party of Lincoln*, 272–273.

19. "In Opposite Camps," *NYDN*, October 21, 1936; "Joe Louis Stumps for Roosevelt, but Forgets to Mention His Name," *NYWT*, September 30, 1936; "Joe Louis Gets a Bit Mixed Up in Speech for F.D.R.," *CT*, October 1, 1936; Hub M. George, "Politics," *DFP*, October 7, 1936; Ollie Stewart, "A Line or Two," *BAA*, October 10, 1936; "Scores N.J. Politicians," *NYA*, October 17, 1936.

20. Hub M. George, "Politics," *DFP*, August 25, 1936; Hub M. George, "Politics," *DFP*, October 30, 1936; Joe Louis with Edna Rust and Art Rust Jr., *Joe Louis: My Life* (Harcourt Brace Jovanovich, 1978), 158. Charles ran for a US congressional seat again in 1938 but lost despite appearances with Louis.

21. Jack Miley, "Louis Is Stooge for GOP Boys," *NYP*, October 30, 1940; Watson to Rainey; Oscar R. Ewing to Edwin M. Watson, September 28, 1940, Box 13, Official File 300, FDR Papers; "Champion Joe Puts His Punch Behind Willkie," *CT*, November 3, 1940.

22. Louis with Rust and Rust, *Joe Louis*, 16, 158–159; "The Willkie Chicago Speech," *The Crisis*, October 1940, 321.

23. "Joe Louis Tours City for Willkie, Misses Lunch," *NYHT*, November 1, 1940; "Joe Louis in Willkie's Corner as His First Political Venture," *DFP*, October 27, 1940; "Joe Louis Scores President, Charging Broken Promise," *LAT*, October 31, 1940.

24. "Jesse Owens Put in to Give Louis a Race," *NYDM*, November 1, 1940.

25. "Champion Joe Puts His Punch Behind Willkie"; "Jesse Owens Dashes to G.O.P. in Colored Vote Race," *Newsweek*, September 12, 1936, 18–19; William J. Baker, *Jesse Owens: An American Life* (Free Press, 1986; repr. University of Illinois Press, 2006), 133–137.

26. Baker, *Jesse Owens*, 137; Jeremy Schaap, *Triumph: The Untold Story of Jesse Owens and Hitler's Olympics* (Mariner Books, 2008), 192–194; "Owens Claims Snub by Roosevelt Not Hitler," *Troy Daily News* (Ohio), October 16, 1936; "Text of Jesse Owens's Address," *BAA*, October 10, 1936; "Owens Was 'Snubbed,'" *PC*, October 17, 1936.

27. Schaap, *Triumph*, 232; Baker, *Jesse Owens*, 141–143, 154–157.

28. Jesse Owens with Paul G. Neimark, *Blackthink: My Life as a Black Man and White Man* (William Morrow and Company, 1970), 40.

29. Paul Gallico, *Farewell to Sport* (A. A. Knopf, 1938; repr. University of Nebraska Press, 2008), 299.

Notes to Chapter Two

30. Baker, *Jesse Owens*, 155; Donald McRae, *Heroes Without a Country: America's Betrayal of Joe Louis and Jesse Owens* (Ecco, 2002), 11–26; "Joe Louis Spends a Quiet Week-End, Beats Jesse Owens," *CD*, July 9, 1938.

31. John Lardner, "Louis Enjoys Politics, But Not with Owens," *WES*, November 4, 1940; Dan Parker, "When Joe Louis and Jess Owens Debate," *NYDM*, November 2, 1940 (Note that the headline and Parker's column referred to Owens as "Jess"); Mark D. Coburn, "America's Great Black Hope," *American Heritage*, October/November 1978, 88.

32. Meyer Berger, "Portrait of a Strong, Very Silent Man," *NYT*, June 14, 1936; Gallico, *Farewell to Sport*, 307.

33. William H. Wiggins Jr., "Boxing's Sambo Twins: Racial Stereotypes in Jack Johnson and Joe Louis Newspaper Cartoons, 1908 to 1938," *Journal of Sport History* 15, no. 3 (Winter 1988): 242–254; Louis with Rust and Rust, *Joe Louis: My Life*, 39; Chris Mead, *Joe Louis: Black Champion in White America* (Scribner, 1985; repr. Dover Publications, 2010), 57.

34. Lester Rodney, "On the Score Board: Looking at Joe Louis the Athlete," *DW*, February 3, 1941.

35. Heywood Broun, "Louis and Lewis," *The Nation*, February 6, 1937; Leon Horowitz, "Take Your Choice," *Champion of Youth*, June 1936, 19.

36. Margery Miller, *Joe Louis: American* (A. A. Wyn, 1945; repr. Hill and Wang, 1951), 122; Joe Louis, *My Life Story* (Duell, Sloan, and Pearce, 1947), 127–128; Alfred Cassey, "Political Observations," *DT*, November 23, 1940; Rigueur, *The Loneliness of Black Republicans*, 16–22.

37. Goodwin, *No Ordinary Time*, 185–186; Jill Watts, *The Black Cabinet: The Untold Story of African Americans and Politics During the Age of Roosevelt* (Grove Press, 2020), 318–319.

38. Watts, *The Black Cabinet*, 319.

39. Watts, *The Black Cabinet*, 320–321; Byron Darnton, "Joe Louis Tours City for Willkie, Misses Lunch," *NYT*, November 1, 1940.

40. Darnton, "Joe Louis Tours"; "Harlem Cheers, Boos Louis," *NYDN*, November 1, 1940; "Boos Fail to Faze Joe Louis as Orator for Republicans," *WES*, November 1, 1940.

41. "Joe Louis Flies Home for 123rd Willkie Speech," *DFP*, November 4, 1940; "Joe Louis Says It'll Be Willkie by a Knockout," *NYHT*, November 4, 1940; "Joe Louis Speaks 4 Times," *NYT*, November 5, 1940.

42. Dunn, *1940*, 263–264; Rigueur, *The Loneliness of Black Republicans*, 24, 319, n. 58; James J. Kenneally, "Black Republicans During the New Deal: The Role of Joseph W. Martin, Jr.," *The Review of Politics* 55, no. 1 (Winter 1993): 133–134.

43. Berger, "Portrait"; Mead, *Joe Louis*, 50. In 1945, sociologists St. Clair Drake and Horace Cayton introduced the idea of the "Race Man" in their book *Black Metropolis: A Study of Life in a Northern City*.

Three: Against the Ropes

1. Joe Louis Barrow Jr. and Barbara Munder, *Joe Louis: 50 Years an American Hero* (McGraw-Hill, 1988), 123.

2. Roi Ottley, *'New World A-Coming': Inside Black America* (Houghton Mifflin Company, 1943), 198.

3. Maya Angelou, *I Know Why the Caged Bird Sings* (Random House, 2015; 1969), 132–135.

4. Gail Lumet Buckley, *The Hornes: An American Family* (Alfred A. Knopf, 1986), 147; Barney Josephson and Terry Trilling-Josephson, *Café Society: The Wrong Place for the Right People* (University of Illinois Press, 2009), 128.

5. "Wife Just Wants to See Joe Fight," *NYDN*, July 8, 1941; Barney Nagler, *Brown Bomber* (The World Publishing Company, 1972), 70; Dan Burley, "The Love Life of Joe Louis," *Ebony*, July 1951, 28.

6. Gerald Astor, *". . . And a Credit to His Race": The Hard Life and Times of Joseph Louis Barrow, a.k.a. Joe Louis* (Saturday Review Press/E. P. Dutton, 1974), 207.

7. Jack Cuddy, "Conn Claims Mental Edge over Louis," *Tampa Tribune*, June 10, 1941. Billy Conn told author Chris Mead that Johnny Ray was "drunk all the time. He's the only Jewish guy I know that was drunk all the time. But he knew more drunk than the other guys knew sober. In the corner he was always drunk." See Mead, *Joe Louis: Black Champion in White America* (Scribner, 1985; repr. Dover Publications, 2010), 173.

8. Caswell Adams, "Louis, Cool and Calculating, Says 'Sure Conn's Fast—So'm I,'" *NYHT*, June 12, 1941; Billy Conn, "Our Billy Talks Great Battle, Says that He'll Fight One, Too," *Pittsburgh Post-Gazette*, June 10, 1941.

9. "Louis Confident of Taming Conn," *NYDM*, June 17, 1941; John Kieran, "Getting Ready for a Big Fight," *NYT*, June 16, 1941; Dick McCann, "Louis 5-11 to KO Conn in 18th Title Defense," *NYDN*, June 18, 1941; Hy Hurwitz, "Conn Kayoed with Title in Grasp," *BG*, June 19, 1941; Victor O. Jones, "Louis Holds Form in Conn Defeat Despite Hecklers," *BG*, June 19, 1941.

10. Daniel M. Daniel, "Six Fights for Louis Feature 1941 Plans of Mike Jacobs," *The Ring*, March 1941, 3–4, 43.

11. Daniel, "Six Fights," 43.

12. Walter Winchell, "On Broadway," *Indianapolis Star*, December 22, 1940.

13. Daniel, "Six Fights," 3; Dan Burley, "At Last, It's Out! Real Dope on When Joe Louis Will Retire," *NYAN*, March 15, 1941.

14. Dan Parker, *NYDM*, news clipping, ca. June 1942; Richard Bak, *Joe Louis: The Great Black Hope* (Da Capo Press, 1998), 183–185; Hype Igoe, "Louis' Dude Ranch Shows Joe at His Best," *The Ring*, August 1941, 19–21.

Notes to Chapter Three

15. "Joe Louis Is Sport's Largest Individual Taxpayer in U.S.," *CD*, March 1, 1941. For a list of the purses won by Louis during his career, see Bak, *Joe Louis*, 297–299.

16. Caswell Adams, "Louis Wins in 7th as Baer Is Disqualified While Pilot Protests After-the-Bell Knockdown," *NYHT*, May 24, 1941; Stanley Frank, "Buddy Baer Proves Himself No Bum," *NYP*, May 24, 1941.

17. Art Carter, "Three Stitches Required to Close Joe's Eye Cut," *BAA*, May 31, 1941; Dick Cox, "Terror Thrill for Joe," *The Ring*, August 1941, 5; Daniel M. Daniel, "Joe Wearing Out," *The Ring*, June 1941, 12.

18. "Louis Set to Start His Drills for Conn," *NYT*, May 29, 1941; Stanley Franks, "Jacobs Hails Conn as Next Champion," *NYP*, June 18, 1941; Mike Vaccaro, *1941: The Greatest Year in Sports* (Doubleday, 2007), 102.

19. "The International Situation," *NYT*, June 18, 1941; "Bid U.S. Prepare for a Long War," *NYT*, June 18, 1941; James P. Dawson, "Louis Is 1 to 4 Choice to Defeat Conn in Match Tonight," *NYT*, June 18, 1941.

20. John Kieran, "This Way for the Big Show," *NYT*, June 18, 1941; "Bomber Realized Conn Was Winning," *NYT*, June 19, 1941.

21. Andrew O'Toole, *Sweet William: The Life of Billy Conn* (University of Illinois Press, 2008), 5–6; Victor O. Jones, "Louis Holds Form in Conn Defeat Despite Hecklers," *BG*, June 19, 1941; James P. Dawson, "Louis, Near Defeat, Stops Conn in 13th and Retains Crown," *NYT*, June 19, 1941; Vaccaro, *1941*, 139.

22. Harry Ferguson, "Mike Jacobs' Granite Heart Cracks; and Conn Gets Kiss," *BG*, June 19, 1941; "Joe Louis Actor," *NYA*, June 28, 1941.

23. Dick McCann, "Louis to Rest till Sept; Four Seek Title Shot," *NYDN*, June 20, 1941; Caswell Adams, "Nova to Battle Louis for Title in September Heavyweight Bout," *NYHT*, June 22, 1941; Jack Mahon, "Army One Thing that May Halt Louis," *Nashville Banner*, June 20, 1941.

24. W. W. Edgar, "Louis Refuses to Fight Wife's Divorce Action," *DFP*, July 3, 1941; "Wife of Joe Louis Sues for Divorce," *NYT*, July 3, 1941; "Joe Louis Answers Wife," *NYT*, July 10, 1941; "Louis Sued for Divorce," *NYAN*, July 5, 1941.

25. Thomas R. Hietala, *The Fight of the Century: Jack Johnson, Joe Louis, and the Struggle for Racial Equality* (M.E. Sharpe, 2002), 305–306; Lem Graves Jr., "From the Press Box," *NJG*, July 12, 1941.

26. Melancholy Jones, "Sports Slants," *ADW*, July 5, 1941; Edgar Rouzeau, "The Sportscope," *NJG*, July 12, 1941; Nell Dodson, "Mrs. Joe Louis Finds Job of Being Wife of World Heavyweight Champ Not So Easy," *ADW*, June 23, 1941.

27. Barrow and Munder, *Joe Louis*, 202–203; Marva Louis, "Why I Quit Joe," *Ebony*, December 1949, 61, 64; Joe Louis with Edna Rust and Art Rust Jr., *Joe Louis: My Life* (Harcourt Brace Jovanovich, 1978).

28. "Louis May Wed Before Bout, and Then He May Not," *CT*, September 24, 1935; Edna Ferguson, "Louis Weds; Harlem Yowls; Bride at Ring," *NYDN*, September 25, 1935.

29. I. F. Coles, "Says Louis Worship Has Made Mobbists," *BAA*, July 2, 1938.

30. Ozzie Neilson, "Joe and Marva Not 2 Love Birds," *BAA*, July 19, 1941; Burley, "The Love Life of Joe Louis," 23; "Joe Louis Said to Be Engaged to Niece of Manager," *PC*, July 6, 1935; Langston Hughes, *The Collected Works of Langston Hughes*, vol. 14: *I Wonder as I Wander* (University of Missouri Press, 2001), 319; Allyson Hobbs, *A Chosen Exile: A History of Racial Passing in American Life* (Harvard University Press, 2014), 137–141; Rollo S. Vest, "K.O. Threatens Joe Louis as Deb Hurls Brick at Car," *PC*, July 20, 1935.

31. "Joe Louis to Wed Is New Rumor," *CD*, September 1, 1935; "Five Portraits of the 19-Year-Old Chicago Stenographer Who Will Soon Become Wife of Joe Louis, Heavyweight Boxer," *BAA*, September 14, 1935; "Joe Already Calls Miss Trotter, His Pretty Fiancée, 'Mrs. Louis,'" *PC*, September 14, 1935; Burley, "The Love Life of Joe Louis," 26; Dodson, "Mrs. Joe Louis Finds Job of Being Wife of World Heavyweight Champ Not So Easy"; David Margolick, *Beyond Glory: Joe Louis vs. Max Schmeling, and a World on the Brink* (Vintage Books, 2005), 68, 100; Jack Diamond, "Baer Hangs Up Mittens," *LAT*, September 25, 1935.

32. Frank Marshall Davis, "Louis Not Doped: Love Rift Spiked," *BAA*, July 4, 1936; Arch Ward, "Talking It Over," *CT*, June 29, 1936; William G. Nunn, "Say Louis Wasn't Worried over Wife's Affairs," *PC*, July 4, 1936.

33. "Joe Gibbons of Joe Louis Fame Shot to Death," *CT*, October 6, 1936; "Open Inquest on Joe Gibbons of Louis Case," *CT*, October 8, 1936; Dan Burley, "Policeman Who Killed Gibbons Held on Manslaughter Charge," *CD*, October 24, 1936; "Witness in Gibbons Case Fatally Shot," *PC*, November 7, 1936; "Slew Cabbie, Cop Freed," *BAA*, November 21, 1936; "Cop Is Held for Killing Louis Rival," *DT*, October 24, 1936.

34. Neilson, "Joe and Marva"; Louis, "Why I Quit Joe," 65; Barrow and Munder, *Joe Louis*, 200–202.

35. Barrow and Munder, *Joe Louis*, 200–201; Louis with Rust and Rust, *Joe Louis*, 149, 156.

36. "Louis Denies Striking Wife," *NYWT*, July 9, 1941; "She Didn't Treat Him Kindly, Joe Louis Says," *NYDN*, July 10, 1941; "Louis' Wife Must Fight," *NYDN*, August 1, 1941; John C. Dancy to Presley Winfield, August 12, 1941, Box 1, 1941 Folder, John C. Dancy Papers, University of Michigan Historical Collections, Bentley Historical Library, Ann Arbor, MI; "Everything Is O.K. With Louises Now," *NYAN*, August 23, 1941.

37. Diana Briggs, "He Is Cold Marva Weeps at Hearing," *CD*, August 23, 1941; "It Was Wife's Zeal with Charge Accounts that Made Louis Mad," *NYDN*, August 19, 1941.

38. Dan Parker quoted from Dan Burley, "Confidentially Yours," *NYAN*, July 12, 1941.

39. "Joe Louises Make Up, He Carries Her from Court," *NYDN*, August 20, 1941; "Joe and Marva Call Off Plans for Divorce," *DFP*, August 20, 1941; "Second Honeymoon for Marva and Joe," *PC*, August 30, 1941.

40. Louis, "Why I Quit Joe," 66–67.

41. Bak, *Joe Louis*, 188; Caswell Adams, "Louis, Now 1-A, Faces Induction After Nova Bout," *NYHT*, September 10, 1941; "Louis Classed 1A for Army Draft," *NYT*, September 10, 1941; Bob Brumbry, "Lush Era of Boxing Goes Out with Louis," *PM*, September 11, 1941; Caswell Adams, "Louis to Resign Title, Planning to Win It Back," *NYHT*, September 20, 1941.

42. "Dancers Riot to Hear Lena," *BAA*, March 1, 1941; "Lena Horne Leaves Broadway for Hollywood," *PC*, October 25, 1941; Bill Rowe, "Notables from Everywhere Attend Big Fight," *PC*, June 29, 1935; Joe Louis with Edna Rust and Art Rust Jr., *Joe Louis: My Life* (Harcourt Brace Jovanovich, 1978), 154–155.

43. James Gavin, *Stormy Weather: The Life of Lena Horne* (Atria, 2009), 77–80; Lena Horne and Richard Schickel, *Lena* (Doubleday, 1965), 109; Gail Lumet Buckley, *The Hornes: An American Family* (Alfred A. Knopf, 1986), 139; James Haskins with Kathleen Benson, *Lena: A Personal and Professional Biography of Lena Horne* (Stein and Day, 1984), 21.

44. Gavin, *Stormy Weather*, 80–82; David W. Stowe, "The Politics of Café Society," *The Journal of American History* 84, no. 4 (March 1998): 1386–1387.

45. Gavin, *Stormy Weather*, 86–89; Lena Horne as told to Helen Artstein and Carlton Moss, *In Person, Lena Horne* (Greenberg, 1950), 187; John Meroney, "How Lena Horne Escaped Hollywood's Blacklist," *The Atlantic*, August 27, 2015; Horne and Schickel, *Lena*, 117–118.

46. Josephson and Trilling-Josephson, *Café Society*, 128.

47. Daniel, "Louis to Switch His Camp to Greenwood," *NYAN*, March 9, 1940.

48. The pictures of Louis and Horne at Greenwood Lake can be found in the Carl Van Vechten Papers Relating to African American Arts and Letters, Beinecke Rare Book and Manuscript Library, Yale University.

49. Martin Duberman, *Paul Robeson* (The New Press, 1989), 72–73; Kelefa Sanneh, "White Mischief: The Passions of Carl Van Vechten," *New Yorker*, February 9, 2014.

Four: King Joe

1. Jimmy Cannon, "Pvt. Cannon's Report on Joe Louis and the Aero Hour," *PM*, September 30, 1941.

2. Caswell Adams, "Introducing—The New Joe Louis," *Saturday Evening Post*, May 10, 1941, 105.

3. Cannon, "Pvt. Cannon's Report."
4. Frank Graham, "Setting the Pace," *The Sun*, October 15, 1941.
5. Ted Carroll, "Nova's Yogi Cult," *The Ring*, October 1941, 8; Richard Bak, *Joe Louis: The Great Black Hope* (Da Capo Press, 1998), 202; John Lardner, "Joe Louis vs. the Cosmos," *Newsweek*, September 1, 1941, 40; Lew Freedman, *Joe Louis: The Life of a Heavyweight* (McFarland, 2013), 188.
6. Lardner, "Joe Louis vs. the Cosmos," 40; Bak, *Joe Louis*, 202; "Joe Louis Unbothered by Yogi Lou Nova," *ADW*, September 23, 1941.
7. Jesse Abramson, "Fans Wear Topcoats, Sweaters, as Cool Weather Chills 56,549," *NYHT*, September 30, 1941; "F.D.R. Gets Fight Details on Train," *PI*, September 30, 1941.
8. Richards Vidmer, "Down in Front," *NYHT*, September 30, 1941; Jimmy Powers, "Louis KO's Nova in 2:59 of 6th," *NYDN*, September 30, 1941.
9. Jimmy Powers, "Louis KO's Nova In 2:59 of 6th"; Lester Rodney, "On the Score Board," *DW*, October 1, 1941; "A Credit to the Nation," *DW*, October 2, 1941.
10. "10,000 in Harlem Hear Louis Thank His Rooters," *BAA*, October 4, 1941.
11. Milton Meltzer, "Robeson, Richard Wright, Basie in Tribute to Joe Louis," *DW*, October 3, 1941.
12. Richard Wright, "Joe Louis Uncovers Dynamite," *New Masses*, October 8, 1935, 19.
13. "King Joe" (Joe Louis Blues) was released by Okeh Records as a 10-inch, 78-rpm record in two parts. It sold 40,000 copies in its first few months. Together, both parts feature eight of Wright's stanzas, but all thirteen of his stanzas are printed in the sheet music. Richard Wright Papers, box 84, folder 975, Yale University Library.
14. Harold Lavine, "Why the Army Gripes," *The Nation*, August 30, 1941, 180.
15. Lavine, "Army Gripes," 180.
16. Matthew F. Delmont, *Half American: The Epic Story of African Americans Fighting World War II at Home and Abroad* (Viking, 2022), 75.
17. Alexa Mills, "A Lynching Kept Out of Sight," *WP*, September 2, 2016; Ulysses Lee, *The Employment of Negro Troops* (U.S. Government Printing Office, 2000), 349.
18. "Ask FDR and Stimson to Probe Soldier Death," *PC*, April 26, 1941; "Ask FDR to Probe Death of Ft. Benning Soldier: Killing Is Called Act of a Mob," *ADW*, April 22, 1941; Mills, "A Lynching Kept Out of Sight."
19. Roy Wilkins, "Wartime Lynchings," *The Crisis*, June 1941, 183.
20. Walter White to Eleanor Roosevelt, September 22, 1941, National Association for the Advancement of Colored People, General Office File,

"Joe Louis—Bout for the Navy 1941–1942," Library of Congress, (hereafter NAACP papers).

21. Walter White to Julian Black, September 23, 1941, General Office File, "Joe Louis—Bout for the Navy 1941–1942," NAACP papers; Walter White to Truman Gibson, September 23, 1941, General Office File, "Joe Louis—Bout for the Navy 1941–1942," NAACP papers.

22. F. H. Osborn to Walter White, October 1, 1941, General Office File, "Joe Louis—Bout for the Navy 1941–1942," NAACP papers.

23. Joe Louis, as told to Meyer Berger and Barney Nagler, "Joe Louis Story," *Life*, November 15, 1948, 136.

24. Joe Louis, "Joe Louis Writes—Army Camp Boxing Tour Starts," *NYP*, October 8, 1941.

25. "Joe Louis Entertains 10,000 at Camp Grant," *CHA*, October 9, 1941; "10,000 Watch Heavyweight Champion's Exhibition at Chanute Field," *CHA*, October 12, 1941; "Draft Board Finds Joe Louis Fit!," *CHA*, October 14, 1941; "Soldiers Show Joe," *NYDN*, October 10, 1941; Joe Louis, "Nervous First Time in Draft Test," *NYP*, October 15, 1941; Frank Mastro, "Louis Passes Army Tests; Awaits November Call," *CT*, October 15, 1941; "Army Life Stops at Camp Grant," *CDN*, October 9, 1941. "Joe Louis Passes His Test for Army," *NYT*, October 15, 1941.

Five: Anchors Aweigh

1. "Louis Boxes at Fort Custer," *NYT*, October 16, 1941; Joe Louis, "Joe Louis Writes—Army Camp Boxing Tour Starts," *NYP*, October 8, 1941.

2. Robert Dallek, *Franklin D. Roosevelt and American Foreign Policy, 1932–1945* (Oxford University Press, 1979), 285; David M. Kennedy, *Freedom from Fear: The American People in Depression and War* (Oxford University Press, 1999), 496–500.

3. Franklin D. Roosevelt, "Navy Day Address," October 27, 1941.

4. Samuel Eliot Morison, *The Battle of the Atlantic, 1939–1943, History of United States Naval Operations in World War II*, volume 1 (Little, Brown, 1947), 94; Joseph Connor Jr., "Sinking the USS *Reuben James*," Warfare History Network, Summer 2017, https://warfarehistorynetwork.com/article/sinking-the-uss-reuben-james/.

5. Matthew Delmont, *Half American: The Epic Story of African Americans Fighting World War II at Home and Abroad* (Viking, 2022), 79–81.

6. Josh White, "Uncle Sam Says," recorded 1941. Permission to quote given by Josh White III.

7. Randy Roberts, "Joe Louis' Decision to Fight for the Segregated Navy Was Deeply Unpopular—Until Pearl Harbor Was Bombed," *The Undefeated*, December 7, 2021; Sherie Mershon and Steven Schlossman, *Foxholes and Color Lines: Desegregating the U.S. Armed Forces* (Johns Hopkins University Press, 1989), 47.

Notes to Chapter Five

8. "Why Fight for the Navy," *Cleveland Call and Post*, November 22, 1941.

9. "Plan Louis–Buddy Baer Return Bout Here," *NYDN*, November 1, 1941; "Buddy Baer to Fight Louis Jan. 2? Jacobs Says 'No,'" *CT*, November 1, 1941.

10. "Nation-Wide Vote Indicating Race Supports Joe," *PC*, November 29, 1941.

11. "Louis Managers Justify Bout for the Navy," *Cleveland Call and Post*, November 29, 1941; Arthur Huff Fauset, "Louis' Managers Astute," *PT*, December 6, 1941.

12. Joe Louis Barrow Jr. and Barbara Munder, *Joe Louis: 50 Years an American Hero* (McGraw-Hill, 1998), 132.

13. James P. Dawson, "Match Arranged for Navy Relief," *NYT*, November 17, 1941; Bob Stedler, "Sport Comment," *BN*, January 8, 1942.

14. Richards Vidmer, "Down in Front," *NYHT*, December 18, 1941.

15. Dan Burley, "Harlem Cold on Louis Bout," *NYAN*, November 8, 1941.

16. Quote from Dan Burley, "Joe Louis Dead Wrong Fighting for Jim Crow Navy," *NYAN*, November 22, 1941. Also see: Dan Burley, "Fans Roused over Louis Fighting for Jim Crow Navy," *NYAN*, November 29, 1941; Dan Burley, "Fans Ask Louis Not to Put Race on the Spot Fighting for Jim Crow Navy," *NYAN*, December 6, 1941.

17. "Nation's Leaders Express Views on Navy Benefit Bout," *PC*, November 22, 1941; "Poll Favors Louis's Navy Fight," *PC*, November 29, 1941; Art Carter, "Joe Hopes Navy Benefit Will Break Barriers," *BAA*, November 22, 1941.

18. Delmont, *Half American*, 85–88.

19. "'Messman Hero' Identified," *PC*, March 14, 1942.

20. David Welky, *Marching Across the Color Line: A. Philip Randolph and Civil Rights in the World War II Era* (Oxford University Press, 2014), 87.

21. Jill Watts, *The Black Cabinet: The Untold Story of African Americans and Politics During the Age of Roosevelt* (Grove Atlantic, 2020), 354–355; "We Are Americans, Too!," *PC*, December 13, 1941.

22. Wendell Smith, "Louis, Navy Fight for Each Other—Nothing Else Matters," *PC*, December 13, 1941.

23. Gilbert Ware, *William Hastie: Grace Under Pressure* (Oxford University Press, 1984), 100–101; Delmont, *Half American*, 89–91.

24. Delmont, *Half American*, 90–91; Roy Wilkins, "Now Is the Time Not to Be Silent," *The Crisis*, January 1942, 7.

25. Vidmer, "Down in Front."

26. "Louis Eases Workouts," *NYT*, December 29, 1941; "'Hope for Best' in Digit Case—Roxborough," *BAA*, December 27, 1941.

27. Part of this section is adapted from Roberts, "Joe Louis' Decision to Fight for the Segregated Navy Was Deeply Unpopular—Until Pearl Harbor Was Bombed."

28. Caswell Adams, "Louis Flattens Trail Mates at Upstate Camp," *NYHT*, January 4, 1942; Caswell Adams, "Louis and Baer Pound Mates in Camp Drills," *NYHT*, January 5, 1942.

29. Tom O'Reilly, "Joe Louis Is 1-A in My Book, Too," *PM*, January 7, 1942.

30. For coverage of the fight, see Caswell Adams, "Louis Knocks Out Buddy Baer in 1st Round at Garden, Keeps World Title," *NYHT*, January 10, 1942; James P. Dawson, "Louis Scores First-Round Knockout Over Buddy Baer in Charity Encounter," *NYT*, January 10, 1942.

31. James P. Dawson, "Louis Scores First-Round Knockout over Buddy Baer in Charity Encounter."

32. Nat Fleischer, "Louis Back at Peak, Gives Savage Display," *The Ring*, March 1942, 6.

33. Bob Brumby, "Louis Volunteers for Army . . . He'll Be Inducted Wednesday," *PM*, January 10, 1942; James P. Dawson, "Louis Summoned to Army Service; Goes In Tomorrow," *NYT*, January 11, 1942.

34. Bob Considine, "On the Line," *NYDM*, January 11, 1942.

35. Dawson, "Louis Summoned."

Six: God's War

1. "It's Pvt. Louis at 11 Tomorrow," *PM*, January 13, 1942; Caswell Adams, "Louis, Surviving Ordeal of Doctors and Cameramen, Dons Gloves for Country Tomorrow," *NYHT*, January 13, 1942; "Army O.K.'s Joe Louis in Final Physical Examination," *BN*, January 12, 1942; "Joe Signs for a Finish Fight," *CT*, January 13, 1942. The stock newsreel footage of Joe's medical exam and his exchange with Abe Taubman can been seen on YouTube, "Joe Louis in the Army AKA Joe Louis Joins Up (1942)."

2. Joe Louis Barrow Physical Examination Record, January 12, 1942, Joe Louis Military Personnel File, Record Group 319, Records of the Army Staff, NARA; "It's Pvt. Louis at 11 Tomorrow."

3. "Louis Gives Check to the Navy Fund," *NYT*, January 14, 1942; "Joe Louis Gives $47,100 Purse, Jacobs $37,229 to Navy Fund," *NYP*, January 13, 1942.

4. James Edmund Boyack, "Hailed as Most Popular Champion; Anxious for Japs," *PC*, January 17, 1942; "Marva's Lonely Without Her Joe," *ADW*, January 25, 1942.

5. Bradley W. Hart, *Hitler's American Friends: The Third Reich's Supporters in the United States* (Thomas Dunne Books, 2018), 21–35; Al Binder, "Find 'Little Germany' Near Upton," *NYDN*, August 30, 1942; Annie Wilkinson, "Camp Siegfried: Hitler's Long Island," *Long Island Press*, August 26, 2019; Marvin D. Miller, *Wunderlich's Salute: The Interrelationship of the German-American Bund, Camp Siegfried, Yaphank, Long Island, and the Young Siegfrieds and Their Relationship with American and Nazi Institutions* (Malamud-Rose, 1983), 204–208.

6. Milton Bracker, "Joe Louis Spends First Day in Camp," *NYT*, January 15, 1942; Dan Parker, "Louis Just Another Guy Named Joe Now," *NYDM*, January 15, 1942; "Bean Soup Gives Joe Louis Taste of Life in Army," *BN*, January 14, 1942.

7. Morris J. MacGregor Jr., *Integration of the Armed Forces, 1940–1945* (United States Army Center for Military History, 1985), 24–25; Ulysses S. Lee, *The Employment of Negro Troops* (Office of the Chief of Military History, U.S. Army, 1966; repr. Center of Military History, 2001), 241–248; Parker, "Louis Just Another Guy."

8. Ollie Stewart, "Army Is Just Like Training Camp, Joe Louis Tells AFRO," *BAA*, January 24, 1942; Ollie Stewart, "Joe Confined to Quarters," *BAA*, January 24, 1942; "'A Day in Camp with the Heavyweight Champ' Shows Joe Preparing for Action!," *PC*, January 24, 1942; Joe Louis, *My Life Story* (Duell, Sloan and Pearce, 1947), 148–150.

9. James E. Boyack, "Buddies Say Joe Is Ideal Soldier," *PC*, January 24, 1942; Glenn Douglass, "This Is the Army," *BAA*, October 30, 1943; "Don't Shake a Nigger's Hand," *PM*, August 6, 1941.

10. Matthew F. Delmont, *Half American: The Epic Story of African Americans Fighting World War II At Home and Abroad* (Viking, 2022), 106, 119; Thomas R. Hietala, *The Fight of the Century: Jack Johnson, Joe Louis, and the Struggle for Racial Equality* (M.E. Sharpe, 2002), 285–286; Mark Whitaker, *Smoketown: The Untold Story of the Other Black Renaissance* (Simon & Schuster, 2018), 173–176.

11. Milton Starr, "Report on Negro Morale," 1942, Box 20, Folder: Minorities—Negro—Negro Morale, Philleo Nash Files, Harry S. Truman Presidential Library, Independence, Missouri.

12. Starr, "Report on Negro Morale." For an insightful discussion of how the Office of War Information framed Joe Louis as a patriotic symbol during the Second World War, see Lauren Rebecca Sklaroff, "Constructing G.I. Joe Louis: Cultural Solutions to the 'Negro Problem' During World War II," *Journal of American History* 89, no. 3 (December 2002): 958–983.

13. Starr, "Report on Negro Morale."

14. Jack Mahon, "Joe Louis Honored by Boxing Writers' Association at Annual Dinner," *Bradford Evening News and Daily Record* (Pennsylvania), January 22, 1942; James Edmund Boyack, "Louis Hailed at Writers' Banquet," *PC*, January 31, 1942. For background on Hoover and the FBI's surveillance of Black Americans between the First and Second World Wars, see Mark Ellis, "J. Edgar Hoover and the 'Red Summer' of 1919," *Journal of American Studies* 28, no. 1 (1994): 39–59, and Kenneth O'Reilly, "The Roosevelt Administration and Black America: Federal Surveillance Policy and Civil Rights During the New Deal and World War II Years," *Phylon* 48, no. 1 (1987): 12–25.

15. Boyack, "Louis Hailed."

Notes to Chapter Six

16. Boyack, "Louis Hailed."

17. "Louis-Simon Bout Listed for March 27 for Army Benefit," *NYHT*, February 26, 1942; Richards Vidmer, "Down in Front: Patriotic Pleasure," *NYHT*, January 2, 1942.

18. Nat Fleischer, "Nat Fleischer Says," *The Ring*, April 1942, 14; Franklin Roosevelt to Kenesaw Mountain Landis, January 15, 1942, President's Personal File 227: Baseball, folder: 1939–1945, Franklin D. Roosevelt Library, Hyde Park, New York.

19. Dick McCann, "Sports Boom on Despite Booms of Guns," *NYDN*, February 12, 1942; Nat Fleischer, "Nat Fleischer Says," *The Ring*, September 1942, 10.

20. "Ft. Dix Soldiers See Louis Spar 4 Rounds," *NYT*, March 9, 1942; "Joe's Plenty Busy at Dix," *NYAN*, March 21, 1942; "Louis Gets Ready for Big Abe Simon," *PC*, March 21, 1942; "Negro and White Troops Clashed Before Dix Riot," *PM*, April 5, 1942.

21. "Garden Benefit Adds $140,000 to Navy Relief," *NYHT*, March 11, 1942; "Navy Show Draws Crowd of 20,000," *NYT*, March 11, 1942; Edgar T. Rouzeau, "'God Is on Our Side'—Joe Louis Reminds 20,000 at Navy Show," *PC*, March 21, 1942.

22. Joe Louis Barrow Jr. and Barbara Munder, *Joe Louis: 50 Years an American Hero* (McGraw-Hill, 1988), 139.

23. Carl Byoir, "Joe Louis Named the War," *Colliers*, May 16, 1942. The Louis poster first appeared in newspapers in June 1942. See, for example, the *Detroit Evening Times*, June 24, 1942; *CE*, June 25, 1942; *NYA*, June 27, 1942.

24. "Where Are Our Soldiers?," *PC*, March 7, 1942; Delmont, *Half American*, 110.

25. Claudia Jones, "Lift Every Voice for Victory," pamphlet published by New Age Publishers, June 1942.

26. "Negroes Have a Big Stake in This War, Says Joe Louis," *DW*, April 2, 1942.

27. Dick McCann, "Joe for Doughboys," *NYDN*, March 27, 1942; Chris Mead, *Joe Louis: Black Champion in White America* (Scribner, 1985; repr. Dover Publications, 2010).

28. Wendell Smith, "Joe in Easy Win over Simon as 18,000 Look On," *PC*, April 4, 1942; Al Buck, "Louis Phones Ailing Trainer; 'I'll Win for Army and Chappie,'" *NYP*, March 27, 1942; Stanley Frank, "Louis Not at Best Against Big Abe," *NYP*, March 28, 1942; Nat Fleischer, "Man of the Hour," *The Ring*, June 1942, 3–4.

29. Edgar T. Rouzeau, "The Sportscope," *NJG*, April 4, 1942; Paul Gallico, "The Fight," *NYDN*, September 24, 1935; Paul Gallico, "The Private Life of Private Joe Louis," *Liberty*, May 23, 1942, 52.

30. Tommy Devine, "Blackburn, Louis' Trainer, Goes Down for Eternal Count," *PP*, April 25, 1942.

31. "Test for J. Johnson," *WP*, May 9, 1909.

32. Truman K. Gibson Jr. with Steve Huntley, *Knocking Down Barriers: My Fight for Black America* (Northwestern University Press, 2005), 72; "His Brother Used Razor," *BG*, December 31, 1908; "Jack Blackburn in Jail in Phila.," *Allentown Leader*, January 15, 1909; "Blackburn Held for Man's Death," *PI*, January 17, 1909; "Fighter Given Fifteen Years," *BG*, June 30, 1909; "Colored Pugilist Who Formerly Lived at Versailles Tries Suicide in Prison," *Lexington Herald-Leader*, February 1, 1909; "'Jack' Blackburn Guilty of Murder," *PI*, June 30, 1909; Geoffrey C. Ward, *Unforgiveable Blackness: The Rise and Fall of Jack Johnson* (Knopf, 2005), 437.

33. Joe Louis with Edna Rust and Art Rust Jr., *Joe Louis: My Life* (Harcourt Brace Jovanovich, 1978), 36; Earl Brown, "Joe Louis," *Life*, June 17, 1940; Joe Louis and Gene Kessler, "Murder with Gloves," *Liberty*, November 23, 1935, 14–16; Ed Van Every, "Louis' Rise Meteoric," *The Ring*, September 1937, 3.

34. Mead, *Joe Louis*, 6.

35. "Blackburn Shooting Aftermath of Attempt to Purchase Home," *PC*, October 26, 1935; Gibson, *Knocking Down Barriers*, 72–73; "Blackburn Exonerated in Fatal Shooting of Tuskegee Graduate," *BD*, November 7, 1935.

36. "Joe Louis Sits Beside Trainer, Jack Acquitted," *PC*, March 14, 1936.

37. Devine, "Blackburn, Louis' Trainer, Goes Down"; "What Boxing Scribes Say About Jack Blackburn," *BAA*, May 2, 1942.

38. Marcy S. Sacks, *Joe Louis: Sports and Race in Twentieth-Century America* (Routledge, 2018), 49.

39. "30,000 Turn Out for Funeral of Blackburn, Louis's Trainer," *NYHT*, April 30, 1942.

40. Kenneth McCormick, "Reading Gets 4 to 5 Years; Will Appeal," *DFP*, January 8, 1942; James Doherty, "Jury Indicts 26 in Policy Rings; Hail Precedent," *CT*, January 31, 1942; Joe Louis as told to Meyer Berger and Barney Nagler, "Joe Louis' Story," *Life*, November 15, 1948, 140.

Seven: War Boxing, Inc.

1. Michael S. Jacobs to Army Emergency Relief, May 16, 1942, Records of the Office of the Secretary of War, Record Group 107, Office of the Assistant Secretary of War, Civilian Aide to the Secretary, Subject File 1940–1947, Box 182, NARA.

2. Dan Parker quoted in "We're in Joe's Corner," *NJG*, June 13, 1942; Jimmy Powers, "The Power House," *NYDN*, May 20, 1942; Gayle Talbot, "Army Cools Jacobs Off on Summer Bout for Louis," *DFP*, May 19, 1942.

3. Robert P. Post, "Big U.S. Force Arrives in Ireland with Tank Units and Heavy Guns; Nazis Stiffen, but Russians Gain," *NYT*, May 19, 1942; Hanson

Notes to Chapter Seven

W. Baldwin, "America at War: The Second Quarter (March–May 1942)," *Foreign Affairs* 20, no. 4 (July 1942): 589–606.

4. "We're in Joe's Corner."

5. Henry McLemore, "48 States-Full of Sentiment Eager and Ready to Second Joe Louis in His Fight to Pay $117,000 Income Taxes," *Austin American-Statesman*, June 9, 1942.

6. Caswell Adams, "Louis Granted Deferment on U.S. Income Tax," *NYHT*, May 30, 1942; "Taxes Kayo Fighter Joe," *YANK: The Army Newspaper*, June 6, 1942; "Yes, Y'Gotta File a Return," *YANK*, June 17, 1942.

7. "Louis Should Step Out of Ring, Become Soldier, Army Feels," *WES*, May 31, 1942; "Army's Ban on Louis Dooms Fight Game," *PC*, June 6, 1942.

8. Dick McCann, "Sports Does Its Bit at PG in Carnival of Stars," *NYDN*, June 15, 1942; Joe Bostic, "Louis Boxes; Receives Scroll," *The People's Voice*, June 20, 1942; Dick McCann, "I Wake Up Screaming," *NYDN*, June 15, 1942.

9. "Louis Ordered to Finish Army Basic Training," *NYHT*, June 19, 1942.

10. "Louis Goes West for Training," *NYDN*, June 23, 1942; Bob Considine, "On the Line," *NYDM*, June 24, 1942.

11. "Robinson on Furlough," *PC*, September 19, 1942; Jackie Robinson as told to Ed Reid, "Jackie Robinson Tells His Story," *Brooklyn Eagle*, August 19, 1949.

12. Jackie Robinson, *Baseball Has Done It*, ed. Charles Dexter (J.B. Lippincott, 1964), 37; Ulysses Lee, *The Employment of Negro Troops* (Office of the Chief of Military History, U.S. Army, 1966; repr. Center of Military History, 2001), 88; Arnold Rampersad, *Jackie Robinson: A Biography* (Ballantine Books, 1997), 90–91; Rachel Robinson and Lee Daniels, *Jackie Robinson: An Intimate Portrait* (Harry N. Abrams, 2014), 28.

13. Rampersad, *Jackie Robinson*, 69, 89, 91; "Chi White Sox Reject Race Players," *PC*, March 21, 1942; Jackie Robinson as told to Alfred Duckett, *I Never Had It Made: An Autobiography of Jackie Robinson* (Putnam, 1972; repr. HarperCollins, 1995), 13; Carl T. Rowan with Jackie Robinson, *Wait Till Next Year: The Life Story of Jackie Robinson* (Random House, 1960), 71.

14. Joe Louis with Edna Rust and Art Rust Jr., *Joe Louis: My Life* (Harcourt Brace Jovanovich, 1978), 179; Joe Louis, "Joe Louis Disapproves Black Muslims' Actions," *BG*, September 20, 1964; Joe Louis as told to Meyer Berger and Barney Nagler, "Joe Louis' Story," *Life*, November 15, 1948, 139.

15. Rampersad, *Jackie Robinson*, 92–93; Truman K. Gibson Jr. with Steve Huntley, *Knocking Down Barriers: My Fight for Black America* (Northwestern University Press, 2005), 235; Richard M. Dalfiume, *Desegregation of the U.S. Armed Forces: Fighting on Two Fronts, 1939–1953* (University of Missouri Press, 1969), 65.

Notes to Chapter Seven

16. Louis with Rust and Rust, *My Life*, 177–178.

17. Rowan with Robinson, *Wait Till Next Year*, 75–76; Robinson as told to Duckett, *I Never Had It Made*, 16–17. Robinson did play at least one game with an all-Black football squad from Fort Riley against a team from Lincoln University, a historically Black school. See "Lincoln All-Stars Tie Fort Riley 11," *MC*, December 4, 1943.

18. Chris Mead, *Joe Louis: Black Champion in White America* (Scribner, 1985; repr. Dover Publications, 2010), 226–227; Carol Briley interview with Truman Gibson, Independence, Missouri, July 27, 2001, Harry S. Truman Presidential Library.

19. Gibson with Huntley, *Knocking Down Barriers*, 12; Jack Roosevelt Robinson Military Personnel File, NARA. In addition to Mead, other biographers of Louis repeat Gibson's story about Robinson assaulting a white officer at Fort Riley. See Richard Bak, *Joe Louis: The Great Black Hope* (Da Capo Press, 1998), 222; Lewis Erenberg, *The Greatest Fight of Our Generation: Louis vs. Schmeling* (Oxford University Press, 2006), 194.

20. Henry McLemore, "Joe Louis Receives 300 Letters a Day, Most of Which Are Touches—Bomber Saving Money," *Honolulu Advertiser*, September 18, 1935.

21. Trina N. Seitz, "The Killing Chair: North Carolina's Experiment in Civility and the Execution of Allen Foster," *The North Carolina Historical Review* 81, no. 1 (January 2004): 59; "Negro Assailant Rushed to Prison," *Durham Herald-Sun*, September 29, 1935; David Margolick, "'Save Me, Joe Louis!,'" *LAT*, November 7, 2005.

22. John A. Parris Jr., "Death Row Upset on Execution Eve," *Raleigh News and Observer*, January 24, 1936; "First Lethal Gas Victim Dies in Torture as Witnesses Quail," *Raleigh News and Observer*, January 25, 1936.

23. "Gas Execution Called Savage," *Charlotte Observer*, January 25, 1936; Ted Benson's *Daily Worker* column was reprinted in the *Pittsburgh Courier*. See Benson, "'The Battle of the Century—Joe Louis vs. Jim Crow,'" *PC*, February 29, 1936.

24. Martin Luther King Jr., *Why We Can't Wait* (New American Library/Harper & Row, 1964), 100–101.

25. King Jr., *Why We Can't Wait*, 101.

26. Caswell Adams, "Jacobs Is Given 'Go-Ahead' for Louis Title Bout," *NYHT*, August 12, 1942; Caswell Adams, "Louis and Conn Will Get Total of $135,451 from Title Match Oct. 12 to Pay Their Debts," *NYHT*, September 19, 1942; Joe Cummiskey, "Of Plans for Million-Dollar Louis-Conn Fight, with a $135,451 'Gouge,'" *BG*, September 25, 1942.

27. Caswell Adams, "Louis to Risk Title Against Conn Oct. 12 with All Receipts Going to Army Relief Fund," *NYHT*, September 9, 1942; "Sport: Flop of the Century," *Time*, October 5, 1942; Jim McCulley, "Louis, Conn Will Battle for Army Relief Oct. 12," *NYDN*, September 9, 1942; "Louis Leaves Fort Riley," *NYT*, September 10, 1942.

28. Wilbur Wood, "Criticism of Sports Writers in Louis-Conn Episode Unfair," *WES*, September 28, 1942; Cummiskey, "Of Plans."

29. For the picture of Jacobs, see "Joe Louis Signs for 22nd Defense of Title," *NYHT*, September 23, 1942; Joe McCarthy, "Sports: Mike Jacobs Wants to Stage G.I. Boxing Show in Ireland," *YANK*, September 23, 1942.

30. "Charge Conn-Louis Go Is 'Mockery of War,'" *NYDN*, September 24, 1942.

31. Bert Andrews, "Stimson 'Shocked,' Investigates Louis-Conn Charity Fight Set-Up," *NYHT*, September 25, 1942; "Louis Fight Plans Shock to Stimson," *NYT*, September 25, 1942.

32. Dan Parker, "Mike Jacobs, Boxing Dictator," *Look*, June 25, 1946, 36, 38; Gibson with Huntley, *Knocking Down Barriers*, 235–236; Diary of Henry L. Stimson, September 24, 1942, Volume 40, Series XIV, Henry Lewis Stimson Papers, Yale University Library.

33. Godfrey Hodgson, *The Colonel: The Life and Wars of Henry Stimson, 1867–1950* (Knopf, 1990), 265–268.

34. Diary of Henry L. Stimson, September 23, 1942, September 24, 1942; Hugh S. Fullerton, "Sports Roundup," *Scranton Times-Tribune*, September 26, 1942; Claude M. Fuess, "An Atlantic Portrait: Henry L. Stimson," *The Atlantic*, September 1941, 335–337; Hodgson, *The Colonel*, 130, 172, 248–249.

35. Diary of Henry L. Stimson, September 25, 1942.

36. George Dixon, "Stimson Calls Fight Off; Stops Louis-Conn Leaves," *NYDN*, September 26, 1942.

37. "Offer by Agent Reported," *NYT*, September 26, 1942; Caswell Adams, "Jacobs Asks Stimson to Permit Fight, Giving All to Army Relief," *NYHT*, September 27, 1942.

38. Dan Parker, "War Is on Level, Not Ballyhoo Stunt!," *NYDM*, September 26, 1942.

39. "Louis Quits Ring," *NYDN*, October 12, 1942.

40. Dick McCann, "'Misunderstood' Louis Says He's Still Champ," *NYDN*, October 13, 1942.

41. "Roxborough and Jacobs Claim Joe Louis Says He Isn't Retiring but Champ Says: 'No More Comment'; Gets 15-Day Furlough," *DFP*, October 13, 1942; Frederick C. Othman, "Latin Painter Forsakes Home for U.S. Beauties," *Rochester Democrat and Chronicle*, November 12, 1942.

Eight: Stormy Weather

1. J. Cullen Fentress, "Down in Front," *CE*, October 22, 1942.

2. Leo C. Rosten, *Hollywood: The Movie Colony, the Movie Makers* (Harcourt, Brace and Company, 1941), 3–5.

3. James Gavin, *Stormy Weather: The Life of Lena Horne* (Atria Books, 2009), 44, 105.

Notes to Chapter Eight

4. Joe Louis, as told to Meyer Berger and Barney Nagler, "My Story—Joe Louis," *Life*, November 8, 1948, 127.

5. Harry Levette, "Hollywood Puts Out Mat of Welcome for Joe Louis," *NJG*, October 31, 1942.

6. Gail Lumet Buckley, *The Hornes: An American Family* (Applause Books, 1986), 148–149; Gavin, *Stormy Weather*, 93.

7. Clayton R. Koppes and Gregory D. Black, "Blacks, Loyalty, and Motion-Picture Propaganda in World War II," *The Journal of American History* 73, no. 2 (September 1986): 392; Donald Bogle, *Toms, Coons, Mulattoes, Mammies, and Bucks: An Interpretive History of Blacks in American Films* (Bloomsbury Academic, 2016).

8. Gavin, *Stormy Weather*, 98–103.

9. Gavin, *Stormy Weather*, 103.

10. For Walter White's dealings with the motion picture industry see White, *A Man Called White: The Autobiography of Walter White* (Viking Press, 1948), 198–205; Clayton R. Koppes and Gregory D. Black, *Hollywood Goes to War: How Politics, Profits and Propaganda Shaped World War II Movies* (University of California Press, 1990), 39–47.

11. White, *A Man Called White*, 199.

12. White, *A Man Called White*, 200; Gavin, *Stormy Weather*, 93.

13. Kenneth Robert Janken, *White: The Biography of Walter White, Mr. NAACP* (The New Press, 2001), 169; Lena Horne and Richard Schickel, *Lena* (Doubleday, 1965), 134.

14. Horne and Schickel, *Lena*, 131–135; Gavin, *Stormy Weather*, 94–104.

15. Neal Gabler, *An Empire of Their Own: How the Jews Invented Hollywood* (Crown, 1988), 79, 97, 209.

16. Horne and Schickel, *Lena*, 132–133.

17. For the basic details of Lena's contract negotiations see Horne and Schickel, *Lena*, 134–135. In some retellings of the story, Lena said that the negotiations were conducted by Freed.

18. Horne and Schickel, *Lena*, 134–135; Donald Bogle, *Lena Horne: Goddess Reclaimed* (Running Press, 2023), 64–65; "MGM Signs Lena Horne for Hit with George Raft," *Pittsburgh Courier*, January 31, 1942; Billy Rowe, "Rowe's Notebook," *PC*, February 28, 1942; Bill Chase, "Meet Lena Horne, the 'New Type' Sepia Movie Star," *NYAN*, June 20, 1942.

19. Scott Eyman, *Lion of Hollywood: The Life and Legend of Louis B. Mayer* (Simon & Schuster, 2005), 320.

20. Gavin, *Stormy Weather*, 113.

21. Gavin, *Stormy Weather*, 62–63.

22. Irene Thirer, "Lena Horne's Double-Duty Career," *NYP*, October 27, 1943; "Lena Horne Still Idol," *PC*, July 3, 1943.

23. "Ebony Interview: Lena Horne," *Ebony*, May 1980, 42.

Notes to Chapter Eight

24. Billy Rowe, "Lena Horne, Joe Louis Spike Marriage Rumors," *PC*, November 14, 1942.

25. Rowe, "Lena Horne, Joe Louis."

26. Marva Louis, "Why I Quit Joe," *Ebony*, December 1949, 61; Gavin, *Stormy Weather*, 138.

27. Sidney Skolsky, "The Week in Review," *Los Angeles Citizen News*, October 24, 1942; Gavin, *Stormy Weather*, 137–139; "Louis Baby a Girl! Name, Marva Joe," *NYDN*, February 9, 1943; Louis, "Why I Quit Joe," 67; "Hollywood News," *NYHT*, February 16, 1943.

28. For background on *This Is the Army*, see James Kaplan, *Irving Berlin: New York Genius* (Yale University Press, 2013), 203–215; Jody Rosen, *White Christmas: The Story of an American Song* (Scribner, 2002), 129–132; Laurence Bergreen, "Irving Berlin: This Is the Army," *Prologue Magazine* 28, no. 2 (Summer 1996), www.archives.gov/publications/prologue/1996/summer/irving-berlin-1.

29. Kaplan, *Irving Berlin*, 204, 215.

30. *This Is the Army*, directed by Michael Curtiz (Warner Brothers, 1943).

31. Stephen Vaughn, "Ronald Reagan and the Struggle for Black Dignity in Cinema, 1937–1953," *Journal of African American History* 87, no. 1 (Winter 2002): 84–86; Bergreen, "Irving Berlin: This Is the Army."

32. Eleanor Berneis, "Review of *This Is the Army*," 1943, Office of War Information Records, Bureau of Motion Pictures, RG 208, box 3527, NARA.

33. Vaughn, "Ronald Reagan," 85.

34. Frederick C. Othman, "Man of the Month: Champion Joe Louis Scared of Hollywood Movie Camera," *Negro Digest*, May 1943, 44.

35. Kaplan, *Irving Berlin*, 216–217.

36. Philip T. Hartung, "This Is the Army," *The Commonweal*, August 27, 1943, 466; William A. Fowlkes, "Colored Actors 'Grin and Jive' in Army Picture," *ADW*, August 27, 1943; Daniel Prentiss, "This Is the Army," *New Masses*, August 17, 1943, 30.

37. Quoted in Buckley, *The Hornes*, 159–160.

38. Gavin, *Stormy Weather*, 108–109.

39. Script review of "Thanks Pal" ("Stormy Weather") by Lillian Bergquist (January 11, 1943), Records of the Office of War Information, Bureau of Motion Pictures, RG 208, Box 3527, NARA; Film Review of *Stormy Weather* by Sally Kaye (May 6, 1943), Records of the Office of War Information, Bureau of Motion Pictures, RG 208, Box 3527, NARA.

40. Film review of *Cabin in the Sky* by Peg Fenwick (January 19, 1943), Records of the Office of War Information, Bureau of Motion Pictures, RG 208, Box 3513, NARA.

41. Horne and Schickel, *Lena*, 135.

42. Gavin, *Stormy Weather*, 138–139.

43. In Joe Louis's memoir, *My Life*, written with Edna and Art Rust, the boxer claimed that his relationship with Lena ended after a heated disagreement over his relationships with other women. Supposedly, Louis became incensed after an argument and he "hit her with a left hook and knocked her on the bed." Then, he said, he "jumped on her and started choking her." This story is highly unlikely. If the heavyweight champion had struck her "with a left hook," Lena would have undoubtedly suffered a broken jaw, and she would not have been able to hide it from her friends or the press. It's important to note that Louis collaborated with the Rusts at a time when he was suffering from severe mental illness and cocaine abuse. Equally important, when reporters asked Lena about the story in Joe's memoir, she denied it ever happened. Furthermore, on multiple occasions, in the late 1940s and 1950s, they were seen publicly embracing each other warmly. It's hard to imagine that if Joe struck her, Lena would ever be seen with him again. For Joe's version of the fight with Lena, see *My Life*, 182–183. For Lena's denials that Joe attacked her, see "Ebony Interview: Lena Horne," 42, and Jacqueline Trescott, "Lena Horne: The Sunshine and Storms of a Legend," *WP*, October 27, 1978.

Nine: The American Gestapo

1. "Call 50 Police to Bridge Riot," *DFP*, June 21, 1943; Alfred McClung Lee and Norman D. Humphrey, *Race Riot: Detroit, 1943* (Octagon Books, 1968), 20–21, 26; Richard Lingeman, *Don't You Know There's a War On? The American Home Front, 1941–1945* (Putnam, 1970; repr. Thunder's Mouth Press, 2003), 326; Matthew F. Delmont, *Half American: The Epic Story of African Americans Fighting World War II at Home and Abroad* (Viking, 2022), 152.

2. A. J. Baime, *The Arsenal of Democracy: FDR, Detroit, and an Epic Quest to Arm an America at War* (Houghton Mifflin Harcourt, 2014), 245; Thurgood Marshall, "The Gestapo in Detroit," *The Crisis*, August 1943, 232; "Race War in Detroit," *Life*, July 5, 1943, 93.

3. "Mobs Rove the City to Stir Trouble," *DFP*, June 22, 1943; Marshall, "The Gestapo in Detroit," 232–233; Baime, *The Arsenal of Democracy*, 246.

4. James S. Pooler, "3 Years of Strife Behind Disorders," *DFP*, June 22, 1943; Baime, *The Arsenal of Democracy*, 247–248.

5. David M. Kennedy, *The American People in World War II: Freedom from Fear Part II* (Oxford University Press, 1999), 345; Delmont, *Half American*, 147–148; Pooler, "3 Years of Strife Behind Disorders."

6. "Joe Louis Coming to Detroit Monday," *DFP*, June 27, 1943; "Joe Louis Wins Decision over Interviewers," *CT*, June 28, 1943; Wendell Smith, "Mrs. Brooks Talks About My Boy Joe," *PC*, March 12, 1949; Don DeLeighbur, "Portrait of Fighting Man," *DT*, July 17, 1943; Richard Deverall to Clarence Glick, "Detroit Race Riots," Second Report, June 28, 1943, OF4245g, Office of

Production Management, Committee on Fair Employment Practices, Detroit 1943–1944, Franklin D. Roosevelt Papers, FDR Library, Hyde Park, New York.

7. Walter White, "Behind the Harlem Riot," *The New Republic*, August 16, 1943, 220–222; DeLeighbur, "Portrait of Fighting Man."

8. Mary McLeod Bethune to Brig. Gen. F.H. Osborn, June 1, 1943, Records of Headquarters Army Service Forces, Special Services Division, General Records, 1941–1945, 353.8, Athletics, RG 160, Box 248, Entry 196A, National Archives, College Park, Maryland.

9. "Louis Starts Army Camp Tour in U.S. and Abroad Aug. 30," *NYHT*, August 17, 1943; Wil Haygood, *Sweet Thunder: The Life and Times of Sugar Ray Robinson* (Alfred A. Knopf, 2009), 56–57.

10. Stanley Frank, "Sugar Boy," *Colliers*, March 7, 1942, 17, 32; Sugar Ray Robinson with Dave Anderson, *Sugar Ray* (Viking Press, 1970; repr. Da Capo Press, 1994), 14; "Businessman Boxer," *Time*, June 25, 1951.

11. Robinson with Anderson, *Sugar Ray*, 9; Walker Smith Consultation Service Report, Camp Sibert, Alabama, March 8, 1944, Walker Smith (Ray Robinson) Official Military Personnel File (OMPF); Walker Smith Personal History, ca. April 1944, Medical Department, US Army, Smith OMPF; Walker Smith, Clinical Abstract, June 5, 1944, Smith OMPF.

12. Dan Burley, "Confidentially Yours," *NYAN*, April 15, 1944; W.C. Heinz, "Why Don't They Like Ray Robinson?," *Saturday Evening Post*, December 9, 1950, 30–31; Haygood, *Sweet Thunder*, 30–32.

13. Haygood, *Sweet Thunder*, 33–36.

14. *The Ring*, June 1942; Frank, "Sugar Boy," 34; Robinson with Anderson, *Sugar Ray*, 110; "Ray Robinson in Army; Will Box LaMotta Friday," *St. Louis Post-Dispatch*, February 23, 1943; "Robinson Down, But Beats Jake," *NYDN*, February 27, 1943. The Robinson–Wilson card was the first time in four years that Jacobs matched two Black boxers in the main event.

15. George Mouzon, "Louis 'K.O.' at Camp Devens," *NYAN*, September 11, 1943; "Highlights on the Joe Louis Tour," press release, War Department Bureau of Public Relations, September 13, 1943; "Louis on Tour," *Life*, September 13, 1943, 34–35.

16. Morris J. MacGregor Jr., *Integration of the Armed Forces, 1940–1965* (Center of Military History, 1981), 37; "Dear Sir" letter from unsigned soldier, Camp Stewart, Georgia, December 14, 1943, Records of the Office of the Secretary of War, Civilian Aide to the Secretary, 1940–1947, RG 107, Box 186, NARA (hereafter, Civilian Aide to the Secretary of War records); Delmont, *Half American*, 66–67.

17. Burley, "Confidentially Yours."

18. Gerald Astor, *". . . And a Credit to His Race": The Hard Life and Times of Joseph Louis Barrow, a.k.a. Joe Louis* (Saturday Review Press/E.P. Dutton &

Co., 1974), 232; "Joe Protests Camp Seating Arrangements," *NJG*, September 18, 1943; Captain Carroll Fitzgerald to Director, Special Services Division, War Department, September 27, 1943, Civilian Aide to the Secretary of War records; "Joe's a Genuine Leader," *NJG*, September 18, 1943.

19. Alfred E. Smith, "Lena Horne Quits USO Tour in Row over Army Jim Crow," *CD*, January 6, 1945; "War Dept. Awaits Probe of Camp JC Against Lena Horne," *BAA*, January 20, 1945; Memorandum, Summary of Information, Intelligence Division, ASF, Domestic and Counterintelligence Branch, Camp Robinson, December 28, 1944, Civilian Aide to the Secretary of War records, Box 186. In her memoir, Horne incorrectly stated that the German POW incident took place at Fort Riley, Kansas, but undoubtedly it occurred at Camp Robinson. See Lena Horne and Richard Schickel, *Lena* (Doubleday, 1965), 175–177.

20. Cpl. Rupert Trimmingham to *YANK*, Fort Huachuca, AZ, April 28, 1944.

21. "Louis Shows Damaging Left to Admiring Fans at Maxwell Field," *NYA*, January 29, 1944; "Marva's Boston Debut Brings $1000 per Week," *BAA*, May 6, 1944.

22. "Louis Marriage 'on the Rocks,'" *NYDN*, September 25, 1943; "Joe Louis, Wife Separate; to Seek Divorce After War," *BAA*, October 2, 1943; Al Monroe, "Marva Tells Why She Split with Joe," *CD*, October 2, 1943; "Anyone Need Singer? Call Mrs. Joe Louis," *NYDN*, October 21, 1943; "Louis Approves of Wife's Tour as Singer, but Hints at Divorce," *NYHT*, January 30, 1944; "Louis to Marry Lena Horne? No Comment by Champ," *NJG*, January 8, 1944.

23. Jack Saunders, "Reveals Secret for Becoming Singer," *PC*, February 12, 1944.

24. Walker Smith Consultation Service Report, Camp Sibert, Alabama, March 8, 1944, Smith OMPF.

25. Walker Smith Consultation Service Report, Camp Sibert, Alabama, March 10, 1944, Smith OMPF; Walker Smith, Sworn Statement, April 16, 1944, Smith OMPF.

26. "Negro Rapist Killed by Gadsden Officers as He Attempts Escape After Identification," *Gadsden Times*, March 12, 1944; "Negro Soldier Sought for Criminal Assault," *Birmingham News*, February 19, 1944; "Police Kill Negro for Attack," *Anniston Star*, March 12, 1944.

27. "Negro Rapist Killed."

28. Emory O. Jackson to Roy Wilkins, March 16, 1944; Emory O. Jackson to Roy Wilkins, March 20, 1944; Emory O. Jackson to Arthur Davis Shores, March 14, 1944. Emory Jackson correspondence can be found in the Raymond McMurray Killing File, Papers of the NAACP, Part 09: Discrimination in the U.S. Armed Forces, Series B: Armed Forces' Legal Files, 1940–1950.

29. Truman K. Gibson to the Assistant Secretary of War, March 31, 1944, Civilian Aide to the Secretary of War records; "Jail Joe Louis, Ray Robinson," *NYAN*, April 1, 1944.

30. Robinson with Anderson, *Sugar Ray*, 122–124; Sugar Ray Robinson, "My Fighting Life," *The Mirror* (Perth, Western Australia), September 8, 1951; Heinz, "Why Don't They Like Ray Robinson?," 182.

31. Joe Louis Barrow testimony to Major Smith W. Brookhart Jr., March 24, 1944, Camp Sibert, Records of the Office of the Inspector General (Army), Confidential Correspondence, 1917–1947, Record Group 159, Box 727, File 333.9 -Camp Sibert.

32. "Jail Joe Louis, Ray Robinson"; "ANP Reports Joe Louis Was Not Jailed in Camp Sibert," *The Weekly Review* (Birmingham), April 15, 1944; Robinson with Anderson, *Sugar Ray*, 122–124. Although Robinson recalled tackling a white MP at Camp Sibert, there is no record of it in his military file.

33. Joe Louis as told to Meyer Berger and Barney Nagler, "Part Two of Joe Louis' Story," *Life*, November 15, 1948, 139.

34. Joe Louis Barrow testimony to Major Smith W. Brookhart.

35. Jules Tygiel, "The Court-Martial of Jackie Robinson," *American Heritage*, 34–39; 2nd Lt. Jack Robinson to Sec. of NAACP, July 24, 1944, Papers of the NAACP, Part 09: Discrimination in the U.S. Armed Forces, Series B: Armed Forces' Legal Files, 1940–1950, Folder: Soldier Trouble, Robinson, Jackie, 1944; The Adjutant General to Commanding Generals, et al., July 8, 1944, Subject: Recreational Facilities, AG 353.8 (5 July 44) OB-S-A-M; Ulysses Lee, *The Employment of Negro Troops* (Office of the Chief of Military History, U.S. Army, 1966; repr. Center of Military History, 2001), 324.

36. Arnold Rampersad, *Jackie Robinson: A Biography* (Ballantine Books, 1998), 102–109.

37. Robinson with Anderson, *Sugar Ray*, 124; Summary of Information Report, "Conditions: Camp Sibert, Alabama," April 3, 1944, Intelligence Division, ASF, Domestic and Counterintelligence Branch, War Department, OF 4245g, Office of Production Management, Committee on Fair Employment Practices, War Department Materials Concerning Minorities, 1944 March–April, MS Franklin D. Roosevelt and Race Relations, 1933–1945, FDR Papers, Roosevelt Presidential Library and Museum, Hyde Park, New York.

38. Personal Medical History of Sgt. Walker Smith, April 6, 1944, Smith OMPF; Walker Smith, Neuropsychiatric Note, written by Captain Robert L. Craig, April 10, 1944, Smith OMPF.

39. "Louis Here on a Visit," *NYT*, March 28, 1944; Robinson with Anderson, *Sugar Ray*, 126; Clinical Abstract, Sgt. Walker Smith, June 3, 1944, Smith

Notes to Chapter Ten

OMPF; Captain Stockbridge H. Barker to Director, Operations Division, Fort Hamilton, NY, March 31, 1944, Smith OMPF; Walker Smith, Neuropsychiatric Note, April 7, 1944, Smith OMPF.

40. Barney Nagler, "Boxing's Bad Boy: Sugar Ray Robinson," *Sport*, October 1947, 35.

41. Barker to Director; Heinz, "Why Don't They Like Ray Robinson?," 182.

42. Statement of Edward F. Flaherty made to Captain Leon A. Michaelis, Fort Hamilton, April 6, 1944, Smith OMPF.

43. Walker Smith, Clinical Abstract; Walker Smith statement, April 15, 1944, Smith OMPF; War Department Investigation of the Alleged Irregular Discharge of ex-Sgt. Walker Smith, Office of the Inspector General, August 7, 1944, Smith OMPF.

44. Walker Smith, History of the Present Illness, April 6, 1944, Smith OMPF; Walker Smith, Neuropsychiatric Note, April 7, 1944, Smith OMPF.

45. Walker Smith, Progress Notes, written by Captain Robert L. Craig, April 10, 1944, Smith OMPF; War Department Investigation of the Alleged Irregular Discharge of ex-Sgt. Walker Smith, Office of the Inspector General, August 7, 1944, Smith OMPF.

46. War Department Investigation of the Alleged Irregular Discharge of ex-Sgt. Walker Smith, Office of the Inspector General, August 7, 1944, Smith OMPF.

47. Walker Smith, Progress Notes, written by Captain Robert L. Craig, May 26, 1944.

48. War Department Investigation of the Alleged Irregular Discharge of ex-Sgt. Walker Smith, Office of the Inspector General, August 7, 1944, Smith OMPF.

49. "Hearst Newspapers to Sponsor Return of Ray Robinson," *Omaha Guide*, September 9, 1944; "Robinson Patient in S.I. Hospital for Past 10 Days," *BE*, April 9, 1944; "Ray Robinson in Hospital Under Arrest," *DT*, April 15, 1944; Heinz, "Why Don't They Like Ray Robinson?"

50. For Heinz's description of D-Day, see "Sun Reporter on U.S. Battleship Tells How Navy Fought on D-Day," in W.C. Heinz, *When We Were One: Stories of World War II* (Da Capo Press, 2002), 3–7.

51. Haygood, *Sweet Thunder*, 94.

Ten: Over There

1. This story is drawn from Pvt. Tom Ephrem, "Wounded GI Risks Sight to Get Glimpse of Joe Louis," *The Ring*, November 1944, 7, and "All for a Look at the Champ," *PC*, June 24, 1944.

2. Captain Fred Maly to the Director, Special Services Division, October 16, 1944, RG 107, Box 182, NARA; "All for a Look."

3. "Louis Counts On Title Bout," *Baltimore Sun*, October 11, 1944; Ephrem, "Wounded GI Risks Sight," 7; Maly to the Director, Special Services Division, October 16, 1944.

4. Joe Williams, "Louis Visiting Wounded G.I.s," *BN*, September 6, 1944.

5. "Louis Arrives in Britain to Give Ring Exhibitions," *NYT*, April 9, 1944; "Louis Reaches Britain to Start Boxing Tour," *NYHT*, April 9, 1944.

6. Maly to the Director, Special Services Division, October 16, 1944.

7. Don Deleighbur, "Louis Has Done His Part and the Army Should Reward Champion by Allowing Him to Fight," *NYAN*, July 22, 1944; Maly to the Director, Special Services Division, October 16, 1944.

8. "Joe Louis Obeying Orders," *The Citizen* (Gloucester, England), April 11, 1944; "Sgt. Barrow Comes To Town," *The Guardian* (London), April 12, 1944; James Butler, "Joe Louis Here—But They Kept It Quiet," *Daily Herald* (London), April 12, 1944; Tom Jackson, "Champ in Uniform," *Evening News* (Manchester, England), April 12, 1944; Sid Feder, "$64 Query—Louis, Title," *WP*, April 12, 1944.

9. "Joe Louis Obeying Orders"; "Joe Louis Now Better'n Ever," *NYDN*, April 12, 1944; "Sergeant Joe Louis Hopes to Box in Berlin," *Evening Standard* (London), April 11, 1944; "Joe Louis Makes London Debut to Cheers of G.I.'s and Press," *NYHT*, April 12, 1944.

10. Randy Dixon, "Honor Louis in England," *PC*, April 22, 1944; Randy Dixon, "Louis Lifts GI's Morale," *PC*, May 6, 1944.

11. "Joe Louis in Cheltenham," *Gloucestershire Echo*, April 17, 1944; "To-Day's Gossip—Joe Louis," *Gloucestershire Echo*, April 17, 1944; "Louis Finds Allies Are 'Ready.' But London's Quiet Palls on Him," *NYHT*, April 16, 1944.

12. For a more detailed look at the debates on both sides of the Atlantic, see Linda Hervieux, *Forgotten: The Untold Story of D-Day's Black Heroes, at Home and at War* (Harper, 2015), 169–193; Matthew F. Delmont, *Half American: The Epic Story of African Americans Fighting World War II at Home and Abroad* (Viking, 2022), 215–244.

13. Hervieux, *Forgotten*, 176, 187, 188.

14. Mark A. Huddle, ed., *Roi Ottley's World War II: The Lost Diary of an African American Journalist* (University of Kansas Press, 2011), 95–98.

15. Kenneth P. Werrell, "Mutiny at Army Air Force Station 569: Bamber Bridge, England, June 1943," *Aerospace Historian* 22, no. 4 (Winter/December 1975): 206; Hervieux, *Forgotten*, 177–178, 185.

16. For a detailed investigation of the Bamber Bridge affair, see Werrell, "Mutiny at Army Air Force Station 569," 202–209.

17. Werrell, "Mutiny," 207.

18. Pamela E. Walck, "Mutiny at Bamber Bridge: How the World War II Press Reported Racial Unrest Among U.S. Troops and Why It Remains in British Memory," *American Journalism* 37, no. 3 (2020): 346–371.

19. Joe Louis, "My Toughest Fight," *Salute*, December 1947, 11–12.

20. Louis, "My Toughest Fight," 11–12; Huddle, ed., *Roi Ottley's World War II*, 98–99.

21. Louis, "My Toughest Fight," 13.

22. Joe Fleming, "Negroes Turn Over Field to AF; Joe Louis Late but Makes It," *Stars and Stripes*, May 2, 1944.

23. Delmont, *Half American*, 216–218.

24. For a fine overview of *The Negro Soldier*, see Thomas Cripps and David Culbert, "*The Negro Soldier* (1944): Film Propaganda in Black and White," *American Quarterly* (Winter 1979): 616–640; Ulysses Lee, *The Employment of Negro Troops* (Office of the Chief of Military History, U.S. Army, 1966; repr. Center of Military History, 2001).

25. Kimberly L. Phillips, *War! What Is It Good For? Black Freedom Struggles and the U.S. Military from World War II to Iraq* (University of North Carolina Press, 2012), eBook, chapter 1.

26. *The Negro Soldier*, directed by Stuart Heisler (War Activities Committee of the Motion Pictures Industry, 1944); Nathan Seeley, "Carlton Moss and African American Cultural Emancipation," *Black Camera: An International Film Journal* 9, no. 2 (Spring 2018): 55.

27. Frank Capra, *The Name Above the Title: An Autobiography* (Macmillan, 1971), 359.

28. Huddle, *Roi Ottley's World War II*, 51, 90.

29. "Joe Louis Display at the Stadium," *Liverpool Daily Post*, July 5, 1944; Art Carter, "Joe Visits Fighter Group, Praises Outfit in Speech," *Washington Afro-American*, September 9, 1944.

30. Captain Fred Maly to Director, Special Services Division, A.S.F., October 16, 1944, NARA, RG 107, Box 182; Tris Dixon, *Damage: The Untold Story of Brain Trauma in Boxing* (Hamilcar, 2021), x, 1–8.

31. "Joe Louis's Tip to British Boxing," *Liverpool Evening Express*, July 4, 1944; "Louis Winding Up Tour; Mediterranean Next Stop," *The Stars and Stripes*, July 14, 1944; "Joe Louis Visits Fliers in Italy," *NJG*, September 2, 1944; "Camera Records Stops on Joe Louis's North African Tour," *BAA*, September 2, 1944; John "Rover" Jordan, "Joe Louis Popular with GI's in Italy," *NJG*, August 12, 1944; Ollie Harrington, "Louis and Boxing Troupe Now Performing in Italy," *PC*, August 26, 1944; Max Johnson, "Injuries, Weight Break Up Joe Louis Boxing Troupe," *BAA*, September 9, 1944; Art Carter, "Joe's Boxing Troupe Tours the 5th Army," *NYAN*, September 30, 1944.

32. Harrington, "Louis and Boxing Troupe."

33. Johnson, "Injuries, Weight."

34. "Countess' Home in Italy Swept by Tides of War," *NYHT*, October 1, 1944; "Fighting Men," *NYDN*, August 15, 1944; Art Carter, "Joe Louis Visits Front Line Foxholes," *Washington Afro-American*, September 30, 1944.

35. Ed Sullivan, "From the GI Joes," *NYDN*, October 1, 1944.

36. For Louis's homecoming, see Louis Effrat, "Joe Louis Returns After Long Tour," *NYT*, October 11, 1944; "Louis Picks Two GI Contenders," *NYDN*, October 11, 1944; Jack Cuddy, "Next Champ Won't Be a 4-F, Grins Furlough-Bound Joe Louis," *DFP*, October 11, 1944.

37. Al Laney, "The Champion Comes Home," *NYHT*, October 11, 1944.

38. "Furlough Awaits Joe Louis," *NYT*, October 12, 1944; Dan Burley, "Return of Joe Louis Stirs Conjectures," *NYAN*, October 21, 1944.

39. "Louis' Manager Must Go to State Prison," *NJG*, October 24, 1944.

40. "Marva Louis," *DT*, October 21, 1944; "Long May They Rave," *NYDN*, July 31, 1944; Marva Louis, "Why I Quit Joe," *Ebony*, December 1949, 67–69; Floyd G. Snelson, "Harlem's Welcome to Marva Recalls Story of Decade Ago," *CD*, March 17, 1944; Don DeLeighbur, "Can Marva Louis Sing a Song . . . ?," *Cleveland Call and Post*, December 11, 1943; "Marva's Boston Debut Brings $1000 per Week," *BAA*, May 6, 1944; "Marva Louis Steps Out to Rival Bomber's Earning Power on Stage," *Cleveland Call and Post*, November 27, 1943.

41. Louis, "Why I Quit Joe," 61; "Louis's Wife Sues Again," *NYHT*, March 21, 1945; "Hearing Next Tuesday on Louis Divorce Suit," *NYHT*, March 23, 1945; "Marva Is Granted Divorce," *PC*, April 7, 1945; Truman K. Gibson Jr. with Steve Huntley, *Knocking Down Barriers: My Fight for Black America* (Northwestern University Press, 2005), 241–242.

42. Louella O. Parsons, "Paul Muni, Claud Rains Will Be Costarred in Film Fantasy," *Modesto Bee*, June 15, 1945.

43. "Louis Bars Fight Talk Until War Is Finished," *NYHT*, October 26, 1944; "Louis Puts War First," *NYT*, October 26, 1944. On November 11, 1944, Louis knocked out Johnny Davis in the first round of a contest scheduled for four rounds. Davis was a novice fighter with three wins and three losses on his professional record. The match was clearly an exhibition, though the New York State Athletic Commission labeled it a title defense. The more important National Boxing Association did not sanction it as a title defense. Newspaper accounts clearly considered it part of a Joe Louis exhibition tour. See "Louis Boxing Tour Lists Five Cities," *NYDN*, November 11, 1944.

44. Gibson, *Knocking Down Barriers*, 239–240; Gerald Astor, ". . . And a Credit to His Race": The Hard Life and Times of Joseph Louis Barrow, a.k.a. Joe Louis* (E.P. Dutton & Co., 1974), 236; "Promotion Gives Fifth Stripe to Joe Louis; Titleholder Is Now a Technical Sergeant," *NYT*, April 10, 1945; "Joe Louis Has 71 Points," *NYT*, July 16, 1945.

45. Captain Fred Maly to Director, Special Services Division, A.S.F., October 16, 1944, National Archives, RG 107, Box 182; "Louis Ends Long Trip," *NYT*, July 7, 1945.

46. "Joe Louis Honored as Model Soldier," *NYT*, September 24, 1945; "Louis Awarded the Legion of Merit for 'Exceptionally Meritorious Conduct,'"

NYHT, September 24, 1945; "Joe Louis, Truman Gibson Get Army Merit Awards," *PC*, September 29, 1945; "Louis Receives Discharge and '46 Bout Looms," *NYHT*, October 2, 1945; "Louis Discharged; to Attend Series," *NYT*, October 2, 1945; "The Champion Collects His Army 'Gate,'" *NYT*, October 3, 1945.

47. Arthur Daley, "Louis and Conn Back by Request," *NYT*, October 17, 1945.

Eleven: Homecoming

1. Bryan Greene, "After Victory in World War II, Black Veterans Continued the Fight for Freedom at Home," *Smithsonian Magazine*, August 30, 2021; Beverly Gage, *G-Man: J. Edgar Hoover and the Making of the American Century* (Viking, 2022), 311; Matthew Delmont, *Half American: The Epic Story of African Americans Fighting World War II at Home and Abroad* (Viking, 2022), 271–278; "Two More Lynchings! Dixie 'Reign of Terror' Spreads," *PC*, August 24, 1946; Evelyn Seeley, "'It's Got to Be . . . Negro, Whites Alongside One Another,'" *PM*, August 16, 1946.

2. Jennifer E. Brooks, *Defining the Peace: World War II Veterans, Race, and the Remaking of Southern Political Tradition* (University of North Carolina Press, 2004), 24; Philip Dray, *At the Hands of Persons Unknown: The Lynching of Black America* (Random House, 2002), 376–383.

3. Enoc P. Waters Jr., "Bloodless Charleston Revolt," *CD*, June 15, 1946; M. L. King Jr., Morehouse College, "Kick Up Dust," *Atlanta Constitution*, August 6, 1946.

4. Kari Frederickson, *Dixiecrat Revolt and the End of the Solid South, 1932–1968* (University of North Carolina Press, 2001), 54; A. J. Baime, *White Lies: The Double Life of Walter F. White and America's Darkest Secret* (Mariner Books, 2022), 272–277; Major Robinson, "Woodard Tells Bitter Story," *CD*, July 27, 1946.

5. "Helping Hands," *NYDN*, August 9, 1946; "Negroes, Whites Form Vet Organization," *The People's Voice*, April 13, 1946; "1946: Year of Great Negro Resistance to Hate Groups," *New Jersey Afro-American*, January 1947; "The Negro Veteran Tests America," *Ebony*, May 1946, 40.

6. Gerald Astor, "*. . . And a Credit to His Race*": *The Hard Life and Times of Joseph Louis Barrow, a.k.a. Joe Louis* (Saturday Review Press/E.P. Dutton, 1974), 259; Neil Scott, "Joe Louis Joins Woodard Benefit," *NYAN*, August 3, 1946.

7. Seeley, "'It's Got to Be.'"

8. Bill Mardo, "In This Corner," *DW*, February 26, 1946; Seeley, "'It's Got to Be.'" Citing his memoir, *Joe Louis: My Life*, Louis's biographers have repeated a false story that he gave a speech at the Woodard benefit at Lewisohn Stadium on August 18, 1946. However, contemporary newspaper accounts reported

that Louis did not attend the benefit. The *New York Herald Tribune* and *New York Amsterdam News* reported that Louis was ill and unable to attend. See "Blinded Negro to Get $22,000 Raised at Rally," *NYHT*, August 19, 1946; Bill Chase, "Performers Had Backstage at Benefit, Too," *NYAN*, August 24, 1946.

9. Barney Nagler, *Brown Bomber* (World Publishing Company, 1972), 157.

10. A. J. Liebling, *The Sweet Science* (Viking Press, 1956; repr. North Point Press, 2004), 35–36; Harvey Breit, "Louis Versus Conn—and 'Old Age,'" *New York Times Magazine*, June 16, 1946, 48; "Louis' Nose Hit in First Workout," *NYT*, May 5, 1946; Grantland Rice, "Joe Louis Must Sharpen Attack to Beat Conn," *BG*, May 22, 1946; "Louis Is off Form in Six-Round Drill," *NYT*, May 29, 1946; Grantland Rice, "Hint Champion Louis Has Done His Training Behind Closed Doors," *BG*, June 9, 1946.

11. Rice, "Hint Champion Louis"; Barney Nagler, "How to Run a Prize Fight," *Collier's*, June 15, 1946, 22; John Field and Earl Brown, "The Boxing Racket," *Life*, June 17, 1946, 103; Joseph C. Nichols, "$100 Ringside Tops Louis-Conn Scale," *NYT*, April 2, 1946.

12. Breit, "Louis Versus Conn—and 'Old Age'"; "Louis Moves East April 24," *CD*, April 27, 1946; Wendell Smith, "Louis Rapidly Getting into Shape in Pompton Lakes Camp," *PC*, May 18, 1946; Wendell Smith, "Punching the Bag," *PC*, May 25, 1946.

13. Jonathan Eig, *Opening Day: The Story of Jackie Robinson's First Season* (Simon & Schuster, 2007), 21–23; Chris Mead, *Joe Louis: Black Champion in White America* (Scribner, 1985; repr. Dover Publications, 2010), 271; Ronald F. Briley, "Where Have You Gone William Bendix? Baseball as a Symbol of American Values in World War II," *Studies in Popular Culture* 8, no. 2 (1985): 27; Jules Tygiel, *Baseball's Great Experiment: Jackie Robinson and His Legacy*, expanded edition (Oxford University Press, 1983; repr. Oxford University Press, 1997), 37–43.

14. Thanks to historian John Thorn for providing a copy of the Frank Young column. See Young, "Dixie Sport Scribes Differ on Robinson," *CD*, November 3, 1945.

15. Tygiel, *Baseball's Great Experiment*, 75; Jackie Robinson, "'Glad of Opportunity and Will Try to Make Good.'—Robinson," *PC*, November 3, 1945; Joseph D. Bibb, "Popular Man's Burden," *PC*, November 24, 1945; "Sports Heroes Try Each Other's Weapons," *NJG*, June 22, 1946; James P. Dawson, "Field Chairs for Bout Sacrifice 7,000 Seats at Yankee Stadium," *NYT*, June 15, 1946; "A Real Champ: Jackie Acclaims Joe Louis at Howard Fete," *Washington Afro-American*, February 6, 1954.

16. "Thousands Hail Joe Louis in a Parade in New York City," *St. Louis Argus*, June 21, 1946; Julius J. Adams, "Louis Day Parade Biggest in All History of Harlem," *NYAN*, June 22, 1946; Hy Turkin, "Louis KO Lights Fuse

to Harlem Celebration," *NYDN*, June 20, 1946; Richard Dier, "Thousands Line Streets as Bojangles Leads Harlem Championship Parade," *Washington Afro-American*, June 22, 1946; Gene Ward, "Harlem, in Holiday Mood, Waits in Vain for Louis," *NYDN*, June 20, 1946.

17. Jimmy Cannon, "What the Army Did to Louis and Conn," *Salute*, April 1946; Whitney Martin, "Tonight Zero Hour for Conn's Five-Year Plan for Revenge," *BG*, June 19, 1946.

18. Elizabeth Faue, *Rethinking the American Labor Movement* (Routledge, 2017), 116; "Television Is Lovely Way to See it Easily," *Toronto Star*, June 20, 1946.

19. James P. Dawson, "Louis 5-14 Choice over Conn Tonight," *NYT*, June 19, 1946; Larry Wolters, "Television Spectator Gets Ringside View and Saves $100," *CT*, June 20, 1946; "Television Is Lovely." Historian Troy Rondinone notes that in 1946, boxing "along with a smattering of other sports programming" accounted for nearly 40 percent of all TV broadcasts. See Rondinone, *Friday Night Fighter: Gaspar Indio Ortega and the Golden Age of Television Boxing* (University of Illinois Press, 2013), 17.

20. Jimmy Cannon, "The Lightning Hits Billy Conn," *The New Republic*, July 1, 1946, 934; Grantland Rice, "Rice Describes Fight as Leading Flop of All World Championships," *BN*, June 20, 1946; Arthur Daley, "Louis Proves His Own Prediction: Conn Could Run, but Couldn't Hide," *NYT*, June 20, 1946; Arthur Daley, "Sports of the Times," *NYT*, June 21, 1946.

21. Steve Snider, "One Louis Punch Puts Billy Conn on Fistic Shelf," *BN*, June 20, 1946; Cannon, "The Lightning Hits Billy Conn," 935. Although Conn announced his retirement after losing to Louis in 1946, he returned for two more fights in 1948.

22. "Joe Is Never Hurt by Retreating Challenger," *DFP*, June 20, 1946; Jim McCulley, "Bomber Elated over Kayo; Billy Retires from Ring," *NYDN*, June 20, 1946.

23. "How Joe Louis Lost 2 Million," *Ebony*, May 1946, 10; Field and Brown, "The Boxing Racket," 103, 114; W.C. Heinz, "What Happened to Joe Louis' $4,000,000!," *Cosmopolitan*, December 1950, 72; "The Blow That K.O.'D Joe Louis," *U.S. News & World Report*, January 25, 1957, 66; Nagler, *Brown Bomber*, 148.

24. Astor, "... *And a Credit to His Race": The Hard Life and Times of Joseph Louis Barrow, a.k.a. Joe Louis*, 250; Joe Louis as told to Edward Linn, "Oh, Where Did My Money Go?," *Saturday Evening Post*, January 7, 1956, 68.

25. Barney Nagler, *James Norris and the Decline of Boxing* (Bobbs-Merrill Company, 1964), 4; Frank Wakefield, "Bison Handles World Champion but Never Wore Boxing Glove," *BN*, February 8, 1946; Nagler, *Brown Bomber*, 149.

26. Sid Feder, "Louis Earns at Rate of $803 per Second," September 20, 1946, *Cincinnati Enquirer*.

27. "Roxborough and Louis Hold Reunion," *DFP*, October 5, 1946; Frank E. Bolden, "Joe Happy as 'Roxie' Is Freed," *PC*, October 12, 1946.

28. "NBA Secretary Claims Jacobs Hurts Boxing," *CT*, February 3, 1946; Field and Brown, "The Boxing Racket," 103, 114.

29. Lee Dunbar, "On the Level," *Oakland Tribune*, October 6, 1946; Paul Carbo, FBI File, Section One.

30. Dan Parker, "Who Is Frankie Carbo?," *The American Weekly*, October 18, 1959; David Remnick, *King of the World: Muhammad Ali and the Rise of an American Hero* (Vintage Books, 1999), 58–60; Steven A. Riess, "Only the Ring Was Square: Frankie Carbo and the Underworld Control of American Boxing," *The International Journal of the History of Sport* 5, no. 1 (1988): 34–35, 41.

31. Nagler, *James Norris and the Decline of Boxing*, 19–20; A. J. Liebling, "The University of Eighth Avenue," *Sports Illustrated*, December 12, 1955, 36; Angelo Dundee with Bert Randolph Sugar, *My View from the Corner: My Life in Boxing* (McGraw-Hill, 2009), 32.

32. Dan Parker, "Mike Jacobs, Boxing Dictator," *Look*, June 25, 1946, 38; Carbo, FBI File, Section One; *Hearings Before the Subcommittee on Antitrust and Monopoly*, Eighty-Sixth Congress, 2nd sess., Part 2: Frank Carbo, December 1960 (US Government Printing Office, 1961), 292.

33. Parker, "Who Is Frankie Carbo?"

34. James P. Dawson, "Promoter Jacobs Gravely Ill Here," *NYT*, December 4, 1946; "Mike Jacobs in Hospital with Brain Hemorrhage," *NYDN*, December 4, 1946; "Mike Jacobs near Death; in Grave Condition After Suffering Brain Hemorrhage," *Daily Herald* (Provo, Utah), December 4, 1946; "Heart Ailment Balks Jacobs' Fight for Life," *CT*, December 8, 1946; Ed Sullivan, "Little Old New York," *NYDN*, December 16, 1946.

35. "Joe Louis Pays Visit to Jacobs in Hospital," *WP*, December 10, 1946; Wendell Smith, "The Sports Beat," *PC*, December 21, 1946; James P. Dawson, "Jacobs' Aides Map Extensive Plans," *NYT*, December 29, 1946.

36. Action Report, Southern Conference for Human Welfare, New York Committee, September 12, 1946, Papers of the NAACP, Part 18, Special Subjects, 1940–1955, Series C: General Office Files, Folder: Southern Conference for Human Welfare, 1945–1947, (hereafter, SCHW folder, NAACP papers).

37. Action Report, SCHW folder, NAACP papers; Joe Louis to Mr. Barrington, September 4, 1946, SCHW folder, NAACP papers; Thomas A. Krueger, *And Promises to Keep: The Southern Conference for Human Welfare, 1938–1948* (Vanderbilt University Press, 1967), 148–150; "Louis at Rally to Aid Southern Welfare," *NYT*, September 20, 1946; John Hudson Jones, "The Champ Touches Off Aid to Dixie Campaign," *DW*, September 20, 1946; "Joe Louis Opens Rally for Aid to Dixieland," *BAA*, September 28, 1946.

38. "South Analyzed at Louis Dinner," *BAA*, December 21, 1946; Chester L. Washington, "Champ Takes Sock at Race Prejudice," *PC*, December 28, 1946.

Notes to Epilogue

39. Washington, "Champ Takes Sock"; Joe Louis, "My Toughest Fight," *Salute*, December 1947, 12–16.

40. Rick Hurt, "Sports Train," *The People's Voice*, March 9, 1946.

41. A. H. Belmont to D. M. Ladd, memorandum, November 6, 1951, Joe Louis, FBI File; Gage, *G-Man*, 441.

42. "War-Bond Sale Boosted at Big Rally in City," *DFP*, June 1, 1942; "35,000 Cheer Joe Louis, Robeson at Music Fest," *CD*, July 31, 1943; Paul Robeson, "Plain Talk: Louis Is Still Our Champion," *The People's Voice*, December 20, 1947.

Epilogue: The Final Round

1. Barney Nagler, *James Norris and the Decline of Boxing* (Bobbs-Merril Company, 1964), 3–6; Barney Nagler, "Louis Says He'll Retire After June Fight," *Bronx Home News*, December 11, 1947.

2. Harry Grayson, "Walcott's Knockdown of Louis Was Other Way Around," *Herald-Journal* (Logan, Utah), December 2, 1947; Jack Cuddy, "Joe Louis Is Favored at 10-1 in 24th Bout in Defense of Title," *BN*, December 5, 1947; Harry Grayson, "Jersey Joe's Story Parallels Braddock's," *Lansing State Journal*, November 30, 1947.

3. Gerald Astor, ". . . And a Credit to His Race": The Hard Life and Times of Joseph Louis Barrow, a.k.a. Joe Louis* (Saturday Review Press/E.P. Dutton, 1974), 244; Grantland Rice, "Outfought, Outfoxed, Weird Decision Saves Crown for Joe Louis," *BN*, December 6, 1947; Gene Ward, "Louis Outpoints Walcott; Fans Boo Decision," *NYDN*, December 6, 1947; Oscar Fraley, "'I Ain't Fighter I Was at 23,' Joe Says After Walcott Bout," *BN*, December 6, 1947. A ringside poll of thirty-two boxing writers indicated that twenty-one had scored the bout for Walcott, ten scored it for Louis, and one called it a draw.

4. Nagler, *James Norris and the Decline of Boxing*, 5–6; Nagler, "Louis Says He'll Retire."

5. Richard Wright, "King Joe" ("Joe Louis Blues"), composed 1941, copyright 1942.

6. "Walcott Only Remembers First Punch—Right to Head," *Bergen Evening Record* (New Jersey), June 26, 1948; Jimmy Powers, "The Powerhouse," *NYDN*, June 26, 1948; "'Referee Beat Me'—Walcott," *BG*, June 26, 1948; Gene Ward, "Louis Kayos Walcott in 2:56 of 11th," *NYDN*, June 26, 1948; Wendell Smith, "So Long, Joe! You Were the Greatest," *PC*, July 3, 1948.

7. Bill Nunn, "An Open Letter to Joe Louis," *PC*, July 3, 1948.

8. Nunn, "Open Letter."

9. Matthew F. Delmont, *Half American: The Epic Story of African Americans Fighting World War II at Home and Abroad* (Viking, 2022), 284–285; Christine Knauer, *Let Us Fight as Free Men: Black Soldiers and Civil Rights* (University of

Pennsylvania Press, 2014), 86, 272, n. 23; "Louis Fights Again—This Time for Non-Jimcro Army," *NJG*, April 17, 1948.

10. Frederick J. Frommer, "Truman Called for Integrating the Military 75 Years Ago—and to Go Further," *WP*, February 2, 2023.

11. President Truman's Address Before the NAACP, June 29, 1947, Truman Library Institute.

12. Knauer, *Let Us Fight as Free Men*, 4; Morris J. MacGregor Jr., *Integration of the Armed Forces, 1940–1945* (United States Army Center for Military History, 1985), 312–313.

13. John McMullan, "Joe Louis, Here, Vacates Heavy Title," *Miami Daily News*, March 1, 1949; Robert Coughlan, "How the IBC Runs Boxing," *Sports Illustrated*, January 17, 1955, 12–13; Russell Sullivan, *Rocky Marciano: The Rock of His Times* (University of Illinois Press, 2005), 52–54. Louis later insisted that the "Mendel Plan," as it became known, originated as his own idea. See Ed Linn, "Tarnished Idol," *Sport*, May 1958, 20.

14. McMullan, "Joe Louis, Here, Vacates Heavy Title"; Nagler, *James Norris and the Decline of Boxing*, 7–8; Martin Kane and James Shepley, "The Case Against the IBC," *Sports Illustrated*, April 23, 1956, 28; "Mike Jacobs, Boxing's Empire-Builder, Dies at 72," *BG*, January 25, 1953; "Jacobs Slaps Today's Pugs," *Brooklyn Eagle*, November 21, 1952; "My Closest Friend, Says Saddened Louis," *BG*, January 25, 1953.

15. Linn, "Tarnished Idol," 20.

16. On the IBC's monopoly, see Coughlan, "How the IBC Runs Boxing," 11–13, 47–50.

17. "Moral Duress Charge Wins Marva Divorce," *Miami Daily News*, February 19, 1949; Marva Louis, "Why I Quit Joe," *Ebony*, December 1949, 69–70.

18. "Joe and Lena Play a Duet," *BAA*, June 18, 1949; Jimmie Fidler, "In Hollywood," *Pasadena Independent*, June 19, 1949; Dan Burley, "The Love Life of Joe Louis," *Ebony*, July 1951, 22.

19. Chris Mead, *Joe Louis: Black Champion in White America* (Scribner, 1985; repr. Dover Publications, 2010), 271; "Joe Louis Testifying in Tax Tangle," *DFP*, June 30, 1955; Louis Lautier, "How Joe Louis' Kids Lost $64,000 to US," *Washington Afro-American*, December 22, 1956.

20. Gene Ward, "Ez Thrashes Louis for Title," *NYDN*, September 28, 1950; Mead, *Joe Louis*, 257.

21. Astor, ". . . *And a Credit to His Race*," 253; "Louis Is Through but 'Positively,'" *NYT*, September 28, 1950.

22. Arthur J. Snider, "Louis Advised to Heed Guidance of Doctors on His Future Plans," *BN*, November 3, 1951; William Nack, "The Rock," *Sports Illustrated*, August 23, 1993, 56–60; Sullivan, *Rocky Marciano*, 76–88.

23. Sullivan, *Rocky Marciano*, 99; Jerry Nason, "Brockton Boxer Clouts Ex-Champ out of Ring," *BG*, October 27, 1951.

24. Jimmy Cannon, "Jimmy Cannon Says," *Newsday* (Suffolk County, NY), November 6, 1951.

25. "Sport: Joe's Fight," *Time*, January 28, 1952; "Joe Louis Will Fight PGA Tournament Ban," *LAT*, January 14, 1952; Norman Bell, "Joe Louis Warring with P.G.A. over Color Line," *Honolulu Star-Bulletin*, January 14, 1952.

26. "Will Joe Louis Be Golf Champ Next?" *Ebony*, December 1948, 13–18; Marion E. Jackson, "Sports of the World," *ADW*, January 11, 1952; George B. Kirsch, *Golf in America* (University of Illinois Press, 2008), 150–151; "Ches Says . . . ," *PC*, January 26, 1952.

27. Kirsch, *Golf in America*, 160; Shirley Povich, "This Morning," *WP*, January 15, 1952.

28. Jimmy Cannon, "Jimmy Cannon Says," *Newsday*, January 15, 1952.

29. Marcy S. Sacks, *Joe Louis: Sports and Race in Twentieth Century America* (Routledge, 2018), 169; "Smith Admits Bias in Reply to Joe Louis," *NJG*, January 19, 1952.

30. "Joe Louis Deserts Golf Fight," *CE*, January 17, 1952; "Ches Says . . . ," *PC*, January 26, 1952; "Sport: Joe's Fight," *Time*, January 28, 1952; "Negro Golf Stars Qualify and Play in Phoenix Golf Open; Louis Fails," *NYAN*, January 26, 1952; Kirsch, *Golf in America*, 161. In his defense for playing the San Diego Open, Louis was criticized for saying, "We have to crawl before we can walk," but Joe insisted he was misquoted.

31. Wendell Smith, "Sports Beat," *PC*, January 26, 1952.

32. "Joe Louis Resents 'Spokesman of Race' Title," *Miami Times*, August 29, 1953.

33. Smith, "Sports Beat."

INDEX

Abramson, Jesse, 97
Adams, Caswell, 94, 122
Ali, Muhammad, 258
All-Sports Carnival (1942), 152
Amateur Athletic Union (AAU), 59, 197, 233
American Dilemma, 6
Andrews, Adolphus, 114, 128–129
Angelou, Maya, 70
anti-lynching law, 54–55, 57, 107, 121, 260
Army, US. *See also* military
   Black officers, 18, 155–157, 226
   boxing exhibitions at military posts, 3–4, 19, 105, 114, 151, 199, 201, 204
   draft (*see* draft)
   draft board, 74, 79, 86–87, 125, 155
   failure to publicize Black soldiers, 139
   Louis's discharge from, 239–240
   Louis's enlistment in, 103–105, 124–125
   Louis's induction into, 17–19, 127–128
   racial tensions, 137–138
   rapid expansion of black men in, 154
   segregation in military, 4, 18–19, 54, 120, 131, 155, 269–271
Army Emergency Relief Fund
   Louis–Conn potential rematch for, 160–167
   Louis–Simon fight (1942), 136, 140–141, 150
   Mike Jacobs and, 149–150, 160–167
   This Is the Army, 180, 182, 186

Army General Classification Test (AGCT), 130–131
Atlantic Charter, 108
Austin, J. C., 146

Baer, Buddy
   Louis fight (1941), 76, 94–95
   Louis fight (1942), 112–124, 135
Baer, Max, 10, 12, 81, 100, 144
Bamber Bridge gunfight, 225–226
Bard, Ralph, 123
Barker, Stockbridge H., 211
Barrow, Joe Louis. *See* Louis, Joe
baseball, 59–60, 136, 155, 249–251
Basie, William "Count," 99
Belle Isle bridge, 191–194
Benson, Ted, 159–160
Berger, Meyer, 62
Berlin, Irving, 180–183
Bernard, Pierre, 96
Bethune, Mary McLeod, 118, 195
Biddle, Francis, 133
Big Four Policy and Numbers House, 35
Binyon, Claude, 182
Black, Julian
   Blackburn funeral, 146
   Brown on, 28–29
   Camp Grant exhibition, 105
   as civic leader, 26
   gate proceeds share, 41
   hiring Blackburn, 143
   indictment, 146
   Louis–Conn fight (1941), 69
   Louis's enlistment, 103
   Louis's military induction, 129

Index

Black, Julian *(continued)*
  Marva Louis, 82–84
  Navy Relief Society match, 113
  payment of suit against Blackburn, 145
  rules on fighter's conduct, 23
Black Americans
  actors, 170–178, 184–186, 188
  in the army (*see* Black soldiers)
  attacks on Black veterans, 243–247
  credentialed Black reporters, 131
  Democratic Party and Black voters, 53–55, 66–67
  discrimination and inequities (*see* Jim Crow)
  exploitation of, 15
  fascism, experience with, 50
  Great Migration, 7, 25
  importance of Louis to, 3, 15–16, 19, 28–29, 100, 268
  Louis as Black hero, 5, 24, 30, 133, 135, 196, 251, 263, 268–269
  lynching (*see* lynching)
  race riots, 15, 191–194, 225, 243
  racial stereotypes in films, 170–171, 173–174, 184, 188–189, 229
  racism (*see* racism)
  soldiers (*see* Black soldiers)
  Wilkins on democracy for Black people, 50–51, 103
Blackburn, Charles Henry "Jack"
  death, 141–142
  funeral, 146
  illness, 121, 140–141
  imprisonment, 143
  influence with Louis, 145–146
  Louis–Conn fight (1941), 72–73
  personal history, 142–147
  shooting of Houser and Cannon, 145
  training Louis, 143–144
Blackburn, Fred, 142–143
Black Freedom Movement, 262
Black Moses, Joe Louis as, 21–22, 25, 70, 146
Black soldiers
  attacks on Black veterans, 243–247
  Buffalo soldiers, 153
  in England, 220, 223–226
  helped by Louis, 6, 155, 279–280
  at Louis fights, 201, 280–281
  lynching of soldiers, 102–103, 270
  The Negro problem, 4, 18, 133
  The Negro Soldier (film), 229–231
Black veterans
  attacks on, 243–247
  lynching of, 243–245, 247, 260–261
blood banks, 4
BMP (Bureau of Motion Pictures), 184, 188
Bocchicchio, Felix, 266
Boman, Fay, 205–206
Bostic, Joe, 152
Bowman, John, 144
boxing. *see also* Louis, Joe, fights of; *specific fighters*
  Boxing Writers' Association, 134
  Carbo influence in, 257–260, 266, 273
  exhibitions (*see* boxing exhibitions)
  exploitation of boxers, 35, 74, 145, 255
  International Boxing Club (IBC), 271–273
  morale boost from, 136–137
  New York State Boxing Commission, 38, 40, 135
  Norris–Wirtz–Carbo triumvirate, 273
  promoters (*see specific individuals*)
  punch-drunk syndrome, 26, 204, 232
  on television, 253
  training techniques, 95–96
  War Boxing, Inc., 161, 166
boxing exhibitions of Louis in the Army
  "All-Sports Carnival," 152
  overseas, 218, 221, 231–232, 235
  seating of Black troops, 201, 227
  Sugar Ray Robinson's removal from, 204
  toll on Louis, 232
  at US military posts, 3–4, 19, 105, 114, 151, 199, 201, 204

Index

Boxing Writers' Association, 134
Braddock, James J., 38–41
Brodhead Naval Armory, 191
Brooks, Lillie Barrow, 12, 29, 193
Broun, Heywood, 9, 64
Brown, Earl, 21–24, 27–31
Brown, Lawrence, 99
Brundage, Avery, 59
Bruseaux, Sheridan, 84
Buck, Walter, 208
Buckley, Gail Lumet, 171
Budge, Don, 152
Bureau of Motion Pictures (BMP), 184, 188
Burley, Dan
   breakfast with Louis, 235–236
   criticism of Louis, 114–116
   on Jacobs concern over Louis's military service, 74
   on Navy Relief Society match, 114–116
   Original Handbook of Harlem Jive, 114
   prize-fighters as kings, 200
   on treatment of Black veterans, 243
Burman, Red, 94
Butler, James, 221

Cabin in the Sky (film), 169, 171, 176–177, 186–188
Café Society, 87–91, 175
Calloway, Cab, 187
Camp Croft, 132
Camp Good, 158
Camp Gordon, 245
Camp Grant, 105
Camp Hood, 209
Camp Lee, 200
Camp Robinson, 200–202
Camp Shanks, 239
Camp Sibert, 204–210
Camp Siegfried, 129–130
Camp Stewart, 200
Camp Upton, 129–132, 134, 136, 141
Cannon, Jimmy
   Conn conversation, 252
   fighting for a paycheck, 276
   on Jim Crow as umpire in baseball, 249
   Louis dressing room conversation (September 1941), 93–94
   on segregationist PGA, 278
Cannon, Lucy, 145
Capps, Alice, 158
Capra, Frank, 229
Carbo, Paul John "Frankie," 257–260, 266, 273
Carnera, Primo, 22, 38, 52, 62, 82, 88, 114, 194
Case, Jack, 198
Cassey, Alfred, 64
censors, 132, 174, 188–189, 194, 226, 247
Chandler, Albert "Happy," 250
Charles, Ezzard, 274–275
chronic traumatic encephalopathy, 232
Churchill, Winston
   FDR meeting (August 1941), 108
   Operation Torch, 164–165
civil rights movement, 245, 262
Clark, Mark, 234
Clarke, M. C., 116
Cohen, Rose, 259
Coles, I. F., 82
Conn, Billy
   debts to Mike Jacobs, 162, 166
   Louis fight (1941), 69–79, 95
   Louis fight (1946), 247–249, 251–255
   potential Louis–Conn rematch, 112, 152–153, 161–167
Considine, Robert, 43–44, 125
Cook, Raymond, 110
Costello, Frank, 259
Cotton Club, 87, 91, 180, 189
Coughlin, Charles, 55
Craig, Robert L., 213–214
Crawford, Lindsay J., 211, 214, 219
Curtiz, Michael, 182, 184–185

Daley, Arthur, 241
Dancy, John C., 85–86
Daniel, Dan, 37, 74, 76

Index

Davis, Benjamin O., Jr., 65–66
Davis, Elmer, 169
Dawson, James P., 253
D-Day, 228
Delmont, Matthew F., 228
Democratic National Committee, 52
Democratic Party, and Black voters, 53–55, 66–67
Dempsey, Jack, 113, 249
Detroit Race Riot (June 1943), 191–194, 225
DiMaggio, Joe, 77, 123
Disabled Veterans' Fund, 215
discrimination
  banned by War Department, 209
  in golf, 277–279
  in military, 6
  New Deal employment programs, 54
  Willkie's pledge to end, 55
Dodson, Nell, 81
Dönitz, Karl, 219
Donovan, Arthur, 76, 95
Dorsey, George and Mae, 244
Double Victory campaign, 154
draft
  Conn, 252
  Jackie Robinson, 155
  Louis message to Congress, 270
  Louis's status, 74, 79, 86–87, 98, 122, 125
  peacetime, 51, 110
  resistance to, 169
  unpopularity of, 101
draft board, 74, 79, 86–87, 125, 155
Du Bois, W. E. B., 5
Dunbar, Lee, 257
Dundee, Angelo, 258
Dunham, Katherine, 187
Dunphy, Don, 70, 78
Dunston, Nebraska, 110
Dykes, Jimmy, 155

Early, Stephen, 65–66
Edens, Roger, 175
Edward J. Neil Memorial Award, 134

Edwards, Harry Stillwell, 21
Eisenhower, Dwight D., 210, 225
election of 1940, presidential, 47–68
Ellison, Ralph, 91
England
  Bamber Bridge gunfight, 225–226
  Joe Louis in, 217–228, 280
  racial tolerance, 223–224
Ephrem, Tom, 218
Espionage Act, 132–133
Executive Order 9981, 270–271

Farley, James A., 135
Farr, Tommy, 222
fascism
  Black experience with, 50
  at Camp Upton, 132
  democracy triumph over, 237
  fight against, 3, 17, 39, 51, 55, 121, 134, 230
  Jim Crow equated with, 139
Feller, Bob, 101, 152
Fentress, J. Cullen, 169
Fields, John, 24
Finnish Relief Fund, 44
Fitzgerald, Carroll, 201
Flaherty, Edward F., 212–213
Fleischer, Nat
  boxing and baseball as needed diversions, 136
  at boxing awards banquet, 135
  Louis–Buddy Baer fight (1941), 76
  Louis–Buddy Baer fight (1942), 124
  Louis–Paychek fight (1940), 44
  Louis–Simon fight (1942), 141
Fleming, Joe, 228
Flynn, Edward J., 52, 55–56, 58
Fort Benning, 102
Fort Devens, 199
Fort Dix, 137–138, 140, 199
Fort Hamilton, 210, 213–215, 240
Fort Henry, 201
Fort Jay, 127, 211–212
Fort Monroe, 201

Index

Fort Riley, 152–158, 160–161, 167–169, 180, 194, 250
Foster, Allen, 158–160
Four Freedoms, 50
Fowlkes, William A., 186
Freed, Arthur, 175–176, 187
Fullerton, Hugh, 165
Fullum, Frank, 268

Gable, Clark, 196, 222
Gainford, George, 197–198, 212
Galento, Tony, 42, 96
Gallico, Paul, 60, 141
gas chamber execution, 159–160
Gavin, James, 89
Gershwin, George, 91
Gibbons, Joe, Jr., 83–84
Gibson, Althea, 278
Gibson, Julie, 89
Gibson, Truman
   as Backburn's defense attorney, 144–145
   on Blackburn, 142
   Fort Riley visits, 155–156, 160–161
   Jackie Robinson story, 157–158
   Jacobs bribe, 239
   on Julian Black, 83
   Louis discharge, 239
   Louis's attorney, 271
   Louis's enlistment, 103
   Louis's living every day, 8
   potential Louis–Conn army relief bout, 160–163
   problems in War Department, 186
   Robinson complaint to, 209–210
Godoy, Arturo, 41–45, 47
Golden Gloves, 26, 198, 233
golf, 7, 79, 95, 105, 154, 276–280
Gone with the Wind (film), 41–42, 176, 185
Goodman, Soll, 204–205
The Good War (Terkel), 220
Gould, Joe, 38, 40–41
Graves, Lem, Jr., 80
Great Depression, 2, 6, 25–26, 54, 64, 158, 237, 257, 266

Great Lakes Mutual Numbers House, 32–33
Great Migration, 7, 25
Green, Eddie, 227
Greenberg, Hank, 105
Greene, Abe, 135
Greenwood Lake, 71, 87, 90, 121–122, 161, 166, 239
Guinyard, Freddie, 105, 129

Hall, Felix, 102
Hammond, John, 71, 88, 99
The Harder They Fall (Schulberg), 259
Harrington, Ollie, 233, 244
Hastie, William H.
   aide to Stimson, 65, 155, 165
   on lynching of black soldiers, 102–103
   potential Louis–Conn army relief bout, 165–166
Hayes, Cleo, 179–180, 189
Haygood, Wil, 196
Hayton, Lennie, 274
heavyweight title, sale of, 271–273
Heinz, W. C., 215–216
Heisler, Stuart, 229
Higgins, Joseph T., 151
Hitler, Adolf
   ambition of, 14
   Lindbergh's admiration for, 49
   Louis on, 94, 140, 244, 277
   Mein Kampf, 14, 109
   Owens on, 59
   persecution of Jews, 112
   Schmeling and, 11, 14, 39
Holliday, Billie, 88–89
Hollywood
   Black actors, 170–178, 184–186, 188
   Joe Louis in, 184–186
   Lena Horne in, 168–178, 186–190
   Louis and Horne together in, 168–19, 171, 178–180
Hoover, Herbert, 53
Hoover, J. Edgar, 132, 135, 262
Hopkins, Harry, 223
Horne, Edwin "Teddy," Jr., 87, 176–177

Index

Horne, Lena
  affair with Louis, 71, 85, 87–92, 168, 178–180, 189–190
  Cabin in the Sky (film), 169, 171, 176–177, 186–188
  in Hollywood, 168–178, 186–190
  "Joe Louis Day" festival, 251
  Louis–Conn fight (1941), 71
  Louis marriage rumors, 179, 189–190, 203, 238
  Louis–Schmeling fight (1936), 12
  Panama Hattie (film), 187, 190
  photographs, 89–92
  proposed tour of military camps, 195–196
  relationship with Louis (1949), 273–274
  Stormy Weather (film), 187–188
  USO tour of southern camps, 201–202
Householder, Eugene R., 120
Houser, Enoch, 144–145
Hughes, Langston, 13, 83, 91
Hurt, Nick, 262

I Know Why the Caged Bird Sings (Angelou), 70
Improved Benevolent and Protective Order of Elks of the World, 52–53
International Boxing Club (IBC), 271–273
isolationists, 47–49, 67
Italian Theater, 233–234

Jackson, Delilah, 187
Jacobs, Joe, 39
Jacobs, Mike
  bribe to Gibson, 239
  Carbo and, 257–260
  Conn debts to, 162, 166
  contract with Louis, 26, 37–38
  control of boxing industry, 256–257
  deal making by, 36–38
  death, 272
  decline in match attendance, 137
  Disabled Veterans' Fund, 215
  exploitation of Louis's financial ignorance, 74–75
  Gould, deal with, 40–41
  health crises, 259–260, 272
  Look magazine profile, 258
  Louis–Braddock fight (1937), 38–41
  Louis–Buddy Baer fight (1942), 112–114
  Louis–Conn fight (1941), 73–79
  Louis–Conn fight (1946), 240–241, 248–249, 252–254
  Louis–Nova fight (1941), 95, 97
  Louis's debts to, 95, 150, 161–162, 166, 210–211, 236, 254–255
  Louis's draft status, 74, 87
  Louis's enlistment, 124
  Louis's fight schedule, 73–75
  Louis–Simon fight (1942), 136
  Louis's military induction, 129
  Navy Relief Society match/donation, 128–129
  O'Toole's charges against, 163
  potential Army Emergency Relief fight, 149–150, 160–167
  retirement announcement by Louis, 167–168
  robbery of, 36
  Twentieth Century Sporting Club, 41, 44, 79, 137, 162, 241, 272
  war bonds, 127
Jeffries, Edward J., 193
Jeffries, Jim, 15
Jenkins, Burris, Jr., 14
Jews
  elimination from professional boxing in Germany, 39
  persecution in Germany, 13, 51, 112
  in Roosevelt's broad coalition, 67
  significance of Louis–Schmeling 1938 fight, 3
Jim Crow
  Alfred Edgar Smith on, 119
  Blackburn on, 145
  degradation of, 50, 88, 142, 154, 237
  fascism equated with, 139

Index

inequities of, 237
Louis on fighting, 261
military, 4, 17, 103, 110, 113, 115, 120–121, 131, 200–201, 207–209, 224, 269
transplantation into Britain, 224
Willkie's opposition to, 94
Joe Louis: American (Miller), 10
Joe Louis Enterprises, Inc., 274
Johnson, Jack, 15, 23–24, 82–83, 142–143
Johnson, Joseph, 110
Jones, Claudia, 139–140
Jones, Edward D., 226
Jones, Louis, 88, 178
Jones, Theodore, 274
Josephson, Barney, 88–90

Kells, Clarence H., 240
Kelly, Harry, 193
Kennedy, Rufus, 84
Key, Alice, 189
Kieran, John, 162, 166
King, Martin Luther, Jr., 160, 245
"King Joe" (song), 93, 99–100
Kirsch, George, 277
Knox, Frank, 111, 116, 123
Korean War, 277
Ku Klux Klan, 64, 140, 193, 244

labor strikes, 252–253
Landis, Kenesaw Mountain, 136, 155
Landon, Alf, 58–59
Laney, Al, 235
Lavine, Harold, 101
Le Berthon, Ted, 186–187
Legion of Merit, 240
"Lend-a-Hand-to-Dixieland" fund drive, 261
Lend-Lease Act, 74
Leslie, Joan, 182
Lewis, David Levering, 91
Liebling, A. J., 258
Life magazine profile (June 1940), 21–24, 27–31

Lindbergh, Charles, 49
Linn, Ed, 255, 273
Little Troc, 172, 175
London, Joe Louis in, 220–222, 231
Louis, Jacqueline, 180, 203, 235, 237–238
Louis, Joe
  as activist, 7, 246, 262, 279
  affairs, 28, 71, 85, 87–92, 168, 178–180, 189–190, 273
  army boxing exhibition tours, 3–4, 19, 105, 114, 151, 199, 201, 204
  army poster, 138–139
  in army propaganda, 4, 7, 128, 133–134, 184, 196
  Army Relief Fund donation, 149–150
  as Black hero, 5, 24, 30, 133, 135, 196, 251, 263, 268–269
  as Black Moses, 21–22, 25, 70, 146
  Black soldiers at fights of, 201, 280–281
  Black soldiers helped by, 6, 155, 279–280
  celebrity of, 4, 81, 95, 114, 169, 179, 196, 237, 238, 251
  charity matches of, 112–124, 128–129 (*see also* Army Emergency Relief Fund)
  childhood of, 7, 25
  civil rights speech by (December 1946), 260–261
  on Conn, 73, 153, 240
  debts to John Roxborough, 75, 150, 162, 236, 254
  debts to Mike Jacobs, 95, 150, 161–162, 166, 210–211, 236, 254–255
  discharge from army, 239–240
  divorce, 79–81, 85–87, 238, 273–274
  draft status, 74, 79, 86–87, 98, 122, 125
  early years, 7–8, 25–26
  Edward J. Neil Memorial Award, 134
  in England, 217–228, 280
  enlistment of, 103–105, 124–125

333

Index

Louis, Joe *(continued)*
  exploitation of, 7, 33, 35, 74–75, 145, 255
  fighting style of, 146
  fights (*see* Louis, Joe, fights of)
  financial problems of, 41, 74–75, 151, 255, 274
  folktales about, 158–160
  funeral, 1–2, 5–6
  as golfer, 7, 79, 95, 105, 154, 276–280
  Hitler, comments on, 94, 140, 244, 277
  in Hollywood, 184–186
  horse farm, 75, 107, 153
  hospital visits, 217–219, 234–235
  hustlers surrounding, 37, 163
  induction into army, 17–19, 127–128
  Jackie Robinson and, 149, 153–158, 160, 249–251
  Jack Johnson and, 15, 23, 82, 143
  "Joe Louis Day" festival in Harlem, 251
  Lena Horne and, 12, 71, 189–190, 203, 238, 251, 273–274
  marriage to Marva Trotter, 81–82 (*see also* Louis, Marva)
  on Max Schmeling, 10, 18
  memorial service for, 5–6
  NAACP donations, 30, 63
  Navy Relief Society donation, 124, 128–129
  obituaries, 6
  overseas military tour of Joe Louis, 217–235
  political views of, 56–58, 64–68
  popularity of, 19, 21, 58, 114, 123, 151, 251
  Republican Party support by, 56–58, 64–68
  retirement announcement, 167–168
  retirement of, 271
  sale of heavyweight title, 271–273
  tax debt, 75, 149–151, 153, 254–256, 274
  use in propaganda, 4, 7, 128, 133–134, 184, 196
  War Department use of, 4, 98, 103, 140, 180, 193–194, 196, 199, 210, 219–220
  wedding, 81–82
Louis, Joe, fights of
  Baer, Buddy (1941), 76, 94–95
  Baer, Buddy (1942), 112–124, 135
  Baer, Max (1935), 81, 100, 144
  Braddock (1937), 41
  Bum of the Month Club, 74, 94, 101
  Burman (1941), 94
  Carnera (1935), 22, 38, 52, 62, 82, 88, 114, 194
  Charles (1950), 274–275
  Conn (1941), 69–79, 95
  Conn (1946), 247–249, 251–255
  gates/purses from, 27, 75
  Godoy (1940), 41–45, 47
  Louis–Conn fight rematch, 240–241
  Marciano (1951), 275–276
  Mauriello (1946), 256
  McCoy (1940), 75, 94
  Musto (1941), 94
  Nova (1941), 95–98
  Paychek (1940), 44–45
  pre-professional, 26
  Schmeling (1936), 38, 43, 58, 71, 83
  Schmeling (1938), 10–11, 14–16, 60, 64, 75, 93, 97, 113, 230
  Simon (1942), 94, 136, 140–141, 150, 239
  television broadcast, 253
  Walcott (1947), 265–267
  Walcott (1948), 268
Louis, Marva, 79–87, 95
  absence of Joe Louis, 179–180, 203, 235, 238, 273
  affairs of Joe Louis, 8, 85, 87
  alimony, 86, 255
  birth of Jacqueline, 180
  Chicago draft board, 79, 86–87
  competition with Lena Horne, 203
  divorce, 79–81, 85–87, 238, 273–274

Index

Joe Gibbons and, 83–84
Joe Louis's military induction, 129
as liability, 83
life in husband's shadow, 81, 237
Louis–Conn fight (1941), 71–72
pregnancy, 168–169
at Schmeling fight (1936), 12
singing, 203, 237
as soldier's wife, 168
wedding, 81–82
Luce, Henry, 21, 30
lynching
anti-lynching law, 54–55, 57, 107, 121, 260
Black soldiers, 102–103, 270
Black veterans, 243–245, 247, 260–261
Maya Angelou on, 70
of Raymond McMurray, 206
NAACP protests against, 244
by police, 206
Roy Wilkins on, 120

MacDonald, Janet, 32–33
MacLeish, Archibald, 132
Major League Baseball, 136, 155, 249–251
Malcolm, Roger and Dorothy, 244
Maly, Fred
on attendance at Louis exhibitions, 218–219
on Jackie Robinson, 250
on Louis hospital visits, 218
praise for Louis, 218–220, 235, 239–240
on racial conflicts, 220
on Sugar Ray Robinson, 204–205
toll of exhibitions on Louis, 232
Marbles, Alice, 152
Marciano, Rocky, 275–276
Marshall, George C., 120, 164, 180, 229
Marshall, Thurgood, 193
Martin, Clyde, 105
Martin, Joseph W., 58
Martin, Whitney, 252

Martland, Harrison, 232
Mauriello, Tami, 256
Mayer, Louis B., 175–177, 189
McArthur, George, 129
McBride, William, 32–33
McCarthy, Joe, 162–163
McCoy, Al, 75, 94
McDaniel, Hattie, 172, 177, 189
McLemore, Henry, 151
McMurray, Raymond, 205–207
McNulty, John, 266
McQueen, Butterfly, 177
Mead, Chris, 157
Mein Kampf (Hitler), 14, 109
Mendel, Harry, 271
Metro-Goldwin-Mayer (MGM), 168–170, 175–178, 189, 274
Miles, Marshall Davis, 255–256
Miley, Jack, 56–57
military. *see also* Army, US
overseas tour of Joe Louis, 217–235
racial animosity of white soldiers, 101
racial policies in US Navy, 110–111, 113, 115–116, 118
racism in, 4, 120, 140, 269
rapid expansion of Black men in, 154
segregation, 4, 18–19, 54, 120, 131, 155, 269–271
military posts
boxing exhibitions, 3–4, 19, 105, 114, 151, 199, 201, 204
Horne's USO tour of Southern, 201–202
Louis and Robinson (1943), 194–196, 199–204
Louis's tour of, 105, 114, 121, 246, 260
Miller, Doris "Dorie," 117–118
Miller, Margery, 10–11
Mills, Fred, 219–220
Minnelli, Vincente, 187
mob rule, 50–51, 237
mob violence, 244, 246–247, 270
Mocambo, 186–187
Monroe, Lucy, 123

335

Index

Moore's Ford Bridge, 244, 261
Morale Division, 103, 105, 125, 131
Moss, Carlton, 230
movie industry, 169–190
movies
    Cabin in the Sky, 169, 171, 176–177, 186–188
    Gone with the Wind, 41–42, 176, 185
    The Negro Soldier, 229–230
    Panama Hattie, 187, 190
    racial stereotypes in, 170–171, 173–174, 184, 188–189, 229
    The Spirit of Youth (film), 24
    Stormy Weather, 187–188
    This Is the Army, 2, 180–186, 195
    Why We Fight (documentary), 229
Murder, Inc., 257
Murphy, George B., 17–18, 183, 185
Mussolini, Benito, 47–48
Musto, Tony "Baby Tank," 94
Mutual Broadcasting System, 70–71
Myrdal, Gunnar, 6

NAACP (National Association for the Advancement of Colored People)
    Louis's donations to, 63
    Mary McLeod Bethune, 19
    The Negro Soldier (film), 229–230
    Ollie Harrington, 244
    protests against segregation and lynching, 244
    Roy Wilkins, 33, 50, 103
    Truman's address to, 270
    Walter White, 4, 30–31, 98, 173, 175
Nagler, Barney, 170, 266–267
National Council of Negro Women, 118
National Negro Congress, 17
Native Son (Wright), 99
Navy, US
    Navy Relief Society fundraiser, 138
    Navy Relief Society match/donation, 112–124, 128–129
    racial policies, 110–111, 113, 115–116, 118

Nazi Germany
    Battle of the Atlantic, 219
    espionage, 77
Negro Leagues, 59–60
Negro problem, 4, 18, 133
The Negro Soldier (film), 229–231
New Deal, 17, 54–55, 57–58, 64
New World A-Coming': Inside Black America (Ottley), 29
New York State Boxing Commission, 38, 40, 135
Nicholas Brothers, 187
Nicholson, George, 152, 196, 199, 219, 221, 231–233
Nielson, Ozzie, 84–85
Norris, James D., 271–273
Nova, Lou, 79, 87, 90, 95–98
Nunn, William G. "Bill," 69, 268–269
Nye, Gerald P., 173

Office of Facts and Figures, 132–133
Office of War Information (OWI)
    Bureau of Motion Pictures (BMP), 184, 188
    The Negro Soldier (film), 229–230
    propaganda, use of Louis for, 133–134, 139
officer candidate school (OCS), 155–157
OHIO acronym, 101
Operation Overload, 210
Operation Roundup, 164
Operation Torch, 164–165
organized crime, 257
Original Handbook of Harlem Jive (Burley), 114
Orwell, George, 223–224
Osborn, Frederick H., 104–105, 195–196
Othman, Frederick C., 185
O'Toole, Donald, 163
Ottley, Roi
    Louis–Conn fight (1941), 70
    on meeting of Black press, 132
    on *The Negro Soldier* (film), 231

Index

New World A-Coming': Inside Black America, 29
race relations in Britain, 224
Owens, Jesse, 53, 58–61, 67
OWI. *See* Office of War Information

Panama Hattie (film), 187, 190
Parker, Dan
  on Carbo, 258–259
  depiction of Louis, 61–62, 68
  on draftee inductions, 130
  imagined Louis–Owens debate, 61–62
  on Joe–Marva Louis divorce, 86
  on potential Louis–Conn army relief bout, 166–167
Parris, John, Jr., 159
Parsons, Louella, 238
Patterson, Robert F., 140, 165–166
Paychek, Johnny, 44–45
Pearl Harbor, 77, 117–118, 121, 136–137, 154, 172, 181
Pegler, Westbrook, 12
Perfetti, Dom, 198
PGA (Professional Golf Association), 276–280
Phelan, John J., 135–136
Pillion, Maude, 142–143
Polk, Alonzo, 142–143
Polk, Mattie, 143
poll tax, 121, 260–261, 270
Pompton Lakes, 7, 62, 90, 239, 246, 248–249, 251
Porter, Cole, 190
poster, 138–139
Povich, Shirley, 278
Powers, Jimmy, 33, 42, 98
POWs, German, 201–202
presidential election (1940), 47–68
President's Committee on Civil Rights, 270
Prinz, LeRoy, 185
Professional Golf Association (PGA), 276–280

propaganda
  by Black press, 132
  Black soldier, 4
  Elmer Davis on, 169
  Louis use in, 4, 7, 128, 133–134, 184, 196
  movies and, 169, 173–174, 229
  Office of War Information (OWI), 133–134
punch-drunk syndrome, 26, 204, 232

race riots, 15, 191–194, 225, 243
racial stereotypes in films, 170–171, 173–174, 184, 188–189, 229
racism
  Louis efforts against, 6, 113, 156, 208, 247, 280
  Louis's anger/frustration over, 63
  in military, 4, 120, 140, 269
  Nazi, 4, 120, 140
  in show business, 89, 184
Rainey, Julian, 52
Randolph, A. Philip, 269
Ray, Ebeneezer, 23, 30
Ray, Johnny, 72, 78
Reading, Richard, Jr., 32
Reading, Richard "Little Dick," Sr., 32–33
Reagan, Osmond P., 205–206
Reagan, Ronald, 182
Remnick, David, 257
Republican Party
  Black support for, 53–59, 65
  Louis support for, 56–58, 64–68
retirement announcement by Louis, 167–168
Rice, Grantland, 161–162, 266
Rickard, George "Tex," 37
Rickey, Branch, 249–251
Robeson, Paul
  Café Society, 89
  on Joe Louis, 263
  praise for Lena Horne, 175
  proposed tour of military camps, 195–196

Index

Robeson, Paul *(continued)*
  silencing, 140
  singing "King Joe," 99–100
  supporter of Soviet Union, 262–263
  at Van Vechten's gathering, 91
Robinson, Bill "Bojangles," 172, 187
Robinson, Casey, 182
Robinson, Donald, 155–156
Robinson, Edna Mae, 212
Robinson, Jack Roosevelt "Jackie"
  bus protest, 209
  court-martial, 157–158, 160, 209
  at Fort Robinson, 153–158
  integration of baseball, 155, 249–251
  on Joe Louis, 149, 154
  Louis's support of, 249–251
Robinson, Rachel, 154
Robinson, Sugar Ray
  alias taken by, 198
  amateur career, 197–198
  army induction, 198–199
  contract with Jacobs, 272
  desertion, 211–215
  early life, 196
  friendship with Louis, 2, 249, 251
  health, 204–205, 210–216
  LaMotta fight, 198–199
  at Louis–Charles fight, 275
  Louis's use of car, 236
  MP tackled by, 207–208
  tour of army camps, 195–196, 199–204
Rodney, Lester, 41–42, 63
Roosevelt, Eleanor, 103–105, 191
Roosevelt, Franklin, Jr., 48
Roosevelt, Franklin D.
  Black Cabinet, 195
  Churchill meeting (August 1941), 108
  declaration of war, 120
  Detroit riots, 193
  ending diplomatic relations with Germany, 77
  Four Freedoms, 50
  green light letter to Major League Baseball, 136
  Louis meeting (1940), 52–53
  Louis–Nova fight (1941), 97
  lynching of black soldiers, 102–103
  Navy Day speech, 109
  Negro officers, 156
  New Deal, 17, 54–55, 57–58, 64
  Operation Torch, 164–165
  presidential campaign (1940), 47–68
  state of emergency declaration, 17
  University of Virginia commencement speech (1940), 47–49
Rouzeau, Edgar T., 80–81
Rowe, Billy, 6, 19, 112–113, 138, 179
Roxborough, Charles, 34, 56, 64
Roxborough, Elsie, 82–83
Roxborough, John
  advice to Louis, 228
  Blackburn funeral, 146
  Brown on, 28–29
  as civic leader, 26, 34
  conviction, 146
  draft status of Louis, 79
  gate proceeds share, 41
  hiring Blackburn, 143
  indictment (1940), 33–34
  influence on Louis, 236
  on *Life* profile of Louis, 31
  on Louis and politics, 47, 56–57
  Louis–Conn fight (1941), 69–70
  Louis's debts to, 75, 150, 162, 236, 254
  Louis's enlistment, 103, 124
  Louis's image management, 22–24, 31
  Marva Louis and, 80, 82
  Navy Relief Society match, 113
  as numbers operator, 35, 121
  payment of suit against Blackburn, 145
  prison, 236, 255
  purse percentage, 34–35
  relationship with Louis, 34–35
  retirement announcement by Louis, 167
  silence on civil rights, 63–64
Runyon, Damon, 39
Rust, Art, Jr., 156

Index

Rust, Edna, 156
Rutherford, Ann, 176

Schiff, Dorothy, 56
Schmeling, Max
  boxing career, 11–12
  Louis fight (1936), 38, 43, 58, 71, 83
  Louis fight (1938), 10–11, 14–16, 60, 64, 75, 93, 97, 113, 230
  military service, 9–12, 16, 219
  as Nazi proxy/icon, 9, 11, 14–15, 38–39
  potential Braddock fight, 38–40
  reported death, 9–10, 16
Schulberg, Budd, 259
Scottsboro Nine, 64
Seamon, Mannie, 153, 248
segregation
  American South, 199–200
  military, 4, 18–19, 52, 54, 101, 120, 131, 155, 269–271
  NAACP protests against, 244
  pervasive, 50
  PGA policy, 277
Selective Service, 51–52, 54
Shanley, Robert, 183
Sharkey, Jack, 12
Shekerjian, Haig, 208
Shull, Lynwood, 245
Simon, Abe, 94, 136, 138, 140–141, 150–151, 239
Sinatra, Frank, 222, 261, 265
Sissle, Noble, 13
Sloan, James M., 65–66
Smith, Alfred Edgar, 119–120
Smith, Horton, 277–279
Smith, Leila, 196–197
Smith, Walker, Jr. *See* Robinson, Sugar Ray
Smith, Wendell
  on John Roxborough, 34
  on Louis and US Navy, 119
  Louis–Schmeling fight, 13
  Louis–Simon fight, 141
  Louis's stand against PGA, 279–280
Snipes, Maceo, 244

Southern Conference for Human Welfare, 260
Special Service Division, 218, 220, 235, 240
Spiller, Bill, 278–279
The Spirit of Youth (film), 24
Starr, Milton, 133–134
Stepin Fetchit, 172
Stewart, James R., 107
Stewart, Jimmy, 196
Stewart, Ollie, 131–132
Stillman's Gym, 258
Stimson, Henry L.
  on army charity bout, 163–166
  Hastie as aide to, 65, 155, 165
  on Louis's public appearances, 152
  lynching of black soldiers, 102–103
  on military racial policy, 120
  Murphy's urging on Louis fighting in US Army, 17–18
  Negro officers, 156
  racism, 18
  segregation in armed forces, 18, 165
  war preparation, 77
Stormy Weather (film), 187–188
Strauss, Sol, 272
Sullivan, Ed, 260
Supplee, H. Clay, 125
Surles, Alexander D., 152, 161–162, 165–166

Taubman, Abraham, 127
Taylor, Luther "Dummy," 62
television, 253
Terkel, Studs, 220
This Is the Army (film), 2, 180–186, 195
Time, 21–22, 30, 48, 77
Tipton, Leo, 192
Trimmingham, Rupert, 202
Trotter, Walter C., 82
Truman, Harry, 270
Trumbo, Dalton, 171
Tunney, Gene, 115, 123, 134–135, 249
Twentieth Century Sporting Club, 41, 44, 79, 137, 162, 241, 272

Index

U-boat, 108–109, 210, 219
"Uncle Sam Says" (song), 110–111
Uncle Tom, 22, 31, 73, 116, 172, 261
United Colored Democrats, 55
United Negro and Allied Veterans of America, 246, 262
uprising of 1946, 244–245
USO tour, Lena Horne's, 201–202
USS *Greer*, 87, 108–109
USS *Kearny*, 107–109
USS *Missouri*, 240
USS *Nevada*, 215
USS *Reuben James*, 109–110, 111
USS *West Virginia*, 117

Van Every, Edward, 24–25
Vann, Robert, 52
Van Vechten, Carl, 90–92
Vidmer, Richards, 43, 97, 114, 136
Vietnam War, 5
voting rights, 6, 260–261

Walcott, Joe
   Charles fight (1949), 275
   Charles fight (1951), 275
   Louis fight (1947), 265–267
   Louis fight (1948), 268
Walker, James J. "Jimmy," 135
Waller, Fats, 187
Wanger, Walter, 174
war bonds, 127, 134, 203, 263
War Boxing, Inc., 161, 166
War Department
   Army General Classification Test (AGCT), 130–131
   Army Relief Fund bout, 150–152, 160–163, 166
   Black volunteers turned away by, 51
   censors, 194, 226
   death of Felix Hall, 102–103
   discrimination prohibition, 209
   failure to publicize Black soldiers, 139
   Lena Horne USO tour, 202
   The Negro Soldier (film), 230
   segregation policy, 4, 18, 54

Special Service Division, 218, 220, 229, 235, 240
Sugar Ray Robinson, 212
use of Louis, 4, 98, 103, 140, 180, 193–194, 196, 199, 210, 219–220
Warner, Jack, 182
Washington, Chester, 22, 51
Weiss, Sid, 234
Wesley, Carter, 80
"What the Well-Dressed Man in Harlem Will Wear" (song), 182–186
White, Josh, 89, 110
White, Walter
   on cultural importance of Louis, 4
   Harrington's suggestion, 233
   influence in Hollywood, 173–174
   Lena Horne and, 173–177
   Liederkranz Hall meeting (October 1941), 99
   on *Life* profile of Louis, 30–31
   Louis's enlistment, 103–105
   on Navy racial policies, 116
   on role of Louis in the war, 98
   on treatment of Black veterans, 243–244
white supremacy, 3, 6, 11, 16, 246
Why We Fight (documentary), 229
Wilkins, Roy
   defense of Roxborough, 33–34
   on democracy for Black people, 50–51, 103, 120–121
   Jackson correspondence with, 206
   "The Negro Wants Full Equality," 217
Willkie, Wendell
   election results, 67
   influence in Hollywood, 173–174
   Louis–Buddy Baer fight, 123–124
   Louis's campaigning for, 56–58, 61–62, 66–68, 93, 246
   opposition to Jim Crow, 94
   pledge to end discrimination, 55
Wilson, Earl, 84
Wilson, George "California Jackie," 196
Wilson, Jackie, 198
Winchell, Walter, 138, 277
Wirtz, Arthur, 271–273

Index

Wood, Wilber, 161
Woodard, Isaac, 245–247, 261
Woodson, Waverly, Jr., 228
Works Progress Administration (WPA), 64, 67
World War II
  Battle of the Atlantic, 219
  D-Day, 228
  defeats in the Pacific, 181
  end, 238–240
  German POWs, 201–202
  Italian Theater, 233–234
  Louis in, 2–5, 217–235
  overseas tour of Joe Louis, 217–235
  Pearl Harbor, 77, 117–118, 121, 136–137, 154, 172, 181
  Roosevelt's University of Virginia commencement speech (1940), 47–49

USS *Greer*, 87, 108–109
USS *Kearny*, 107–109
USS *Reuben James*, 109–110, 111
Wright, Richard, 140, 267
  cleansing power of Joe Louis, 100
  "King Joe," 93, 99–100
  Liederkranz Hall meeting (October 1941), 99
  Louis–Schmeling fight (1938), 15–16
  radical meaning of Louis, 11

Yaphank, 129–130
Yip! Yip! Yaphank (revue), 180
Young, Frank, 250

Zanuck, Darryl, 174
Zanzibar, 234, 237

Johnny Smith is the J. C. "Bud" Shaw Professor of Sports History at Georgia Tech. Author of *Jumpman*, he lives in Atlanta, Georgia.

Randy Roberts is the 150th Anniversary Distinguished Professor of History at Purdue University. He lives in Lafayette, Indiana.

They are coauthors of *Blood Brothers*, *A Season in the Sun*, and *War Fever*.

RAISING READERS
Books Build Bright Futures

Thank you for reading this book and for being a reader of books in general. We are so grateful to share being part of a community of readers with you, and we hope you will join us in passing our love of books on to the next generation of readers.

Did you know that reading for enjoyment is the single biggest predictor of a child's future happiness and success?

More than family circumstances, parents' educational background, or income, reading impacts a child's future academic performance, emotional well-being, communication skills, economic security, ambition, and happiness.

Studies show that kids reading for enjoyment in the US is in rapid decline:

- In 2012, 53% of 9-year-olds read almost every day. Just 10 years later, in 2022, the number had fallen to 39%.
- In 2012, 27% of 13-year-olds read for fun daily. By 2023, that number was just 14%.

TOGETHER, WE CAN COMMIT TO RAISING READERS AND CHANGE THIS TREND. HOW?

- Read to children in your life daily.
- Model reading as a fun activity.
- Reduce screen time.
- Start a family, school, or community book club.
- Visit bookstores and libraries regularly.
- Listen to audiobooks.
- Read the book before you see the movie.
- Encourage your child to read aloud to a pet or stuffed animal.
- Give books as gifts.
- Donate books to families and communities in need.

Books build bright futures, and Raising Readers is our shared responsibility.

For more information, visit JoinRaisingReaders.com

Sources: National Endowment for the Arts, National Assessment of Educational Progress, WorldBookDay.org, Nielsen BookData's 2023 "Understanding the Children's Book Consumer"